AMERICAN LITERATURE'S WAR ON CRIME

LITERATURE NOW

LITERATURE NOW

Matthew Hart, David James, and Rebecca L. Walkowitz, Series Editors

Literature Now offers a distinct vision of late-twentieth- and early-twenty-first-century literary culture. Addressing contemporary literature and the ways we understand its meaning, the series includes books that are comparative and transnational in scope as well as those that focus on national and regional literary cultures.

Keegan Cook Finberg, *Poetry in General: Literary Experimentalism and U.S. Public Forms*

Jennifer Scappetone, *Poetry After Barbarism: The Invention of Motherless Tongues and Resistance to Fascism*

Alexander Manshel, *Writing Backwards: Historical Fiction and the Reshaping of the American Canon*

Glenda Carpio, *Migrant Aesthetics: Contemporary Fiction, Global Migration, and the Limits of Empathy*

John Brooks, *The Racial Unfamiliar: Illegibility in Black Literature and Culture*

Vidyan Ravinthiran, *Worlds Woven Together: Essays on Poetry and Poetics*

Ellen Jones, *Literature in Motion: Translating Multilingualism Across the Americas*

Thomas Heise, *The Gentrification Plot: New York and the Postindustrial Crime Novel*

Sunny Xiang, *Tonal Intelligence: The Aesthetics of Asian Inscrutability During the Long Cold War*

Jessica Pressman, *Bookishness: Loving Books in a Digital Age*

Heather Houser, *Infowhelm: Environmental Art and Literature in an Age of Data*

Christy Wampole, *Degenerative Realism: Novel and Nation in Twenty-First-Century France*

Sarah Chihaya, Merve Emre, Katherine Hill, and Jill Richards, *The Ferrante Letters: An Experiment in Collective Criticism*

Peter Morey, *Islamophobia and the Novel*

Gloria Fisk, *Orhan Pamuk and the Good of World Literature*

For a complete list of books in the series, please see the Columbia University Press website.

American Literature's War on Crime

NOVELS AND THE HIDDEN HISTORY
OF MASS INCARCERATION

Theodore Martin

Columbia University Press
New York

Columbia University Press
Publishers Since 1893
New York   Chichester, West Sussex
cup.columbia.edu
Copyright © 2026 Columbia University Press
All rights reserved

Library of Congress Cataloging-in-Publication Data
Names: Martin, Theodore author
Title: American literature's war on crime : novels and the hidden history of mass incarceration / Theodore Martin.
Description: New York : Columbia University Press, 2026. | Series: Literature now | Includes bibliographical references and index.
Identifiers: LCCN 2025036328 (print) | LCCN 2025036329 (ebook) | ISBN 9780231211802 hardback | ISBN 9780231211819 trade paperback | ISBN 9780231559072 ebook | ISBN 9780231565561 PDF
Subjects: LCSH: Crime in literature | Imprisonment in literature | American fiction—20th century—History and criticism | American fiction—21st century—History and criticism | LCGFT: Literary criticism
Classification: LCC PS374.C75 M37 2026 (print) | LCC PS374.C75 (ebook)
LC record available at https://lccn.loc.gov/2025036328
LC ebook record available at https://lccn.loc.gov/2025036329

Cover design: Kimberly Glyder
Cover art: Shutterstock

GPSR Authorized Representative: Easy Access System Europe, Mustamäe tee 50, 10621 Tallinn, Estonia, gpsr.requests@easproject.com

CONTENTS

Introduction: Crime and Fiction   1

1. Invisible Men, 1940–1966   23

2. Riot Acts, 1967–1974   67

3. Detecting Domestic Violence, 1975–2000   105

4. Two Paths for Pathology, 1984–1998   151

5. The Novel in the Age of Mass Incarceration, 1992–2023   185

    Epilogue: And the Law Won   235

ACKNOWLEDGMENTS   243
APPENDIX: CAST OF CRIME NOVELS   245
NOTES   249
INDEX   291

AMERICAN LITERATURE'S WAR ON CRIME

Introduction

CRIME AND FICTION

Read a book? No; no; God, no!

—*SAVAGE HOLIDAY* (1954)

This book is about the role that books played in the buildup to mass incarceration. From the 1950s to the 2010s, in response to a cascade of political and economic upheavals, the United States embarked on an unprecedented social experiment of punitive public policy, an expanded criminal code, intensified policing, and massive prison-building. In this period, the police and the prison became arguably the two defining institutions of American society, while crime became one of the most durable issues in the nation's electoral politics. By now, we know a great deal about the political, legal, racial, and economic processes that laid the groundwork for what became the crisis of mass incarceration. *American Literature's War on Crime* investigates how readers and writers of fiction participated in those processes and made their own contributions to that crisis. It begins from an obvious but easily overlooked fact: that the evolution of the U.S. crime war occurred against a backdrop in which millions of American citizens had their heads in what are generally called crime novels— one of the past century's most enduring and bankable literary genres. I wrote this book because I wanted to understand where reading habits and crime politics intersected. What follows is the story of how America's road to becoming the world's largest jailer was paved with novels.

The aim of this book is to uncover the substantial part that novelists played in explaining the War on Crime—unpacking its underlying ideas about criminality, race, class, and gender—to a diverse reading public. What did it mean to read fiction about crime in an era defined by the reign of tough-on-crime attitudes that singled out Black, Brown, and poor communities? What did novelists think they were doing when they chose to write about cops and criminals during a period of unprecedented prison expansion and police militarization? How did American literature's portraits of criminality either confirm or contest the criminal stereotypes circulating widely through mainstream media and public discourse? In short, how did novels sometimes resist, and more often assist, the rise of mass incarceration in America?

These are the questions *American Literature's War on Crime* sets out to answer. To do so, it analyzes more than seventy works of fiction about crime written between 1940 and 2024. These works range from mass-market genre fiction (by Jim Thompson, Ed McBain, Donald Goines, Mary Higgins Clark, Sister Souljah, and Stephen King, among others) to so-called literary or elevated genre fiction (by authors such as John A. Williams, Richard Price, Margaret Atwood, and Walter Mosley) to mainstays of the American literary canon (Richard Wright, Toni Cade Bambara, Don DeLillo, Colson Whitehead). Through readings of these authors and many more, I make two core arguments. First, I contend that the War on Crime exerted a sweeping influence on the course of American fiction generally and American crime fiction specifically. A great deal of postwar literature, I will show, was molded by the radical reorganization of police power, legal procedure, social welfare, and racial ideology that took place under the sign of the crime war. Accordingly, this book makes the case that we ought to understand the War on Crime as a unique and pivotal period not only of social history but of literary history as well. The War on Crime altered the form and the content of American literature. It changed the kinds of crimes, the types of characters, the characterizations of policing, the conceptions of race, the procedures of judgment, and the conventions of crime-solving that defined major subgenres of crime writing—from police procedurals and vigilante narratives to feminist detective novels and serial killer stories—in the second half of the twentieth century. By studying this array of narrative transformations, my intent is to show how the War on Crime lodged itself at the center of American literature's political unconscious.

INTRODUCTION

Second, I argue that American crime writing was not just unconsciously or passively shaped by U.S. crime policy; it was also an active attempt to shape that policy. Simply put, literature had its own distinctive role to play in the War on Crime. Crime novels, this book proposes, were a key setting in which the country's rapidly changing ideologies of crime control were variously tested, contested, and corroborated. I read the genre of crime fiction as disputed cultural terrain—a kind of literary battleground—where divergent explanations of crime vied for readers' attention. Novels competed with one another to teach readers how (or whether) to accept the conflations of crime, class, and race that hastened the rise of the American carceral state. In sum, works of fiction made the War on Crime comprehensible, consumable, digestible—but in different ways for different audiences. Crime fiction, as this book understands it, was not a belated or second-order representation of the nation's crime war. It was one of several concurrent theaters in which that war was waged.

In 1965, President Lyndon Johnson launched what he called an "active combat against crime," radically overhauling the federal government's role in policing.[1] With this, the War on Crime had officially begun. But this was no short-term policy shift. The motives behind the war had begun to take shape decades earlier, and the effects of its policies were still being felt well into the twenty-first century. In this sense, we can think of the War on Crime as designating not an isolated event but a whole era of American history: a period, stretching from the 1940s to the 2010s, in which crime became a vital keyword in the drama of American democracy and the machinery of mass incarceration was set fatally in motion.[2]

This era began just after World War II, when anxieties about criminal disorder became a key component of the public response to changing urban demographics (a result of the Second Great Migration and white flight to the suburbs) and to burgeoning civil rights activism. By the middle of the 1960s, mainstream America was in a state of steady alarm over reports of rising crime rates and televised images of urban uprisings. In response, the Johnson administration turned away from its nascent antipoverty programs and launched the War on Crime. This dramatically transformed the practice of policing in the United States, which became increasingly focused on the surveillance and containment of working-class communities of color. Over the next few decades, Johnson's War on Crime flowed seamlessly into Nixon's and Reagan's Wars on Drugs, which targeted Black and Brown drug users and dealers for harsh punishment while shielding white suburban families from the consequences of punitive drug laws. At the same time, a national focus on the problem of violence against women funneled additional money into police departments and further intensified state surveillance of working-class families. In the 1980s, the powder keg of mass incarceration finally exploded. Between 1973 and 1983, the number of Americans in prison or jail jumped from fewer than 200,000 to more than 400,000. It kept growing from there. The number topped one million in 1989. It hit two million in 2002.[3] Over the course of just a few decades, the United States had created the largest prison population in the world—a population remarkable for its unprecedented size as well as for its shocking concentration of low-income people of color, especially African Americans. The world we live in now, of pervasive policing and titanic rates of imprisonment, is a world that was long in the making. It was made by the War on Crime.

The legal scholars Jonathan Simon, Ian Haney López, and Mary Louise Frampton contend that the War on Crime fundamentally "remade our society."[4] The historian Heather Ann Thompson has argued that crime policy was responsible for "some of the most dramatic political, economic, and social transformations of the postwar period."[5] The sociologist Stuart Schrader makes the case for putting "the prison at the center of the social and political history of the past four decades."[6] All of these claims are invitations to consider crime control as one of the primary forces shaping American society after World War II. Taking a cue from these scholars and borrowing a phrase from the historian Elizabeth Hinton, we may think of the postwar period as the "long War on Crime."[7] What happens when we view this particular slice of American history specifically through the lens of crime? Such a viewpoint allows us to see the connections between the dismantling of Jim Crow, the advance of deindustrialization, the contraction of the welfare state, the repressive response to political radicalism, the collapse of the family wage, the intensification of segregated urban poverty, and the massive growth of the prison system—historical processes that were all routed through and regulated by new techniques of law enforcement. This book uses the concept of the long War on Crime to name this prolonged period of social transformation stretching from the 1940s to the twenty-first century: a period in which political and economic turmoil was managed through the ever-more-tightly aligned procedures of criminalization, racialization, and incarceration.

What was "crime," in the eyes of those fighting a war against it? The answer is not so simple. What constitutes a criminal act is extremely fungible and historically mutable, not to mention highly dependent on variables of gender, race, and class. In truth, crime is a code word. Crime is how a culture talks about its fundamental arrangements of social inequality. You might say that discourses of crime register the modern world's fear of the very conditions of marginalization and immiseration that it has itself created. Categories of criminality function discursively to "rename real situations linked to poverty and transgression."[8] They also function materially to manage "the behaviors of poor and nonwhite people."[9] Crime, in this sense, is both a means of redescribing an unequal society and a "primary tool for social control."[10] This tool works to reinforce and even generate hierarchies of class and race.[11]

Criminalization—that is, the process of deciding what types of actions and what kinds of people count as criminal—has long been used to harass the jobless, subdue the working class, and subordinate particular ethnic and racial groups. As early as the fourteenth century, the juridical category of vagrancy emerged as a way to control "a wide variety of marginal populations—including the poor, the unemployed, sex workers, itinerant performers, and strangers—perceived to pose the threat of potential future criminality."[12] Vagrancy laws later migrated to the United States, where they functioned as part of the Black Codes and "became a surrogate for slavery" in the Reconstruction South.[13] By the turn of the twentieth century, as Saidiya Hartman has vividly documented, wayward minor laws targeted free Black women in Northern cities by criminalizing such normal activities as "drinking, dancing, dating (especially interracial liaisons), having sex, going to parties and cabarets, inviting men to your room, and roaming the street."[14] In short, definitions of crime and choices about which crimes to enforce have evolved alongside the changing shape of inequality, exploitation, and repression.

With this in mind, we can begin to understand the War on Crime as the particular way that the United States forged both new terms and new tools to manage the conditions of racial and economic stratification in the postwar, postindustrial era. Rioter, radical, pusher, prisoner, superpredator, inner-city dweller, gang member, welfare queen: These dramatis personae of the crime war established a whole new vocabulary for talking about race and class in America. Part of what is important about these criminal types is that they solidify racial stereotypes without using racial terms. "Criminal justice reproduces racism in a coded . . . fashion," Christian Parenti has argued, a process that helps make racism "ideologically palatable" in a post–Jim Crow era committed to the fiction of color blindness.[15] Yet there is no question that the crime war's unique cast of characters has always been deeply racialized. In fact, it developed specifically as a way of characterizing low-income Black communities.

In the formative years of the War on Crime, politicians' and policymakers' central concern was "controlling crime in black urban neighborhoods."[16] The national obsession with crime in Black communities had its origins in the profound demographic, geographic, and economic shifts that occurred at midcentury. The demographic character of American cities changed substantially after 1945, as millions of African Americans escaped segregation and racial terror in the South and migrated to the industrial North. As this mass migration took place, redlining, white flight, industrial contraction, and suburban development left Black residents confined to increasingly isolated and under-resourced areas of cities.[17] The historian Thomas Sugrue argues that the "emergence of persistent, concentrated, racialized poverty" in postindustrial cities was a fundamentally new feature of American social life starting in the 1950s. "Central-city residence, race, joblessness, and poverty have become inextricably intertwined in postindustrial urban America," he writes.[18] The novel entanglement of these categories was both described and justified by the public's fixation on crime. The collective fantasy of segregated urban neighborhoods overrun by crime not only birthed the War on Crime but did so in specifically racialized terms. By the early 1960s, Hinton suggests, "notions of black criminality" were "considered an objective truth and a statistically irrefutable fact."[19] The highly dubious "fact" of Black criminality—which was, in truth, a reductive renaming of the structural problems of deindustrialization, class stratification, and urban crisis that couldn't be addressed as such—would serve as the public face of U.S. crime policy for the rest of the century.[20]

INTRODUCTION

"Capitalism requires inequality and racism enshrines it," the sociologist Ruth Wilson Gilmore teaches us.[21] The War on Crime is a particularly vivid manifestation of this complicated truth: a war on "deindustrialized cities' working or workless poor" that started as, and still often looks like, a race war.[22] The crime war is how U.S. society renamed and responded to the shifting dynamics of racialization and class composition after 1945.[23] Invoking the famous dictum of Stuart Hall, Gilmore says it as well as anyone: "If . . . race is the modality through which class is lived, then mass incarceration is class war."[24]

American Literature's War on Crime is a literary history of this unique form of class war that, justified by crime, was perforce routed through race. By focusing on the new type of crime governance that grew specifically out of the attempt to manage poverty and inequality in urban African American communities after World War II, this book ends up probing an additional legacy of the War on Crime: its binary, Black-and-white understanding of race. To be clear, policing and prisons are in no way problems solely for Black Americans. The early twenty-first century has seen increasing rates of imprisonment for Hispanic Americans, poor white Americans, immigrants, and women. Latine people are now "the largest ethnic or racial group in the federal prison system," mainly as a result of federal courts' intensified focus on immigration-related offenses.[25] Meanwhile, the penal machinery initially constructed for the urban drug war was steadily exported to predominately white rural counties, which became not only the preferred sites for new prison construction but also the primary contributors to skyrocketing rates of people held in jails.[26] Today, Idaho, Wyoming, West Virginia, and Montana each incarcerate a higher share of their residents than California, New Jersey, or New York.[27]

Nevertheless, the historical record leaves little doubt that the era of the War on Crime was initiated by a set of punitive state interventions into working-class Black neighborhoods. Consequently, for most of the twentieth century, domestic crime policy tended to view the American social order predominately in terms of Black and white. In the crucial years of its formation, consolidation, and bipartisan reign, the War on Crime was most often waged through ideologies and images linking Blackness to crime. Such ideologies were ready at hand, having been a part of American cultural life since at least the nineteenth century.[28] Accordingly, in this book, I have chosen to assemble a literary and historical archive that concentrates primarily, though not exclusively, on the processes of Black criminalization that underwrote the crime war. This approach in no way exhausts the ways that race and class have operated throughout either the history of the crime war or the history of postwar crime fiction.[29] It is, however, an important way to begin to tell the story of how those two histories converged.

What does any of this have to do with novels? Good question. Let's start here: Crime, perhaps more than any other social issue, is a story we tell ourselves. The more the story circulates, the less it feels like a story.[30] But it is. Crime is not simply a quantifiable fact or a concrete event. It is a whole affective atmosphere: an expansive haze of inchoate feelings and unspoken beliefs, which is shaped into shared narratives. These narratives declare that crime rates are on the rise and that citizens should be worried; they teach that crime happens in particular places and because of particular types of people; they indicate what social disorder looks like and who can be relied on to fix it. The tales we tell about crime are as important to how it is policed and legislated as what the facts say about it. This book therefore approaches crime as something that is simultaneously real and fictional. By *fictional* I do not necessarily mean *fake*. I mean, rather, something that is built from the basic elements of plot and narrative and so shares essential DNA with written works of fiction.

Many scholars before me have pointed out that the problem of crime seems to bridge fiction and reality. Beliefs about crime involve "ceaseless migrations across the fact/fiction divide."[31] Famous criminals have often relied on knowledge of investigative procedure gleaned from popular culture, further "eroding the distinctions between fact and fiction."[32] Writing itself ("form, trope, and scriptive practices") was a key factor in the creation of modern policing.[33] But don't just take it from a bunch of literary critics. Sociologists, criminologists, and historians have also acknowledged that crime has an essential imaginative and rhetorical dimension. For the cohort of social scientists behind the classic book *Policing the Crisis*, crime control measures turned out to be dictated less by the "fact" of crime than by "the way crime is perceived."[34] For the historian Dominique Kalifa, descriptions of the criminal classes are best understood not as a reflection of

INTRODUCTION

"the real world" but as a "cultural construction," part of a "social imaginary" that is "incarnated in plots and recounted in stories."[35] When it comes to crime, figments frequently function as facts. The fictional is rendered social. Imagination can make policy.[36] Sometimes such relays between reality and fiction seem almost too perfect. In 1842, Edgar Allan Poe wrote a fictional detective story, "The Mystery of Marie Rogêt," that was an attempt to solve a real crime. In 1995, the famous FBI criminal profiler John E. Douglas explained that his approach to solving real crimes was indebted to the work of the fiction writer Edgar Allan Poe.[37]

Culture and media are thus not incidental to the way we think about crime. They are an essential part of it.[38] This is most obvious in the case of news media, which has an outsize influence on how the public thinks about the prevalence of crime and the typology of criminals.[39] Governments have recognized this and acted accordingly. In the 1980s, the Reagan administration waged its drug war partly through television and newspapers.[40] But news coverage is not alone in shaping the public response to crime. The criminologist Nicole Rafter argues that "crime films draw from and in turn shape social thought about crime."[41] The editors of *Crime TV: Streaming Criminology in Popular Culture* contend that "most people get their information and knowledge about crime and justice from TV shows, movies, and other popular outlets."[42] Research in the fields of sociology and criminology has amply backed up these claims.[43] Perhaps it should not be surprising that so many of the ideas and beliefs people have about the criminal legal system come from fictional sources. As the critic Mark Seltzer reminds us, "making others believe is . . . what making up fictions does."[44]

As one of several cultural forms situated within the vast mediasphere of crime storytelling, novels have garnered far less attention in studies of the relation between crime and culture than film, television, and, more recently, podcasts. That's an unfortunate oversight, given how essential the format of print fiction was to the development and dissemination of crime narrative in the twentieth century. From dime novels to pulp magazines to mass-market paperbacks, print attracted readers in large part by peddling stories about crime.[45] Since the 1940s, crime fiction has been one of the major genres sustaining the publishing industry.[46] By the late twentieth century, the crime novel had become far and away the most common genre category on weekly bestseller lists—a phenomenon that the novelist and critic Patrick Anderson has dubbed "the triumph of the thriller."[47] Although novels themselves are no longer the cultural powerhouse they once were, it is nevertheless the case that a significant portion of what people do still read—whether as print books, e-books, or audio books—are crime novels. What was true in the time of pulps and paperback originals remains true today: Crime fiction sells. The genre has been a constant presence in U.S. culture for nearly a century. *American Literature's War on Crime* takes the long view of this massive and massively successful genre. In doing so, it is able to ask an important question about the history of the genre's continuous growth and perennial popularity: What has the veritable flood of crime novels published since midcentury had to do with the deluge of policing and imprisonment that engulfed the country during that same span?

The five chapters of this book highlight five pivotal moments in the War on Crime and show how novels jockeyed for position to explain to readers what was really going on in those moments. Crime novels, as I read them, offered competing stories about crime—what it is, who commits it, why to fear it—and fought to convince readers which of those stories they ought to believe. Is race a reliable marker of criminality (chapter 1)? Is a riot a crime or a political act (chapter 2)? Can the police be trusted to handle violence against women (chapter 3)? Is addiction a crime or an illness (chapter 4)? Is prison a humane form of punishment (chapter 5)? Each of these questions represents the core dilemma—or, put differently, the structuring fiction—around which both the crime novels and the crime policy of the era orbited. Piecing together how novels navigated these central debates of the crime war, I argue that crime fiction constituted the site of a sustained cultural dialogue where opposing depictions of criminals, explanations of crime, and justifications for imprisonment vied for hegemony.

By and large, novelists seemed to know what they were doing. A common theme in the crime literature of this period is the role that fictional narratives play in shaping people's beliefs about crime. In Patricia Highsmith's *Strangers on a Train* (1950), one character chides another for his unrealistic assumptions: "You read too many detective stories."[48] In Brian Garfield's *Death Wish* (1972), the naïve protagonist realizes he has never seen a crime committed—"had never seen a bookie, never known a gangster . . . had never seen drugs change hands"—other than "on television or in the movies."[49] In Lawrence Block's *A Walk Among the Tombstones*

(1992), a character who teams up with a detective expects to see "a car chase and a shoot-out or some shit like that," only to conclude, "Maybe I spend too much time in front of the television set."[50] In Donna Tartt's *The Secret History* (1992), the narrator admits that a particular fact about the legal system is something "I knew, from television."[51] In Toni Cade Bambara's *Those Bones Are Not My Child* (1999), one character has "read enough mystery novels to know" how a criminal investigation is supposed to work. Another of Bambara's characters is saddened to realize that, contrary to what pop culture had promised her, "There'd be no Virgil Tibbs arriving on the scene all scientific and articulate, bringing the culprits to justice and leading her boy safely home."[52] Virgil Tibbs himself would have agreed. In *Death for a Playmate* (1969), John Ball's famous detective has to suppress his frustration with people who assume that police work will be "just like the shows on TV."[53]

Novelists from this period were clearly self-conscious about their declining cultural prestige in a world that was increasingly dominated by television and film. They sought to counter this by reminding readers that what we think we know about crime is in fact mediated by media of all kinds, novels included. Broadly speaking, recurrent moments like those in the previous paragraph belong to the long history of reflexivity in the novel.[54] They also indicate crime fiction's persistent awareness of the fictional underpinnings of crime. The reflexivity that we see in these examples is simultaneously an acknowledgment of crime's essential fictionality and a promise, however improbable, to give readers a more realistic (meaning less fictional) account of it. What these texts repeatedly tell us is that if we're reading or watching the wrong things—if we "spend too much time in front of the television set"—we're likely to have the wrong idea of what crime is. Crime novels positioned themselves as a potential corrective. They vowed to teach readers better.

A vivid example of this tendency appears on the first page of every book in Ed McBain's 87th Precinct series of police procedurals (which ran for an astounding fifty years). The 87th Precinct novels always begin with the same three sentences, set apart on their own dedicated page: "The city in these pages is imaginary. The people, the places, are all fictitious. Only the police routine is based on established investigatory technique."[55] Here McBain simultaneously confesses the fictitiousness of his books and asserts their authenticity. This double move allows McBain to position his "imaginary" stories as reliable windows onto the "established" reality of police practice. In a sense, these sentences would go on to become an implicit frame for practically every crime novel written under the cloud of the crime war: a kind of shadow agreement between author and reader that a given fiction about crime and policing will deliver a minimum amount of authenticated fact. McBain's disclaimer is only one instance of the many ways that crime novels deliberately index their own pedagogical imperative, their function as corrective lessons for readers steeped in the unreliability and misinformation of the crime mediascape. The novels I examine in this book are no doubt fantasies themselves, often misleading in their own right. But we will want to pay close attention to how and why this tradition of fiction has labored to convince its readers that, through the very act of reading, they stand to learn something more accurate and thus more edifying about what crime really is.

Perhaps this is why the protagonist of Richard Wright's *Savage Holiday* (1954) refuses to read novels at all. Recently retired, and soon to become an unwitting murderer, he wonders what to do with all his new spare time. Should he "read a book? No; no; God, no! He would have resented some novelist's trying to project upon him some foolish flight of fantasy."[56] Wright is only half-joking when he describes novels as attempts by writers to "project" some sort of "fantasy" or set of ideas onto readers. For as much as these lines traffic in a bit of easy irony (a resentment toward novelists expressed by a character in a novel), they also indicate Wright's awareness that crime novels play a key role in shaping the belief systems—or more cynically, constructing the fantasy worlds—of their readers. The hero of Wright's novel doesn't want to read a novel because he doesn't want to have his worldview affected by what he reads. He does not want to be swayed by fiction. To fear literature for this reason is also to admit its power. Every crime novel has its own story to tell about the nature, causes, and consequences of crime. The criminal who stars in *Savage Holiday* didn't want to risk being influenced by that kind of story, but many, many readers in the War on Crime era were willing to take the chance. *American Literature's War on Crime* follows in the footsteps of those intrepid readers. It seeks to reconstruct what it was like to be conscripted into the crime war—to be taught to love it or hate it or defend it or question it—through the reading of novels. You might say it is an effort to find out what the protagonist of *Savage Holiday* was so afraid of.

INTRODUCTION

At this point readers of this book might find themselves wondering: What even *is* a crime novel? The category is no doubt unwieldy and imprecise. Crime fiction is, as the critic Thomas Heise says evenly, "an elastic, fluid, and heterogeneous genre."[57] Often it feels as if we simply know a crime novel when we see one. The phrase *crime fiction* once primarily meant *detective fiction*, yet it came to encompass a range of psychological thrillers that adopt the perspectives of victims and perpetrators. It tends to imply a certain kind of mass production—formulaic plots, repetitive series, airport paperbacks—but also includes an increasing number of more prestigious or "literary" authors, not to mention authors whose work for pulp presses was later absorbed into the literary canon (Raymond Chandler, Chester Himes, Patricia Highsmith). Every time crime fiction is boiled down to one thing—one set of narrative conventions, one rung on the cultural hierarchy—it turns out to be several other things as well.

I should say from the outset that this book is not especially interested in policing the borders of this particular genre. Instead, I strive to read as widely as possible across the numerous subgenres, myriad formulas, various readerships, and varying degrees of cultural prestige that make up the notoriously baggy category of crime fiction. Most of the books I discuss in *American Literature's War on Crime* do fall within the bounds of the most familiar definitions of the genre: mass-market detective novels, police procedurals, and thrillers. With those novels forming a substantial base for each chapter, I then move to broaden my field of vision, wondering where other genres that tell stories about cops, criminals, and prisons (naturalist fiction, speculative fiction, postmodern fiction, and more) fit within the larger puzzle of the literary crime war. The chapters that follow thus leapfrog from the psychological thrillers of Dorothy B. Hughes to the police procedurals of Joseph Wambaugh to the domestic suspense novels of Mary Higgins Clark to the serial killer fiction of Patricia Cornwell to the feminist detective novels of Barbara Neely. I study fiction that was marketed to white audiences, to Black audiences, to conservative audiences, and to liberal ones. I discuss writers who are massively popular (Sue Grafton, Stephen King), critically respected (John A. Williams, Toni Cade Bambara), and largely forgotten (Nancy Pickard, John Katzenbach). I analyze a number of works that it may seem outlandish to categorize as crime novels at all (Ralph Ellison's *Invisible Man*, Don DeLillo's *White Noise*, Jesmyn Ward's *Sing, Unburied, Sing*). From the point of view of this book, all of this and more can be thought of as crime fiction.

Such an expansive, big-tent approach to the genre is not a unique scholarly innovation, and it isn't meant to be.[58] Still, some readers may find my book's definition of crime fiction unusual or even strained, encompassing as it does the popular and the prestigious, the marginal and the mainstream, the conventional (cops and killers) and the atypical (*White Noise*, really?), not to mention novels that seem, by any measure of common sense, to belong to different genres entirely, such as melodrama, historical fiction, science fiction, or the gothic. My intention in treating the genre in so loose and open a manner is *not* to imply that differences of form, reception, audience, marketing, and canonicity don't matter. Rather, my aim is to find a way to chart the series of literary dialogues about crime that took place both *within* and *across* different narrative formulas, different publishing spheres, and different communities of readers. The War on Crime is the name of the territory that these dialogues surveyed and traversed. Crime fiction, as I employ the phrase, is the name of the map.

The premise of this book is that if we want to fully understand how postwar American writers adapted to a world that was being transformed by new ideologies of crime control and new modes of police power, we need a more capacious way of talking about what counts as a crime novel. To this end, *American Literature's War on Crime* may be thought of as an attempt to recenter the *crime* part of the phrase *crime fiction*. What if we were to make the social history of crime—rather than the aesthetic history of a particular cluster of formal conventions (private eyes, mean streets, locked rooms)—the key to defining the crime novel? Unlocking the genre in this way enables us to notice something fairly remarkable: how an enormous variety of literary texts found themselves addressing the same set of questions concerning crime, class, race, and policing—questions whose more common shorthand, for the past sixty years, has been the War on Crime. From the middle of the twentieth century to the first decades of the twenty-first, a large number of novelists, drawing on an array of genre conventions and working within a range of publishing situations, all contributed to a sustained conversation about the nature of crime. Repurposed as a way to capture this large-scale literary conversation, the category of crime fiction becomes a critical tool for tracking

INTRODUCTION

how the defining policies, ideologies, procedures, and debates of the War on Crime were absorbed into, and refashioned within, the pages of popular fiction.

Excellent books have already been written about crime fiction and the liberal state,[59] race and the detective novel,[60] literature and prison,[61] the cultural construction of racial criminality,[62] Black pulp fiction,[63] the surveillance of Black writers,[64] and the literary response to Broken Windows policing.[65] Building on these pathbreaking traditions of scholarship on race, crime, and genre, *American Literature's War on Crime* offers the first comprehensive study of the relation between American fiction and the policies that produced mass incarceration.[66] My aim is to rewrite the literary history of crime fiction after 1940, revealing how the genre developed in lockstep with the institutions and ideologies of punishment in postwar America.

The novels I study in this book helped forge the world—the imagined worlds and worldviews—in which mass incarceration flourished. Yet they did so in different ways and often to opposing ends. If crime novels are always trying to tell us something about crime, that doesn't mean they're all telling us the same thing. I've proposed that in the years of the crime war, the genre of crime fiction operated as contested terrain: a kind of cultural battleground where writers vied to tell competing stories about the nature of crime, policing, and punishment. The debates and disagreements that played out in fiction show us the tensions that coursed beneath public support for the War on Crime: how different communities of readers and writers developed different explanations of and responses to the national conversations around crime. It would be a mistake to assume that all crime novels did one thing or had one predictable (pro-police, pro-prison) political function. They didn't. Instead, literary texts allow us to glimpse *the process of ideological struggle* over policing and incarceration: the messy and uneven process by which a set of ideas about and justifications for the carceral state steadily gained traction in American culture. During the long War on Crime, crime fiction was a vital cultural site where disputes about crime and punishment could be publicly staged, and where an uneasy but ultimately decisive consensus around police and prison expansion was slowly hammered out.

My understanding of crime fiction as politically contested terrain operates across various scales of reading. First, an individual text may contain its own internal contradictions in understanding crime (*The New Centurions* preaches color blindness but criminalizes race; *The Green Mile* laments prison but also accepts it). Next, two corresponding texts or two contemporaneous subgenres might engage in a specific dialogue or disagreement about crime (police procedurals viewed riots as threats to civilization, while Black revolutionary novels depicted them as collective political gestures). But it is only at a still broader scale that that we can see the whole history of postwar crime fiction as a sustained space of cultural contestation: an ongoing battle to tell readers what crime—and the War on Crime—is and isn't. Call this the *totalizing view* of how a genre interfaces with history. It is this totalizing view that the whole of *American Literature's War on Crime* seeks to bring into focus. For better or for worse, the view at this scale is not going to be either confirmed or falsified by a single text; nor does it depend on the self-reported experience of any one reader. Instead, it requires us to read many novels across many decades in order to make out a broader literary–historical pattern. What we gain from studying that pattern is a panoramic view of how postwar U.S. literature was informed by, and in turn helped to form, the cultural logic of the crime war.

For obvious reasons, then, this book's major claims would not be convincingly substantiated by readings of a small handful of privileged texts. To make a more convincing case about how literature participated in the defining debates of the long War on Crime, this book required a larger archive. In the chapters that follow, I've done my best to assemble one that is big enough to be persuasive yet manageable enough to be read in interesting ways. Unavoidably, a larger archive requires some tradeoffs. The more texts there are to analyze, the less space there is to talk about each one. *American Literature's War on Crime* moves swiftly across a number of novels in order to try to paint a fuller picture of literature's enmeshment in the politics of crime. My hope is that readers will ultimately be convinced that the compromise impelled by this approach is worth it: that we might choose to risk a foreshortened account of any single novel in order to achieve a more sweeping view of how eight decades of continual crime war remade an entire literary genre.

Seventy is a lot of novels. It's still not enough. Crime fiction is a bottomless pit of a genre. Erle Stanley Gardner, creator of the famous fictional defense lawyer Perry Mason, once referred to himself as a "fiction factory."[67] Yet the sheer uninterrupted production of crime fiction over almost a century may bring to mind less an assembly line than a perpetual-motion machine. I don't know exactly how many mystery and detective novels have been published in that time, but I do know that it would be impossible for one person, unaided by computers, to read them all. The risk of writing a book such as this one, then, is that my desire to assemble a generously sized archive may be misconstrued as a promise of comprehensiveness. So allow me to issue a caution, in the form of a confession: This book is not comprehensive. A few of the noteworthy twentieth- and twenty-first-century crime novelists who do not appear in the following pages include David Goodis, Margaret Millar, Iceberg Slim, Tony Hillerman, Rolando Hinojosa, John Grisham, Nikki Baker, Megan Abbott, and James Patterson. The list goes on. Some of these absences involve authors whose significance I thought could be better explained through frameworks that lie outside the scope of this book. Others are the result of my deliberate choice in certain cases to highlight lesser-known or more unexpected texts over those that have already received scholarly attention on similar grounds. Still others are simply regrettable oversights.

But the novels treated in the coming chapters were not selected at random. In building the archive that would serve as the foundation for this book, I was driven by two main priorities. First, I sought to cover as much ground as possible by selecting works by famous as well as forgotten crime writers, mass-market novels as well as literary ones, bestsellers as well as books long out of print; and by making sure these works represented many of the best known subgenres of postwar crime writing, including the criminal-centered thriller, the police procedural, the vigilante novel, the feminist detective novel, domestic suspense fiction, and serial killer fiction. Second, I zeroed in on what I take to be the essential storylines of the War on Crime and prioritized the novels that best typify how writers themselves took up and fleshed out those storylines. The result is one critic's attempt, extensive but hardly exhaustive, to map the relays between crime fiction and crime policy in the era of mass incarceration.

That map unfurls over five chapters. They tell a continuous chronological story about the development of the War on Crime and the rise of mass incarceration. In the 1940s and '50s, Black criminalization intensified in the face of urban demographic change and civil rights struggle (chapter 1).

In the 1960s and '70s, civil unrest and the rise of Black radicalism spurred the official launch of the War on Crime (chapter 2). From the 1970s to the 1990s, violence against women became an issue of national concern and transformed how feminist activists viewed the police (chapter 3). In the 1980s and '90s, the War on Drugs marked a new phase in the criminalization of urban communities of color (chapter 4). And in the 1990s and 2000s, mass incarceration became both a full-blown crisis and an accepted feature of American society (chapter 5). Each chapter recounts a key episode in America's long War on Crime—and does so by documenting how that episode was narrated, as it unfolded, by crime novels.

Chapter 1, "Invisible Men, 1940–1966," explains how the seeds of the War on Crime were sown in the demographic, economic, and political upheavals of the 1940s and '50s. The changing racial demographics of urban areas, diminishing employment prospects for Black workers in the industrial North, and intensifying civil rights activism all combined to tie criminality to race in the public imagination. In response to the rapid spread of new ideologies of Black criminality, midcentury crime fiction relentlessly probed the limits of criminal visibility. It did so by organizing itself around one recurring question: What is a criminal supposed to look like? This chapter demonstrates how that question coursed through paperback thrillers about undetected psychopaths by Patricia Highsmith, Jim Thompson, Dorothy B. Hughes, Robert Bloch, and Chester Himes; canonical works of African American fiction by Ralph Ellison, Richard Wright, and Ann Petry; white-authored novels about Black criminals by Charles Willeford, Evan Hunter, and Hughes; and Black-authored novels about white criminals by Petry, Wright, and Himes. Ultimately, my aim is to show how the tenacious link between racial and criminal visibility in the postwar, pre–Civil Rights era dictated the formal development of the crime novel while also policing who was able to write about what kind of crime. Generally speaking, midcentury crime novels knew that people could not identify criminals just by looking at them. But these novels also understood that they were part of a society that increasingly believed it could.

Chapter 2, "Riot Acts, 1967–1974," introduces the War on Crime and documents its considerable influence on crime novels in the 1960s and '70s. Johnson's crime war was a response to a multitude of factors, foremost among them the proliferation of uprisings in segregated neighborhoods of American cities. The conflation of crime and revolt, I argue, played a major

INTRODUCTION

role in the development of the era's crime fiction, which pioneered several new literary character types designed to stake out key positions in the roiling debates about the causes and consequences of urban rebellion. The chapter covers the invention of the beat cop procedural by Joseph Wambaugh; the riot reportage of John Hersey; novels about Black revolutionaries by John Ball, Ernest Tidyman, Sam Greenlee, John A. Williams, John Edgar Wideman, and Gil Scott-Heron; and vigilante fiction by Donald Goines and Brian Garfield. As the figures of the beat cop, the revolutionary, and the vigilante became familiar characters in the era's crime fiction, they became the mouthpieces for a series of directly competing claims about the nature of riot, race, and crime rates. They rushed to give readers different answers to the question of what—or whom—the newly launched War on Crime was really a war against.

Chapter 3, "Detecting Domestic Violence, 1975–2000," demonstrates how debates about the role of the state in policing gender-based violence shaped women's crime writing. Between the 1970s and the 1990s, a dramatic change occurred in how the legal system responded to violence against women. Domestic violence was transformed from an issue routinely ignored by the police to a cornerstone of the War on Crime. This chapter traces how that transformation—and the complex disagreements it spurred within the feminist movement—was reflected in several new kinds of crime fiction that were written by and marketed primarily to women. I begin by uncovering the role that depictions of domestic violence played in feminist private eye novels by Sue Grafton, Sara Paretsky, Nancy Pickard, Patricia Cornwell, and Barbara Neely. I then show how anxieties about family values and family violence were registered in domestic suspense fiction by Mary Higgins Clark and Toni Cade Bambara. Finally, I turn to Eleanor Taylor Bland's and Linda Fairstein's novels about female police officers and prosecutors, reading them as early literary expressions of what has come to be known as carceral feminism. Should women partner with the police in order to combat gender-based violence? This was a question that divided activists from the very start of the feminist antiviolence movement. It was also a question that determined the course of female crime fiction in the late twentieth century.

Chapter 4, "Two Paths for Pathology, 1984–1998," recounts how the War on Crime became the War on Drugs and asks: If the stereotypical criminals of the era were young Black men, why were so many novelists in the

1980s and '90s writing about white serial killers? My answer is that the character types of the serial killer and the drug addict were more closely linked than people realize. That link was rooted in a culture that was trying to decide whether addiction was a crime or an illness—and whether illness itself was a problem better managed by the health care system or the criminal justice system. As these questions were answered in the form of harsh antidrug laws, crime writers began to test the boundaries separating crime, sickness, and pathology. They wanted to understand where to draw the line between crime politics and medical ethics. This chapter explores how that line was drawn in serial killer novels by James Ellroy, Walter Mosley, Patricia Cornwell, Lawrence Block, Barbara Neely, Joyce Carol Oates, and Don DeLillo; and in crime narratives set in hospitals by Barbara D'Amato, Sue Grafton, Sara Paretsky, Richard Price, and Octavia Butler. The chapter ends by situating the War on Drugs in the broader context of deindustrialization, arguing that the literary figure of the psychopath ultimately became an emblem of how the sickness of an entire economic system could be successfully hidden behind the pathologization of the urban poor.

Finally, chapter 5, "The Novel in the Age of Mass Incarceration, 1992–2023," tells the story of how American novelists slowly but steadily awakened to the crisis of a growing prison population. I chart the course by which mass incarceration—as a novel phenomenon in U.S. history, and as a new set of terms and concepts for describing that phenomenon—made its way into mainstream fiction. From the 1990s to the 2020s, different subgenres of crime fiction worked in different ways to cultivate in their readers a particular ethical or affective stance toward the prison system. The chapter analyzes wrongful-conviction narratives by Stephen King and John Katzenbach; detective novels by Michael Nava, Walter Mosley, and Sara Paretsky; pioneering works of street literature by Sister Souljah and Vickie Stringer; historical novels by Colson Whitehead and Jesmyn Ward; and speculative fiction by Margaret Atwood, George Saunders, and Nana Kwame Adjei-Brenyah. While crime novels initially responded to concerns about mass imprisonment by fixating on feelings of guilt and complicity, recent prison fiction—written after mass incarceration had become a fully entrenched part of public discourse—has labored to answer a pair of more far-reaching questions about the vast carceral network that undergirds our present. Was mass incarceration inevitable? Or did we once have the freedom to make a different choice?

For a complete list of the literary works discussed in each chapter, consult the appendix.

———

This book is a work of literary history. That means it studies the development of novels over time. As befits a book whose main subject is the history of literature, the years designated in each chapter's title refer not to political events but to the span of publication dates of the novels discussed in that particular chapter. Framing the chapters this way allows me to foreground what might be called the *literary coordinates* of the War on Crime that constitute this book's main contribution to an already rich and extensive conversation among scholars, writers, theorists, and activists about mass incarceration in America. It allows us to see how, as times changed, the nature and substance of novels about crime changed with them.

This book is also a work of literary historicism. That means it studies how the development of novels takes place in relation, and often in response, to social circumstances. Literature no doubt develops according to its own internal clock; yet that clock is clearly synchronized with broader contexts. This book is an attempt to understand how such acts of synchronization occur—and to explain why, whether as scholars or citizens or simple lovers of fiction, we ought to care that they do. Although it has long been common to view literary works as superfluous or superficial or superstructural or second-order adornments laid decoratively atop the real world, the fact of the matter is that they are also, in a very real sense, a part of that world: objects fabricated from within it, bearing its traces.[68] It follows that the reading of fiction should not immediately be assumed to offer some kind of escape or protection from the concrete realities and practical concerns of our world. What reading really provides, I would venture, is just a different set of directions for getting there. Consider this book an atlas of the myriad routes by which crime novels convey us back to the wider world of law and order and crime and punishment that both occasions and transfixes them.

American Literature's War on Crime believes that we can learn something new about how mass incarceration flourished by studying novels, and that we can learn something new about novels by studying how they participated in the formative debates of the crime war. It is true that crime is no mere fiction. Yet fiction is one of the primary ways a culture tells itself the story of what crime is and what should be done about it. The history of postwar crime fiction can thus be understood as a secret history of the stories that helped transform the United States into a carceral state. Let's find out what those stories had to say.

1

INVISIBLE MEN, 1940–1966

nobody knows what a murderer looks like

—*STRANGERS ON A TRAIN* (1950)

DOUBLE VISION

One of the most noteworthy features of mid-twentieth-century American crime fiction is the sheer number of novels starring charismatic murderers. From Norman Bates to Bigger Thomas to Tom Ripley, many of American literature's most famous criminal sociopaths were birthed in midcentury fiction.[1] Why? What was the era's literary preoccupation with criminality all about? This chapter argues that midcentury novels about criminals were really about the deepening entanglement of three distinct concepts: criminality, visibility, and race.[2] Can you identify a criminal just from looking at them? My contention is that this question became newly central to both American society and American literature in the postwar, pre–Civil Rights era: an era when racial prejudice found its most effective expression in the language of crime.

The War on Crime did not officially materialize until the middle of the 1960s. But its seeds were planted well before then, amid the immense geographic, demographic, and economic upheavals wrought by the Second Great Migration and the Civil Rights movement. Those upheavals locked in a set of enduring ideas about the link between race and crime. In the postwar decades, new myths about Black criminality sprouted up across the American social landscape. Such myths would go on to play a central role in the remaking of urban crime policy after 1965. But they took root first in the 1940s and '50s, when changing economic and social conditions significantly altered the politics of race. From Northern suburbs to Southern elites all the way to the halls of Congress, a large and varied chorus of voices rose above the din to proclaim that Black crime was the nation's primary problem.

The problem wasn't really crime, though. It was jobs. Hundreds of thousands of manufacturing jobs began to disappear from Northern cities in the 1950s, just as a large Black population arrived from the South looking for freedom from Jim Crow oppression and for places to work.[3] Employment discrimination and the concentration of Black workers in precarious low-wage jobs meant that as unemployment rates started to rise, they did so first and most precipitously for Black workers in Northern cities. By 1955, the Black unemployment rate had surged to double the rate for whites.[4] As this happened, U.S. cities became home to a new class of the permanently unemployed that was largely made up of African Americans.[5]

Chronic unemployment, a consequence of industrial contraction, plant relocation, labor-market segmentation, deskilling, and outright discrimination, fed stereotypes about the criminal disorder of nonwhite urban communities. The simple fact of outdoor gatherings among Black men unable to find work became, as the historian Thomas Sugrue documents, "a scene that whites found threatening."[6] The public visibility of the unemployed Black worker (an image that might otherwise have been taken as a harbinger of the economic downturn that would soon affect working-class communities of all colors) was thus mistaken for a crime scene. An economic threat, unemployment, was sublimated into anxiety about the threat of Black criminality. Urban America was now generally seen as "black, antineighborly, and uninhabitable."[7] Police presence in segregated urban neighborhoods grew, and killings by police became increasingly common. In a famous petition submitted to the United Nations in 1951 titled *We Charge Genocide*, the Civil Rights Congress argued that since the 1930s, "most of the violence against Negroes" had moved from "the countryside" to cities, and was now perpetrated not by mobs but by cops. "Once the classic method of lynching was the rope," the CRC wrote. "Now it is the policeman's bullet."[8] As Black urban neighborhoods felt the first shudders of deindustrialization and confronted a new wave of lethal policing, white workers, the firms that employed them, and the social services that supported them shifted to the suburbs. Crime was one of the most common excuses that white families gave for moving out of cities.[9] In this way, the term became a code word for a much wider complex of deteriorating social conditions—including the absence of adequate jobs, housing, and schools—that white flight and public divestment had locked into segregated urban cores. Taking stock of the situation in the early 1950s, William L. Patterson, the leader of the Civil Rights Congress, noted that there seemed to be a "conscious attempt to place the brand of criminality" on Black communities in general, and on "Negro youth" in particular.[10]

As civil rights activism gained energy and visibility in this period, it too was folded into preexisting narratives about Black crime. Organized acts of protest and civil disobedience were frequently held up as examples of lawlessness and added to crime statistics. Meanwhile, Jim Crow politicians loudly insisted that integration itself was an incubator of crime. As the political scientist Naomi Murakawa has influentially argued, by the end of the 1950s, intense debates over civil rights had produced an unlikely bipartisan consensus that the urgent issue of Black citizenship was, at its core, a crime problem. For their part, Republicans and Southern Democrats argued that integration and civil rights organizing caused crime and emboldened criminals. Northern Democrats argued the reverse: that crime was a *result* of racial oppression and white mob violence in the South, which led to what they viewed as "justifiable anger," often expressed as violence, on the part of African Americans. The two sides may have disagreed on the solution, but both "accepted black aggression as the center of the debate."[11] The notion of Black criminality could be taken as evidence of the danger of abolishing Jim Crow or of the need to do so, but in either case, it was taken as a fact. No matter which side of the aisle a person sat on, there was little political effort or incentive to distinguish civil rights activism from petty crime.

Things had not always been so. In the late nineteenth and early twentieth centuries, the answer to the question *what does a criminal look like?* was more likely to center on working-class European immigrants, who were then visually stamped with associations of crime and vice. But those associations began to loosen in the 1920s and '30s, the historian Khalil Gibran Muhammad has argued, as the "national attention on white hoodlums and ethnic gangsters during Prohibition gradually receded" in the wake of the Great Depression. The waning interest in white ethnic criminals was bound up with important changes to the presumed visibility of the criminal classes. In the mid-1920s, second-generation immigrants "were perceived as the most dangerous criminals because they moved easily beyond the slums of their birth and the ethnicity of their parents."[12] That is to say, working-class criminals were considered dangerous because they could no longer be counted on to look different from middle-class white people. Now whiteness was not something that visually marked urban criminality; it was something that concealed it. Interestingly, however, this did not make the general public more afraid of white criminals; instead, it aroused sympathy for them. The de-ethnicization of second-generation immigrants made them seem not worryingly undetectable but simply more white, which in turn made them appear less inherently criminal and more deserving of economic aid and legal protection. Criminal justice reforms in the 1920s and '30s bore this out, as public outcry coupled with the broader rehabilitative ideals of the New Deal helped overturn policies designed to punish repeat offenders, most of whom were white men.[13]

As "the children of the foreign born became more 'white,'" Muhammad argues, "whites became less 'criminal.'"[14] The twinned de-ethnicization and decriminalization of the white working class in the early twentieth century had far-reaching consequences.[15] Just a few decades later, it would be possible for the sociologist Daniel Bell to make his famous argument that organized crime was simply a "stepladder of social ascent" for European immigrant communities: a means of social mobility and an entrypoint to middle-class respectability.[16] White ethnic crime came to be seen, in Bell's well-known phrase, as "an American way of life." Meanwhile, the dissociation of crime from both white poverty and European ethnicity left it attached to one prominent visual shorthand: race. In the early 1940s, the FBI's *Uniform Crime Reports*—the century's flawed but widely-accepted standard-bearer for statistical understandings of crime—eliminated the category of "Foreign-born white" altogether. With this, Muhammad asserts, the stereotype of European immigrant criminality fully vanished, and "blackness now stood as the singular mark of a criminal."[17]

The matter of how criminality was visually and therefore racially marked became, in turn, one of the most commonly told stories in midcentury crime fiction. This is not to say that crime novels simply reproduced en masse a single set of stereotypes about Black criminals. They didn't. Rather, crime novels found themselves obsessed with—and increasingly organized around—a single recurring question: What is a criminal supposed to look like? The question was the driving force behind several major developments in American crime writing in the 1940s and '50s. This chapter charts those developments in four parts. First, I show how pulp thrillers about undetected psychopaths depended on unspoken but vital assumptions about racial visibility. Second, I demonstrate how those same assumptions about race and crime dictated the terms of African American literature's vexed dialogue with the discipline of sociology. And in the third and fourth sections, I assess two seemingly opposed but in fact tightly entwined literary trends of the period: white authors writing from the perspective of falsely accused Black criminals, and Black authors writing from the point of view of white criminals. Overall, my aim is to show how the tenacious link between racial and criminal visibility dictated the formal development of the crime novel while also policing who got to write about what kind of crime. The color line in midcentury crime fiction was a line separating both the look of literary criminals and the identities of those writing about them. As we shall see, this line turned out to be permeable in some ways, uncrossable in others. And the critical reputations and commercial fortunes of some of the era's most important writers hung in the balance.

AGAINST TYPE

In midcentury crime thrillers that use criminals as protagonists, the distinguishing feature of the criminal is that no one suspects him or her to be one. Take Patricia Highsmith's *Strangers on a Train* (1950). The entire point of Guy Haines and Charles Bruno—the two strangers who meet on a train and end up involved in a double murder—is that they do not look like criminals. Guy, according to Bruno, was not "the kind of fellow to plan a murder with." Bruno himself does not necessarily seem like that kind of fellow either; he is white and wealthy and "anyone seeing him would have judged him a young man of responsibility and character, probably with a promising future." Even Guy has a hard time believing him capable of murder: "Supposing Bruno had done it? He couldn't have, of course, but just supposing he had?" The novel repeatedly states that neither man looks the way one would expect a murderer to look. Indeed, this is the substance of Guy's great epiphany about himself in the finale: "He didn't look like a murderer... in his clean white shirtsleeves and his silk tie and his dark blue trousers, and maybe even his strained face didn't look like a murderer's to anybody else." Guy muses aloud, "That's the mistake... that nobody knows what a murderer looks like. A murderer looks like anybody!"[18]

The cultural frisson of a murderous criminal who could look "like anybody" was a unifying theme in the era's crime thrillers. In Highsmith's *The Talented Mr. Ripley* (1955), the law fails to detect Tom Ripley because he doesn't fit the type: "The police think it's some outsider who dropped by occasionally to pick up his mail, because none of the dopes in this house look like criminal types."[19] In Jim Thompson's *The Killer Inside Me* (1952)—a novel that his pulp publisher Lion Books tried to nominate for the National Book Award[20]—the psychotic sheriff Lou Ford hides behind a façade of aw-shucks politeness and folk wisdom: "A typical Western-county peace officer, that was me. Maybe friendlier-looking than the average. Maybe a little cleaner cut. But typical."[21] In Dorothy B. Hughes's *In a Lonely Place* (1947), one of the genre's great feminist critiques of male violence, serial killer Dix Steele is presented in almost identical terms: just "an average young fellow" who "look[s] just as normal as you or me, more normal probably." As one eyewitness says, "She was sure he couldn't be the strangler; he wasn't that kind of a man at all."[22] In Robert Bloch's landmark novel *Psycho* (1959), even Norman Bates doesn't seem like the murdering type; characters describe him as "no murderer," not "the type who'd ever pull any fast ones." Indeed, everyone who meets Bates is reassured by his appearance, from Mary Crane (who "made up her mind very quickly, once she saw the fat bespectacled face and heard the soft, hesitant voice. There wouldn't be any trouble") to her boyfriend Sam, who after meeting Norman feels "ashamed" for ever suspecting him: "He sounded so—so damned *ordinary!*"[23]

The structuring conceit in all of these novels, obsessed as they are with the unseen pathologies of the "ordinary," the "average," and the "typical," is that one could never know what a criminal might look like. This sounds like a fitting expression of the anxieties that characterized the early decades of the Cold War and gave rise to the Red Scare, as American society became fixated on the invisible threat of communism, the specter of an "enemy within" that could not necessarily be detected from without.

Yet as *the* defining gimmick of the midcentury suspense novel, the surprise revelation that criminals could not be identified from their outer appearance would only really have worked—would only have succeeded in being a surprise—if readers to some extent believed the opposite. Characters like Norman Bates are the enemies within, the criminals we can't see. In that case, who were the criminals readers assumed they *could* see?

In his first conversation with Bruno in *Strangers on a Train*, Guy grows increasingly frustrated with his new friend's obsession with murder: "You read too many detective stories," he tells him. "They're good," Bruno insists. "They show that all kinds of people can murder." Guy replies, "I've always thought that's exactly why they're bad." What makes detective fiction bad, according to Guy, is that it universalizes criminality, associating it with "all kinds of people." In other words, it gives the impression that there are not particular criminal types. Guy, by contrast, believes there *are* criminal types: "A certain type turned to crime. And who would know from Bruno's hands, or his room, or his ugly wistful face that he had stolen?" What type turns to crime? Whose hands or face—in contrast to Bruno's—could convey directly that they belong to a criminal? Despite Guy's later claim that "nobody knows what a murderer looks like," there is one social context mentioned in the novel that suggests that people do know. That context is a lynching. "People might collectively lynch a murderer," Guy says in the novel's final scene, an apparent non sequitur, to which his companion drunkenly replies, "Never hold with lynchings.... Gives the whole South a bad name."[24] This unexpected reference to racial terror in the South—state-sanctioned crime that most frequently justified itself through false accusations of Black men—provides an answer to the lingering question of what exactly a criminal is supposed to look like in *Strangers on a Train*. The reason that "nobody knows" that Guy and Bruno are criminals is because they are middle-class and white. The stereotypical criminal stalking the midcentury American imagination, by contrast, was neither of those things.

Highsmith was no stranger to the stereotype of the nonwhite criminal. As her biographer Andrew Wilson recounts, Highsmith, a well-known antisemite, also harbored an "irrational hatred" of Black people, and by the 1960s had become convinced that "blacks and Puerto Ricans" were responsible for rising crime in New York City.[25] In a letter written in 1971,

Highsmith speculated that continued integration would lead to a future New York overrun by Black people "hanging from 50th story windows, plugging their neighbors... before taking the lift down to fleece their pockets." This hyperbolic scene, verging on absurdity, sounds as if it were lifted from a Chester Himes novel. (In fact, Himes's *The Real Cool Killers* from 1959 revolves around the shooting of a zip gun from an apartment window.) But Highsmith did not believe herself to be exaggerating: "It has already happened to Newark, New Jersey—which is now almost cleared of whites; they have a black mayor, even, and the highest crime and dope and welfare rate in all the USA."[26]

This was hardly a fringe view. As we've already seen, the notion that integration would lead to crime was a common argument against the Civil Rights movement. It also had roots in a longer tradition of racial criminalization. African Americans have long been, in the words of W.E.B. Du Bois, "accused and taunted with being criminals." As Du Bois wrote in *The Crisis* in 1932, "Nothing in the world is easier in the United States than to accuse a black man of crime."[27] And nothing is harder in *Strangers on a Train* than to accuse a white architect. Being deposed about Miriam's murder, "Guy was sure that his own straightforwardness alone had absolved him from any suspicion."[28] Guy's faith in the link between the "straightforwardness" of his presentation and the certainty of being exonerated doubles as the novel's whole unstated but unmistakable premise: a commentary on, if not an affirmation of, the class and racial codes that dictate who can and cannot be assumed, just from looking at them, to be a criminal.

To be sure, crime fiction has long equated villainy with racial difference.[29] The first detective story written in English was Edgar Allan Poe's "The Murders in the Rue Morgue" (1841), the tale of an orangutan that brutally murders two women, which Poe based on a series of articles he had read in the *Philadelphia Saturday News and Literary Gazette* about, respectively, an orangutan in the London Zoo, an escaped ape in New York City, and a Black man named Edward Coleman who murdered his wife.[30] Poe's thinly veiled allegory of racial anxiety would become an explicit feature of the distinctly American tradition of hardboiled fiction that flourished in the 1920s and '30s, which, as many critics have pointed out, revolved around the affirmation of white male authority, often at the expense of people of color.[31] Dashiell Hammett's Continental Op drinks laudanum and dreams of trying to kill a "small brown man" wearing "an immense sombrero."[32] Raymond Chandler's Pete Anglich—a precursor to Philip Marlowe—dispatches a purple-suited Black man who breaks into his hotel room.[33] Carroll John Daly's Race Williams defeats the Ku Klux Klan, only to find himself pretending to be a member.[34]

The midcentury crime thriller's intensified interest in the drama of the hidden white criminal was less a departure from this tradition, I would suggest, than the other side of the same coin. These are novels whose central mystery is why no one can believe the killer is actually a killer; and the repeated solution to this mystery is that *looking like a killer* is actually a racial category. In these novels, what it means for someone to look or not look like a criminal is inextricable from the era's dominant ideology of racial difference, which rendered Blackness uniquely visible and whiteness conveniently invisible. This ideology is at play in something as apparently innocuous as the title to Jim Thompson's best known novel. In *The Killer Inside Me*, the murderous psycho is presented from the start as a separate being that lives "inside" sheriff Lou Ford. Ford's exterior and his interior don't match; the killer is *in* him but not him—and so, we might surmise, not white. Too much of a stretch? Maybe. In this particular historical moment, however, the strange image of a criminal concealed within you who doesn't resemble you was in fact closely connected to ideas of whiteness and Blackness. The image evoked by Thompson's title bears an uncanny resemblance to Norman Mailer's infamous concept of "The White Negro," popularized in his essay of that title, which was published just a few years after *The Killer Inside Me*. In that essay— as appalling as ever, but widely read at the time—Mailer argued that the tendency among white hipsters to "encourage" their inner "psychopath" was really a form of minstrelsy: a way of imitating what Mailer considered the innate "psychopathy" of Black culture.[35] For Mailer, the very idea of the white psychopath involved a kind of inverted racial masquerade, something like inside-out blackface.[36] He saw white criminality as something within a person that didn't racially resemble that person. In that sense, he could just as easily have titled his essay "The Black Killer Inside Me." Meanwhile, Thompson's killer sheriff Lou Ford is the perfect example of what Mailer would call in the same essay "a psychic outlaw," meaning that his criminality is a matter of inner disposition rather than outward legibility.[37] It's "inside" his head, not on his skin. The point is that you'd never know it just from looking at him.

Other midcentury crime novelists similarly grasped that the white psycho's capacity to remain unseen was at root a racial construct. Robert Bloch's *Psycho*, for instance, actually tells the story of not one but two unsuspected criminals (no, not Mrs. Bates). Norman Bates's victim Mary Crane has herself just stolen $40,000 from her boss at the Lowery Agency, and as with Bates, nobody can believe she could have done it: "That was the worst part: accepting Mary in the role of a thief. Mary wasn't that kind of person." Here again we see how the genre's language of criminality was tied to type, to the idea that only a certain "kind of person" committed crime. Yet in Mary's case, there's a twist. Her sister Lila and her boyfriend Sam are right: Mary really isn't that kind of person. Just before she is murdered, Mary has second thoughts about what she has done. She decides to return all the money after imploring herself, "*Come clean, Mary. Come clean as snow.*" The snow metaphor is revealing. Whiteness is the key to Mary's reclaimed innocence. Giving up the criminal identity that never seemed to fit her in the first place, she ultimately affirms a set of implacable facts not simply about the "kind of person" she is but about the type of skin and body she has, which she assesses immediately before taking the most famous shower in American fiction: "For a moment she stood before the mirror set in the door and took stock of herself... the body was free, white, and twenty-one."[38] No longer having an unsuspected thief hidden "inside" her, Mary Crane of Fort Worth, Texas, can now properly match her inner self (which, having repented, is "clean as snow") to her outer appearance. She is finally "free"—from the threat of prison as well as from suspicion—and that freedom is inextricable from the "white" exterior of her body.

Dorothy Hughes, too, was thinking about the presumed innocence of whiteness when she wrote *In a Lonely Place*. It is no coincidence that Dix's white anonymity—the largely successful concealment of his psychopathic nature behind the fact that he "looked like a thousand other" white middle-class men in Los Angeles—is finally unraveled by a scene of racial seeing. Central to Dix's double life, no less than to his sense of self, is his ability to come and go "without being observed." At a key moment toward the end of the novel, however, he realizes that "he wasn't unobserved. A yahoo was trimming the hedge just beyond his doors. A little measly

Mexican fellow in faded overalls, a battered hat bending his ears, a mustache drooping over his mouth. The shears were bigger than the man. Clip, clip, clip clip, the shears chopped with Dix's approaching footsteps. The fellow looked up as Dix reached the back door. "'Allo,' he said brightly."[39]

This moment of being seen marks the beginning of Dix's unraveling. He soon notices another gardener watching him ("the Virginibus Arms had suddenly gone in for gardening in a big way"), and all of a sudden lawyers and cops are ringing his doorbell, a car might be following him ("it couldn't be. The two men in the sedan were ordinary"), additional unfamiliar people appear around his apartment complex—in short, he feels *noticed*. At one point Dix lies down on his bed, "trying to quiet his thoughts, pleading to any gods who might heed to give him rest. And he heard it begin, clip-clip, clip-clip. Outside his windows, clip-clip, clip-clip. . . . It had begun and it wouldn't stop. It would go on, louder and louder, sharper and sharper. . . . He began to weep." A kind of rewrite of "The Tell-Tale Heart" for the midcentury apartment complex, here Dix's repressed guilt is brought to the surface not by the beating of a heart but by the incessant clipping of a gardener's shears. But why the gardener? Throughout Hughes's novel, Dix's own acts of observation are regularly connected to race: the Mexican gardener, a "young colored" waiter, even a striking moment when Dix is caught off-guard by the sight of a woman who reminds him of his first victim and to whom he refers as "the little brown girl."[40] In all of these instances, Dix's ability to remain unseen as the novel's killer is contrasted with his ability to see others specifically by seeing them through their race.

The connection between visibility and racialization seems, indeed, to be the very thing that secures Dix's own invisibility—until it doesn't. Dix has spent most of the novel enjoying the privilege of invisibility while calling special attention to the racial visibility of the minority workers around him. The moment when Dix is watched and greeted by the gardener he labels as "Mexican" is the moment when the tables are turned: the person Dix has seen through racialization now sees him. It is telling that Hughes uses this pivotal scene to set in motion the novel's entire extended climax, which will culminate in Dix's being unmasked and apprehended, finally seen for who he really is. If the moment of being noticed marks the beginning of his downfall, that is because it is the moment when he is subjected to the very procedures of racialized visibility from which he had thought his whiteness exempted him. It turns out that the people of color whom Dix was seeing while imagining himself "unobserved" were seeing him back the whole time.

Ultimately, it was left to Chester Himes to fully unpack the political implications of the undetectable-murderer genre.[41] Himes's *Run Man Run* (written in the late 1950s and published in 1966) is the story of a psychotic white policeman named Matt Walker who, in the novel's opening, wanders past an Automat, where he ends up murdering two Black porters whom he accuses of stealing his car. Another porter, Jimmy Johnson, witnesses the killings and spends the rest of the book running from Walker, who is trying to kill him too. Like all the other white criminals I've discussed in this section, Walker's defining characteristic is that he "doesn't look like a killer." As a result of this elemental assumption about criminal appearance, no one believes Johnson's story about the murders: not the police, not his lawyer, and not even his girlfriend, Linda Lou, who finds it hard to accept something "so unbelievable." Having met Walker herself, she just "couldn't believe he'd murder two defenseless colored men and shoot at Jimmy without warning." As she puts it to Johnson, "It'd just make it easier for us to get a case against him and get others to believe you too if he looked more like the type who'd do such a thing." The problem is that Walker doesn't. Once again, the perception of criminality is inseparable from a particular kind of typification. Walker knows this, and he spends the bulk of the novel confident that people will believe him to be innocent precisely because of how he looks: "No one would ever think of him as a maniac."[42]

Meanwhile, the person who does look "like the type" is Johnson himself. Walker capitalizes on this by attempting to frame him for the Automat murders. Johnson's presence in the narrative—as a working-class Black man who is at once Walker's disbelieved victim and his plausible scapegoat—adds a new layer to Himes's version of the nobody-believes-he's-a-killer story, one that was only implied in the other novels I've considered thus far. Alternating between Walker's perspective and Johnson's, Himes makes explicit how the widespread presumption of white innocence (the natural expectation that a white cop doesn't look like a psychopath) depends on the equally widespread belief in Black guilt. In the opening pages of the novel, Walker, stumbling drunk, assumes that he has misplaced his car until he randomly catches sight of one of the porters. The "sight of a Negro made him think that his car had been stolen instead of lost. He couldn't have said why, but he was suddenly sure of it." The sudden unconscious connection between the "sight of a Negro" and the idea of stealing highlights the powerful logic of visibility that connects race to crime throughout the novel. When Walker accuses the porter of stealing the car, it is based on the premise, the porter realizes, that "being a Negro made him automatically suspect." This sort of automatic suspicion is the equal and opposite force of Walker's own "unbelievable" criminality. "He's a white detective and I'm just a poor colored porter," Johnson laments later. As he comes to realize, the privilege of innocence and the burden of guilt are rigidly distributed along exactly these lines. Johnson decides that the whole question of crime is "just a matter of what people want to believe."[43] And what most people wanted to believe about criminality at this time was that it could be visibly detected on the surface of another person's skin.

Himes knew this firsthand. In 1955, only days before departing the United States for France, where he would live for the rest of his life, Himes was having a farewell meal with his fellow janitors at the Automat where they worked when an aggressive police officer confronted the group, angrily accusing them of having stolen his car.[44] Himes was able to escape his encounter unscathed. Then he wrote a novel about it. With *Run Man Run*, Himes was trying to understand why it was that the barely submerged violence of an unhinged white cop could be so effortlessly laundered, in American society, into groundless criminal suspicion foisted on a group of Black workers. To answer this question, he borrowed the tools of a distinctly midcentury literary genre that had, in a more coded way, been narrating it all along.

The story of the undetectable murderer that was told repeatedly across the pulp crime thrillers of the 1940s and '50s—the story of the person who just *didn't look like the type* to be a criminal—was always, at its core, a story about race. The invisibility of the white criminal depended on the visual linkage of Blackness to crime. Literary explorations of the former were thus inextricable from popular beliefs about the latter. From Hughes to Himes, midcentury thrillers highlighted criminals who couldn't be seen as criminals precisely to the extent that they were seen as "typical," "average," and white. These novels confessed that crime could happen anywhere, be committed by anyone. It was just a matter of what, or who, you were willing to let yourself see.

THE SOCIOLOGIST AND THE CRIME NOVELIST

The antihero of *In a Lonely Place* pities the detective looking for him: "Poor guy. Going around in circles trying to find an invisible man."[45] As for the most famous invisible man in American letters—the unnamed narrator of Ralph Ellison's *Invisible Man* (1952)—he has a rather different experience. It is not, despite the tempting misreading of the novel's title, that he can't be seen at all. It's more that, when he is seen, he is most likely to be seen as a criminal. When the narrator walks to the trash to get rid of a package, someone spies him and says suspiciously, "You some kind of confidence man or dope peddler or something?" Later, he dresses in a style that he knows others will "see . . . simply as a criminal." In the novel's climactic scene, he descends into the underground sewer while trying to elude two white men who are chasing him while shouting, "What'd you steal?" And at the very start of the novel, the narrator lashes out at a white man who calls him "an insulting name," only to find that the newspaper reports the incident as a mugging.[46] For Ellison, it was essential to convey that racial criminality was a way of seeing and being seen. In *Invisible Man*, criminalization is how Black existence, otherwise ignored, is made visible to and by white society.

The question of how this mode of racial seeing was established and experienced became a pressing one for many African American novelists at midcentury. It was a question that lay at the heart at another landmark work of fiction: Richard Wright's *Native Son* (1940). Wright grew up reading detective stories in pulp magazines like *Flynn's Detective Weekly* and the *Argosy All-Story Magazine*, and his biographer Michel Fabre goes so far as to suggest that Wright "owes his spiritual survival in racist Mississippi and . . . his vocation as a writer to detective stories, popular fiction, and dime novels."[47] This personal attachment to pulp crime genres had a notable influence on the composition of *Native Son*, even as the novel set out to give a much different explanation for the causes of crime. Bigger Thomas is, to be sure, one of American literature's most well-known criminals. It is easy to forget, however, that part of the point of Wright's novel is that Bigger is already seen as a criminal before he even meets Mary Dalton, whom he will eventually kill. As we learn during Bigger's first foray into the Dalton family's wealthy neighborhood, this is a world in which Blackness is criminalized in advance: "Suppose a policeman saw him wandering in a white neighborhood like this? It would be thought that he was trying to rob or rape somebody." Bigger is acutely aware of race as a concept brought into being by criminalization. The "feeling he had had all his life: he was black and had done wrong" is vindicated when Bigger finds himself standing in a room full of reporters and police who are looking for Mary's body. The "white faces all about him," Bigger believes, do not necessarily think him capable of having "killed a rich white girl." But they already see him as a some kind of criminal: "They might think he would steal a dime, rape a woman, get drunk, or cut somebody."[48]

In the novel's climactic courtroom scene, the prosecutor Buckley explains that the point of punishing Bigger is "for the protection of our society, our homes and our loves." It is crime control. Thus does Bigger's violent attempt at self-determination end up merely fueling white society's racist fantasy of being overrun by Black criminals—the "fear," as Buckley puts it in court, "that at this very moment some half-human black ape may be climbing through the windows of our homes to rape, murder, and burn our daughters!" At the end of *Native Son*, Bigger seems to realize that what really defines him is this feedback loop of racial criminalization, not his own violent assertion of agency. "They wouldn't let me live and I killed," Bigger tells his communist lawyer Max, speaking the novel's most famous lines. "I didn't want to kill! . . . But what I killed for, I *am*! It must have been pretty deep in me to make me kill!"[49]

What has always interested me about these lines is how uncomfortably they echo the era's essentialist view of Black criminality: the notion that Bigger's violent impulse is "deep in" him and that his act is therefore interchangeable with his identity ("what I killed for, I *am*"). That echo may be what Max hears, too, as he listens to Bigger, his "eyes . . . full of terror" and "his body mov[ing] nervously."[50] The critic Abdul JanMohamed has read Bigger's lines here as a "moral affirmation of his desire and his life . . . an affirmation of his actions and, hence, his agency," and I can certainly see why.[51] But it's odd that Bigger jumps so quickly from affirming his actions to affirming an essentialist claim about his identity, and odder still that he does so while making clear that he doesn't really believe that claim himself ("it *must have been* pretty deep in me," he says, as if as repeating something he has been told). That's why I think that what Wright has chosen to have Bigger attest to in this heartbreaking scene is the sheer voraciousness of the myth of Black criminality. What Bigger is saying to Max is that there is no act of Black resistance such a myth can't swallow, no form of Black being—no utterance of "I am"—for which it can't claim to speak.

In her breakthrough novel *The Street* (1946), Ann Petry took up the issue of racial criminalization in a similar way. As Wright had done six years earlier, Petry based her novel—an exposé of poverty and violence in Harlem—on a news clipping about a crime.[52] Also like Wright, she had a more personal connection to genres of crime writing. Petry's husband was a mystery writer, and her first published piece of fiction, "Marie of the Cabin Club," was a crime story.[53] Fusing Petry's familiarity with mystery fiction with her background in progressive journalism and social work, *The Street* is a novel about the sexism, racism, and economic deprivation that underlie white society's view of "colored people as naturally criminal." Lutie Johnson is a working mother raising her son in Harlem, a world that Petry represents as dually defined by Black male unemployment and Black female overwork. When Lutie fights off a sexual assault by her building's superintendent, he retaliates by coercing her son into stealing mail and getting him arrested. Desperate for money to hire a lawyer, Lutie turns to her boyfriend Boots, only to discover that he intends to pimp her out to his white boss. Realizing that Boots is "like these streets that trap all of us—vicious, dangerous," Lutie kills him. She acknowledges that the pressure has been building in her for a while: "It hadn't even been self-defense. The impulse to violence had been in her for a long time, growing, feeding, until finally she had blown up in a thousand pieces."[54] The novel ends with Lutie escaping to Chicago, leaving her son behind.

Like Bigger, what Lutie really confronts in this final scene is the experience of an action raised to an essence, a contingent moment elevated to a mode of being: "For the first time the full implication of what she had done swept over her. She was a murderer." Lutie's thought that *she was a murderer* echoes Bigger's *what I killed for, I am*: lines that I read less as confessions or affirmations than as moments of recognition about what it means to be condemned to live under a regime of racial essentialism ("she was," "I am") whose key lever is criminalization. Unlike Bigger, however,

Lutie confronts an additional fact whose implications are decidedly gendered. She recognizes that such a regime views Black criminality as not only ontological but also heritable: "A kid whose mother was a murderer didn't stand any chance at all. Everyone he came in contact with would believe that sooner or later he, too, could turn criminal."[55] A Black woman like Lutie is subject to the operations of racial criminalization twice over, seen not only as a criminal but also as a woman who will pass that criminality on to her child.

In their parallel endings, *The Street* and *Native Son* emphasize the tragic ways that violence can be misread as evidence of innate Black pathology. Interestingly enough, the same misreading shaped the reception of both novels. The historian Lawrence P. Jackson notes the "curious" fact that, despite Petry's repeated condemnations of white people in *The Street*, "Somehow white liberals managed to love the book." Part of that, he goes on, seems to have been rooted in their "smug presumption" that Lutie's real problems were caused by other Black people.[56] Reviewing *The Street* for the *Nation*, Diana Trilling read it as proof of the fact that "there is nothing inherently virtuous . . . about being a member of a mistreated minority."[57] The possibility that white liberals would take Petry's novel as a referendum on the virtue—or lack thereof—of an entire race was precisely what made some Black critics nervous about it. In his review for *The Crisis*, James Ivey complained that "there is hardly a decent character in the book" and insisted that "the total picture is a distortion." He continued, "Harlem is not the seething cesspool of sluts, pimps, juvenile delinquents, and clucks pictured in this novel. There are normal and responsible people in the community but you would never suspect it from reading this book."[58]

For Ivey, the trouble with *The Street* was that it encouraged readers to "suspect" that every resident of Harlem was a criminal. In one sense, this is a puzzling complaint, as if the problem with a work of fiction could be that it is too fictional (a "distortion" of reality). But this was precisely the problem that haunted the midcentury fiction of Black urban life, a problem—as we can see from Ivey's focus on "sluts, pimps, [and] juvenile delinquents"—rooted specifically in the challenges Black writers faced when writing stories that sought to represent incidents of crime. Ivey's complaint pinpoints a pressing worry that loomed over novelistic production at midcentury. Would literary explorations of racial criminalization simply be mistaken for sociological confirmation of stereotypes about Black criminals?

The worry was understandable, not least because, at the time, sociologists played a major role in disseminating ideas about racial difference. The most influential and widely read sociological treatise on the problem of race in midcentury America was Gunnar Myrdal's *An American Dilemma: The Negro Problem and Modern Democracy*. Myrdal, a Swedish economist, had been hired by the Carnegie Corporation in 1937 to write a report on U.S. race relations. He and his team of researchers published their 1,400-page findings in two volumes in 1944. The conception of the so-called race problem articulated in *An American Dilemma* shaped an entire generation of liberal thinking; the book was cited everywhere from the 1947 Report of the President's Committee on Civil Rights to the Supreme Court's 1954 decision in *Brown v. Board of Education*. *An American Dilemma* famously argued that anti-Black racism was "at bottom . . . a moral dilemma" lodged in "the minds of white . . . Americans." At the center of that moral and mental dilemma, it turns out, was the indelible image of Black criminality. *An American Dilemma* spends literally hundreds of pages wrestling with "the popular belief that all Negroes are inherently criminal." If Myrdal did not fully succeed in demystifying such a belief, that's likely because he himself was unsure about the extent to which it was actually mistaken. Myrdal was at pains to challenge "the stereotyped notion . . . that Negroes have a criminal tendency," yet he was unable to do so without adding some sort of qualification. "Negroes seem to be no more aggressive than whites," he writes at one point—"Except for the sullen criminal youths found mainly in Northern cities." Later he writes, "There are no reasons to assume that Negroes are endowed with a greater innate propensity to violence than other people," though there is still an "excess of physical assaults—and of altercations—within the Negro community." Myrdal did not think that readers should believe Black people were either "culturally" or "biologically more criminal than whites," yet he gave them many reasons to continue to believe it, stating that "relatively unfixed moral standards serve to encourage crimes inflicted by Negroes on other Negroes," that "Certain traits . . . more developed in the Negro as a consequence of his slavery background and his subordinate caste status, have also been conducive to a high Negro crime rate," and that "when the Negro migrates North, he brings his high crime rate along with him."

Myrdal perceptively recognized that crime statistics were deeply flawed ("they do not provide a fair index of Negro crime"), and he understood that notions of biologically innate criminality were scientifically indefensible and morally worthless. But in *An American Dilemma* he utterly failed to fashion a different framework for talking to a white audience about Black criminalization. Instead, he offered a conclusion that could only have sounded ominous to white readers who already feared imaginary Black criminals: "The truth is that Negroes *generally do not feel they have unqualified moral obligations to white people.*"[59]

"Modern African American crime fiction begins with *Native Son*," a prominent scholar has suggested.[60] The other thing that began with *Native Son* was the tendency to conflate Black fiction with sociological fact. The literary historian Joseph Darda argues that "liberal institutions such as the Book-of-the-Month Club, the Rosenwald Fund, and social science departments" instructed the novel's earliest readers to view Bigger as a "sociological case" study of a Black criminal determined by his environment.[61] The Chicago school of sociology was a well-known influence on the writing of *Native Son*.[62] Wright was mentored by the University of Chicago sociologist Louis Wirth and was close friends with Horace Cayton, whose 1945 book *Black Metropolis* was the first ethnographic study of Black urban life in the North. Cayton asked Wright to contribute the introduction to *Black Metropolis*; in that oft-cited piece, Wright credited the "huge mountains of fact piled up by the Department of Sociology at the University of Chicago" for giving him his "first concrete vision of the forces that molded the urban Negro's body and soul." He concluded that "sincere art and honest science were not that far apart."[63] That sense of kinship between the novelist and the social scientist—what Jackson calls "the uniting of sociology and fiction" that reshaped both disciplines in the 1940s—stayed with Wright.[64] Meditating on the process of writing *Native Son*, he imagined himself inhabiting both roles: "Why should I not, like a scientist in a laboratory, use my imagination and invent test-tube situations, place Bigger in them, and, following the guidance of my own hopes and fears, what I had learned and remembered, work out in fictional form an emotional statement and resolution of this problem?"[65] But if *Native Son* was a model for how the novelist might think of himself as a scientist free to experiment, it was also, more reductively, an invitation to see literature as a mere vehicle for conveying the findings of empirical research. "Wirth and his colleagues sought to share sociological knowledge with the masses," Darda explains, "and they looked to Wright's race novel as a model for how to reach them."[66]

The unprecedented commercial success of *Native Son*, coupled with Wright's vocal acknowledgment of the influence of sociology on his writing, had far-reaching consequences for the field of African American literature, which found itself increasingly constrained by an expectation of sociological accuracy and ethnographic authenticity. Through institutions like the Julius Rosenwald Fund, which supported some of the most well-known Black writers of the period, literary patronage in the 1940s and '50s was predominantly devoted to supporting what Jodi Melamed has called "the sociological race novel," a kind of fiction that was "presumed to retrieve and transmit sociologically accurate information about African American life conditions and psychology."[67] Accordingly, liberal readers were encouraged to read a novel like *Native Son* primarily, in Darda's words, "as an education in black life"—an education meant to be mined from the "mountains" of sociological evidence on which Wright claimed his novel had been built.[68]

It was only a matter of time before the relation between sociology and Black literature came full circle. One of Myrdal's key claims in *An American Dilemma* was that "not only occasional acts of violence but much laziness, carelessness, unreliability, petty stealing and lying are undoubtedly to be explained as concealed aggression."[69] Where did Myrdal get the idea that African American life was defined by "concealed aggression?" He got it, he says, from *Native Son*:

> In the growing generation of Negroes, there are a good many individuals like Bigger Thomas, the hero of Richard Wright's popular novel, *Native Son*. They can be seen walking the streets unemployed; standing around on the corners; or laughing, playing, and fighting in the joints and pool-rooms everywhere in the Negro slums of American cities. They have a bearing of their whole body, a way of carrying their hats, a way of looking cheeky and talking coolly, and a general recklessness about their own and others' personal security and property, which gives one a feeling that carelessness, asociality, and fear have reached their zenith.[70]

If Wright once provocatively imagined *Native Son* as a fictional "laboratory," a place to experiment with the mixing of social science and literary art, Myrdal unceremoniously closed the loop, reading the work of fiction as a direct sociological study of the criminal habits, acts, and attitudes ("recklessness," "carelessness," "asociality") of an entire generation of young Black men. Despite Wright's embrace of sociology, he still considered the main achievement of *Native Son* to be its imaginative rendering of Bigger's interiority, a realm that he believed could be plumbed by literature alone ("I wanted the reader to feel that there was nothing between him and Bigger; that the story was a special *premiere* given in his own private theater").[71] Yet Myrdal seems to have read *Native Son* entirely for its exterior descriptions: the image of men "standing around," the "bearing" of their bodies, their "way of carrying" a hat. In fully collapsing the distinction between sociology and literature, he managed to transform *Native Son* from a fictional exploration of Black consciousness into factual evidence of the inevitability of Black crime. The special irony of this misreading is that it is a version of what happens to Bigger himself. What Bigger killed for, he found himself defined by. Bigger's attempt to explore the possibility of agency through violence ended up being absorbed back into society's essentialist beliefs about Black criminality. Wright's attempt turned out pretty much the same way.

It is not immediately clear how troubled Wright was by this way of reading *Native Son*. He is said to have admired *An American Dilemma*, and later in his life he became friends with Gunnar and Alva Myrdal; he even dedicated his 1957 book *Pagan Spain* to them. Yet a lingering discomfort with *Native Son*'s sociological reception seems to have played a role in the very next piece of fiction he began writing. From 1941 to 1942, Wright worked feverishly on a new novel called *The Man Who Lived Underground*, whose protagonist, Fred Daniels, is not a criminal conditioned by his impoverished environment but an innocent Black man beaten and tortured by the police into confessing to a crime he did not commit. The interrogation scene ("'Tell us what you did.' 'I . . . I–I ain't done n–n–nothing . . .' A fist exploded between his eyes") occupies fifty-four excruciating pages, fully a third of the entire novel; it is immensely difficult to read.[72] Clearly, Wright wanted his readers to confront a very different way of understanding the coercive production of the myth of Black criminality. Yet as excited as Wright was about his planned follow-up to *Native Son*—"I have never written anything in my life that stemmed more from sheer inspiration," he said of *The Man Who Lived Underground*—the book was never published as he intended it during his lifetime.[73] A heavily condensed version, with no trace of the interrogation scene, appeared as a short story in the collection *Eight Men*, but only after Wright's publisher Harper & Brothers declined the novel, in part for its overly frank depiction of police violence.[74] Everyone wants sociological authenticity until they don't.

By the middle of the 1940s, *Native Son* had become a "cultural flash point for issues of race," as Jackson recounts, and white liberals alongside "well-to-do and aspiring blacks were expected to rebuke Bigger Thomas" as criminal and amoral, someone incapable of exemplifying Black cultural values.[75] Chester Himes staged this rebuke in a key scene in *If He Hollers Let Him Go* (1945), another classic midcentury work of African American literature that fused the traditions of protest fiction and crime fiction. Wright himself wrote an early review of Himes's debut novel, comparing it favorably "with the novels of James M. Cain."[76] The comparison to one of the era's most famous crime writers seems particularly relevant given the terms on which Wright's own novel is discussed by the fictional characters of *If He Hollers*. As one of Himes's characters puts it, "All Wright did was write a vicious crime story.... *Native Son* turned my stomach. It just proved what the white Southerner has always said about us; that our men are rapists and murderers." The protagonist, Bob Jones—a stand-in for Himes himself—stubbornly defends *Native Son*: "Well, you couldn't pick a better person than Bigger Thomas to prove the point."[77] But the defense falls flat. Himes had accurately diagnosed the disheartening fact that Wright's Black crime novel was doomed to be indicted on two seemingly incompatible grounds: either readers dismissed it as lurid pulp ("a vicious crime story") or misconstrued it as literal sociology ("it just proved what the white Southerner has always said about us"). It was either too generic or too real. Liberal readers, Himes concluded, could not see any other way to understand how African American literature might make imaginative or political use of crime. In a by-now predictable twist, Himes's own novel fell victim to the same fate. According to Jackson, reviewers of *If He Hollers* "thought Himes had written something that was significant but 'harsh' and 'sociological,' or not exactly art."[78]

From critics' fixation on the "sociological" aspects of *The Street* and *If He Hollers* to *Native Son*'s outright co-optation by liberal sociologists, we see the peculiar challenges that crime posed as a literary subject for Black writers at midcentury. The character of the Black criminal was now the site of a complicated and far-reaching novelistic dilemma: how to come to terms with a literary figure who was as likely to be used to perpetuate the era's racial discourse on crime as to contest it. Was it possible to write about the complexities of radical violence and Black criminalization without "just prov[ing]" what white society already thought about Black criminals? On the final page of *The Street*, as she sits on the train that will allow her to elude capture for her killing of Boots, Lutie has a rather unexpected thought: "What possible good has it done to teach people like me to write?" Meant to sum up the general futility of Lutie's situation—whatever education and employment she had access to was not enough to help her avoid the consequences of "that god-damned street"—the thought may also reflect Petry's ambivalent feelings about her own act of writing this particular type of novel. While *The Street* may seem an unusual crime novel in some respects, a more conventional version of the genre occasionally flashes into view in Petry's text. At one point, the villainous building super deceives Lutie's son Bub into stealing mail. "This is some detective work catching crooks," Supe tells Bub. "There's these crooks and the police need help to catch them." Ironically, it is the fantasy of doing "some detective work" that tricks Bub into breaking the law. This fantasy, inseparable from the logic of the detective genre, is one that Bub finds especially comforting: "This was the reality. This great, warm, open space was where he really belonged. Supe was captain of the detectives and he, Bub, was his most valued henchman."[79] Bub is thus trapped, in part, by the trappings of genre. He is caught by the improbable belief that, as a young, poor Black man in Harlem, he will be able to help "catch the crooks" rather than be labeled a crook himself. Between Bub's experience of "detective work" as the ultimate deception and Lutie's concluding thought that writing has done her no "possible good," what *The Street* finally conveys is Petry's abiding suspicion that crime writing might be, for Black writers, a cruel trick—a way to get themselves entangled, like Bub, in a plot that only fuels white society's frantic search for Black criminals.

BLACK MASK

A kind of ethnographic trap thus ensnared midcentury African American fiction. Black novelists were pressured to represent Black experience authentically yet could also be accused of reinforcing Black stereotypes—stereotypes centered principally, as we have seen, on crime. Faced with this catch-22, Wright, Petry, and Himes all shifted away, at least temporarily, from writing about the character of the Black criminal. This opened up a new literary niche for white crime novelists who were similarly struggling to come to terms with the racial politics of crime at midcentury. In the 1950s and '60s, some of the most noteworthy works of fiction about Black criminality were written by white authors. These genre experiments in cross-racial identification were inspired by the dawning awareness that the mechanisms of suspicion, surveillance, and criminalization—the basic rudiments of the crime novel—worked differently for Black Americans. As I'll show in this section, the white-authored novel of Black crime offers a revealing glimpse into the ways that white authors used the genre of crime fiction not only to explain the racial violence of the criminal legal system but also, in differing and complex ways, to explain it away.

In 1955 Charles Willeford published *Pick-Up*, his second novel, as a Beacon paperback original. The novel later entered the canon of postwar crime fiction through the Library of America, which selected *Pick-Up* for its *Crime Novels: American Noir of the 1950s* omnibus (a collection edited, as fate would have it, by Jim Thompson's biographer, Robert Polito). *Pick-Up* tells the story of Harry Jordan, a painter and former soldier who begins an affair with an alluring alcoholic woman named Helen Meredith. The depressive couple make a suicide pact. When the time comes to fulfill it, Harry strangles Helen as planned but fails to kill himself ("Harry Jordan was a failure in everything he tried. Even suicide"). Still hoping to die, Harry confesses to killing Helen and asks to be sent to the gas chamber. Then, in a plot twist, Harry is told that all the charges have been dropped and he is free to go: Helen has been found to have died from natural causes rather than the strangling. This first twist is followed by a second, disclosed only in the novel's last lines, when Harry, who has not made a single mention of race at any point before, describes himself as "a tall, lonely Negro. Walking in the rain."[80]

This ending is peculiar, to say the least. "It's not immediately apparent what Willeford's motive for this stunt was," the critic Sean McCann notes dryly.[81] At minimum, these final sentences shade in the disguised contexts of racist insults and interracial sex panic that Willeford has coyly redacted from his narrative, such as one scene where "three workmen... made a few choice nasty remarks about Helen and me," or another where a policeman repeatedly calls Harry "boy." There's also a "weird, mixed-up dream" Harry has:

> In my dream I was running rapidly down an enormous piano keyboard. The white keys made music beneath my hurried feet as I stepped on them, but the black keys were stuck together with glue and didn't play. Trying to escape the discordant music of the white keys I tried to run on the black keys, slipping and sliding to keep my balance. Although I couldn't see the end of the keyboard I felt that I must reach the end and that it was possible if I could only run fast enough and hard enough. My foot slipped on a rounded black key and I fell heavily, sideways, and my sprawled body covered three of the large white keys with a sharp, harsh discord. The notes were loud and ugly.[82]

Harry's dream is definitely about racial integration. The white keys sound "loud and ugly" without the black keys, and the black keys, glued together, can't play at all. Harry tries to stick solely to the black keys in order to "reach the end" of whatever he's trying to accomplish, but along the way he slips; his fall back into the realm of the white keys produces "a sharp, harsh discord." Harry's presence in the white world is thus "discordant"—he doesn't fit in—while the possibility of achievement in the Black world is highly restricted, constrained by the "glue" of Jim Crow. Where does Harry belong? Although this dream seems to imply a basic awareness of how racial oppression shapes Harry's world, it is also an argument for racial integration and against self-segregation. It is a warning to Harry not to stick exclusively to the black keys.

Perhaps most importantly, it's a dream. For Willeford, racial tension appears to exist primarily at the level of the psyche; only in Harry's unconscious mind does race pose a problem of social organization. In the waking reality that makes up the rest of the novel, Harry interacts quite harmoniously with the white world. The music he makes with the white keys of American society is not discordant in the least. This was Willeford's true aim in *Pick-Up*: to write a novel that supported integration by demonstrating the minimal role that race could be expected to play in determining a man's life. The real significance of the final twist, then, is that as a way of reframing the rest of the novel, it has no significance.

Being Black changes very little for Harry, whose life bears a striking resemblance to Willeford's own. Both men became painters while in the army, attended art school with the help of the G.I. Bill, and were "offered a teaching job at a private school." The autobiographical link between the white writer Willeford and his Black main character is meant to support Willeford's claim that racial oppression doesn't make that much of a difference. Just play the whole piano! The psychiatrist at the mental hospital asks Harry at one point if he "felt persecuted"—clearly a racially inflected word—after being fired from his job. Harry is quick to reassure him: "Oh, no, nothing like that."[83]

Indeed, the complete (and in the end far-fetched) absence of racial persecution from *Pick-Up*'s fictional world is most evident in Willeford's depiction of Harry's excessively equitable treatment by the institutions of mental health and criminal justice, which work together to absolve him of all responsibility for Helen's death and to send him on his way with a little cash in his pocket without once subjecting him to discrimination on account of his race. This is, to my mind, the most fascinating and bizarre aspect of *Pick-Up*: Harry's ability to move unobstructed through what McCann archly describes as "an efficient and surprisingly just legal system."[84] The justice Harry gets is surprising indeed—so much so that it is perhaps better described as implausible. But don't take my word for it. Harry himself is incredulous when he receives word of his release: "But if I didn't actually kill her . . . I must have at least hastened her death! And if so, that makes me guilty, doesn't it?" Harry's lawyer replies that it doesn't. The lawyer seeks to reassure Harry by explaining that he "read the full M.E. report" and that Helen "was in pretty bad shape. Malnutrition, I don't remember what all." The medical conclusion is that "she'd have died anyway."[85]

She'd have died anyway: not exactly an airtight legal defense. Harry's own lawyer breezily acknowledges the absurdity of the situation: "Why, this is the easiest case I've ever had. Usually my clients go to jail!" Almost anyone else would have gone to jail. Why doesn't Harry? This preposterous plot twist may signal the difficulty Willeford was having in trying to produce the sound of racial harmony using the instrument of the crime novel. Despite wanting to demonstrate the fundamental color blindness of American institutions, Willeford's novel ultimately collides with the basic implausibility of Harry's freedom, an implausibility that *Pick-Up*, with its astoundingly weak claim that Helen would "have died anyway" and its embarrassed acknowledgment that almost any other person in Harry's position would "usually . . . go to jail," barely bothers to hide. Remember, Harry is a Black man who has freely confessed to strangling a white woman. Willeford's need to give Harry his freedom—meant to clinch the point that race doesn't make a difference in the application of the law—finally runs afoul of the laws of narrative probability, to say nothing of the laws of the American judicial system. Choosing to write a crime novel about one Black man's experience of being treated with maximum solicitousness and fairness by what Harry himself calls "blind justice," Willeford ended up with a story that, not to put too fine a point on it, makes very little sense.[86] As one white writer's attempt to adopt the fictional perspective of a Black man, *Pick-Up* does not convey much about the lived experience of racial oppression. It does, however, help produce a more complete picture of the ways that white writers were trying—and sometimes failing—to understand racial criminalization at midcentury. It's not that Willeford (unlike, say, Highsmith) assumed all Black men were criminals. It's that he couldn't bring himself to believe that assumptions about Black criminality meaningfully shaped the lives of Black Americans at all.

"White crime writing in the fifties is resolutely integrationist," the critic Leonard Cassuto has suggested, an attitude he finds exemplified by white writers such as Ross Macdonald and John Ball, whose novels feature white detectives teaming up with Black detectives or working on behalf of Black clients.[87] *Pick-Up* clearly shares this integrationist bent, unfurling the fantasy of a color blind legal system capable of playing "the white keys" and "the black keys" in reasonable harmony. Yet the novel also demonstrates that many white crime novelists of the era were thinking about more than just Black and white cooperation—they were also thinking about what it would be like to be inside the head of a Black protagonist falsely accused of a crime. For his part, Willeford mobilized cross-racial interiority in order to make the counterintuitive and ultimately reactionary suggestion that racial criminalization didn't make much of a difference after all. Other popular writers of the time came to more complex, if not always less problematic, conclusions about the role that the presumption of guilt played in shaping Black life in midcentury America.

In 1954 the writer born in Harlem as Salvatore Lombino and now using the pen name Evan Hunter made a splash with the publication of *The*

Blackboard Jungle, a sensationalist novel based on Hunter's own experience teaching at an integrated vocational school in the Bronx. The publishing-house copy on the back of the 1955 Pocket Books Cardinal edition describes the book as "the first novel to dramatize one of the top social problems of our day." That problem was juvenile delinquency. But it turns out that Hunter had more than one of the day's "top social problems" on his mind. In the same year that *Blackboard Jungle* appeared, Hunter published a largely overlooked novel called *Runaway Black*. (The novel had been turned down by Herbert Alexander, the editor of Pocket Books, who "hadn't much liked" the manuscript; it ended up being published by Fawcett Gold Medal under yet another of Lombino's pseudonyms, Richard Marsten.[88]) *Runaway Black* was about the problems of racial criminalization and police violence in Harlem, and it was an attempt to describe those problems from the point of view of a Black protagonist. As such, it remains a fascinating record of the narrative contortions Hunter was forced to perform as he sought to diagnose what might be wrong with the relationship between race and policing.[89]

Runaway Black tells the story of Harlem resident Johnny Lane, who is stopped by the cops one afternoon and questioned about a murder he didn't commit. Realizing that he's about to be framed—"He read the logic like the writing on the wall"—Lane knocks down the officers and flees. He spends the rest of the novel on the run, asking a variety of friends, acquaintances, and strangers to harbor him. Afraid of being implicated in Lane's guilt, they often refuse to help. But his run from the police is unexpectedly reframed just forty pages into the novel, when another man being interrogated at the station confesses to the murder of which Lane has been accused. Lane has been cleared; he just doesn't know it, and the brutish cop in charge of the investigation doesn't care to tell him ("The word'll get around, sooner or later . . . Let him find out the good news by himself"). The fact of Lane's official exculpation turns his desperate attempt to outrun the cops from tragedy—an innocent man trying to avoid being locked up, or worse, for something he didn't do—into farce: "The patrolman burst out laughing. 'He thinks the law is still after him! Ain't that something?'" Another character puts it more succinctly: "He's running for nothing!"[90]

The farce of Lane's pointless running reorients Hunter's novel in two interesting ways. First, it allows Hunter to slyly restore the police to the position of heroes by focusing on a good cop who spends the bulk of the novel trying to deliver Lane the news about his innocence. Sergeant David Trachetti, poor guy, isn't even properly appreciated by the neighborhood he polices, where "an old couple . . . stared at him hostilely. He was white, and he was a cop, and that made him a double menace. Trachetti felt the coldness of their stares at the back of his neck, and he wondered again why the hell he was bothering. Did any of them appreciate it? Hell, he might very well get knifed."[91] As a white cop in Harlem, Trachetti is presented as both undervalued and unafraid, willing to move through a city whose Blackness is represented as synonymous with violence (the perpetual risk of "get[ting] knifed"). Who is left to "appreciate" this overlooked man but Hunter's readers? Trachetti's heroism also reinforces the putative comedy of Lane's situation, as he is now on the lam not from a racist police force that framed him but from a friendly cop who is earnestly trying to locate him in order to tell him he has nothing to run from.

While the cops (at least one, anyway) are trying to help Lane, it is the citizens of Harlem who are presented as bearing the primary responsibility for his plight. This is the novel's second interesting reorientation. Misled by gossip, rumor, and self-interest, most of the friends Lane seeks are unwilling or unable to believe he's innocent ("I only know what I hear, Johnny"). A young pharmacist named Frankie Parker calls the police when Lane shows up at his workplace seeking medical help. Lane, Parker reasons, "had certainly seemed guilty yesterday. . . . Was he supposed to take a chance helping Johnny when he *might* have been guilty, when he certainly *looked* guilty?" While the character of Trachetti is tirelessly trying to locate Lane in order to tell him he's innocent, Parker, upon learning the truth, wishes he could tell him but decides he can't: "I couldn't face him, not after that."[92] So he decides to pass the news on to the first customer who walks in, hoping it will get back to Lane. The problem is that the customer, Hank Sands, turns out to be the novel's villain, a grotesque character who keeps the information about Lane's innocence secret, using it to manipulate and sexually exploit Lane's girlfriend Cindy. At this point, *Runaway Black* reveals itself to be a rather different book than one might have assumed. It is not actually a novel about a falsely accused Black man trying to elude the cops. It is instead about a legally cleared Black man who is on the run for no reason, and who almost dies from an untreated wound on his arm not because of the racism of the police but because of the embarrassed self-interest and outright vindictiveness of everyday residents of Harlem.

In a strange scene early in the novel, a patrolman brags that "I know more about Harlem than three-fourths of the [people] in it." Is it possible that Hunter, born and raised in Harlem, felt the same way? *Runaway Black* at times positions itself as a primer on Harlem life for white readers presumed not to live there. "In Harlem," the wall-breaking narrator explains at one point, "*ofay* was simply pig Latin for 'foe.'" As for the people who did live there, one gets the sense that Hunter didn't think they fully understood their own situation. "You live right here," the patrolman continues, "and you don't know what the hell's going on right under your nose." What did Hunter think was actually "going on" in Harlem? In *Runaway Black*, Harlem is a place where being on the run is more of an existential condition than a legal one ("Johnny Lane had just realized with sudden clarity that he'd actually been running his whole life"), and where the police aren't as much to blame for it as the people who "live right here" tend to think.[93]

Perhaps Hunter really did think the cops in Harlem weren't getting a fair shake. Or perhaps he, like Lane in the opening pages of *Runaway Black*, simply saw "the writing on the wall" for his own career. The violence and racism endemic to American policing would not have been convenient points for a novelist who was one year away from reinventing himself as Ed McBain, creator of the 87th Precinct series, one of the longest-running and most consistently popular series of police procedural novels ever written. As Hunter/McBain recounts in the introduction to the republication of his first 87th Precinct novel, *Cop Hater*, "I wanted to use a *lot* of cops as my hero."[94] *Runaway Black* essentially cleared the grounds for the expansive cop mythography of the 87th Precinct series by turning the tragedy of Black criminalization into farce, selling readers the fantasy that the matter of running from the police may somehow not have anything to do with the police themselves. To separate the experiences of poor Black people from their harassment by the police was to free readers to sympathize with the plight of the former while still rooting for the latter. "This whole goddamn city is full of cop haters," says a cop in *Cop Hater* (1956).[95] This can be understood not just as a political problem afflicting society but also as a literary problem afflicting McBain: If he wanted to write a police novel, readers would need to be willing to root for the police. *Runaway Black* was McBain's attempt to resolve the problem. Before he could inaugurate a new era of police representation with *Cop Hater*, Hunter used *Runaway Black* to both diagnose and correct the error of hating cops.

Where Willeford used his cross-racial novel of Black criminalization to wish away racial disparity altogether, and Hunter used his to acknowledge such disparities but to distinguish them from the generally professional, respectable behavior of the police, the noir writer Dorothy Hughes at least recognized that racial hierarchy continued to exist and that policing was a primary way of maintaining it. The protagonist of her novel *The Expendable Man* (1963) is a wealthy Black doctor, Hugh Densmore, who is falsely accused of killing a young white woman named Iris. Densmore is framed for the crime by Iris's boyfriend Fred Othy, a white working-class bus driver who murdered Iris after convincing her to have an illegal abortion. The frame nearly works because the police are so willing to believe in Densmore's guilt. Even the marshal who claims a kind of postracial color blindness in light of recent civil rights protests ("there's not going to be any color business in this case," he insists) still has "a hard time believing that a Negro doctor had the ideals and ethics of a white doctor." By the novel's end, Densmore has come to understand that American policing is rooted in the racialization of the very concepts of guilt and innocence. "The police wanted to believe Fred O., he was one of their own, not a dark alien stranger," Densmore realizes. As for Densmore himself, although he is cleared in the book's final pages, he remains haunted by the "innocent guilt" he now recognizes is inscribed into race.[96]

Hughes's title is an obvious nod to Ralph Ellison. One character namechecks the famous novelist explicitly: "In our country, more often than not, we are what Ellison so well describes as invisible." In *The Expendable Man*, however, as in Hughes's earlier novel *In a Lonely Place*, invisibility is better understood as the defining characteristic of white criminals who are capable of remaining unseen by the public and the police. It is Fred Othy who is, in Densmore's words, "the invisible man."[97] Densmore is the expendable one. The term indicates Hughes's interest in the relation between race and social disposability. Her novel is an attempt to understand why the police find it so easy to criminalize innocent Black people, as if society had no other use for them.

Yet *The Expendable Man* is not simply about the forms of racial expendability produced by the legal system and manifested by the police. It is also a novel about class, specifically how racial criminalization threatens the fragile gains of an emerging Black professional class. Densmore is an "educated, civilized man" with "a big Cadillac and money." Throughout the ordeal of his false accusation, he is gripped by the fear not so much of prison but of public shame. As he explains to his lawyer, "the headlines will scream: Dr. Densmore Accused of Abortion. That's what will be remembered, not that I was proven innocent." As a successful doctor, Densmore's experience of Black criminalization is felt primarily as a threatened loss of status: "Once Hugh was arrested, once his name became public property, his family was shamed, his medical future without hope."[98]

Part of the novel's point is that Densmore's class does not protect him—as it would a white professional—from the structural injustice and personal bigotry of a corrupted legal system. But it's hard for Hughes to make this point without sounding some awkwardly elitist notes. She writes at one point that "this was Hugh Densmore and not some poor shabby guy they'd picked off the street or out of a shack." The problem with lamenting that Densmore's class position isn't enough to protect him is that it quickly slides into the complaint that it *should* be enough: that class status should be enough to put one man above suspicion, while shabbiness alone could be sufficient to indict another. In *The Expendable Man* such shabbiness is the shared possession, if not the birthright, of Fred Othy as well as Doc Jopher, the poor white doctor who performed Iris's abortion and who does happen to live in a shack. Both of these characters are physically marked by their poverty in a way that Hughes depicts as virtually synonymous with their criminality. "There was little evidence of a decent living in this broken-down house and the broken-down segment of man visible in the doorway," Densmore observes during his climactic meeting with Doc Jopher—clear evidence of the bad doctor's willingness to take money for performing illegal abortions. As for Othy, Densmore's first encounter with him is even more visually stark: "When he saw the face, Hugh's pulse quickened. He knew this was the right man. It wasn't a good face, it was bony, the complexion bad, pasty despite Arizona sun. The mouth was mean with small unclean teeth."[99] Here the "unclean teeth" and "bad, pasty" complexion—not merely the man's whiteness but his poor whiteness—are enough to make Densmore certain in his knowledge that this is the criminal he's been looking for. Apparently Othy is not so invisible after all.

The Expendable Man's emphasis on the visual codes of social class culminates in a bizarre sequence of class masquerade. In order to coax a confession from Doc Jopher, Densmore decides he must perform the part of a poor Black Southerner seeking an abortion for his girlfriend. He borrows some ill-fitting clothes, feigns a strong accent, and acts "obsequious," all of which "helped give him the appearance he needed, that of a poor lout wearing hand-me-downs."[100] To finally incriminate the stereotypical white poverty embodied by both Othy and Jopher, Densmore, it would seem, must become a stereotype himself.

But who is duping whom here? Clearly, Densmore's outlandish performance is meant to further debase a figure like Doc Jopher, who exposes the prejudice he otherwise denies ("It ain't that I'm bigoted," he protests) precisely through his willingness to believe that the kind of exaggerated stereotype Densmore is playacting here is real.[101] But isn't the reader being asked to believe in something distressingly similar: that is, in the reality of the class stereotype embodied not by Densmore but by Doc Jopher? It's as if Hughes, admirably seeking to discredit and dislodge the visual regime of Black criminalization, can do so only by reasserting the visibility of white poverty. Some group, it seems, needs to symbolize criminality. Hughes has simply swapped one for another. She was not the only midcentury author to do so. The critic Rachel Watson has described the ways that the blame for racial inequality in the Jim Crow era was frequently "displaced onto poor whites" in political as well as literary discourse; the most famous example is Harper Lee's classic novel of racial liberalism, *To Kill a Mockingbird*.[102]

In the final pages of *The Expendable Man*, Densmore reflects on his brush with the law by emphasizing the newly reinforced security of his social position: "He was no longer the expendable one."[103] No matter how many times I read Hughes's novel, I always pause on this line. Hughes is telling us that there *is* still an expendable man in the case; it just "no longer" happens to be Densmore. (Presumably it is now Fred Othy, he of the poverty-stricken complexion and incriminating teeth.) Is this good news or bad news? I honestly have no idea whether Hughes means this is as a radical critique of the entire American legal system (which, she astutely intimates, both requires and creates expendable populations through varying intersections of race and class) or as the low-hanging fruit of narrative reassurance for the reader schooled by racial liberalism to worry about individuals, not systems (at least Densmore is okay!). Should it really be cause for celebration that the burden of expendability has simply been shifted from Black to white and from well-off to poor?

Whatever Hughes thinks is the answer to that question, she indicates that a certain kind of professional class identity is essential to her novel—and likely to her sense of the people who would be reading it. In the book's climactic scene, Densmore has finally been arrested and seems on the verge of being framed for Iris's murder . . . until he is rescued and redeemed by none other than Doc Jopher. While Jopher is initially inclined to blame Densmore in order to save himself, eventually he decides to tell the police the truth. "Othy brought the girl to me," he admits. "He waited while I took care of her." Jopher's confession happens swiftly and unexpectedly, immediately after he is insulted by Fred Othy, who dismissively tells the police, "You going to listen to . . . a drunk old hoss doctor?" Hughes's narrator isn't sure what causes Jopher finally to "sing" but has a good guess: "It could have been the professional insult."

In short, it is Jopher's concealed but enduring professional identity that explains his final gesture of solidarity with Densmore—who is, of course, *Doctor* Densmore to you. Indeed, Densmore had already been pained by Jopher's professional decline; when he visits the shack, the first thing he thinks, mournfully, is that this ruined man was "once a student with aspirations, once a Doctor of Medicine." Yet the idea of the professional fall from grace implies the possibility of a restoration; Jopher is still, after all, an educated man "of Medicine." He justifies his illegal abortion practice in exactly such professionalized terms: "I can't stand to hear [the girls] crying when I'm a doctor and know I can help them."[104] Read in this way, what the climactic scene of *The Expendable Man* ultimately depicts is a pair of educated medical professionals expressing their professional class solidarity by joining forces in the fight against a racist police department and a racist, woman-killing bus driver. If Hughes's novel has been premised from the start on the idea that the problem of Black criminalization cuts across class lines, it concludes by suggesting that the solution to this problem resides in the systems of education and professionalization that (after *Brown v. Board of Education*) were now poised to cut across racial ones. By the end of the book, Dr. Densmore and Doc Jopher are no longer differentiated as Black and white or rich and poor. Instead, they are banded together as two men whose shared level of educational attainment (each "a Doctor of Medicine" with the diploma to prove it) allows them to see what the working-class cops and public transportation drivers of the world cannot: that eradicating the scourge of American racism is a task best left to licensed professionals.

Hughes shrewdly diagnosed how Black criminalization operated through social institutions and became entrenched in American culture. But she also made a calculated bet that her novel's educated white readership would be most amenable to that diagnosis when it was expressed in class terms: terms that assured readers of their fundamental similarity to a middle-class professional like Densmore and of their essential difference from the poor, prejudiced whites who are, Hughes strongly implies, the real obstacle to racial justice in America. Ultimately, *The Expendable Man* suggests that the trick to inhabiting the consciousness of a different person is to think of it as class consciousness. The possibility of sympathetic identification among educated professionals has, indeed, been the beating heart of Hughes's novel all along. Not for nothing did she decide to give her falsely accused Black protagonist—*Hugh* Densmore—her own name.

Read together, *Pick-Up*, *Runaway Black*, and *The Expendable Man* indicate a turning point in the literary history of the crime novel: a moment when white crime writers felt increasingly compelled to imagine what the criminal justice system looked like from the perspective of the people of color who were most likely to be victims of it. Writing through the eyes of Black protagonists accused of a crime but eventually exonerated, Willeford, Hunter, and Hughes developed a narrative form that they thought could diagnose and dissect, rather than unthinkingly perpetuate, the myth of Black criminality. Yet these same writers were also prevented by everything from the precepts of racial liberalism to the demands of the literary marketplace to the limitations of their own racial and class positions from finding the most effective ways to challenge that myth. These novels make it clear that by the 1950s and '60s, the genre of crime fiction could no longer plausibly claim to be color blind. Nevertheless, what white writers saw when they attempted to shed their blinders to racial criminalization was not necessarily the whole picture.

WHITE LIES

By the time white novelists decided to try putting themselves in the shoes of falsely accused Black protagonists, a number of major African American authors—including those responsible for some of our most enduring literary depictions of racialized criminals—had grown leery of the topic.

Between 1947 and 1954, Richard Wright, Ann Petry, and Chester Himes all wrote crime novels centered on white characters. All three novels were criminally overlooked in their authors' lifetimes. The books cost their writers a sizable amount of capital in terms of their relationships with readers as well as publishers.[105] So why did they write them? Critics have explained the brief burst of midcentury "white-life novels" in a variety of ways.[106] Emily Bernard explains that this body of fiction (which includes novels by James Baldwin, Zora Neale Hurston, and Frank Yerby) was at the time referred to as "raceless writing," a phrase that falsely implied that the absence of Black characters meant the absence of race *tout court*. Bernard argues that this implication was in fact what Black authors were writing against; they depicted "white characters in order to destabilize conventional assumptions about whiteness and universality."[107] Paula Rabinowitz describes this as a moment when Black "writers, stung by the sobriquet of 'Negro writers' and trying to get out from under the shadow of Richard Wright . . . sought to broaden, which in publishing meant whiten, their perceived subject matter."[108] Joseph Darda contends that white-life fiction was the preferred literary form of liberal funding institutions, which saw such fiction as a herald of integration.[109] And Lawrence Jackson suggests that it was a product of the pressures of the literary marketplace. African American novelists, he writes, "could not escape the publishing climate. The conservative wisdom held that black writers could not make a career of writing books with black characters and selling them to white audiences."[110]

This all sounds right. Still, it's worth asking why so many Black-authored novels about white characters took the form specifically of crime novels. By the end of the 1940s, it was clear that what was popularly known as the "race novel"—the sociological or ethnographic novel of Black life—was more likely to confirm than to contest the increasingly stubborn linkage between Blackness and criminality. Black novelists decided they needed another approach. One solution was to subtract the Black characters and keep the crime. What would happen to racial criminality when the race being criminalized was white?

Ann Petry was one writer who wanted to find out. One year after the appearance of *The Street*, she published *Country Place* (1947), a grim melodrama of infidelity, scandal, and attempted murder in a white New England town. After serving in World War II, Johnnie Roane returns home to Lennox, Connecticut to find that his wife, Glory, has begun an affair with the town womanizer, Ed Barrell. As a powerful storm descends on Lennox, things spiral out of control: Johnnie tracks Glory and Ed to a cabin in the woods, planning to kill them (eventually, he just punches Ed in the face and leaves); at the same time, Glory's scheming mother Lil hatches a plan to kill her wealthy, diabetic mother-in-law Mrs. Gramby for the inheritance money. Mrs. Gramby survives Lil's attempted murder by chocolate long enough to update her will, which now deeds the family home to her three servants, including her maid Neola, the novel's sole Black character. The novel ends with Lil exploding in a racist tirade aimed at the now upwardly mobile servants as well as the Jewish lawyer who prepared the new will. While Lil is ranting, a heartbroken Johnnie Roane boards a train to New York City, choosing to leave behind the gossip and prejudice of his poisoned hometown.

Rabinowitz suggests that "*Country Place* required a convoluted plot of murder and greed that, had [Petry] not made her characters white, might have been deflected onto what she described as the 'social criticism' novel of race and its pathologies."[111] This is a key point. *Country Place* is not simply Petry's attempt to avoid deflection onto racial pathology. It is an attempt to shift the entire way of thinking about criminal pathology from Black to white. Bernard puts it this way: "*Country Place* employs yet another strategy meant to challenge dominant stereotypes about black degeneracy, and that is to counter them with suggestions about white degeneracy."[112] In *Country Place*, no white character is free from the stain of degenerate criminality. Lil is an attempted murderer, Glory an adulteress; Ed Barrell is said to resemble "a newsreel showing Mussolini." Mrs. Gramby is the matriarch of a family for which criminality is part of the bloodline; a Gramby "was hanged for murder about a hundred years ago." Meanwhile, the war hero Johnnie rapes and strangles his wife on his first night home. In short, everyone is implicated in what the book's narrator, Doc Fraser, the local pharmacist, calls the "vein of violence running under the surface" of the town.[113]

What did readers make of all this? Reviews of the book were mixed. It is clear that the main issue shaping the reception of *Country Place* was the question of Petry's authority to write it. Who was Ann Petry, acclaimed surveyor of the struggles of urban Black life in Harlem, to offer such a thoroughgoing indictment of the hidden criminality of small-town white America? The back cover of the 1950 Signet edition of *Country Place* anticipates this reaction with a telling biographical note: "Ann Petry grew up in Old Saybrook, Connecticut, where her family has owned a drugstore for fifty years. As a result, the New England milieu of her new novel is entirely familiar to her."[114] These overly intimate sentences protest too much. They index the publisher's anxiety that readers would think Petry *not* familiar with—and thus unqualified to write about—white New England. The issue of familiarity was, of course, an issue of race. It was a worry about whether Petry had the cultural authority to write about characters who didn't look like her.

The final scene of Petry's novel savvily anticipates this concern. As Doc and the Weasel (the town cabdriver, an irrepressible gossip) have a brief farewell conversation in the pharmacy, the narrator makes seemingly random mention of a nearby item: "There is a mirror on the cigar counter, one of those standing mirrors that men use for shaving. I placed it there in the hope that someone would buy it. It didn't sell. But I let it stay on the counter because the customers, male and female alike, enjoy admiring their faces in it."[115] An opportunity for paying customers to gaze at their own faces: This seems like a pretty good description of how Petry imagined *Country Place* itself. Her novel sought to reflect back to white readers who they really were, the "vein of violence" and criminality that shaped them through and through. But the irony was that it was a mirror held up to white readers by an author who did not herself racially mirror them. Petry seems to have recognized that the viability of some sort of honest self-reflection might ultimately depend on who readers believed was behind the mirror. That's why, in this final scene, no one is behind it. It's just sitting there on Doc's counter, where customers might chance a look at themselves when they think no one is watching. Petry understood that the success of *Country Place* as a mirror of white violence required the parlor trick of making readers momentarily forget about the woman who was holding that mirror up to them.

Over the course of his career, Richard Wright, too, became increasingly fixated on how to shatter the presumed mirroring of Blackness and crime. His 1953 opus *The Outsider*—written while Wright was in exile in France—tells the story of a Black murderer who abjures racial identification. "Being a Negro," the novel explains of its antihero, Cross Damon, "was the least important thing in his life." *The Outsider* is at heart an existentialist fantasy about the radical freedom afforded by the refusal of all social ties, including racial identity and "racial struggle." That fantasy is realized through motiveless—meaning *not* environmentally conditioned (contra *Native Son*)—crime. Damon murders not out of rage but in order to demonstrate that he feels no social obligation to obey social injunctions against murder. Damon "had cynically scorned, wantonly violated every commitment that civilized men owe ... to those with whom they live. That, in essence, was his crime. The rest of his brutal and bloody thrashings about were the mere offshoots of that one central, cardinal fact."[116]

Wright hoped that *The Outsider* would depose *Native Son* as the standard-bearer of African American literature, replacing the earlier novel's ideas about social and economic determination with an existentialist vision of absolute Black freedom. But *The Outsider* had the bad luck of coming out just a few months after *Invisible Man*, and up against the backdrop of Ralph Ellison's immediate literary celebrity, Wright's novel failed to have the impact he hoped. Ultimately, he decided that its ideas about an existential criminality that was still marked as Black did not go far enough.[117] One year after the critical and commercial failure of *The Outsider*, he published an even more unpopular crime novel, *Savage Holiday* (1954). It was the only novel Wright ever composed that featured no Black characters.

Savage Holiday tells the story of a middle-aged white man named Erskine Fowler, a recently fired insurance executive who accidentally kills a young boy in his apartment building and then, in a fit of repressed sexual jealousy, intentionally stabs the boy's mother. In a 1960 interview, Wright said of *Savage Holiday*, "I picked a white American businessman to attempt a demonstration of a universal problem."[118] Wright seems here to surrender to the idea that only white characters could be sites of universal identification, whereas minority characters were likely to be seen as speaking for a particular community. But if we read this quote in relation to the sociological and formal problem Wright had been grappling with in his fiction for the previous fifteen years—the problem of crime—we can interpret it in a slightly different way. What Wright was trying to do in *Savage Holiday* was suggest that crime itself was a "universal problem," not a racially particularized one. However, it no longer seemed sufficient to him to demonstrate this simply by critiquing or refuting the stereotype of the Black criminal, which had already been refuted in the literature and social science of the previous few decades, to no avail. So Wright made the same decision Petry did. He set out to show that white people could be criminals, too.

The drama of *Savage Holiday*, however, is not whether Erskine will turn out to be a murderer. It is whether anyone will believe that he is. Wright is less than optimistic. When Erskine walks into a police station at the novel's conclusion and announces, "I want to surrender.... I just killed a woman," the policeman asks, "You're sure that you're not drunk?" This back-and-forth goes on for several pages, with the policeman insisting, "Mr. Fowler, you look like a solid citizen to me." As we have seen throughout this chapter, a society committed to the presumption of white innocence—to the "look" of "solid citizen[s]"—must be equally committed to the presumption of Black guilt. That commitment is made clear when, after a woman reports having seen something suspicious before the young boy's death, the racist building super remarks that "it's a wonder she didn't say" she had seen a Black man.[119]

False accusations of illusory Black figures repeatedly hover at the edges of this novel about the foundations of the white criminal mind. The lingering presence of racialized suspicion suggests that Wright may have sensed the deeper futility of his literary project: the limits of crime fiction's capacity to reframe the entrenched cultural discourse about crime. Suffice it to say that his novel does not speak highly of novels. On the first day of Erskine's forced retirement, he wonders what he's going to do with all his free time: "What ... did he want to do at this moment? ... Read a book? No; no; God, no!"[120] This apparently tossed-off moment of literary self-consciousness acquires a more savagely poignant meaning in the context of *Savage Holiday*, which was, if nothing else, a book that few people wanted to read. Wright's regular publisher, Harper, rejected it; eventually it was put out by the less prestigious paperback press Avon, only to be ignored by readers. The book went quickly out of print. After the ordeal with *Savage Holiday*, Wright's former editor Edward Aswell wrote a letter to Wright to dissuade him from continuing to work on what he had proposed to be the project's two sequels.[121] Aswell encouraged Wright to instead pursue "something that you can write about with intuitive knowledge and something with which you can make effective use of your own experience."[122] This sentence gives the game away. Surely, Wright could be expected to have no more "intuitive knowledge" and personal "experience" of the Black murderers of *Native Son* and *The Outsider* than he had of the white murderer of *Savage Holiday*. Yet Aswell, like the larger reading public, saw a career-defining difference between Wright's fiction about Black crime and his fiction about white crime.[123] This difference would only have made sense if one assumed—drawing on the dominant view of African American fiction as essentially sociological or ethnographic—that what it took to write about Black criminality was not experience in being a criminal but only experience in being Black.

Wright took Aswell's advice and abandoned the trilogy. To the end of his life, he "believed that what his agent and publishers held against *Savage Holiday* was that he had crossed the color line and written about white people."[124] But he hadn't simply written about white people. He had written about a white criminal. The ill-fated publication history of Wright's self-described attempt to write a "universal" novel confirms that the most profound insight to be gleaned from *Savage Holiday* is not that all people—even white people—are criminals. It's that, when it came to a novel about non-Black criminality written by an author famous for his depiction of a poor Black criminal, no one was particularly interested in reading it.

Early in his career, Chester Himes was forced to learn a similar lesson. He got his start writing short fiction for magazines while he was in prison. Those initial stories were centered exclusively on white characters, which were easier to get published, helping the young Himes establish an audience.[125] But that was in the 1930s. Two decades later, Himes spent years trying to find a publisher for the prison novel he had long been laboring on, which grew out of some of those early magazine stories. *Yesterday Will Make You Cry* was an autobiographical account of Himes's own experience, told from the perspective of a white prisoner named Jimmy Monroe. Of trying to sell the manuscript, Himes wrote, "A few Hollywood people knew of me from *Esquire* . . . but no one suspected I was black. When they saw my face, I was finished, period."[126] After multiple rejections, rewritings, and retitlings, the book finally appeared in heavily expurgated form as *Cast the First Stone* in 1953. The published version bore little resemblance to Himes's original vision, and it was a critical and commercial flop. By 1972, the publisher's copy on the back of the Signet reprint was describing Himes's book as "a ruthlessly honest novel of a young black's agonizing discovery of his own emotions." This is a stunning error, to which Melvin Van Peebles calls attention in his introduction to the republication of the original manuscript of *Yesterday Will Make You Cry*. "What damn 'young black's agonizing discovery?'" he writes. "Jimmy Monroe, Chester's central character, was white!" Van Peebles reads this as further evidence of the social constraints that forced Black novelists to write exclusively about Black experience: "The writer of the blurb (twenty years later) still couldn't leap over the ingrained racial assumptions that all a black writer could write about was another black."[127] The book's prison setting is an important piece of the puzzle, too. Part of the mistaken assumption about Himes's prison novel was that a Black novelist writing about the topics of crime and punishment would naturally be writing about Black criminals. Signet seems to have decided that if that wasn't actually the case, they would simply market the book as if it were.

By the 1950s, African American novelists were acutely aware that they were writing in the midst of historical circumstances that conspired to make *Black*, *crime*, and *crime fiction* appear as a chain of commonsense equivalences, and thus a set of interchangeable terms. That interchangeability was precisely what novels like *Country Place*, *Savage Holiday*, and *Yesterday Will Make You Cry* set out to contest. Ironically, it also turned out to be the primary obstacle to each novel's reception. For his part, Himes was so frustrated with the publishing difficulties and poor reviews of his early novels that he felt he had no choice but to leave the United States. He boarded a steamer to Paris in December 1955 and, like Wright, lived abroad for the rest of his life. (Just before he left, Himes had the frightening run-in with the sinister cop that became the basis for *Run Man Run*.)

The same years that saw Himes pushed out of his own country by an indifferent publishing industry and racist law enforcement saw the successful launch of the career of a young Patricia Highsmith. The two writers' opposing fortunes were not entirely unrelated. Highsmith had written the bulk of *Strangers on a Train* while on fellowship at the Yaddo writer's colony in 1948—where she lived across the hall from none other than Chester Himes. Himes was, in the estimation of his biographer, the "hands-down expert in crime and murder" at Yaddo the year that he and Highsmith were there together.[128] But Highsmith never credited him, nor did she recall discussing much about fiction with him at all.

Years later, Highsmith wrote an unsigned review of Himes's 1964 detective novel *Cotton Comes to Harlem* for the *Times Literary Supplement*, praising the novel for its humor, for its ability to "poke fun at white and black alike," and for its "mellowed" tone—a welcome improvement, she wrote, over Himes's earlier "black-versus-white" work, which Highsmith claimed was too full of "bitterness, tragedy, and above all hatred."[129] Most notable of all, Highsmith commended *Cotton Comes to Harlem* for its sociological authenticity. "There is the real feel of Harlem," she declared, "in his two layabouts happily sampling a half-bottle of found whiskey, which turns out to be something else; and in an eerie purse-snatching act, achieved by cutting away the back of a woman's skirt with a sharp razor while she is held rapt by a man who is telling her of a dream he had about Jesus." Does Highsmith really think that these two pieces of absurdist slapstick are authentic examples of "the real feel of Harlem?" That's a depressing thought. Firmly ensconced in the high surrealist phase of his career, Himes was still being read as a racial realist—and the notion of such realism continued to rest, as Highsmith's review makes clear, on the assumed linkage of "real" Black life to poverty ("layabouts") and crime ("purse-snatching"). I argued at the start of this chapter that the whole premise of a novel like *Strangers on a Train*—about the undetectability of two white middle-class criminals—depended on this linkage. If that is true, it helps explain why, a dozen years later, Highsmith was still invested in propagating it. As for Himes, whether he actually gave Highsmith some tips for writing about white criminals in their time at Yaddo or simply wanted to try his own hand at tackling the topic in *Yesterday Will Make You Cry*, his contributions were rendered as invisible as the killer in a Highsmith novel.[130]

In crime novels of the time, invisibility was both the point and the rub. "Nobody knows what a murderer looks like," Guy Haines thinks at the end of *Strangers on a Train*. "What's a murderer supposed to look like?" Jimmy Johnson wonders in *Run Man Run*.[131] Whatever else one writer may or may not have borrowed from the other, Highsmith and Himes clearly shared a common interest in how criminals were presumed to "look." They were not alone. From the 1940s to the 1960s, as African Americans moved en masse to industrialized cities and the struggle to end Jim Crow became a national movement, white America's perception of what crime was and what kinds of people committed it became ever more narrowly circumscribed by race. The processes of demographic realignment and civil rights struggle combined to make racial criminalization essential to the structuring of U.S. society. Inextricable from those processes, the era's crime novels relentlessly probed the limits of criminal visibility. What *are* criminals "supposed to look like?" What about the authors who write about them? Caught between the ideology of racial criminality that dominated the social sphere and the ideology of racial authenticity that dominated the literary sphere, crime writers correctly deduced that nobody really can know "what a murderer looks like." But they also saw that many people assumed they could know. This push and pull provides the solution to the mystery of the midcentury crime novel. The story of the criminal who could look "like anybody!" gained its formidable literary power from the fact that it was circulating in a society where exactly the opposite was true.[132]

2

RIOT ACTS, 1967–1974

> Someone had to guard the city.
>
> —*DEATH WISH* (1972)

WAR STORY

Is a riot a political act or a criminal one? This question was at the center of American public discourse and policy debate in the 1960s. It was also a question that remade the decade's crime fiction. Few crime novels of the time were untouched by the increasingly blurred relation between street crime and rebellion—especially as that relationship became one of the period's predominant ways of conceptualizing, and criminalizing, race.[1] Consider, for instance, George V. Higgins's classic novel of organized crime in Boston, *The Friends of Eddie Coyle* (1972). At the start, Eddie Coyle, a white criminal in need of guns, finds himself haggling with a stubborn gun dealer, Jackie Brown. Jackie explains that business is booming: "I had a guy seriously ask me, could I get him a few machineguns. He'd go a buck and a half apiece for as many as I could get." The mention of machine guns piques Coyle's interest; he interrupts Jackie to ask, "What color was he?"[2]

Coyle never gets an answer. Yet, one chapter later, now in need of a favor, Coyle tells a cop that he may have some useful information to trade. "Suppose," says Coyle to Detective Foley, "you had a reliable informer that put you onto a colored gentleman that was buying some machineguns." Coyle has clearly invented the detail about the buyer's race. Why? What

Higgins wants us to see is how Coyle capitalizes on a chain of equivalences so plausible, as far as the police are concerned, as to appear basically inevitable: "machineguns" really means armed revolt, and armed revolt really means Black militants. "He knows I'm a cop, of course," the detective tells another cop, "and he knows I'm a federal cop, so he's got to figure I got a hard-on for the Panthers. Not that he ever said Panthers. But Eddie's not stupid."[3] What it means to be not stupid in *The Friends of Eddie Coyle* is to understand how criminality was racialized in the 1960s and '70s by dint of being radicalized.

Black radicalism offered a useful distraction from, among other things, white organized crime. "The Panthers're the best thing ever happened to the Mafia," opines another of *Eddie Coyle*'s characters.[4] This fact is not only a thematic interest in Higgins's novel. It is the book's formal principle. The MacGuffin of Black militancy drives the novel's plot for more than a hundred pages, as the police search for Black radicals who don't exist instead of for a group of white bank robbers who do. Coyle's odd question in the opening pages—"What color was he?"—thus turns out to be the key to understanding the narrative form of a novel whose plot is structured entirely around the distinction between Black radicals and white Mafia operatives. In this way, *The Friends of Eddie Coyle* slyly narrates the essence of an era in which the public imagination was preoccupied by the fantasized links between race, militancy, and criminality.

The fantasy of the racialized and radicalized criminal bore little relation to the realities of crime. It was instrumental, however, in shaping the reality of President Lyndon Johnson's War on Crime, officially launched in 1965. In the early to mid 1960s, worsening poverty and unemployment, constant media coverage of rising rates of crime and drug use, the increased visibility of the civil rights and Black Power movements, and hundreds of uprisings in cities all contributed to a federally orchestrated response to what Johnson called the "public malady" of urban crime.[5] As these conditions, anxieties, and ideologies coalesced into a crime war, they profoundly altered what it meant to read and write the fiction of crime and punishment.

The War on Crime was forged in the crucible of revolt. In an address to Congress in the spring of 1965, Johnson lamented that lawlessness had "become a malignant enemy in America's midst" and announced his plans to begin an "active combat against crime." As the administration saw it, crime was "no longer merely a local problem" but a national one, and federal initiatives were now required "to intensify our crime prevention and crime-fighting at all levels of government."[6] Several months later—and one month before the first piece of War on Crime legislation was unanimously approved by Congress—police brutality during a traffic stop in the Watts neighborhood of Los Angeles led to one of the largest urban insurrections in American history. The Watts rebellion lasted six days, involved thirty-five thousand African American residents, resulted in the mobilization of sixteen thousand National Guard soldiers and LAPD officers, led to more than three thousand arrests, and left thirty-four people dead. Over the next three years, uprisings would take place in more than two hundred and fifty U.S. cities, often in response to similar incidents of police violence.

After Watts, the issue of what was then called street crime became increasingly blurred with fears of rebellion.[7] The watchword of the day, "crime in the streets," was effectively synonymous with what Barry Goldwater, in the 1964 speech that introduced his presidential campaign, called "mobs in the street."[8] By the summer of 1967, polls showed that riots now outranked the Vietnam War as a major public concern; a year later, the number one domestic priority according to polling was "crime and lawlessness."[9] The rise of what is now widely known as law-and-order politics was thus deeply tied to perceptions of urban civil disorder. In public discourse, the term *crime* more often than not meant *riot*, and rioters in turn were consistently cast as criminals. The equation of rioter to criminal was made explicit by Johnson himself in his nationally televised address during the 1967 Detroit uprising, in which he proclaimed that "the looting, arson, plunder, and pillage which have occurred are not part of the civil rights protest. There is no American right to loot stores, or to burn buildings, or to fire rifles from the rooftops. That is crime." Johnson assured his viewers that the "criminals who committed these acts of violence against the people deserve to be punished."[10]

The urban uprisings that swept the nation in the mid-to-late 1960s—political responses to poverty, unemployment, welfare disinvestment, and police harassment in segregated communities—were, as Elizabeth Hinton has influentially shown, central to shaping both the policies of and the rationale for the War on Crime.[11] In 1965, Johnson convened the National Commission on Law Enforcement and Administration of Justice, or the Crime Commission, headed by Attorney General Nicholas Katzenbach. The commission had been Katzenbach's idea, who thought it necessary to study crime and "rioting by Negroes."[12] After the uprisings in Detroit and Newark two years later, Johnson convened another commission, the National Advisory Committee on Violence and Civil Disorders, this one chaired by Illinois governor Otto Kerner, which was tasked with explaining the causes of the riots and making suggestions for how to prevent them. When its findings were published in 1968, the Kerner Report became a bestseller. It remains best known for the stark diagnosis offered in its opening lines: "This is our basic conclusion: Our Nation is moving toward two societies, one black, one white—separate and unequal."[13] Hinton argues that, in the case of both commissions, the study of the uprisings ended up serving mainly as a pretext to strengthen federal crime policy, singling out "black urban neighborhoods as the primary targets for the federal government's punitive intervention."[14] The conjoined concepts of crime and riot thus worked together to justify the government's strategic shift from welfare policy to policing in inner cities, where, by the mid 1960s, the programs of Johnson's War on Poverty were largely understood to have failed.

This is how the War on Crime came to be founded on the conflation of rioter, criminal, and African American. As the general public panicked about rising crime rates, media reports about the threat posed by drug addicts, and televised images of Black protesters, the Johnson administration responded with the Law Enforcement Assistance Act of 1965 and the Omnibus Crime Control and Safe Streets Act of 1968. These founding pieces of War on Crime legislation directed federal funds to state and local police departments, with the aims of professionalizing, modernizing, and above all militarizing the police. Between 1969 and 1976, the budget for the Law Enforcement Assistance Administration (LEAA)—a federal agency created by the Safe Streets Act, whose purpose was to dispense block grants to states for crime prevention—grew from $63 million to $800 million.[15] Amid this massive expansion of the federal crime-fighting budget, riot control was a task the LEAA "disproportionately favored with funding."[16]

The *war* part of the War on Crime was more than a metaphor. A key goal of the Safe Streets Act was to enable local police departments to acquire weapons and technology from the military.[17] Through Johnson's crime control acts, police departments received funds that they used to procure "military-grade rifles, tanks, riot gear, walkie-talkies, helicopters, and bulletproof vests."[18] Police militarization took place not only against the backdrop of the Vietnam War, but also in response to the growing fear that urban uprisings at home would turn into a full-blown race war—a fear that Hinton suggests was "the fundamental force underlying federal policy-making beginning with Watts in 1965."[19] The unease was further stoked by government officials' belief that the uprisings were somehow linked to Black militants.[20] This was the final piece of the puzzle. The architects of the War on Crime worried that rioters might be the front line in a larger militant battle. So they framed riots as a social ill that could only be cured by a police force that functioned more like a military.

This chapter shows how the War on Crime directly informed the crime novels of the 1960s and '70s.[21] After 1965, the simple act of writing fiction about crime was suddenly inextricable from controversial questions about poverty, race, militancy, and militarization. The conditions that produced the crime war also fostered new kinds of crime stories. In what follows, I trace the emergence of a new set of literary character types—the beat cop, the Black revolutionary, and the vigilante—that were designed to stake out key positions in the country's heated debates about civil unrest. Despite targeting different readerships and drawing on different literary traditions, the police procedurals, Black radical novels, and vigilante fiction of this moment all voiced a common frustration with the government's inability to prevent crime and ameliorate poverty. Yet these closely connected subgenres offered deeply divergent accounts of the causes and consequences of urban rebellion. Capable of serving both radical and conservative ends, the fiction of the early War on Crime era functioned as a contested literary site for managing competing cultural explanations of why marginalized communities were in revolt, and whether or not that made them criminals.

BEAT HAPPENING

Now one of the most ubiquitous forms in American popular culture, the police procedural barely existed before the 1940s. Until then, the American crime novel was far more likely to feature a private investigator than a police officer. It was only after World War II, building on the popularity of radio shows such as *Dragnet*, that the police novel become a recognizable subgenre of mystery fiction.[22] The police procedurals of the 1950s—popularized by writers like Ed McBain, who began his long-running 87th Precinct series in 1956 with the novel *Cop Hater*—emerged in concert with a new set of ideas about the professionalized, technocratic labor of modern policing.[23] McBain's pioneering procedurals proceeded from the assumption that, as he writes in *Cop Hater*, although "police work is like any other kind of work," it is nevertheless "a little difficult for a layman to understand every facet of police investigation." He and other authors set out to make the technical procedures of policing more understandable to lay readers, from the delicate, complex techniques of the "lab boys" in forensics ("The plaster of paris mixture was stirred and then carefully applied to the prepared print. It was applied with a spoon in small portions. When the print was covered to a thickness of about one-third of an inch, the boys spread pieces of twine and sticks onto the plaster to reinforce it, taking care that the debris did not touch the bottom of the print and destroy its details") to the administrative paperwork involved in the "less interesting and more mundane matters to deal with in a precinct."[24]

In the 1960s, McBain's 87th Precinct books sat on shelves alongside the novels of John Ball, a white writer famous for his creation of the fictional Black detective Virgil Tibbs. Ball made Tibbs a proud member of the Los Angeles Police Department, and in the second novel to feature the popular character, *Death for a Playmate* (1969, also known as *Johnny Get Your Gun*), his thoughts turned specifically to the reputation of the police in the aftermath of Watts. Tibbs is investigating a case involving a nine-year-old white boy named Johnny McGuire, who has stolen his father's gun in order to seek revenge on a bully; in the process, Johnny seems to have accidentally shot and killed a teenager whose brother, Miles Orthcutt, is a well-known Black militant. (It turns out the teenager was actually killed by someone else acting at the same time, but that's a longer story.) Tibbs thus becomes centrally concerned not only with the fate of a missing and armed nine-year-old boy but also with the possibility that the militant Miles Orthcutt will "whip up a first-class riot." Still, Tibbs's fear is allayed by "the fact that police riot-handling tactics had improved considerably since the days of the terror in Watts." Ball really wants his readers to understand just how much the LAPD's approach to riots has "improved," so he says the same thing sixteen pages later: "The police had made great strides in crowd handling since the outbreak of violence in Watts a few years previously." In due course, when Orthcutt gives a fiery speech to a crowd, the police wait patiently, respecting his right to free assembly, while the sergeant explains to his assembled officers, "So long as [Orthcutt] confines himself to protest, demanding Negro rights and things like that, he's within the law." When the cops do decide that Orthcutt has crossed the line to inciting a riot, they proceed to disperse the crowd in a safe and orderly fashion. Ball reassures us, "The police break-up of the crowd proceeded smoothly" and "expertly," no doubt "the result of experience gained during the Watts riot."[25]

Yeah, right. Yet this fantasy of police professionalism and by-the-book procedure, even in such explosive conditions as the handling of mass protests, was very much in line with the guiding ideology of the police procedural in the 1950s and '60s. At the very end of *Death for a Playmate*, Ball admits that the larger aim of Tibbs's police work—which has involved assisting the poor, racist McGuire family, who are prejudiced against him—has been to change skeptical communities' opinions of the police. After Tibbs rescues their son Johnny and prevents another L.A. rebellion, Tibbs's captain scolds Johnny's father for ever having doubted the effectiveness and necessity of policing: "I am inclined to believe that you have undergone something of a change of heart concerning police officers and the public service we are trying to render."[26] A similar interest in shaping public opinion about the police was already in play in McBain's *Cop Hater*, whose ending reveals that the entire idea of a "cop hater" who is executing members of the 87th Precinct was really a red herring. Instead, a random couple wanted "to make it look as if a cop hater was loose" in order to provide cover for their murder of the woman's brutish husband (who happened to be a cop). The point of the plot twist is to impress upon a reader how unlikely cop-hating actually is. When one of the surviving detectives of the 87th Precinct confronts the real killer in the novel's final pages, the officer asks him, "Don't you like cops?" The gunman replies, "I love them."[27]

By the late 1960s, however, a new literary image of the police—and a new narrative about the work of policing riots—was emerging to challenge versions like McBain's and Ball's, which had focused on the mind-changing charms of rule-bound professionalism and technocratic efficiency. On this new view, by contrast, the police were less calm professionals smoothly offering a "public service" and more hardened warriors on the front lines of a fight for the fate of civilization. This vision of warrior police forged in the fires of riot was most influentially peddled by Joseph Wambaugh. His debut novel *The New Centurions* (1970) reinvented the procedural genre in one fell swoop, erasing every trace of the classic mystery narrative and reorienting it around a new populist hero: the beat cop. The literary historian Christopher P. Wilson calls Wambaugh "the cultural figure perhaps most responsible for creating the modern mass-cultural image of the paramilitary patrol cop."[28] As such, Wambaugh offers an indispensable case study in how the paramilitary imperatives of riot control during the War on Crime altered the course of the police novel.

Based on Wambaugh's own experience as an LAPD patrolman (he eventually rose to sergeant), *The New Centurions* traces the lives of three Los Angeles cops in a series of plotless, disconnected episodes that chart their transformation from academy cadets in 1960 to jaded veterans in 1965. *The New Centurions* was immensely popular upon its publication. It was also profoundly partisan; the novel often reads more like an LAPD public-relations pamphlet than a novel. This kind of synergy between policing and its media representations was par for the course during William Parker's infamous tenure as LAPD police chief. (It was Parker who devised and implemented his department's tight control over scripts for the *Dragnet* television series in the 1950s; among other things, characters on the show were prohibited from ever using the word *cop*, which cops like Parker considered a slur.[29]) Unsurprisingly, Wambaugh's novel was a largely unfiltered mouthpiece for all the department's major talking points. *The New Centurions* laments the Supreme Court's protection of the rights of the accused ("the court is lying in wait for bad cases like *Mapp vs. Ohio* so they can restrict police power a little more"). It defends police brutality ("Police brutality means to act as an ordinary prudent person, without a policeman's self-discipline, would surely act under the stresses of police work."). It promotes victims' rights ("The judges and the probation officers and social workers and everybody else think mainly about the suspect . . . but you and me are the only ones who see what he does to his victims"). It complains about the "ignorant bastards" of the press who criticize the police for shooting rioters. It steadfastly denies that race plays a role in policing ("I treat everyone the same, white or black").[30] And all the while, it conjures up a steady parade of criminal characters who are primarily poor and Black.

Indeed, the most conspicuous thing one notices in reading *The New Centurions* is the tension between its fixation on the racial specificity of criminals and its doubtfulness about the social significance of race. A central tenet of LAPD ideology at this time was the insistence that race played no role whatsoever in the activities of policing. Parker was famous not simply for rejecting accusations of police racism but for altering the very meaning of what it meant to be a minority in America. "I think the greatest dislocated minority in America today are the police," he once said with a straight face.[31] In *The New Centurions*, the meaninglessness of minority status and racial difference is the novel's repeated refrain: "An asshole is an asshole, they're just a little darker here"; "People are all murderous bastards, they're just a little darker down here."[32] Sentences like these transform race into color in order to insist on the superficiality of racial difference as an index of social inequality. Some people may be "a little darker" than others, but the important point, *The New Centurions* assures us, is that because everyone is "an asshole," everyone will be treated equally badly by the police.

Yet this repeated insistence on the color blindness of policing and on human beings' universal propensity for doing ill is hard to square with the novel's singular focus on the crimes and policing of Black people. One character sums up the book's basic premise early on: "Lots of crime when you have lots of Negroes." Another character complains of his assignment to a beat in a "high crime rate" Black neighborhood, "Every day down here is like ten days in a white division."[33] *The New Centurions* thus finds itself in a tricky position, clinging to the meaninglessness of race as a factor in policing while taking the purported criminality of Black neighborhoods as its main narrative premise. How Wambaugh resolved this paradox tells us a lot about the emergent anticrime ideologies of the period, and about what it took for the police procedural to formally reorient itself around those ideologies.[34]

The tough-on-crime policies of the late 1960s and early 1970s were, the historian Julilly Kohler-Hausmann argues, rooted in beliefs about "the inherent ungovernability of the poor in African American and Latino communities."[35] The concept of ungovernability offered a newly coded way of talking about race and class. And for *The New Centurions*, as for much of the American public at the time, what ungovernability most resembled was riot. The novel's final section is titled "August 1965" and takes place during the Watts uprising. The most revealing thing about Wambaugh's account of the rebellion—which he experienced firsthand as a patrolman—is that he says nothing about what might have caused it. In the narrative universe of *The New Centurions*, the Watts uprising has no identifiable origin, and not even a clear beginning. When it is first mentioned in the opening sentences of the book's final section, it is already in progress—as if its occurrence were so preordained it did not need to be introduced at all. Emerging without causation or explanation, the riot appears as exactly the thing most Americans presumed it to be: the inexplicable yet inevitable criminal outburst of an impoverished nonwhite community.[36] This sense of inevitability is built directly into the structure of Wambaugh's novel. Three hundred pages earlier, in a scene set in the summer of 1960, the veteran Kilvinsky says to his rookie partner, Gus, "You're going to have an impossible job in the next five years or I miss my guess."[37] That guess is, to say the least, a bit on the nose.[38] Terminating exactly five years later in Watts, the narrative arc of *The New Centurions* is meticulously designed to make clear that Kilvinsky's guess is not a guess at all, but a historically verified claim about the seemingly inevitable criminal disorder that defines Black urban neighborhoods.

In the novel's climactic depiction of Watts, Wambaugh's narrator reports that "thousands of felonies were being committed with impunity." It's hard to know which he thinks is worse, the felonies or the impunity. Either way, it's the number that interests me. Wambaugh's quantitative rhetoric of crime is paired with aggregate depictions of the people committing those felonies: "Roving bands of Negroes, men, women, and children screamed and jeered and looted."[39] Between the composite "bands" of rioters and the enumeration of their crimes ("thousands of felonies"), Wambaugh has given the ideology of ungovernability one last, important twist. *The New Centurions* is a lesson in how to write crime fiction for an era dominated by the discourse of crime rates.

The criminal imaginary of the moment was indeed centrally data-driven.[40] "Throughout the 1960s and 1970s," Elizabeth Hinton explains, "flawed statistical data overstated the problem of crime in African American communities and produced a distorted picture of American crime."[41] Despite their significant flaws, however, the era's crime statistics shaped both the public perception of crime and the state's putative solutions to it.⁴² Measured by the FBI's *Uniform Crime Reports*, the nation's crime rate grew by double digits each year from 1965 to 1969, with every increase the focus of extensive and often inflammatory media coverage.⁴³ Yet the popular obsession with crime rates was only the tip of the iceberg. Underneath it was the beginning of the more nefarious turn to algorithmic policing. Computer programs and data analysis became key facets of crime control as early as the 1970s, when the LEAA funded the development of computerized systems to track crime and facilitate information sharing. Pilot programs in St. Louis and other cities, for instance, used federal funds to develop a computer program that could predict crime before it occurred.⁴⁴ LEAA funding also fueled the out-of-control growth of criminal databases, which by the late 1990s held as many as fifty-five million files across local, state, and federal agencies.⁴⁵ More recent innovations in digitized crime control and predictive policing—systems like New York City's CompStat and Chicago's CLEARmap—thus have their origins in the early years of the War on Crime, when the public uproar over rising crime rates went hand in hand with the federal government's attempt to fuse crime fighting with data collection.

The central role of statistics in the War on Crime explains why Wambaugh's reinvention of the police procedural took the particular form that it did. *The New Centurions* pioneered a literary form capable of expressing the *tendential* and *aggregative* nature of crime in the era of its statistical ascendancy. That form is fashioned from the narrative logic of the beat—a geographical unit that today still plays a primary role in the collection and deployment of crime data.⁴⁶ Wambaugh used the scale of the beat to frame a narrative in which crime could appear constant, cumulative, and geographically contained. In this way, *The New Centurions* offers itself up as a kind of alternative crime report, one in which the steady accumulation of unrelated criminal episodes becomes the basis for a pseudo-statistical profile of racialized space—an on-the-ground plotting of the "high crime rate" that, Wambaugh tells us, distinguishes Black neighborhoods from white ones. Thus is Black criminalization made to appear a matter of statistical likelihood rather than racial ontology. The beat narrative conceals race by remapping it as a rate.

This secret of racial concealment is itself unveiled at the very end of Wambaugh's novel. In the final chapter, the three protagonists, beat cops

Roy, Serge, and Gus, sit together reflecting on their shared experience in Watts and their evolving friendship. Sensing a new bond among them, the men open up to each other, a process of emotional sharing that culminates in racial revelation. Roy, feeling "drawn to both of them," is suddenly moved to disclose to his friends that his fiancée is Black. A few pages later, Serge, apparently moved in the same way, reveals that he has been passing as white for all this time but is in fact Mexican. "'I'll be damned, that never occurred to me,' said Roy, looking at Serge for some Mexican features and finding none."[47] How do we explain this bizarre depiction of an episode of male bonding that proceeds specifically from the disclosure of nonwhite racial identities and affinities? On the surface, Wambaugh is laboring to depict the breezy acceptance of diversity among the riot cops: See? Serge is Mexican, and his friends don't even care! Yet we might also read this scene as a kind of return of the repressed. Throughout the novel, crime data and beat geographies have suppressed race, which now, in the book's final pages, can't help but bubble back up to the surface. The relief the men feel in finally being able to confess to each other the racial secrets of their personal lives is also their relief at finally being able to divulge the unspoken secret of policing itself. The secret is that, the patrolmen's own previous denials notwithstanding, an obsession with racial difference has been at the heart of beat policing all along.

Crime data helped launder racial prejudice. In doing so, it became a crucial tool for reconciling the ongoing process of Black criminalization with the legal enshrinement of color blindness. The emergence of the beat cop novel reflects a moment when American culture was responding to the victories of the Civil Rights movement by embracing a more quantified—and thus allegedly race-neutral—view of crime. In the episodic logic of the beat patrol, Wambaugh lighted on the perfect narrative form for converting isolated criminal incidents into the cumulative, color-blind expression of a particular group's alleged tendency toward crime. What *The New Centurions* finally both fictionalizes and formalizes for its readers is a seemingly endless string of police encounters with those agents of disorder who may technically come in all colors but who are, according to the unspoken laws of the novel's hidden statistical imaginary, most likely to look like the residents of Watts.

TRIAL PERIOD

For Wambaugh, the perceived lawlessness in Watts was the master symbol of an American society facing collapse. "Things were breaking apart," thinks one of the cops during the uprising, the fulfillment of the Kilvinsky character's prediction earlier in the novel that "civilization" was "in jeopardy."[48] The insistence that the fate of civilization hung in the balance was a factor in the white conservative response to the uprisings and a key component of the decade's law-and-order imaginary.[49] Amid the widespread sense of anarchy, chaos, and civilizational breakdown conjured by rebellions like the one in Watts, Wambaugh longed for the reassertion of authority. For him, authority meant violence. "Only deadly force could destroy this thing," another of Wambaugh's heroized cops thinks, "and he was glad they were shooting looters."[50]

The idea that the police should have shot more people during riots was not a fringe opinion at the time, nor indeed was it a fictional one. "I saw more crime transpire that day than I saw all two years I been on the force. And there was nothing I could do about it," a Detroit patrolman complained to journalist John Hersey after the 1967 uprising in that city. The problem, this man believed, was that the police weren't violent enough: "If they're breaking into these places here, they should be made examples of, if you shoot a few of them there, you know, the serious violators there." Another cop Hersey interviewed insisted that the entire uprising could have been prevented if they had simply begun "by shooting the people that were at fault" on the first day.[51]

These interviews appeared in *The Algiers Motel Incident* (1968), Hersey's investigative account of what was, even by the desensitized standards of the late 1960s, a particularly shocking episode of police murder: the cold-blooded executions of three young Black men by cops during the Detroit uprising. Although it is not a work of crime fiction, *The Algiers Motel Incident* is perhaps the most well-known piece of literature written about the urban rebellions of the 1960s. For that reason alone, it would seem remiss not to discuss it in these pages. But Hersey's book offers us something more specific: a glimpse into how liberal writers committed to legal procedure were attempting to respond to the perception of anarchy and lawlessness that conservative writers like Wambaugh would so successfully seize on. A veritable don of American letters when he wrote *The Algiers Motel Incident*, Hersey stands as an important case study in how liberal literary institutions were reckoning with their own commitment—aesthetic no less than ideological—to the law.

The Algiers Motel Incident is a heartfelt yet unusual book, at once a painstaking reconstruction of the events leading to the murders and a confusing patchwork of quotations transcribed directly from taped interviews. Hersey had been asked to help write what would become the Kerner Report but declined out of a reluctance to surrender control over his research and writing. Instead, he wrote what amounted to his own personal shadow version of the *Report of the National Advisory Commission on Civil Disorders*. Built out of dozens of interviews Hersey conducted in Detroit shortly after the riot and composed primarily of fragments of oral testimony organized and juxtaposed in ways whose meaning is often difficult to decipher, *Algiers* offers a kaleidoscopic account of what Hersey viewed as a pivotal yet dizzyingly complex episode in American history. Justifying his own appearance in and sporadic commentary on the narrative—a surprising move for a writer who embodied the old guard of omniscient journalism, against which the New Journalists were then in the process of rebelling—Hersey writes that his account was "too urgent, too complex, too dangerous to too many people to be told in a way that might leave doubts strewn along its path." This is somewhat misleading, however. The book positively brims with doubts, confusion, and conflicting testimonies, and the central story that Hersey tells about the event itself is extremely difficult to follow. Aware of these difficulties, he nevertheless hoped that readers would be willing to follow his avowedly nonobjective and frequently confusing story all the way "to its unresolved ending."[52]

The problem of irresolution, as both a narrative problem and a legal one, lies at the heart of Hersey's book. This was in part a problem of his own making. *The Algiers Motel Incident* relies extensively on firsthand testimonials that repeatedly contradict one another. Yet Hersey rarely intervenes to offer guidance on how to interpret those contradictions. He also largely withholds commentary on the things that his interview subjects say. As a result, pages upon pages are given over to the voices of cops whose self-justifications, prevarications, and undisguised prejudice are left not only unchallenged but unacknowledged. It is hard at first to know exactly what Hersey was trying do with these compositional imperatives.

Yet there is, I think, a clear analog and likely inspiration for his book's bewildering narrative form: the American judicial process itself.

Hersey explains some of the reasoning behind his formal choices early on. "Events," he insists, "could not be described as if witnessed from above by an all-seeing eye opening on an all-knowing novelistic mind." Instead, "The story would have to be told as much as possible in the words of the participants."[53] Here the novel form itself is aligned with a kind of "all-seeing" and "all-knowing" judgment that places it closer to theological justice than to the modern system of law. If rejecting the presumption to know and see all meant rejecting the traditional form of the novel, then Hersey needed a different, more democratic form on which to model his narrative. What sort of form could provide a model for the need to remain open-minded and not jump to conclusions in advance, before weighing all available evidence and hearing all relevant testimony in "the words of the participants" themselves? The obvious answer to this question is: a trial. This is pretty much what *The Algiers Motel Incident* is—a literary version of a jury trial, with readers cast as jury members. This is why it turns out to be the reader, not Hersey, who is tasked with sifting through the torrent of conflicting testimony and, at the end of the "unresolved" story, forming their own conclusions about the proper attribution of innocence and guilt.

I do not doubt that Hersey believed that his readers would come to an essentially just and like-minded conclusion about the Algiers murders and the larger system of structural racism they exposed. "There is plenty of guilt lying around for the taking," he writes. Yet this faith in the just outcome that could emerge from an efficiently run trial—a faith reflected, I am suggesting, in Hersey's use of the trial as a model for his book's entire open-ended narrative form—is a somewhat peculiar belief for this particular book to have, considering that one of the main threads running through it is that the American court system was becoming increasingly difficult to defend. Hersey repeatedly describes the "unequal justice" that African Americans confronted in the legal system, a system effectively designed to discount Black experience and Black testimony. The contemporary American legal system was not only depressingly byzantine (a "maze," Hersey calls it). It was also a system that "almost invariably prefers the unreliable testimony of whites to the unreliable testimony of blacks." As a result of this, most of the Black residents of Detroit interviewed by Hersey were not inclined to have much faith in the courts. Michael Clark, a witness to the Algiers killings, is, "like all his friends... cynical to the soles of his feet about the judicial process." Robert Pollard, the brother of Auburey Pollard, one of the murdered men, says it himself: "They don't have no type of justice in court." Pollard's canny analysis of the court system is that it is a system of racial and economic subjugation masquerading as a site of impartial moral judgment. "Justice," Pollard explains to Hersey, "is a way of keeping a person from getting any more than he's got."[54]

Throughout *The Algiers Motel Incident*, Hersey dutifully reports his interview subjects' justified cynicism toward the judicial process. Did Hersey share their views? That is harder to say. Near the end of the book, he quotes the statement of a newly formed "coalition of business, education, labor, and civil-rights leaders" in Detroit: "The issue raised by the Algiers Motel case is... no less than the credibility of our system of justice as embodied in our criminal courts." Because of this, the statement continues, "a full and fair examination of the Algiers Motel case is essential to arresting" the "decline in respect for the rule of law."[55] I think these lines offer significant insight into Hersey's own conception of the mission of his book. He was doing his part to help restore a justice system whose credibility he understood to be in dangerous decline.

What Hersey never seems to have considered was whether that credibility might already be long gone—as men like Pollard and Clark had testified to him. *The Algiers Motel Incident* was no doubt a sincere effort on Hersey's part to offer the "full and fair examination of the Algiers Motel case" that the legal system had at that point been unable to do. Hersey shared the belief that a fuller, fairer examination of the case could help restore "respect for the rule of law" that had otherwise been eroded. Yet, in examining the case, Hersey revealed the thoroughgoing extent of that respect's erosion. He also re-created many of the structural flaws of the very justice system he saw himself as trying to redeem. The "legal maze" of tangled court cases and illogical decisions that Hersey laments is reproduced in miniature in his own book, a labyrinthine investigation that tells us from the start it will offer no clear answers or just resolution and, true to its word, does not. One of the "mythic themes of racial strife in the United States," Hersey writes early on, is "ambiguous justice in the courts" for African Americans.[56] Yet *The Algiers Motel Incident* is nothing if not a formal embodiment of the ambiguity and unreliability that defines the American justice system. In this respect, Hersey's book ends up seeming more like a mirror of this longstanding aspect of racial injustice than a solution to it.

We have already seen how a more conservative literary figure like Wambaugh fixated on the threat of lawlessness associated with the uprisings of the 1960s. This fixation was shared by Wambaugh's fellow real-life cops, including those interviewed in *The Algiers Motel Incident*. In their view, the metaphorical "murder" of the law (as the character modeled on LAPD Chief Parker puts it in *The New Centurions*) was more concerning than the literal killing of civilians.[57] Hersey was clearly horrified by this calculation. But he, too, was writing both in and about a moment when the rule of law seemed to hang in the balance. And he shared the concern. Although Hersey located the problem of lawlessness not in the behavior of protesters (as did Wambaugh and much of the general public) but in the structural flaws of an unequal legal system, he nevertheless found himself clinging to that system as the only dependable formal principle for representing his own research into the events of the Detroit uprising and the Algiers killings. In this way, *The Algiers Motel Incident* turns out to be a telling record of the limits of the liberal imagination in the era of urban rebellion. This was an imagination sympathetic to the vivid and widespread distrust of the legal system's ability to treat Black people fairly—yet still convinced that the antidote to that distrust was destined to be found within the system itself.

REVOLUTIONIZING THE CRIME NOVEL

Whatever his book's faults, Hersey was at least trying to convey to his readers some sense of the systemic factors underlying the long, hot summers of the 1960s. The "summer rebellions," he wrote in *The Algiers Motel Incident*, were caused by four things: "unequal justice, unequal employment opportunities, unequal housing, unequal education."[58] Unfortunately, convincing readers that the uprisings had anything to do with inequality at all—let alone four kinds of inequality—was an uphill battle. One survey from the time indicated that not even one-fifth of white respondents believed that the nation's uprisings were caused by police violence.[59] Another showed that only 5 percent of white people thought the uprisings were consequences of discrimination and racism.[60]

Indeed, the standard view of riots was and remains that they don't have causes at all. As one of Wambaugh's characters notes derisively, "I wonder how long experts will screw around with their cause theories."[61] The general assumption is that riots lie beyond the realm of either rational explanation or intentional calculation.[62] Viewed as irrational, apolitical, and criminal, the urban revolts of the 1960s were rarely interpreted as political acts. Yet, ironically, they were often blamed on political agitators. In the wake of Watts, the McCone Commission "indicted the civil rights movement in general, and local activists in particular, for fueling outrage."[63] After Detroit, the Johnson White House intensely debated whether the nation's urban unrest was part of a conspiracy by Black militants.[64] The Detroit *News* published a front-page article on an alleged "nationwide" conspiracy of sniper attacks organized by "the network of the Black Power movement," and Detroit mayor Jerome Cavanagh at one point attributed the city's riot to "the work of revolutionaries who belong to the black extremist movements."[65] Time and again, public officials insisted on "linking urban uprisings to rising black militancy."[66] The criminalization of riot was thus based, paradoxically, both on the denial of riots as political expressions and on the fear of the growing influence of Black radical politics.

The fear of Black radicalism, and the blinkered way such fear framed mass protest, was a major theme in several famous novels written by white authors from the point of view of Black detectives. Ball's *Death for a Playmate* is paradigmatic in this regard. As Ball paints him, Virgil Tibbs can scarcely contain his scorn for Black radicalism, a scorn so wide it encompasses fictional people as well as real ones: "First it had been Stokley Carmichael who, in Tibbs's opinion, had set the Negro cause back by a generation. Then there had been Rap Brown with his fiery demands for violence and his gospel of hate. After that there had been Eldridge Cleaver. It would be hard for anyone to top that trio, but Miles Orthcutt had risen to the challenge." Through his "flaming personality" and "impassioned oratory," Orthcutt (the one fictional figure in this list) presents himself as a savior to "a vast mob of Black faces." Ball's metaphorical descriptions of Orthcutt are shocking in their own right. He is "like a panther without a leash"; his words are weapons ("Orthcutt was hurling out sentences . . . like verbal grenades"); even his clothes convey violence ("The African garments which he wore were a violent splash of geometric color"). As Tibbs sees it, the danger of Orthcutt's "violent" fashion choices and "verbal grenades" lies in their capacity to incite crowds to rebel. Tibbs repeatedly contrasts these rebellions with the nonviolent legacy of Martin Luther King. In his view, Black radicals betrayed that legacy when they "cried for black power and started riots that ripped apart the Negro sections in Newark and Detroit." As for the uprisings themselves, Tibbs does not consider them true reflections of the will of the people. On the contrary, they are merely evidence that "decent responsible citizens" have allowed themselves to be "temporarily whipped up by a professional agitator."[67] It is no coincidence that the phrase "professional agitator" appears at least half a dozen times in Ball's novel. The point is not simply that someone like Orthcutt is an agitator; the point is that he's a professional—meaning that the mass gatherings he organizes are not an expression of his authentic beliefs. They're just part of his job description.

Similar anxieties about the cynical professionalism of Black militants were voiced in *Shaft* (1970), which, before it became a classic of Blaxploitation cinema, started life as a book by the white novelist Ernest Tidyman.[68] The back cover of my 1971 Bantam edition introduces the titular detective as "a black Bogart who says the revolution is a new way to chase chicks." That John Shaft was first advertised to readers as a vehicle for questioning the authenticity of Black radicalism makes clear how Tidyman's protagonist reflected a certain liberal wariness about discourses of revolution. The novel recounts Shaft's attempt to rescue the kidnapped daughter of a Harlem drug kingpin named Knocks Persons. The search for nineteen-year-old Beatrice Persons eventually leads Shaft to Italian mobsters who are trying to take over some of Knocks's territory. Along the way, Shaft begrudgingly enlists the help of a Black militant leader named Ben Buford, "who was there in Detroit when it was burning, in Watts when it was burning, in Bedford-Stuyvestant when it was burning." The charismatic Buford is, in Shaft's view, a "goddamn phony." Shaft finds Buford's incendiary rhetoric—"the voice of his violence"—not only fake but dangerous, likely to lead "the sheep to the slaughter." He thinks "there might also be insanity" in Buford's eyes.[69]

Shaft distinguishes himself from Buford by being pragmatic rather than political and reasonable rather than insane. Shaft is an "opportunist," an "uninvolved and detached observer," a "middle-man." In the end, he uses these qualities to badger and guilt Buford into using his revolutionary army to practical and "detached" ends. The result is a baroque scheme whereby Buford's men essentially stage a fake riot in order to incite white violence and offer cover for Shaft to burn down the building where Beatrice is being held. (The cops find this to be "the god-damndest [sic] riot they've ever seen" because there's "nobody to fight except white people.") In the final pages of the novel, Shaft ends up being exonerated by a grand jury, with an assist from the police commissioner himself, who credits Shaft with using a fake uprising to help prevent a real one. The commissioner testifies on Shaft's behalf "in payment for the tanks that would not roll the streets." This comes as a relief to both Shaft and the police brass. The novel as a whole has been haunted by the awareness that, as one cop puts it early on, "there is a revolution going on in this city and every other city." In Tidyman's telling, the state doesn't want to respond with repressive violence but will if it has to. He thus spins a fantasy in which revolutionary fervor is redirected and state violence becomes unnecessary. In this fantasy of de-escalation, Shaft's superpower is his ability to prevent the steep human and financial costs of urban uprisings by convincing a group of "belligerent separatists" that "the Revolution wasn't going to work."[70] While Ball depicts the Black revolutionary leader as an imposing but easily vanquished villain—an emperor with a great speaking voice and no clothes—Tidyman represents him as a misguided ally still capable of being won over to the liberal middle ground of the "middle-man." Buford is resistant at first but eventually comes around to Shaft's point of view. He stops hoarding his revolutionary group's resources and manpower and agrees to put them to more local, pragmatic uses—such as loaning them out to a lone private detective who needs some assistance cracking his case.

For African American novelists writing in the same years, the status of militancy in an age of urban insurrection was a more nuanced and complex preoccupation, tinged with hope as well as wariness. "I have . . . been working on the most violent story I have ever attempted," Chester Himes said of his final, unfinished novel *Plan B*, "about an organized black rebellion that is extremely bloody and violent, as any such rebellion must be."[71] From the early 1960s to the mid 1970s, Himes was just one of a number of Black writers—including Sam Greenlee, John A. Williams, John Edgar Wideman, Gil Scott-Heron, Julian Moreau, Chuck Stone, Barry Beckham, Blyden Jackson, Joseph Nazel, Roland S. Jefferson, Nivi-Kofi Easley, and

John O. Killens—who wrote novels starring Black revolutionaries. (Notably, Killens was also a jury member in the People's Tribunal that was organized in response to the killings at the Algiers Motel.[72]) These books were part and parcel of what Valerie Babb has described as "the increasing radicalization that would emerge in much black expression of the 1960s–1970s." This literary radicalization occurred in tandem with the rise of the Black Power movement and of organizations like the Black Panther Party.[73] As the historian Ashley D. Farmer has argued, the Black Panthers played a particularly important role in popularizing the figure of the Black male revolutionary.[74] The figure quickly became a key character type in the era's fiction. Indeed, so fertile was the cross-pollination between Black radical literature and Black radical politics in this period that it became a full-blown publishing phenomenon, as publishers sought to capitalize on the "growing African American market for revolutionary literature."[75]

Commentators have shown how this body of revolutionary literature frequently drew on the genre tropes of speculative and science fiction.[76] But it also responded to the political conditions of its present in a less future-focused way: through debates about crime. After all, this was an era shaped not only by Black radicalization but also by the perceived interchangeability of the radical and the criminal. For many writers, the story of what it might take to foment a revolution had thus, in the age of the War on Crime, become impossible to separate from the story of what it meant to be presumed a criminal. Highlighting the troubled relationship between the stock character of the Black criminal and the emergent figure of the Black revolutionary, these novels show us how future-oriented Black radical fiction remained deeply entangled with the present-day politics of crime control.

The progression from street crime to organized rebellion was most directly and unapologetically imagined in Sam Greenlee's *The Spook Who Sat by the Door* (1969), which tells the story of Dan Freeman, a disaffected ex–CIA agent turned social worker who secretly begins training street gangs in Chicago to wage guerrilla war against the U.S. government. The book struggled to find an American publisher (it came out in England first), and once it did, it was "criticized as a manual for revolutionaries" and dismissed for being overly instrumentalist.[77] Greenlee did not mind the criticism. He viewed *Spook* not simply as a novel but as "a handbook on urban guerrilla warfare, organization, supply, and propaganda." He decided to write it "so that the people who would do it, would do it right."[78] Having worked as a foreign service officer for the United States Information Agency, Greenlee was also attuned to the global coordinates of Black and anticolonial revolt. To do the revolution "right," Freeman, the protagonist of *Spook*, "studied the reports of the guerrilla fight in Algeria, particularly as confined to urban centers; the guerrilla war against the Huks in the Philippines; the guerrilla war against the Malayan Communists; the tactics of the Viet Cong; the theories of Giap and Mao Tse-tung." As Freeman says to the group he is training, "what do you think five hundred well-trained revolutionaries can do to this town?"[79]

Whatever they can do in the novel, their ability to do it is largely underwritten by both the political discourses and the generic conventions of crime. *Spook* explicitly riffs on the tradition of crime fiction; Freeman's nemesis is a detective whose nickname is "the Sherlock of the South Side." Yet *Spook* can be read as a crime novel as much for its relation to the prevailing discourses on crime and riot as for its literary allusions. Indeed, Freeman's revolutionary strategy is tied up with the decade's crime politics at every step. To provide himself professional cover, Freeman "made speeches in the white suburbs concerning juvenile delinquency . . . and spiced them with the white man's statistics concerning Negro crime." Arguing for the necessity of revolutionary politics, Freeman debates a friend who insists, in the exact language of Lyndon Johnson's 1968 omnibus crime bill, that "the streets have to be safe." And as the spark for revolution itself, Freeman realizes he "need only wait for . . . an arrogant, head-whipping cop to spark the riots."[80]

Greenlee's speculative narrative about riot as the starting point for revolution is thus best understood in the context of the government's military mobilization in response to urban unrest—a process that, as the author recognized, had already effectively rendered poor African Americans enemies of the state. The worldview enshrined in the War on Crime was profoundly shaped by the language and logic of the military counterinsurgency then being perpetrated abroad, most visibly in Vietnam.[81] Police in Watts thought of themselves as being at war. LAPD Chief Parker described the situation there as "very much like fighting the Viet Cong."[82] The uprising in Detroit was described in exactly the same way. As the *Detroit News* put it, "It was as though the Viet Cong had infiltrated the riot-blackened streets."[83] According to *Newsweek*, rioters in Detroit had "turned the nation's fifth largest city into a theater of war."[84] It is little surprise, then, that in *Spook*, Freeman understands his revolutionary plot as its own kind of conflict: "The war had begun"; "He awaited the effects of his escalation of the war." And it is no coincidence that the military's counterinsurgent response is given a code name that connects it right back to the ideological machinery of urban policing: "Operation Law and Order."[85] In this light, it becomes clear that Greenlee's recasting of the urban poor as trained guerrilla fighters was simply an attempt to take literally the way inner-city residents were already being portrayed and policed. Simply put, his literary response to the War on Crime was to imagine what it would look like for the criminalized lower classes to wage war back.

How the government might respond to Black revolution weighed similarly on the mind of novelist John A. Williams. Williams is best known for *The Man Who Cried I Am* (1967), his expansive masterpiece about the world of midcentury Black writers. And *The Man Who Cried I Am* is now best remembered for the conspiracy unveiled in its final pages, when the protagonist, Max Reddick, uncovers the "King Alfred Plan," a government contingency plan to detain Black Americans in concentration camps "in the event of widespread and continuing and coordinated racial disturbances." Written in the style of an imagined National Security Council memo, the plan describes how "Demonstrations and rioting . . . have placed the peace and stability of the nation in dire jeopardy." As the memo sees it, the Black "Minority has adopted an almost military posture," meaning that "racial war must be considered inevitable."[86] If *The Spook Who Sat by the Door* is about how riots could serve as the building blocks for organized rebellion, *The Man Who Cried I Am* is about how the federal government already viewed riots in exactly those terms and had readied a response. Where Greenlee conceived his novel as a "handbook" devoted to the practicalities of insurgency, Williams's six pages of fictionalized government documents, memos, lists, and maps depict the bureaucratic minutiae of counterinsurgency.

Although the King Alfred Plan is devised as a response to what the government perceives as the "dire" spread of militarized Black radicalism, Reddick, ironically, only becomes radicalized after discovering it. The plan thus becomes the basis for Reddick's ability to finally imagine the very thing it was put in place to prevent: a large-scale Black revolution. "Black bodies will jam the streets," Reddick thinks. "But those bodies, while they still have life, would be heading downtown this time. No more Harlem. East Cleveland. Lynch Street. Watts. Southside. Downtown. Those people are going to tear up that unreal tranquility that exists in the United States." Here, Reddick imagines the revolutionary energy of the riots channeled outward, out of Black neighborhoods and aimed instead at the structuring myths ("unreal tranquility") that undergird American life. "The clash is inevitable," Reddick realizes after reading the pages of the plan. "The unprotesting, unembattled die." So he decides to protest and to battle. His final act in the novel—before being assassinated by CIA agents—is to call the militant Minister Q (a fictionalized version of Malcolm X) and read him the details of the King Alfred Plan, in the hopes that those details will help him and other Black leaders organize the "coordinated" rebellion that the government had assumed was already taking place in the streets.[87]

What interests me most about Reddick's militant awakening in the closing pages of The Man Who Cried I Am is the fact that it comes to him partly in the language of criminality. As he reads the King Alfred Plan, Reddick finds himself thinking back to one of his first assignments as a young journalist: an interview with Moses Boatwright, a Black, Harvard-educated philosophy major imprisoned for killing and eating a white man.[88] (Reddick pitches the story to his paper as "just the Negro angle. I mean, was there something in his being black that made him do this?"). During their interview, Reddick and Boatwright have a cryptic exchange about Boatwright's motives. "I'm starting to see, Moses," Reddick says placatingly, but Boatwright chides him, "you are not seeing *precisely*. . . . I was born seeing precisely." Years later, now faced with the chilling details of the government's plan to round up Black people and put them in concentration camps, Reddick thinks to himself: "It is still eat, drink and be murderous, for tomorrow I may be among the murdered. This seeing precisely, Max told himself, is a bitch! Moses Boatwright. Seeing precisely." As a way of framing Reddick's dawning revolutionary consciousness, the repetition of this phrase from the Boatwright interview is significant. What Reddick is now able to "see precisely" in the pages of the King Alfred Plan is, the novel suggests, the same thing that Boatwright himself had already seen about the world he lived in: not just the racial violence that underpinned American society, but also the logic in responding by being "murderous" oneself. At this climactic moment in the novel, Reddick comes to see himself as a point of intersection between the militancy of Minister Q and the criminality of Moses Boatwright—an embodiment of what Williams seems to have tentatively imagined as the complementarity, if not the interchangeability, of organized rebellion and individual criminal transgression. For Reddick, murder is a model for militancy. Both are attempts to carve a space of freedom out of a regime of racial violence. "By my acts I decided how I would die," Boatwright explains to Reddick during their interview.[89] Reddick doesn't see it at first, but he sees it precisely in the pages of the King Alfred Plan. Boatwright's decision—and the murderous act that made it possible—makes a lot more sense to him once he realizes that on any given day, people who look like him "may be among the murdered" themselves.

Williams's follow-up novel, *Sons of Darkness, Sons of Light* (1969), betrayed a growing unease with the link between criminality and militancy, however. *Sons of Darkness* is a novel about what it looks like when a member of the professional class "run[s] out of nonviolence."[90] (Williams's good friend Himes praised it for capturing "the dilemma of the black middle class in the certain uprising of the black masses."[91]) The novel tells the story of Eugene Browning, a Black professional who works for the Institute for Racial Justice. When the novel opens, Browning has just learned that a white policeman has shot an unarmed Black teenager. Knowing that the crime is likely to go unpunished, but wary of the violent repression that accompanies riots (when "the state legislatures and the Congress" would do what they always "did after every rebellion—draw the noose tighter and tighter"), Browning seeks a more radical response to the problem of state-sanctioned white violence.[92] He hires a hit man to assassinate the cop.

Browning's decision is less a brief for organized revolt, however, than it is for a kind of radical secrecy: for the anonymous and, above all, individual criminal act. The assassination is Browning's "own little act of violence," an act that he believes should ideally involve "one black man and not five hundred." "Power, real power," he thinks, "resided in anonymity." *Sons of Darkness* thus strategically reimagines revolutionary violence as a matter of individual consciousness: a kind of criminal interiority or secret guilt lodged within Browning's mind alone. Drawing on a literary tradition of psychological crime fiction that runs from Dostoevsky to Richard Wright and Patricia Highsmith, Williams harnesses free indirect discourse and focalized narration to imagine the inner consequences not simply of Browning's decision to have the officer assassinated but also of his inability to tell anyone that he did so: "He should have told the doctor that he too believed in violence.... Browning longed to share his secret with someone, ached to set it down."[93]

Browning's longing shifts the arena of radical violence from the external world to the internal one. In this way, he becomes tethered to a political act whose message is compromised precisely to the extent that it can't be communicated to anyone. Which is exactly what happens: Browning's "simple, selective violent act, calculated to deliver a message," is predictably misread, leading to paramilitary-style attacks by police on Black neighborhoods and the apparent onset of an all-out race war. Ending on this uncertain note, Williams signals his doubt as to whether any kind of violence, no matter how well organized or secretly devised, can avoid producing an even worse "murderous reaction" by the state. But there is equally a lesson here, at the novel's end, about the figure of the secretive, solitary criminal that Browning imagines himself to be. As Browning reconciles with his wife in the book's final chapter, Williams draws our attention less to the political consequences of his radical act than to the guilty solitude to which the act condemned him. "Shit," Browning confesses to his wife, "I've been lonely myself."[94] This long-delayed confession, the finally soothed "ache" of Browning's hitherto unshareable secret, makes clear that Williams's skepticism of violence has both a political and a personal dimension. In the end, *Sons of Darkness* rejects revolutionary violence not only because it invites intensified racial oppression by the state but also because it has forced a Black man like Browning—so sincerely intent on fighting that oppression—to keep a secret that makes him feel like a criminal.[95]

The criminal isolation, as opposed to political solidarity, produced by revolutionary violence was also the focus of John Edgar Wideman's *The Lynchers* (1973), a neomodernist stream-of-consciousness novel that obliquely narrates the plot of four men—Littleman, Wilkerson, Saunders, and Rice—to lynch a white cop and use the public spectacle to spark a revolution. Although *The Lynchers* seems at first sympathetic to the Black nationalist motivations behind the lynching, Wideman ultimately views these men less as political actors than as common criminals. "If they were going to talk about killing," Wilkerson realizes early on, "they had to believe in each other as killers." Later, Saunders is described as "ripe for killing... murder was in his blood."[96] In moments like these, Wideman rewrites militant action as a kind of criminal identity, implying that the tactics of political violence may in the end be indistinguishable from the inner constitution of criminality (the "murder" in one's "blood").

It is no accident that the narrative of *The Lynchers* is bookended by radio reports of senseless, apolitical violence. Early in the novel, Wilkerson's father, Orin, hears news of the murder of Sharon Tate ("Somebody had killed the pregnant movie star.... A damned shame. Somebody crazy did it"). Toward the novel's end, in an obvious parallel, Rice hears news on the radio that Orin Wilkerson himself has been arrested for stabbing a friend during a drunken argument in a vacant lot. These invocations of pointless violence foreshadow the novel's conclusion, which chaotically devolves into a series of misdirected crimes: Rice shoots the younger Wilkerson in a fit of paranoia; Saunders is driven nearly to homicidal madness when Wilkerson never arrives to meet him; and Littleman, having been injured by the police and falsely charged, naturally, with "fomenting a riot," is imprisoned in a mental hospital.[97] Thus, in *The Lynchers*, does the violence of revolutionary desire cause the downfall of so many would-be revolutionaries.

Even the radical poet Gil Scott-Heron worried about how to tell the difference between a revolutionary organization and a criminal one. Scott-Heron's first published work was a mystery novel titled *The Vulture*, published in 1970 by a small New York City press (which would publish Scott-Heron's better-known debut book of poetry, *Small Talk at 125th and Lenox*, later that year). *The Vulture* revolves around the mysterious death of a small-time pill dealer named John Lee and is narrated, *Rashomon*-style, by four different men who knew him and may have been involved in his death. One of those narrators is an activist and revolutionary named Tommy Hall, who works for a community organization called BAMBU (Black American Men for Black Unity), a group that is equal parts Black Panther Party and Black Arts Repertory Theater/School. Speaking on behalf of the group at a local school, Hall explains that BAMBU's aim is to "foster a cultural revolution" through the opening of community centers, which will facilitate education in Black history and culture, political organizing, economic support, and self-defense, among other things. Yet at a clandestine meeting with BAMBU leadership late one night, Hall is given a different glimpse of what the organization is really about. "Just how much of a revolutionary are you, Brother Hall?" the voice of an unseen figure asks him. Reminded that "Brother Malcolm said that there is no such thing as a *bloodless* revolution," Hall is asked to help "rid black people" of the "great plague" of drug addiction. He is to do this by assassinating drug dealers. Accepting a small box with a pistol and shells in it, Hall leaves the meeting intending to follow through on his assignment. (As it turns out, he doesn't actually kill anyone.) But the scene ends with another twist: BAMBU is not actually trying to stamp out the drug trade in New York City. The group is trying to take it over. In the scene's last lines, the unseen voice addresses the other BAMBU leaders in the room: "Don't worry, gentlemen. With the help of young men like Brother Hall, soon BAMBU will be in control of all drug traffic in New York City." The voice then emits a "maniacal laugh" and repeats a slogan that is now blood-drenched in irony: "Black Power!"[98]

The two-sided nature of the organization—one-half community organizing, the other half drug trafficking—has been coyly hinted at earlier in the novel through the circulation of popular rolling papers that are mysteriously stamped with the word "*Bambú.*" Still, discovering that "Black Power!" has become the ironized rallying cry of a secretive crime syndicate is bound to be disconcerting. This may seem an especially strange move for a writer who would, that same year, pen probably the most famous revolutionary poem of the Black Power era, "The Revolution Will Not Be Televised." But Scott-Heron had a complicated relationship to Black radicalism. He was sympathetic to the cause of revolution but uncomfortable with the ideological rigidities of the movement. In his book of poems *Small Talk at 125th and Lenox*, Scott-Heron criticized "you would-be Black revolutionaries" who "deal in too many externals . . . Always afros, handshakes and dashikis," even as he chose to place a two-page photograph of a Black Panther Party headquarters at the book's center.[99]

What *The Vulture*'s surprising plot twist reveals is that Scott-Heron's misgivings were about not only the "externals" or superficialities of self-righteous radicals, but also the potential hazards of revolutionary discourse itself. BAMBU uses the very idea of revolutionary identification—*just how much of a revolutionary are you?*—as a lever to press Hall into service for the criminal side of the operation, and Hall himself uses the same ideas to help himself come to terms with his unexpected assignment. "Revolution was on my mind," Hall says. "I had been willing to stain my soul with the blood of another *man* in order to free those who needed freedom most. I felt good. I felt as though I was right. I felt alive." But of course, what readers know while Hall does not is that he isn't acting to further the revolution, and he isn't working in service of "those who needed freedom"; he is a hit man for a drug trafficking ring. Scott-Heron certainly did not think that the cause of Black revolution was a crime. But he was clearly concerned that the language of who was and wasn't a proper revolutionary ("Are you a fair-weather revolutionary?" the BAMBU leader's voice taunts Hall; "Does the man read Mao or Fanon?" Scott-Heron mockingly ventriloquizes in *Small Talk*) could too easily become a front: a pretext for modes of violence that might be more criminal than political.[100]

By the early 1970s, there was indeed growing disillusionment with the idea of a Black revolution that seemed increasingly unlikely to come to pass. Even the Black Panther Party had begun to "deemphasize armed revolution" and "demilitarize its image" in those years.[101] This may explain why the optimism of Greenlee's speculative revolution so quickly curdles into the ambivalence of Scott-Heron's mystery plot and the outright cynicism of Wideman's cautionary tale. More specific reservations are voiced in these books as well, from equivocation about the role of the middle class in a rebellion of the masses (*Sons of Darkness, Sons of Light*) to suspicion of top-down forms of institutional organizing (*The Vulture*). Still, at a fundamental level, all five of these novels recognized that it was impossible to talk about revolution without talking about crime. Why was that? The answer is tied to the very real ways that Black protest and politicization—from the leaderless uprisings referred to as riots to militant organizations such as the Panthers—had been framed as matters of law enforcement. For African Americans, the mere act of criticizing the state had become a crime. To see this one need look no further than the longstanding FBI surveillance of Black activists and writers that expanded and intensified in the 1950s and '60s. As William J. Maxwell explains in his groundbreaking literary history of federal policing, "A who's who of black protest was spied on, often infiltrated, and sometimes formally indicted by Hoover's FBI."[102] A character in *The Lynchers* sums up this state of affairs aptly: Black people "may survive, but if they ask for more, they are criminals."[103]

The criminalization of Black political demand—of "ask[ing] for more," in Wideman's words—helps explain why all of the novelists discussed in this section considered the story of Black revolution inseparable from both the politics of crime control and the form of the crime novel.[104] Scott-Heron, for one, remained committed to writing a murder mystery even after a potential publisher told him that his audience wouldn't be interested in the genre.[105] Williams, meanwhile, claimed that he wrote *Sons of Darkness* mainly out of financial exigency—"*Sons*," he said, "was one of those books you do to keep eating"[106]—yet he was forced to withstand reviews of the novel that praised its political insight while complaining of its "clumsy and rather tentative plot."[107] Publishers and reviewers alike, apparently, were wary of Black writers' attempts to make use of the formal conventions and "clumsy" plots of the crime genre. For the writers themselves, however, the genre of the crime novel—a literary tradition further invoked by Greenlee's reference to "Sherlock" in Chicago, by Williams's depiction of the remorseless murderer Moses Boatwright, and by Wideman's modernist exploration of the depths of a guilty conscience—represented a crucial instrument for grappling with the disturbing problem of political criminalization.[108] What the genre enabled was a way of reassessing the distinction between political action and criminal activity. The result of this reassessment, however, was hardly a foregone conclusion. In Greenlee's rendering, the moral panic over street crime seemed a useful cover for the clandestine project of revolution. Scott-Heron, conversely, worried that revolution might also be a useful cover for organized crime. And to Williams and Wideman, the blurry line between revolutionary and criminal appeared most damaging to the psychic life of the would-be revolutionary himself. Yet despite their significant political disagreements, all of these novels were organized around the same fundamental dilemma: how to disentangle the inner commitments of Black radicalism from the social construction of Black criminality. In the shadow of the War on Crime, Black revolutionary fiction merged with crime fiction in order to confront the alarming fact that society could not tell the difference between a common criminal and a committed revolutionary. Yet this compound literary form remained haunted by the possibility that, at times, it couldn't necessarily keep that difference straight itself.

RENEWED VIGILANCE

Donald Goines's *Crime Partners* (1974) introduced readers to a different kind of revolutionary criminal. The novel's hero—who starred in three subsequent novels by Goines, all written under the pseudonym Al C. Clark and published by the infamous white-owned publisher Holloway House—is Kenyatta, the leader of a revolutionary organization that trains militants on a farm outside Detroit. Named after Jomo Kenyatta, the first president of Kenya after colonial rule, Goines's Kenyatta has a headquarters decorated with "pictures of Che, Ho Chi Minh, and other men of color who were dedicated leaders in various revolutions."[109] Goines was a key figure in the development of Black pulp fiction. Heavily influenced by Iceberg Slim, his predecessor at Holloway House, Goines updated Slim's formula for an era of Black Power and a new Black readership.[110] Many critics have attributed his massive and ongoing popularity to his innovative fusion of pulp and politics. L. H. Stallings reads Goines's oeuvre as an extended political commentary on "the process of decolonization following enslavement," while Justin Gifford argues that the Kenyatta series in particular "combined popular entertainment and militant black politics in ways unrepresented in American literature before."[111] Other scholars, however, have suggested that the "universally bleak and pessimistic outlook" of Goines's work lacks a clear political focus.[112] The book historian Kinohi Nishikawa goes so far as to suggest that the author "was not writing politics" at all. For Nishikawa, the Kenyatta novels express only "Goines's stone-cold cynicism about Black Power."[113]

I'm less interested in choosing a side in this debate than I am in understanding why Goines's politics would be so hard to parse in the first place. The answer has something to do with how the relation between radical politics and anticrime politics was being transformed in the early 1970s. To be sure, *Crime Partners* is a less politically straightforward text than the revolutionary heroes on Kenyatta's walls would have us think. Though he is driven by the Black Power-inflected "rally cry" of "Death to Whitey," Kenyatta is also "trying to clean up the ghettos of dope pushers and pimps." The goal, as Kenyatta puts it, is to rid the city of both "dopepushers and race-hatin' cops."[114] Rendered in these terms, Kenyatta is not simply fighting the racial violence of the state. He is also taking the state's place in the policing of crime in Black neighborhoods. Kenyatta thus embodies a kind of militant politics whose agenda has shifted from large-scale social transformation to local patrols. Such a shift calls forth a revolutionary figure—Kenyatta himself—who could also plausibly be described as a vigilante.

Goines's vision of the Black vigilante was intimately tied to the early years of the War on Crime, when the overpolicing of urban uprisings went hand in hand with the underpolicing of a mounting drug crisis. The rising crime rates of the late 1960s were frequently blamed on addicts and dealers. Heroin use is estimated to have "increased tenfold during the 1960s," rising to the level of roughly half a million users in 1970. By 1971, Richard Nixon famously asserted that "America's Public Enemy Number One is drug abuse."[115] Both users and sellers of heroin were concentrated primarily in poor, racially segregated parts of major cities, a fact that community organizations blamed on state neglect and police indifference. The evidence of a drug epidemic that had been allowed to thrive in inner cities prompted some African American groups, including the NAACP, to call for increased policing and harsher punishments for drug dealers.[116] Other activists and organizers decided, as the historian Michael Javen Fortner puts it, "to take matters in their own hands."[117] A grassroots vigilante movement grew quickly in Harlem in the late 1960s and lasted through the 1970s. Local vigilante groups cultivated an unlikely alliance between working- and middle-class African Americans and Black militants, Fortner argues, as both sides "considered vigilantism a necessary response to junkies and pushers."[118]

Part revolutionary, part vigilante, Goines's Kenyatta testifies directly to the messy history of drugs, race, and underpolicing. As one of the most famous characters in Black crime fiction, Kenyatta captures the complexities of an era in which the broadly transformative aims of Black revolutionary movements were increasingly tempered by the need to respond to local concerns about public safety and the state's refusal to police drug markets. Those same complexities are registered in *The Vulture*, which likewise imagines a pair of solutions to the "great plague" of drug addiction in Black communities: rehabilitate the addicts, assassinate the dealers ("BAMBU has started an extensive rehabilitation program for the users of drugs.... We have also started a movement to get rid of the pushers and sellers"). As we saw in the previous section, Scott-Heron adds a further twist: BAMBU's murders are not actually an attempt to stop the sale of narcotics but to corner the market on them. Yet the template for Goines's revolutionary vigilantism is already there in *The Vulture*. With no other viable solution in sight, the earnest activist Tommy Hall is willing to be convinced that being "a dedicated man to the cause of uplifting black people" requires being dedicated to the cause of killing off neighborhood drug dealers.[119]

However, if the crisis of urban drug use helped spawn a new kind of Black vigilantism meant to fill the practical void left by police neglect, it also served to create a less radical and more unambiguously punitive figure who happens to be one of the most recognizable products of American popular culture in the 1970s: the white vigilante. The era's most infamous fictional vigilante was immortalized onscreen by Charles Bronson but first created by Brian Garfield in his 1972 novel *Death Wish*. *Death Wish* tells the story of a white accountant named Paul Benjamin, who, after his wife is killed and his daughter traumatized during a home invasion, starts killing petty criminals on the streets of New York. Garfield famously hated the film adaptation of his book, claiming that it shamelessly romanticized the vigilantism that he had been attempting to criticize. Those who have read the novel may find this a somewhat puzzling account of its political intent. That's because it is far less focused on the dangers of vigilantes than it is on the failures of liberal crime policy that made vigilantism seem necessary in the first place. "Someone had to guard the city," Paul thinks. "Obviously the cops weren't doing it. . . . *Then it's up to me, isn't it?*" The inability of the state to effectively safeguard urban space leaves a regular guy like Paul to do the guarding himself. The failures of liberalism, as the novel enumerates them, include the indulgences of the welfare state and permissiveness toward radical protest, both of which, Garfield insists, foster crime. "These young scum grow up in a welfare state where they see that violence goes unpunished," opines one character with whom Paul comes to agree. Another connects neighborhood integration to Black militancy: "They don't just want to move in next door to you, they want to burn your fucking *house* down." Ultimately, Paul comes to the conclusion that "permissive societies were like permissive parents: they produced hellish children."[120]

The gendered obsession with liberal permissiveness was deeply ingrained in the political rhetoric of the time, especially in New York City.

Studying the archive of letters written to New York governor Nelson Rockefeller in the early 1970s, Julilly Kohler-Hausmann finds that correspondents frequently lamented the permissiveness of government policies and associated it with the extension of rights to minority communities. The criticism of permissiveness was thus both racialized and gendered. As Kohler-Hausmann details, "The rhetoric in these letters often belittled and discredited welfare state and therapeutic programs by linking them with attributes typically associated with bad mothering." The feminization of permissiveness—with its maternal production of what Paul describes as all those "hellish children"—prompted an equally gendered response: "Again and again, citizens called for 'tough' responses to these problems."[121] The character in *Death Wish* who first recommends vigilantism to Paul calls for pretty much the same thing: "You got to get tough with the bastards, it's the only thing they understand."[122]

Responding to the liberal permissiveness and feminized lack of toughness that putatively fostered crime, *Death Wish* turns out to be yet another crime novel about the relation between criminality and radicalism, but with a twist. It is the story of what the novel dubs "the right-wing radicalization of Paul Benjamin."[123] Garfield's counternarrative of radicalization reimagines the radical not as a type of racialized criminality but as a bulwark against the perceived proliferation of racialized criminal types.

A perversely inverted image of the era's Black radical novels, *Death Wish* testifies to the crisis of a historical moment at which crime and its solutions were becoming harder to tell apart. Militant attempts to fight inequality in American society were discredited as instances of crime, which the state then used as justification to deploy its own tools of counterinsurgent violence. And still, to many anxious observers wringing their hands over the supposed lack of toughness in American social policy, those tools did not seem violent enough.[124] Such are the multiple, conflicting ways that criminality, riot, and radicalism converged as the defining terms of both crime policy and crime fiction in the 1960s and '70s. The literary character of the Black revolutionary represented a radical rewriting of the criminalized rioter but—as Goines, Scott-Heron, and Garfield all demonstrated—was haunted by the conservative shadow figure of the vigilante. Sometimes militancy could look a lot like militarization. Toward the end of *Death Wish*, Paul imagines himself as "the first of the Resistance—the first soldier of the underground."[125] There are two revealing historical ironies to this line. The first is that it shamelessly borrows the language of the era's militant movements, reimagining revolution (the "underground" of a capital-*r* "Resistance") now not as a tactic of the oppressed but as a tactic to shore up oppression. The second irony is that—as Paul himself would surely have known—seven years into the War on Crime, he was hardly the first armed soldier to put boots on the ground in the Black neighborhoods of an American city.

STRANGER THAN FICTION

In *Death Wish*, the motivating force behind Paul's "right-wing radicalization" is his realization that urban crime is a real rather than a fictional concern. This inspires what is easily the oddest passage in the novel:

> He had never seen real violence except on television or in the movies. Until [his wife's murder] had happened, he had been secretly convinced that a good part of it was fictitious ... he did not really believe, in a personal way, that hoodlums and killers existed.... Sometimes it was hard to escape the feeling that the pages of the *Daily News* and the *Mirror* were filled not with fact-news but with the lurid fantasies of pulp-fiction writers.... Now he had to get used to an entire new universe of reality.[126]

Why would a novel so committed to convincing us of the "reality" of crime draw so much attention to its status as a work of fiction—indeed, as a work of the very kind of "pulp-fiction" that Paul claims is to blame for his own misreading of the facts of crime reporting? At minimum, this reads like a glimmer of hesitation on Garfield's part, a moment of uncertainty about which universe the public crisis of crime actually belongs to: the "universe of reality" or the universe of fiction. And there's more. For the knots of real and fake in the passage point to a yet grimmer possibility, one that Garfield certainly recognized and perhaps actively courted: that citizens would ultimately be convinced of the public menace posed by street crime not because it was real but because they saw it "on television or in the movies"—or, more to the point, because they read about it in a novel like *Death Wish*.

What Garfield tentatively confesses here is something I believe all the writers I've discussed in this chapter suspected: that the crisis of crime was in part a crisis of perception, and that literature might have a significant role to play in shaping that perception. The most striking example of fiction's impact on popular belief in this period involved *The Man Who Cried I Am*, a novel whose incendiary conclusion led Williams's editor at Little, Brown, Harry Sions, to predict that the book would have a very real effect on the world—that it "would create not one Watts, but hundreds."[127] *The Man Who Cried I Am* didn't quite do that, but, as the critic Merve Emre has tracked, the novel did succeed in convincing a great number of its readers that the King Alfred Plan was real. The mistaking (if it was a mistake) of the plan for reality was encouraged in large part by Williams himself, who helped design a promotional pamphlet for the book meant to look like a classified excerpt of the King Alfred Plan; he then left copies on the subway for people to find.[128] Just a few years later, the King Alfred Plan was being discussed at Congressional hearings and in federal courtrooms.[129]

A more unhappy instance of literature's enmeshment in the era's debates about crime, riot, and policing involves *The Algiers Motel Incident*, which, in a tragic irony, was introduced as evidence at the trial of one of the officers accused of the Algiers killings as part of a motion to secure a change of venue. The claim was that the existence of Hersey's book had possibly biased potential jurors. The motion was successful, and the officer's trial ended up being moved to a whiter and more conservative Michigan district. Once there, he was swiftly acquitted.[130] But the afterlives of Hersey's and Williams's books are only the most literal examples. More broadly, we need to understand what Lyndon Johnson himself was forced to admit in 1967: that the "public malady" of the day was not just crime but also "the fear of crime."[131] Crime, as I argued in this book's introduction, is not a straightforward statistical fact. It is bound up with more complex processes of storytelling, belief, and feeling—including a feeling such as fear. All of the texts I have discussed in this chapter were efforts to shape how people felt and what they believed about crime. Christopher P. Wilson has memorably described crime narrative in the late twentieth century as a vehicle for teaching "citizens...to 'learn to live' with crime."[132] Before readers could learn how to live with it, however, they had to be instructed—per *Death Wish*—that crime was a problem at all. Wambaugh's beat cop whose daily walk anecdotally confirms the existence of so many Black criminals; Goines's and Garfield's vigilantes punishing those whom a permissive state would not; the Black radicals of Greenlee,

Williams, Wideman, and Scott-Heron working to differentiate their acts from crimes: Each of these main characters was a vehicle for conveying to readers exactly what kind of problem the so-called crime problem was supposed to be. Each was an attempt to explain what the newly launched War on Crime was really a war against. Hardened criminals? Assembled rioters? "Professional agitators?" Idealistic revolutionaries? Black neighborhoods? John A. Williams, for one, was clear-eyed about fiction's role in adjudicating such questions. As he saw it, neither *The Man Who Cried I Am* nor the viral marketing campaign he launched on its behalf were, in his own words, "cheap publicity." They were not literary but literal declarations of the truth of a world built on the racial violence of urban policing. "We know that the Army and National Guard as well as local police are undergoing riot training," Williams explained in defense of his invention of the fictional King Alfred Plan. "What in the hell is cheap about the truth?"[133]

As the beat cop, the revolutionary, and the vigilante rose to prominence in the crime novels of the 1960s and '70s, these characters became the mouthpieces for a series of directly competing claims about the basic reality of crime. The "entire new universe of reality" that Paul Benjamin thinks he has discovered in *Death Wish* was a universe of racialized urban crime whose reality remained, in fact, an open question. This was a universe shaped as much by the fear of crime as by the fact of it. Look closer: Even in a novel as nervous as *Death Wish*, the much-ballyhooed reality of crime rarely surfaces. In one key scene, Paul goes out "hunting," hoping to be mugged so he can retaliate and shoot a criminal; but for several pages and across many city blocks, no one mugs him ("Two youths on the curb—Puerto Ricans in thin windbreakers. *Okay, come on*. But they only watched him go past"). Indeed, it often seems that Paul's entire journey of revenge is aimed predominantly at young Black and Brown men whose fundamental crime does not involve committing one but simply making people like Paul fear that they might. In another scene Paul again walks the city unmolested: "The fear settled in his bowels again when he walked the single crosstown block to West End Avenue. No one accosted him, he reached the apartment without incident; but he was covered with oily sweat. *I just don't want to feel like this, he thought. Is it so much to ask?*"[134] Somehow, the less real crime becomes, the more Paul is gripped, all the way down to his bowels, by the fear of it. What we learn in a scene like this is that Paul's anticrime politics are not about facts at all. They're about feelings. He says so himself: *"I just don't want to feel like this."*

The historian Michael Flamm has argued that the key error of liberal strategy in the 1960s was not to take the feeling of fear seriously enough. Liberals' skepticism about the reliability of crime statistics, he contends, "distracted them from a larger reality. Simply put, the fear was real."[135] But of course what made the fear of crime real was not necessarily real crime. Flamm's "larger reality," like Garfield's "new universe of reality," was inextricable from a set of fictions that were both ideological and literary. These are the fictions that the novels surveyed in this chapter help us to see. The fear of crime in the 1960s and '70s was stoked by a set of stock social types—the Black criminal, the Black rioter, the Black radical—that circulated widely in American popular discourse. It was further reinforced by a set of literary characters—the jaded beat cop; the ex-liberal vigilante; the authentic and the inauthentic revolutionary—who claimed to be able to give readers an up-close view of the lived reality of rising crime. And so it came to be that, in the formative years of the War on Crime, the supremely consequential task of separating fact from fiction on the issue of crime was performed in no small part by crime fiction itself.

3

DETECTING DOMESTIC VIOLENCE, 1975-2000

Throwing him in jail don't change a thing he's done to me.
—*BLANCHE AMONG THE TALENTED TENTH* (1994)

DIFFERENT CRIME, SAME WAR

One of the most commercially successful genres of crime writing in the late twentieth century was domestic suspense fiction, which featured plots of women and children in danger, often from abusive husbands. Mary Higgins Clark, who would come to be known as the "queen of suspense," helped established the template for the genre in her novel *Where Are the Children?* (1975), written when the issues of domestic violence and child abuse were just beginning to enter public consciousness. Several publishers rejected the manuscript before it found a home with Simon & Schuster. "Child molestation was pretty much a taboo subject," Clark would later write, and publishers "feared the subject of children in that kind of jeopardy might upset their women readers."[1] But *Where Are the Children?* was an unexpected hit. The novel tells the story of Nancy Eldredge, a happily married mother of two who lives in Cape Cod and has a secret. Seven years before, she was convicted of killing her two children, which drove her former husband, Carl, to commit suicide. At her trial, Nancy was found guilty but beat the charge on a technicality. Afterward she changed her name, dyed her hair, and started a new life in Cape Cod. Now her two new children have disappeared and Nancy once again falls under suspicion. In the end, the villain turns out to be Nancy's first husband, Carl, who faked his own death and has returned to torment Nancy and abduct her new children. We learn that when they were married, Carl had been drugging Nancy and molesting their daughter; when Nancy figured out what was happening, he killed their children and framed her. In Cape Cod, a crack team comprising a retired lawyer, a retired psychiatrist, and Nancy's new husband, Ray—three highly professionalized men—work together to help Nancy uncover the buried trauma of her abuse, clear her name, and rescue her children.

In the novel's climactic scene, Nancy realizes under hypnosis that she had been a victim of domestic abuse. "I was in a cage," she explains, "had to get out." But how are women like Nancy supposed to get out of abusive situations? *Where Are the Children?* isn't entirely sure how to answer that. The legal system cannot be fully trusted. It has already found Nancy guilty of a crime she didn't commit, and it is no coincidence that the retired lawyer helping Nancy is writing a book called *Verdict in Doubt*, in which he relitigates "ten controversial criminal trials," often rejecting the original verdict. The police seem unlikely to be much help, either. The local police chief—the meaningfully named Jed Coffin—is a narrow-minded misogynist. He assumes women just tend to "go off the deep end," and he is flatly unwilling to believe Nancy's account of her abuse, which he thinks sounds "pretty hysterical." Coffin believes that Nancy's accusations are simply an effort to blame her ex-husband "for the fact that she wanted out of their marriage."[2] Between Nancy's dubious trial and her gaslighting by a police chief whose name hints at death, Clark appears to have concluded that neither the courts nor the cops were equipped to handle women's experiences of abuse and violence in the home.

However, for Clark, as well as for a majority of anti–domestic violence activists in the 1970s, this did not mean that law enforcement solutions for women should be rejected altogether. It meant that the legal system's response to gendered violence needed to be improved. *Where Are the Children?* conveys this more optimistic belief through a pair of odd but unmissable references. Early in this novel whose plot turns on multiple concealed identities (Nancy has changed her name and appearance, as has Carl), a character passingly remarks that "people do look like other people.... remember that guy ... who was a dead ringer for Lyndon Johnson?" Later, weirdly, another character says almost exactly the same thing: "Lots of people look like someone else. His own uncle ... was a dead ringer for Barry Goldwater."[3] What on earth are the two major party candidates from the 1964 presidential election doing in Clark's 1975 novel about family abuse?

The answer, as may be obvious from reading this book's previous chapter, concerns the War on Crime—a war that both Johnson and Goldwater helped design. When Goldwater turned "crime in the streets" into a central campaign issue in 1964, he set the terms of a national conversation that Johnson went on to amplify. Johnson crushed Goldwater in the general election yet picked up where Goldwater left off; less than a year after his victory, his administration launched its War on Crime. But neither Goldwater nor Johnson was thinking about the kind of domestic and sexual crime that affected women. The first decade of War on Crime policy had little interest in what might be happening to women and children behind the closed doors of private homes. This is why, in *Where Are the Children?*, the two politicians appear as ersatz lookalikes. They represent figures who *look like* they could have done something to protect women like Nancy Eldredge—but didn't. The phoniness of Goldwater and Johnson as they appear in Clark's novel conveys the fact that their anticrime rhetoric did not account for the experiences of women vulnerable to gender-based violence. Despite their tough-on-crime talk, these politicians had done nothing to keep women safe. As far as women were concerned, they were second-rate stand-ins. *Where Are the Children?* was trying to say that, ten years into the anticrime revolution sparked by figures like Johnson and Goldwater, there was still no war on crimes against women. Clark was implying that there should be.

In its otherwise curious references to the men who started the War on Crime, *Where Are the Children?* captures the complexities that feminist writers and activists faced as they sought to draw attention to the crisis of violence against women. Clark was hardly alone in noting, in the 1970s, that the American legal system—in the midst of an unprecedented expansion thanks to Johnson's infusion of federal cash into local enforcement agencies—had a major blind spot. Nor was she alone in wondering what it would take to turn what had so far been a cheap imitation of a war for women's safety into a real one. Yet the still-unfolding consequences of the War on Crime raised a set of difficult questions that would be sharply debated in the ensuing decades. Would women actually be helped by such a war? Or would they be harmed by it?

This chapter uncovers how questions about gender, violence, and the politics of crime control shaped women's crime fiction.[4] Starting in the mid-1970s, crime novels written by and for women became, for the first time, a significant part of the publishing ecosystem. In the 1970s, Clark demonstrated the immense commercial potential of domestic suspense fiction. In the 1980s, there was an explosion of feminist-leaning mystery novels featuring female detectives. And in the 1990s, more novels began to focus on female police officers and prosecutors. By the end of the century, novelists such as Clark and Sue Grafton had established themselves as "among the most bankable of best-selling writers," securing advances and garnering sales on par with Stephen King, Michael Crichton, and other male genre writers.[5] The publishing revolution in women's crime writing that took place between the 1970s and the 1990s was inseparable, I propose, from what the political scientist Marie Gottschalk has described as a "mini-revolution" in how the legal system handled violence against women and how the public understood it.[6] My aim is to show how these two revolutions informed and intensified one another, as female crime novelists developed a running commentary on the complicated relation between women's liberation, male violence, and the police. Simply as a matter of theme, representations of gender-based violence were a common feature of crime novels written by women across a range of subgenres in these decades. But the thematic representation of this kind of violence opened onto a more complex and uncertain reckoning with what it meant to fight male violence by partnering with the carceral state. Ultimately, this chapter argues that women's crime writing in the late twentieth century is best understood as an attempt to come to terms with the tense accommodation between feminist ideals and carceral ideology.

Until the early 1970s, domestic violence was considered a private issue outside the purview of law enforcement. As the legal scholar Mimi E. Kim explains, "Police called to intervene in domestic violence did little to stop the violence," and many police departments "were guided by an explicit 'avoid arrest' policy in matters of family violence, a policy aimed at avoiding undue embarrassment of perpetrators of violence or fracturing a yet intact family."[7] The situation changed as feminist activists successfully drew attention to the plight of battered women, to the problem of family violence, and to the prevalence of sexual assault. The anti–domestic violence movement began in 1973 with the creation of crisis hotlines for victims; the following year the first battered women's shelter opened in the United States.[8] The country's first rape crisis shelters had opened a few years earlier. Working alongside the antirape movement, which developed around the same time, the anti–domestic violence movement spurred a profound shift in public awareness of the problem of violence against women. It also had a lasting impact on the American legal system. In 1975, the National Organization for Women created a task force focused specifically on the issue of domestic violence.[9] In 1976, two major class-action lawsuits were filed on behalf of women against police departments in Oakland, California, and New York City for failing to protect battered women; both lawsuits were settled with consent decrees that marked the first steps toward instituting mandatory-arrest policies in domestic violence complaints. In 1978, the federal Commission on Civil Rights held a series of hearings on the problem of "wife abuse," which brought a whole new level of national attention to what activists had been describing as the " 'hidden epidemic' of battering."[10] The hearings led to the formation of the National Coalition against Domestic Violence in 1978, to the creation of the Office of Domestic Violence in 1979, and to a series of far-reaching changes in how the courts handled charges of domestic abuse. In the first half of the 1970s, domestic violence was barely considered a crime; by 1984, "49 states and the District of Columbia had enacted some form of legislation to provide legal remedies for domestic violence."[11] But as Kim assesses it, "The success of the anti-violence social movement eventually led to its unintended opposite," with the movement folded into the machinery of "a masculinist punitive state."[12] The legal scholar and former public defender Aya Gruber glosses this arc more bluntly, suggesting that "in a few short years, the battered women's movement transformed from a radical antiauthoritarian movement into a propolicing, proprosecution lobby."[13]

This transformation was buttressed, if not encouraged, by the Law Enforcement Assistance Administration, or LEAA—the federal crime control office created as part of the Johnson administration's 1968 Safe Streets Act. The LEAA established the Family Violence Program in 1977, which disbursed more money to domestic violence programs than did any other government agency. Gottschalk suggests that the LEAA effectively "pioneered the federal response to battered women." The outcome was double-edged. On one hand, it helped direct "national attention to the enormity of the problem of violence against women and underscored a woman's right to safety." On the other hand, "it identified law enforcement as the primary arena for addressing the problem."[14] After the LEAA took control of the domestic violence issue, women's shelters were required to cooperate with the police in order to secure federal funding. Most did so, given that they were unlikely to find financial support anywhere else. Funding for services for battered women declined during Ronald Reagan's first presidential term, but started to rise again after the passage of the Family Violence and Prevention Act in 1984. By this point, a number of previously divergent interests and movements—including the antiviolence movement, the victim's-rights movement, police departments, and the federal government—had come together to elevate "the issue of domestic violence" into "a powerful symbol of the war on crime."[15]

Policies such as mandatory arrest and no-drop prosecution (which prohibits prosecutors from dropping domestic violence charges and legally mandates victims' cooperation with prosecutors, even against their wishes) quickly became common tools in the policing of intimate partner violence. By the middle of the 1980s, activists had rallied around the idea that "arrest is best," and "a pro-arrest stance had become the consensus opinion among domestic violence activists in the United States."[16] Yet this opinion did not go unchallenged. More radical wings of the feminist movement remained wary of partnering with the criminal legal system and advocating for punitive solutions. This was especially the case for feminists of color. Put simply, it was not clear whether solutions crafted by and for middle-class white women would really work for other groups of women who had a very different idea of what the police would do once they showed up. The activist and scholar Beth E. Richie explains that "legal and legislative reform work" became the dominant focus of the antiviolence movement despite the fact that "notable objections" were being raised by Black feminists, who remained sharply attuned to "the state's inability and/or unwillingness to protect women from repeated abuse."[17]

Such objections had been voiced in both the antiviolence and the antirape movements from the beginning. Throughout the 1970s, both movements were "characterized by battles over whether or not to pursue strategies and resources specifically tied to law enforcement."[18] In 1974, the New York Radical Feminists insisted that "rape is not a law-and-order issue."[19] In 1977, Santa Cruz Women Against Rape published "an open letter to the anti-rape movement," which expressed serious misgivings about the movement's reliance on the police and the courts. The letter argued that "attempts at 'good relations' with the criminal justice system have served to co-opt our movement, and have led to the belief (or hope) that the criminal justice system can solve the problem of rape. Yet, the sexist and racist nature of the criminal justice system only makes the problem worse."[20] The point that prison was more a perpetuation of patriarchal violence than a solution to it was also made by Assata Shakur in her landmark 1978 essay "Women in Prison," which noted the overwhelming prevalence of abusive backgrounds among incarcerated women. "There are no criminals here at Riker's Island Correctional Institution for Women (New York), only victims," Shakur wrote. "Most of the women (over 95%) are black and Puerto Rican. Many were abused children. Most have been abused by men and all have been abused by 'the system.'"[21] As Angela Y. Davis, Gina Dent, Erica R. Meiners, and Beth E. Richie have detailed more recently, contemporary feminist activists continue to make the case that "prison is quite literally a form of gender violence," an extension of women's experiences of interpersonal abuse.[22]

In 1991, the influential legal scholar Kimberlé Crenshaw published a critique of the antiviolence movement, arguing that it was a mistake to take gender—and the experience of gender-based violence—as a universalizing political identity without reference to race or class. Poor women of color, Crenshaw argued, experienced domestic violence and sexual assault differently than other classes of women. As a result, their experiences were not necessarily reflected in or aided by the solutions proposed by mainstream feminism. The "seemingly universalistic appeal" of the claim that battering was a problem affecting all women equally only ended up redirecting attention to middle- and upper-class white women.[23] In the early days of the anti–domestic violence movement, abuse was frequently described as a "hidden epidemic." But partner abuse had long been associated with poor communities of color; it was only "hidden" in the cases of wealthier white families. As Crenshaw saw it, new ways of talking about domestic violence worked "primarily as a political appeal to rally white elites." This political appeal had a very specific policy aim: more policing. The aim was not universally embraced. "Women of color," Crenshaw noted, "are often reluctant to call the police," because doing so would "subject their private lives to the scrutiny and control of a police force that is frequently hostile."[24]

Feminists of color continued to mount strong challenges to the "arrest is best" consensus of the mainstream antiviolence movement. In 2000, a group of activists who had grown deeply disillusioned with the carceral turn in antiviolence organizing founded INCITE! Women of Color Against Violence.[25] In 2001, INCITE! joined with the prison abolitionist group Critical Resistance to coauthor a "Statement on Gender Violence and the Prison Industrial Complex," which argued for a much-needed collaboration between antiviolence organizing and anti-prison organizing. The issues of gender-based violence and the prison system's violence could not be separated. Activists needed strategies for fighting violence against women without relying on the carceral state, and they needed ways of fighting against the carceral state without sidelining the experiences of survivors of sexual and domestic violence or discounting the need to create safe environments for women.

INCITE! and Critical Resistance worked together to advance a key premise: that "*as an overall strategy for ending violence, criminalization has not worked.*" The groups pointed out, "Despite an exponential increase in the number of men in prisons, women are not any safer, and the rates of sexual assault and domestic violence have not decreased."[26] In fact, pro-criminalization policies such as mandatory arrest and no-drop prosecution not only failed to reduce violence against women. These policies actively endangered them. "For many women, particularly those who are poor and racial minorities, mandatory policies have made them worse off," the political scientist Kristin Bumiller has written.[27] What Richie calls the "over-reliance on the criminal legal system and law enforcement strategies" in the antiviolence movement had many negative effects on the everyday lives of women throughout the 1980s and '90s, making it more common for women to be arrested and incarcerated and more likely for state agencies to remove their children.[28] Mandatory arrest policies require police to make an arrest at every domestic disturbance to which they are called, even if this means arresting battered women. Women thus became victims of the very laws intended to safeguard them. The passage of mandatory arrest laws in California saw arrests of women rise by 400 percent; elsewhere, they increased by as much as a factor of twelve.[29] It is not a coincidence that by the 1990s, women—primarily working-class women of color—had become the fastest-growing segment of the prison population.

Nor is it incidental that as many as 95 percent of incarcerated women are survivors of gender-based violence.[30] The criminalization of domestic violence launched a vicious cycle of arrest and imprisonment that pulled in not only abusers but also the abused. As the legal scholar Leigh Goodmark has emphatically argued, criminal justice reforms pertaining to violence against women ended up doing "immeasurable damage" to the very people they were intended to protect.[31]

What Angela Davis in 1981 called the "crisis dimensions" of gendered violence was very real.[32] How to properly address that crisis was a question with high stakes. It was also a source of deep disagreement. This chapter explores how those disagreements played out in an unlikely but highly visible arena: crime fiction by women. Crime novelists writing about gendered violence in the heyday of antiviolence activism found themselves implicated in the same debates that fractured the movement. How did crime fiction about battered women understand the relation between interpersonal violence and state violence? How did feminist crime writers balance the putatively universalizing fact of violence against women with the disparities of race and class? How did these writers weigh the allure and the peril of partnering with the police? How did they understand their own role in the buildup of the prison state? I pursue these questions across three major subgenres of women's crime writing.[33] The first part of the chapter reveals the important but often overlooked role that representations of domestic violence played in the development of women's detective fiction.[34] The second part situates domestic suspense fiction and child endangerment narratives in the context of neoconservative family values and racial stereotypes about negligent mothers. The third part turns to police and prosecutor fiction in order to see how women's crime fiction eventually internalized the tenets of what has come to be known as carceral feminism. Read together, these subgenres illustrate the significant points of intersection between popular fiction, feminist activism, and crime control policy from the early 1970s to the late 1990s. These three commercially successful and formally significant styles of crime fiction were a product of the way that gendered violence became, during those decades, three things it had not been before: a problem of national concern; a new priority for police departments; and an issue that transformed the aims and alliances of contemporary feminism.

A IS FOR ABUSE

Before 1980, the literary character of the female detective scarcely existed. One critic estimates that there were just thirteen female detectives in the crime literature of the 1970s. Two decades later, the number had grown to more than three hundred.[35] As *Publishers Weekly* observed in 1990, "the woman as tough professional investigator has been the single most striking development in the detective novel in the past decade."[36] A key figure in that development was the Chicago social worker turned detective novelist Sara Paretsky, creator of the V. I. Warshawski series. In 1986, Paretsky helped found Sisters in Crime, a still-active literary organization whose mission is "to promote the ongoing advancement, recognition and professional development of women crime writers."[37] The organization was a response to the fact that, as Paretsky put it, female mystery writers "were being ignored by libraries and bookstores."[38] The year after Sisters in Crime was founded, Paretsky was named a "woman of the year" by *Ms.* magazine.[39]

The rise of detective fiction by women in the 1980s had a lot to do with the feminist activism of the preceding decades. Priscilla L. Walton and Manina Jones, the authors of *Detective Agency*, an excellent study of female detective fiction, observe with some weariness that it is a "critical commonplace" to point out the genre's connections to second-wave feminism. Nevertheless, they add, it is "a commonplace whose truth must be acknowledged."[40] The critic Lee Horsley agrees that women's crime writing grew out of "the experience and the ideals of the liberal feminist activism of the 1960s and 1970s."[41] Many of the writers themselves emphasized this link. As Sue Grafton once explained in an interview, "I am a feminist from way back."[42] By the mid-1980s, it made perfect sense for the feminist publishing house The Crossing Press—best known at that point for reprinting feminist classics such as Audre Lorde's *Zami: A New Spelling of My Name* (1982)—to create an imprint called WomanSleuth, which carved out an inclusive publishing space for women's detective fiction with a radical edge. Early entries in the WomanSleuth series included Mary Wings's *She Came Too Late* (1987), one of the first lesbian detective novels, and Dolores Komo's *Clio Browne: Private Investigator* (1988), one of the first mystery novels to feature a Black female detective.[43] Through imprints like WomanSleuth as well as through mainstream commercial publishers, the female detective novels of the 1980s and '90s carried the ideals of second-wave feminism into the Reagan era, offering a vision of women's social and financial autonomy that directly challenged the explicit antifeminist ethos of neoconservatism.

This is the most commonly told story about what *Publishers Weekly* called the "striking development" of the female private eye in late twentieth century American literature, and it is an important one. But women's detective novels in this period developed not only out of a general feminist ethos but also in conversation with a more specific and contentious public policy issue, an issue that had dramatic consequences for the future of the feminist movement itself. That issue was domestic violence. In a sizable number of women's detective novels, the violence of male partners—husbands, boyfriends, love interests—plays a major role in the plot, either in the detective's professional investigation or in the final epiphany the detective has about her own personal life, and often in both. We gain a new and more precise understanding of the genre, then, by reading it as an attempt to participate in the activist-led effort to raise public awareness about the problem of domestic abuse. The hardboiled private eye—a character famously described by the 1920s pulp writer Carroll John Daly as a "halfway house between the dicks and the crooks"[44]—had always been a figure of ambivalence about the state's role in managing social crisis.[45] The female private eyes who rose to prominence in U.S. fiction in the 1980s and '90s extended this classic figuration of ambivalence toward the state into the realm of intimate partner abuse, where a pair of pressing questions was being debated by activists as well as novelists. What sort of punishment did abusers deserve? And who should get to decide that—women or the police?

Any conversation about how women's detective novels took up the issue of domestic violence should be required to start with Nancy Pickard's appropriately-titled Pocket Books paperback *Marriage Is Murder* (1987), the first detective novel to explicitly discuss the contemporaneous political and policy debates around partner violence. Though now largely forgotten, Pickard was a well-known and award-winning mystery writer in the 1980s; she also served as the second president of the Sisters in Crime organization, after Paretsky. Pointedly topical, *Marriage Is Murder* stars Pickard's recurring series character Jenny Cain, a white amateur detective whose small hometown in Massachusetts is suddenly overrun by a twofold epidemic: of revelations about abusive husbands and of the unexplained murders of those same husbands. Cain's fiancé Geof Bushfield is a cop who is considering quitting his job because of how little his department has been able to do to stem the tide of domestic violence. "I've been called out to that house twice," he laments, "and I still didn't do a damn thing to prevent this from happening."[46] Other major characters in the novel include a radical feminist who runs a battered women's shelter; a pair of married academic sociologists who study the root causes of domestic violence; and Geof's new partner on the police force, recently transferred from Boston, who in a surprise twist turns out to be an abusive husband himself.

Marriage Is Murder was an attempt to show readers a world defined by the ubiquity of domestic violence. Cain is forced to see this world but wishes she didn't have to: "I felt like crawling back into bed and closing my eyes to this vision of the world that revealed black eyes, sobbing women, cynical cops, and dead men." Realizing she can't close her eyes to it, Cain, who in her day job directs a charitable foundation, decides to take action in a way that is professionally natural for her. She assembles a task force of "community advisors"—the shelter director, police officers, sociologists, and social workers—"to investigate the causes of domestic violence." The meetings of this new task force, which Cain dubs SAFE, provide Pickard several opportunities to lecture on the underlying causes of partner violence ("it is not merely an individual, but also a societal problem"; "Domestic violence frequently accompanies unstable social conditions"; "so many of [the men] are pressured by financial problems"). In the end, though, the task force isn't part of the solution to the mystery of who is killing the town's abusive husbands. In fact, oddly, it turns out to be part of the problem. Although each dead man's battered wife is initially suspected of being a murderer, the real killer is revealed to be Professor Henry Ingram, one half of the social-scientist couple who study domestic abuse and help lead Cain's task force. As Cain explains in the novel's final pages, "Ironically, it was SAFE that galvanized him into killing more ... SAFE fed Henry's sense of personal mission, that mission being to 'save' the women by killing the men, even if it brought suspicion onto the women themselves."[47]

In the novel's climax, Henry is killed by his own wife, Kathy, also a domestic violence researcher. Kathy kills Henry because his serial murder of other abusers represents its own kind of hidden violence shaping their marriage. You could say that Henry is avenged by the very figure for which he had helped advocate: the female victim of violence acting in self-defense. In this way, Pickard's novel calls attention to the forms of male violence that circulate not only in instances of abuse but also in the responses of patriarchal institutions. The sociologist who studies the problem and makes policy recommendations turns out to be a violent killer, while one of the cops trying to solve the killings is revealed to be an abuser himself.[48] For Pickard, it would seem, the male fantasy of "saving" battered women—whether by studying abuse or policing abusers—only serves to duplicate the same kind of violence that such women faced from their partners in the first place.

Five years earlier, Sue Grafton had published her debut crime novel, *A Is for Alibi*, which became one of the most influential and commercially successful entries in the genre of women's detective fiction. Grafton, too, used the genre to tell a story about discovering the crisis of domestic abuse. At the start of *A Is for Alibi*, detective Kinsey Millhone agrees to take the case of Nikki Fife, a white woman who has just been released from prison after serving an eight-year sentence for murdering her husband, Laurence, a serial adulterer. Nikki claims she didn't do it and wants Millhone to find out who did. Millhone's investigation peels back a layered plot involving embezzlement and the additional murders of two women who worked for Laurence's law firm. In the end, Millhone learns that Laurence was murdered not by Nikki, his second wife, but by Gwen, his first, who sought revenge for Laurence's emotional manipulation. Millhone also realizes that the man with whom she's become romantically involved over the course of the book—Laurence's law partner Charlie Scorsoni—is a murderer himself.

Grafton wrote *A Is for Alibi* while involved in a difficult custody dispute with her ex-husband. She has joked that she chose to write the novel rather than killing him. At first glance, the novel does read like a form of wish-fulfillment: Gwen seeks revenge on her ex-husband because of the way he exploited the legal system to steal custody of their kids, and she kills him using a method (oleander powder in allergy capsules) that Grafton claims she thought of using on her own ex.[49] But as Gwen's story of her relationship with Laurence unfolds alongside Millhone's dawning awareness of the truth about her romance with Charlie, a different concern comes into view. In Grafton's novel, what "A" really stands for is abuse.

Gwen is initially depicted as a disaffected housewife who seems ripped from the pages of *The Feminine Mystique*. "I was the dutiful wife, and I mean I played the part with dedication few could match," Gwen tells Millhone. "I cooked elegant meals. I made lists. I cleaned the house. I raised the kids." Gwen was, in her own estimation, "kind of like a Barbie doll." But if Gwen at first seems modeled on the Friedanian rhetoric of the early 1960s, her account of her marriage to Laurence eventually comes to be couched in more disturbing and violent terms. This shift situates Grafton's novel squarely within the antiviolence activism of the late 1970s. There was, Gwen observes, something "really fucked" about her marriage. Laurence "was a very controlling person . . . rather aggressive." Of her divorce settlement, Gwen says, "I got beat up." Only later do we understand that this is not merely a metaphor. As Gwen explains to Millhone after confessing to her ex-husband's murder, Laurence "ruined my life, took my kids, robbed me blind, insulted, abused—oh my God, you have no idea."[50] The key revelation here is that Gwen is not simply an unhappy housewife; she is, in her own words, an abuse survivor. Understood thus, the role of the female detective changes substantially. Kinsey Millhone's job has not been, as she thought, to bring a perpetrator to justice. It is to bring the hidden experience of domestic violence to light. "You have no idea," Gwen says of what she's been through. The point of reading *A Is for Alibi* is that now we do.

The problem of abuse turns out to be an invisible thread tying together the various parts and plots of Grafton's novel. Millhone's love interest, Charlie, mentions that he grew up with an abusive father who beat his mother. Millhone's first homicide investigation, she explains, involved a woman who "pleaded temporary insanity"[51]—a defense strategy first used in the 1977 trial of Francine Hughes, an abused woman accused of killing her husband.[52] Most centrally, the arc of *A Is for Alibi* traces Millhone's steady realization that she, too, is dating a man who is secretly violent. Millhone is both attracted to Charlie and "afraid of him." He vibrates with violent energy, "ominous and marked with danger signs." He seems filled with "misdirected rage." At the start of their relationship, Millhone assumes these intimations of danger and violence are part of the attraction. Only later does she realize they were the warning signs of a real threat to her safety. In the novel's climactic sequence, Charlie tries to kill Millhone with a ten-inch butcher knife—a tidy symbol of the violence of the domestic sphere that is hidden in plain sight—while simultaneously gaslighting her about the danger he poses to her: "Kinsey, you don't have to be afraid of me. My God, don't you know that?" The approach works, Millhone admits: "His tone was insistent, gentle, persuasive, hurt. Was I just imagining everything? . . . Maybe I was crazy. Maybe I was making a fool of myself."[53] Here the genre novel's conventional climactic chase scene is overlaid with the tragic narrative of the abuse survivor's self-doubt. In the novel's final pages, Millhone overcomes her doubt and kills Charlie in self-defense. In doing so, she learns what the novel has been trying to teach her, and us, all along: how to recognize the all-too-common warning signs of domestic abuse.

Millhone's killing of Charlie brings the plot of *A Is for Alibi* full circle by putting her in Gwen's shoes. The two characters turn out to be unlikely doubles. Both women kill romantic partners who abused them; both "got pushed too hard and . . . broke," as Millhone herself puts it.[54] The doubling of the female detective and the battered woman was a common literary device at the time. In Sara Paretsky's *Bitter Medicine* (1987), the detective V. I. Warshawski describes herself, after a fight with some local gang members, as looking "like a wife-abuse casualty."[55] As in *A Is for Alibi*, this isn't just a metaphor; it's also an ominous bit of foreshadowing. Like Kinsey Millhone, Warshawski in *Bitter Medicine* discovers that the criminal she's pursuing is also the man with whom she's become romantically entangled. The same discovery—of violence concealed within the detective's own romantic relationship—happens to several other canonical female private eyes of the era.[56] This repeated plot device was a way to underscore the apparent universality of the problem of partner violence. Domestic abuse was, according to the discourse of activists in the 1980s, something that "*could happen to anyone.*"[57] Detective novels turned this into a narrative form that was reused time and again: a tough investigator working on a case of violence against women discovers that she is vulnerable to the same kind of violence in her own personal life. Kinsey Millhone succinctly sums up the revelation that many other female private eyes would go on to have: "Maybe I didn't need protection, I thought. As it turned out, I was wrong."[58]

V. I. Warshawski thinks the same thing, and she, too, learns that she was wrong. In *Bitter Medicine*, Warshawski believes she is separate from the case she's investigating, which involves the fatal mistreatment of a young Latina woman, Consuelo, at a local hospital. She then discovers that the doctor she's dating is the man responsible for Consuelo's death and for the subsequent cover-up. This plot twist allows Paretsky to highlight the link between the institutional neglect of women—especially poor women of color—and male violence in the context of interpersonal relationships. It also enables her to emphasize the structuring irony of the female detective's dual position. Warshawski, protector of women, is also a woman who needs protection herself.

A similar interest in varying scales and sites of gendered violence—the institutional and the interpersonal—informs the novels of Patricia Cornwell, whose series character Kay Scarpetta was one of the most popular female investigators of the 1990s. Cornwell found particular success by fusing the familiar tradition of hardboiled detective fiction with the emerging cultural fascination with serial killers and medical forensics. In her debut novel, *Postmortem* (1990), Scarpetta investigates a serial killer who rapes and strangles women in their homes. Scarpetta feels a personal connection to the case because the victims remind her of herself. Like her, they are all (except for one) professional white women who live alone. Scarpetta's identification with these women is another example of the common doubling between the female investigator and the victims of gendered violence for whom she's working. The idea of what Cornwell at one point calls "an unchivalrous world" in which women are broadly vulnerable to male violence is clinched in the novel's final twist, where we learn that the serial killer is a 911 operator.[59] It was the women's very attempts to seek help from local authorities that led them to be killed. With this twist, Cornwell's novel joins those of Grafton, Paretsky, and Pickard, which are united by their skepticism toward institutional solutions to gendered violence. In *Postmortem*, as in the other novels I've discussed, the problem is not just that women are unsafe. The problem is that the very systems designed to protect women from violence—courts, hospitals, emergency services—end up perpetuating and sometimes directly perpetrating that violence.

Postmortem further situates itself within the feminist lineage of women's crime fiction through a secondary plot that will sound familiar: Scarpetta discovers that the man she's dating—Bill Blotz, a handsome, charismatic widower who is the state's lead criminal prosecutor—is a serial date rapist who may have driven his wife to suicide. The primary and secondary plots of the novel allow Cornwell to explore two distinct but linked ideas about how to protect women from violent men. Whereas the psychopathic 911 operator is caught and killed in a showdown with the police, no punishment ever arrives for Bill. At the end of the novel, he breaks up with Scarpetta, who doesn't mention that she knows he's a rapist or confront him about the threat of violence she began to sense in their relationship. The novel ends on an unsatisfying note. While one exaggeratedly monstrous killer of women has been punished, far more mundane and well-adjusted monsters like Bill Blotz are still out there, well insulated against accusations of rape and relationship violence. Recall that Bill is a powerful lawyer, just like Grafton's duo of abusive men in *A Is for Alibi*. In this way, the ultimate if unexpected lesson of *Postmortem* is that violence against women is not the sole preserve of psychopathic serial killers. Nor is it likely to be noticed, let alone resolved, by a patriarchal legal system that is not just metaphorically embodied by violent men but literally staffed by them.

Barbara Neely's Blanche White series—which began in 1992 and eventually earned her the title of Grand Master from the Mystery Writers of America—offers one of the most sustained commentaries on the relation between the female detective and partner violence, focusing specifically on the experiences of Black women. In *Blanche Among the Talented Tenth* (1994), the second novel of the series, Blanche—a domestic worker turned amateur sleuth—is invited to a weekend at a posh Black resort in Maine called Amber Cove. While there, Blanche deals with an extensive amount of colorism and classism while finding herself drawn into the mystery of a gossipy woman, Faith, who died suspiciously in her bathtub. She learns that Faith kept a store of incriminating documents about nearly everyone in Amber Cove, meaning that nearly everyone had reason to murder her. After Blanche finds Faith's stash of documents, she is assaulted by someone who is trying to steal the information back. In the end, Blanche discovers that her attacker is the same man, Stu, who has been courting her. She also determines that Faith wasn't murdered at all; the radio falling into her bathtub really was just a freak accident. Stu's status as the novel's primary villain is thereby reframed. He is guilty not for what he did to Faith (which was nothing), but for what he did to Blanche.

Telling the story of Blanche's discovery of the hidden violence in her own romantic relationship, *Blanche Among the Talented Tenth* repeats the plot structure we've already noticed in Grafton, Paretsky, and Cornwell.

Yet Neely's approach to the issue is at once more allegorical and more direct. In one scene, Blanche is knocked unconscious after chancing upon an intruder in Faith's cabin, later realizing that the intruder was Stu. In another, Blanche finds the same assailant (whose identity is still concealed) in her bedroom; when she sees him, he pushes her down and runs off. On the surface, these incidents of violence occur outside the context of Blanche's and Stu's relationship. They look more like the generic fate of the snooping hardboiled detective (Raymond Chandler's Philip Marlowe, for one, is always being knocked unconscious). It might thus seem a stretch to propose that Neely uses these scenes to start a conversation about domestic abuse. But that's exactly what she does. At the end of the novel, Blanche confronts Stu about all of this, pointing out the contradiction between his expressions of love for her and his acts of violence against her. Stu begs Blanche to stay with him, telling her, "I never meant to hurt you, never." Blanche finds this hard to believe: "That's why you hit me, pushed me, because you didn't want to hurt me, you rotten liar, you shit!" Clearly, this is no longer a conversation about detective work. It's a conversation about relationship violence. Stu "had kissed [Blanche] like he meant it." He had "looked at her" with genuine appreciation and admiration. Yet he had also physically harmed her, "hit her over the head hard enough to knock her out and pushed her with enough force to give her a backache."[60] Neely has thus cleverly reconfigured the question driving her mystery. The drama of the novel's plot arc is not whether Blanche will find the murderer—there was no murder in the first place—but whether she will stay with the man who assaulted her. Spoiler alert: She doesn't.

Neely's commitment to using detective fiction as a vehicle to discuss domestic violence continued throughout the Blanche series. In the series' fourth and best novel, *Blanche Passes Go* (2000), she expands her vision of female detective work as a tool for uncovering the hidden stories of abused women. The novel begins with Blanche returning to her hometown of Fairleigh, North Carolina, where she is forced to reckon with her own traumatic past as a rape survivor. Eventually she becomes involved in a case surrounding the murder of a young white woman named Maybelle, whose body is found in the woods. Blanche initially suspects that the man who raped her years ago may be the same man who killed Maybelle. But what she discovers instead over the course of the novel is the shocking number of women who have experienced domestic and sexual violence. Maybelle was killed by her abusive boyfriend; Blanche's neighbor is repeatedly abused by her partner; and, as Blanche learns in one of the novel's climactic scenes, her own mother was abused by Blanche's father. What begins as a narrow investigation into one violent man ultimately reveals a broad "circle of bruised women." For Blanche, this circle indicates just how widespread the problem of gender-based violence is. She "wondered if there were women in the world who hadn't been slapped, or probed, or punched, or shouted out or down, or at least scared for half a second" by "some man" desperate to assert his authority.[61]

Blanche's poignant discovery of a "circle of bruised women" highlights a theme important to all the books I've been discussing: the perceived universality of women's vulnerability to male violence. Beth Richie calls this the antiviolence movement's "everywoman narrative," which became a key talking point for feminist activists in the 1980s. The everywoman narrative was a double-edged sword. "Originally, this construction of *any woman could be a battered woman*' and *'rape is a threat to every woman*' was a strategic way to avoid individualizing the problem of domestic and sexual violence and to focus on social dimensions of the problem of gender violence," Richie explains. However, universalizing the problem ran the risk of decontextualizing it. The "assumed race and class neutrality of gender violence" threatened to erase the more specific "victimization of lesbians, women of color in low-income communities, and other marginalized groups." Consequently, "when the national discussion became organized around 'it could happen to anyone,' . . . 'anyone' came to mean the women with the most visibility, the most power, and the most public sympathy."[62]

Neely was thoughtfully attuned to the complexity of these dynamics. In *Blanche Passes Go*, she writes with nuance about how the racial violence experienced by Black women might be connected to the classed vulnerability of poor white women—two linked yet also distinct examples of how women's experiences of violence are discounted.[63] Other writers' attempts to depict domestic and sexual violence as problems affecting all women equally would prove thornier. Consider *Postmortem*. In Cornwell's novel, the clue that finally helps the white investigator Kay Scarpetta figure out the serial killer's identity as an emergency dispatcher appears in a bizarre scene in which, talking to a Black victim's family member, she realizes that she can't tell a person's race over the phone. Scarpetta decides that this explains why the killer's victims seemed to be chosen without regard to their race. Taking 911 calls by telephone, he couldn't distinguish white women from Black women. Setting aside what we may think of this as an account of racialization and listening technologies, let's consider it simply as a version of the era's everywoman narrative. Cornwell is trying to suggest that male violence is a threat to any woman regardless of race. But what she actually says here is that this holds true only so long as the women in question *sound white*. Understood thus, the scene of Scarpetta's telephone-based epiphany ends up making a rather different point than the one Cornwell may have intended. It tells us that in discussions of the ostensibly universal crisis of gendered violence, Black women's voices are likely to disappear.

The ways that universalizing narratives of violence against women can silence or elide important differences permeated other novels at the time. In Paretsky's *Bitter Medicine*, abusive, controlling, and otherwise delinquent husbands and boyfriends crop up repeatedly, most often among the novel's working-class Latine characters. Consuelo has a boyfriend named Fabiano, a deadbeat and a gang member whom Consuelo's family loathes. The leader of the gang that Fabiano belongs to is Sergio Rodriguez, and later in the novel Warshawski imagines the "helplessness" and imprisonment that she assumes his wife must feel—a woman Warshawski has never met and whose name she doesn't know.[64] That Fabiano and Sergio are depicted not only as criminals and gang members but also as men who mistreat their wives reveals the troubling racial politics that lurked beneath liberal feminism's view of the domestic violence issue. In the case of both Consuelo and the woman Warshawski knows only as "Mrs. Rodriguez," sympathy for mistreated women depends on a series of simplistic stereotypes about the criminality of nonwhite working-class men. This was a significant shortcoming of the liberal feminist vision of universal female solidarity forged through attention to domestic violence: Sometimes it could seem more like an alibi for racial and class condescension.[65]

The limitations of gender universalism are most strikingly, if complexly, conveyed in Grafton's *A Is for Alibi*, which includes a secondary plot that is at first hard to make sense of. Although she spends most of the novel investigating Laurence's murder on Nikki's dime, Millhone is simultaneously employed on another case, investigating a woman suspected of insurance fraud. The woman, Marcia Threadgill, had told her insurance company that she was injured. But during several stakeouts, Millhone discovers with growing resentment that she appears totally healthy; why, there she is on her small balcony, hanging a flower pot! A simple question arises: Why is the figure of the female insurance defrauder relevant to a novel that is otherwise entirely focused on abused women? One answer is that, in the early 1980s, these figures were two sides of a single coin encompassing public perceptions of female victimhood and female criminality. Millhone criticizes Marcia's garish makeup and repeatedly refers to her as a "cheat." She could just as well have described Marcia as a *welfare queen*, the gendered and racialized figure of institutional fraud who entered public discourse in the mid-1970s, and who was invariably represented in the media as Black or Latina.

As the historian Julilly Kohler-Hausmann tells us, "by 1976, 85 percent of poll respondents agreed that 'too many people on welfare cheat by getting money they are not entitled to.'"[66] This is exactly what Marcia is doing. She is, as Millhone describes her, "cheap at heart," a "mentality, in my opinion, that leads to the cheating of insurance companies and other sly ruses." Millhone is furious about this, and she blames a society willing to condone it: "it pissed me off that" the insurance company was "halfway inclined to look the other way." Indeed, she is far angrier about what Marcia is doing (fraud) than about what Gwen did (revenge killing), a comparison she makes explicitly: "I thought about Gwen without surprise or dismay.... Somehow I was more offended by the minor crimes of a Marcia Threadgill." "Cheaters win all the time," Millhone concludes with resignation. The phrasing here is revealing. Defined as a "cheater," Marcia is made to resemble Laurence (an adulterer) rather than Gwen, which is to say that she is made to seem deserving of punishment rather than our sympathy.

Grafton thus offers her readers two contrasting images of the gendered criminal. Marcia, clearly coded as working class, is criminalized for her "sly ruses" so that Gwen, a wealthy white battered woman, can be forgiven for killing Laurence. In order to challenge one idea of female criminality, the novel must substitute another. The victim of abuse, getting justice for herself when no one else will, is juxtaposed against the undeserving welfare queen. Millhone decides at the end of the novel that what Gwen did was "what the notion of 'justice' was all about." In the same breath, she decides that "Marcia Threadgill was the new standard of morality against which I would now judge all other sins."⁶⁷ Here, at the behest of our detective hero, the moral compass of gendered crime is decisively recalibrated. It is now not retributive violence but insurance fraud that represents the "new standard" for what constitutes female immorality. In order to absolve Gwen, a different type of woman has to be punished. Marcia Threadgill fits the bill. Thus the ostensible universality of women's vulnerability to male violence breaks apart when it collides with the classed and racialized figure of the welfare cheat. Such vulnerability creates solidarity between women like Gwen and Kinsey Millhone only by distancing them from women like Marcia.

Though they frequently speak the language of gender universalism, these novels also evoke the tensions of race and class that sat just beneath the surface of the contemporary conversation about domestic violence.⁶⁸ "Everywoman" did not necessarily mean every woman.⁶⁹ As Richie argues, liberal feminism's emphasis on universalism ultimately "overshadowed the race- and class-specific dimensions of the institutional failure" to protect women.⁷⁰ The contradiction was repeatedly played out in women's detective fiction. All of the novels mentioned in this section insist that intimate partner violence can happen to any woman. Yet they also demonstrate—sometimes deliberately, sometimes unintentionally—that different sorts of women are differently vulnerable, differently victimized, and differently positioned to gain public sympathy.

The racial and class fault lines of the feminist antiviolence movement shaped two very different ideas about what a solution to the crisis of gendered violence ought to look like. One involved the police; the other didn't. As I detail at the end of this chapter, there is no question that policing won. But even as they faltered in their attempts to depict universal solidarity for women, feminist detective novels were clearly uncertain about what role the police should or could play in protecting women. Actually, Neely's Black feminist detective fiction was more than uncertain. Her novels directly articulated an antagonism that was only murkily addressed in earlier crime novels: battered women's suspicion of the police. At the end of *Talented Tenth*, after Blanche breaks it off with Stu, she tells her friend at Amber Cove, "I'm definitely not going to press charges." The friend, a young feminist, is incredulous, but Blanche offers several reasons for her decision. First, she considers the police ineffectual as a tool for deterring male violence: "Far as I'm concerned, teaching self-defense to girls starting in the first grade has got a better chance of stopping men from beating us up than pressing charges." Second, she considers it more of a risk to herself than to the man she's reporting: "How do you think I'll be treated? How seriously do you think the police would take me?" Third, she considers it illogical as a form of punishment: "He's already gotten away with it, honey.... Throwing him in jail don't change a thing he's done to me." The ineffectuality of the police, the pointlessness of prison, and the likelihood—especially for a Black woman—of being disbelieved (or worse) by official institutions all lead Blanche to do everything in her power to "avoid going to the police" to handle issues of partner violence.[71]

This is a recurring theme across the Blanche series. Neely's title character consistently refuses to collaborate with carceral institutions. At one point in *Blanche Passes Go*, Blanche tries to get information from someone by threatening to call the cops. The narrator is quick to underscore the emptiness of the threat. "Only someone who didn't know Blanche," we're told, would think she'd actually do this.[72] Neely's readers, of course, do know Blanche. Because they do, they are invited to share her knowledge that, whatever justice for battered women could look like, it should not involve the police.[73]

Neely's detective novels make explicit what many female crime novelists were more quietly wrestling with in this era: the controversial partnership between the women's movement and the police. Detective fiction offered a powerful template for telling the story of intimate partner violence. This kind of story could not escape the lingering uncertainty about whether women could rely on law enforcement for protection from abusers. In the 1970s and '80s, many activists believed that the main problem was the state's unwillingness to police incidents of domestic violence. By the start of the 1990s, the problem was that police departments were too eager to arrest people for it (including abused women). Spanning this divide, the novels of Neely, Cornwell, Paretsky, Grafton, and Pickard are all unconvinced that law enforcement institutions would be capable of protecting women. This point is most clearly embodied in Neely's Blanche White, for whom the idea of ever having to go to the police to handle an incident of male violence "scares me half to death." Blanche's distrust of the police is in many ways specific to her experience as a working-class

Black woman. Other female detectives of the era seem, at first glance, to be more neutral in their stance toward cops (Pickard's detective is married to one, after all). Yet the very fact that they are themselves private detectives rather than police officers already represents a meaningful distinction. Kinsey Millhone, for one, became a private eye because she "didn't like being a cop"—specifically, Grafton suggests, because it constrained her ability to respond sympathetically to women who acted in self-defense.[74] Meanwhile, there is a notable if unexpected resonance between Neely's critique of the police and Cornwell's plot about a murderous 911 operator. In both cases, it is dangerous if not fatal for a woman to call the police for help. The danger extends to other patriarchal social institutions as well. In *Bitter Medicine*, a hospital's promise of top-of-the-line care for pregnant women turns out to be false advertising, and so an institution tasked with caring for women ends up murdering one instead. In *A Is for Alibi*, the legal system is dominated by abusive men and therefore contaminated by male violence. In *Marriage Is Murder*, the local task force on domestic violence harbors the novel's killer, while the ineffectual police department happens to employ a wife abuser of its own.

In the very years when Congress and the judicial system were finally acknowledging the seriousness of domestic violence, women's detective novels were asking how helpful such government recognition would ultimately turn out to be. Would the claim for improved care for women be nothing but an empty marketing pitch, as it is in *Bitter Medicine*? Would it give abusive men more legal power, as happens in *A Is for Alibi*? Would it make women more vulnerable to state-sanctioned violence, as Cornwell's and Neely's novels imply? Questions like these played a key role in the development of women's detective fiction in the 1980s and '90s. The flourishing of detective novels by women at the end of the twentieth century was not simply an expression of second-wave feminist ideals of equality and autonomy. It was also a product of the feminist movement's contentious decision to partner with law enforcement in the fight against domestic abuse. Who do you call if you want to decipher the gendered violence of everyday life but can't trust the cops? American literature's private detectives have always worked outside the official capacities of the legal system and the state. This helps explain why, around 1980, the female private eye became a privileged figure for imagining alternative forms of protection and justice for battered women.

MISSING CHILDREN AND FAMILY VALUES

One reason that the antiviolence movement was able to be smoothly absorbed into mainstream law-and-order ideology was that, viewed from a certain angle, it could be taken as an expression of concern for the health of the nuclear family. As the Great Society gave way to the era of neoconservative family values, commentators began to lament "the ongoing decline of the American family."[75] In the 1960s, family life was enshrined as a private realm protected from state intervention. By the end of the 1970s, however, activists had succeeded in making family violence an issue of national concern. Although Reagan began his first term by closing the Office of Domestic Violence that Carter had established in 1979, in 1984 his own Task Force on Victims of Crime called for a special investigation into family violence, noting in its report, "The law should not stop at the front door of the family home."[76] Family violence was thus transformed from an issue that lay beyond the reach of the state to one that seemed a natural fit for the ascendant ideology of family values. For advocates, the safety of the family no longer depended on the absence of the state; it required the state.[77] Accordingly, domestic violence legislation was now pitched as an effort to preserve the integrity of the family rather than as a breach of family privacy. This shift depended on a wholesale transformation of the concept of the family into a space of potential crime—populated by battered women, abused children, and teenage delinquents—that required policing.[78] "Efforts to address violence against women and children" frequently end up "idealizing the nuclear family and motherhood," Marie Gottschalk has suggested.[79] That is exactly what happened when the feminist antiviolence movement collided with the conservative ideology of family values.

One place you won't find much in the way of family values is in the pages of female private eye fiction. Many of the era's most famous female detectives go out of their way to resist being cast in the role of mothers. Kinsey Millhone explains how she "got cured of . . . of any desire for motherhood" by one especially grim case.[80] V. I. Warshawski believes that maternity makes women miserable.[81] Blanche White notes that "mothering did not come naturally to her."[82] These attempts to sever the ostensibly natural link between women and motherhood are broadly indicative of a genre that fundamentally distrusts the nuclear family and the essentialist ideologies of gender it requires.

Other types of women's crime writing from this period took a more earnest interest in how notions of motherhood might shape the state's response to gendered violence. In the missing-child narratives of domestic suspense fiction, the figure of the mother became the focus of narrative attention. Such narratives centered on a question that seems at first merely the stuff of genre fiction but was in fact a prime instance of the way gender, class, and racial ideologies in this period were entangled. The question was: Can a mother be a criminal?

We find this question in the novel that helped invent the genre of domestic suspense, Mary Higgins Clark's *Where Are the Children?* For Clark, the question was indicative of American society's refusal to believe women's accounts of abuse. On this point, her novel proves surprisingly prescient. At her trial, Nancy's testimony is described as literally unbelievable, "her protestations of innocence sounding perfunctory and emotionless." The refusal to believe women's testimony plays a pivotal role in the novel's plot twists, as a series of women in Nancy's town start to realize the unlikely but true fact that Carl is still alive, only to find that their husbands will not listen to them. As one skeptical husband says "condescendingly" to his wife, who thinks she has seen Carl lurking around their town, "This is why I say women don't make good witnesses and never should be jurors."[83] Clark presents this gendered dynamic of disbelief as a defining element of cultural assumptions about motherhood. For Clark, the question of who is believed in situations of family violence is inextricable from who is blamed for it. Throughout the novel, everyone is certain that Nancy killed her children, while no one thinks for a moment that it might have been Carl. Thus drawing a connection between the prevalence of family violence and the gendering of credibility, *Where Are the Children?* is ultimately an attempt to debunk the myth of the irresponsible mother—a figure that society holds responsible for the integrity of the family and the safety of the home in large part because it is unwilling to believe her claims about what is actually happening there.

That said, Clark's particular way of debunking maternal irresponsibility is not without its own complications. She writes repeatedly that there is something biologically unnatural about the idea of a mother harming her family: "No good mother spoke of hurting her children"; "How could I have killed them? They were my children!"; "How could I kill them? They are me. I died with them"; "It simply wasn't possible. No mother murdered her flesh and blood."[84] In lines like these, Clark offers an essentialist retort to society's inclination to blame mothers for violence that happens in the family home. Structured around the ongoing mystery of whether or not Nancy really did kill her children, the novel seeks to reestablish a kind of biological common sense about the nature of motherhood, ultimately asserting that any questioning of that biological foundation is ridiculous. One shouldn't even have to ask. A mother hurting her own children, Clark writes reassuringly, "simply wasn't possible."[85]

Narratives of missing or endangered children are always allegories for a crisis of the nuclear family. *Where Are the Children?* is no exception, offering insight into how a certain version of essentialist feminism found common ground with anxieties about the erosion of family values. In Clark's telling, the tendency to dismiss women's experiences of family violence leads directly to a deeper misunderstanding of the gender roles that guarantee the healthy functioning of the nuclear family. This kind of misunderstanding happens when a mother's biological imperative to protect her children is questioned. It also happens when society refuses to cast suspicion on those men who fail to understand how families are supposed to work. One such man is Carl. The problem with Carl is not only that he is a child molester and a wife abuser. It is also that he harbors a fundamental confusion about family roles. Significantly older than Nancy, Carl treats his wife like his daughter (his pet name for Nancy is "little girl"), and he treats his daughter—whom he molests—like his wife. Nancy's new, post-trial life in Cape Cod corrects this alarming slippage in the assignment of roles within a family. Having replaced Carl with a man her own age, Nancy has created a family unit in which the roles of mother and father are clearly defined. Thus clarified, the nuclear family can now be properly protected from both internal and external threats (a point driven home at the end of the novel, as Nancy's husband, Ray, leads the successful mission to rescue Nancy and the children from Carl's secret hideout).

Clark thus uses the child endangerment story as a narrative form for shoring up the ideal of the traditional family. The act of saving the children doubles as the reclamation of a normative vision of middle-class heteronormative family life in which everyone has a clearly assigned role. When Ray rescues Nancy from the roof of Carl's house at the novel's end, she thinks happily to herself, "It would always be like that with Ray. She would always be safe."[86] Having found a husband who understands how each role in a family is meant to be played—the protective man, the maternal woman—Nancy discovers that the nuclear family, properly defined, is not only dependable but perennial. Read in these terms, the pivotal drama of this pioneering domestic suspense novel is how to preserve the safety of the nuclear family. For Clark, the happy resolution of the drama depends on two things: first, turning society's gaze of criminal suspicion away from mothers; and second, turning it toward those abusive men who perversely misunderstand the proper role that each member of a family is meant to play.

Still, despite its essentialist vision of maternal femininity, Clark's novel tells an important story about the way that male violence in the home is so often misperceived as a result of bad mothering. A key facet of the suspense that drives *Where Are the Children?*—suspense being the stylistic feature through which Clark made her name—turns not simply on whether the children will be saved, but on whether Nancy will be able to successfully convince people that she couldn't possibly be the person who harmed them. In the end, Nancy, who is young, beautiful, and white (three qualities the novel mentions many times), does indeed manage to convince people that she is not a criminal but a "good mother" after all.[87] However, for women of other racial backgrounds and other class positions, suspicions of bad mothering were not so easily dispelled.

Just a few years after *Where Are the Children?* became a hit, the title of Clark's novel acquired a very different resonance. Between 1979 and 1981, at least forty Black children disappeared in Atlanta (many estimates are much higher). As the disappearances continued and public anxiety intensified, local television news reporters began posing an ominous question to viewers: "Do you know where your children are?" Despite the uncanny similarity between the title of Clark's bestselling novel and the signature media phrase of what came to be known as the Atlanta child murders, the reassuring arc of the missing child narrative turned out to function much differently in fictional Cape Cod than it did in real-life Atlanta, where almost all of the missing-child cases remain unsolved to this day. That difference was the subject of Toni Cade Bambara's masterful novel *Those Bones Are Not My Child* (1999), a loosely fictionalized account of the Atlanta disappearances that explored the effects of race and class in determining how women, children, and families were treated by a criminal legal system that was supposed to be there to help them. At the end of *Where Are the Children?*, Nancy celebrates the immense amount of institutional support she has received—from the media, from local rescue services, and eventually (if grudgingly) from the police—by literally throwing everyone a party ("When they got home, Nancy insisted that the television crews and reporters be fed too, and Jonathan had thrown his home open to them").[88] Meanwhile, the protagonist of *Those Bones*, Zala Spencer, confronts total institutional indifference to her missing son and wonders caustically, "Did they only look for well-behaved children from two-parent, nonvet homes?"[89]

Bambara began writing *Those Bones Are Not My Child* in 1979 and worked on multiple drafts of it through 1987. She died in 1995 before finishing the novel. The manuscript was subsequently edited by her friend Toni Morrison and published in 1999. *Those Bones* tells the story of the Atlanta disappearances through Zala and her estranged husband, Spence, whose adolescent child Sonny goes missing. Zala's and Spence's attempts to find Sonny connect them to other parents and community groups working to solve Atlanta's many missing-children cases in the face of media and government apathy. Over time, the parents, performing the investigative work that the police refuse to do, untangle an incredibly complicated plot that involves white supremacist hate groups, child-trafficking rings, and a government cover-up—three important facets of the case that, Bambara suggests, were swept under the rug after the arrest of Wayne Williams. Then, three-quarters of the way through the novel, Sonny miraculously reappears. The final sections of *Those Bones* portray Zala continuing to advocate for the cause of the missing children while successfully rebuilding her own nuclear family unit: recovering Sonny, reconciling with Spence.

One aim of *Those Bones* was to uncover the racial and class contexts that were hidden in mainstream novels about missing children—novels like Clark's. For Bambara, the class component is not incidental: "No search party was mobilized to find a poor kid." (As one character puts it, "the job of the police is to protect the interests of the ruling class.") Yet Bambara's novel also has some important things in common with Clark's. Like Clark, Bambara is interested in how stories of missing children invariably became stories about bad parents. "From the start," she writes, "the prime suspects in the Atlanta Missing and Murdered Children's Case were the parents." And both novels further understand how the presumption of the guilty parent is inevitably gendered, rooted in the ease with which law enforcement institutions tend to dismiss women's stories. In *Those Bones*, women are simultaneously blamed ("It's another way of blaming . . . mothers in general") and discounted ("For nearly a year, mothers had been put off and trivialized . . . as female hysterics"). Viewed through the eyes of the state, parenting itself becomes feminized: Zala thinks to herself that *"the parents, including my husband, we were all hysterical women."* For Bambara, the feminization of the concerned parent is not only tied to the expression of gendered affects such as hysteria and worry; it is also linked to the process by which mothers in particular become objects of suspicion for their potentially pathological parenting behaviors. From the very beginning of the novel, Bambara maps out the vicious cycle whereby missing Black children become evidence of maternal neglect and neglect becomes an excuse to blame Black mothers for their children's disappearance. For example: "The mother of Anthony Bernard Carter was arrested, released, tailed, questioned, dogged for months, and visited at all hours of the night until she was forced to move. The media kept harping on the fact that she was a poor, young Black woman who had only one child, 'only one,' as though that were sufficient grounds for suspicion, if not prosecution."[90] In passages such as this, *Those Bones* spotlights the same question being asked in *Where Are the Children?*: Can a mother be a criminal? Where Clark remained confident in middle-class white mothers' capacity to successfully deflect the question and allay suspicion, however, Bambara's characters are forced to confront the more intractable legacy of American culture's longstanding criminalization of working-class Black mothers.

Suspicion of nonwhite mothers played a key role in the early construction of the War on Crime. Politicians in the Goldwater and Johnson years placed "black and Latina women's parenting at the root of crime, urban unrest, and racial and economic inequality."[91] The obsession with bad mothering in Black families was most infamously expressed in Daniel Patrick Moynihan's notorious government report *The Negro Family: A Case for National Action* (1965). The Moynihan Report helped cement the idea of Black families' cultural pathology in the popular imagination. Its author defined African American life as a "tangle of pathology" including poverty and crime, and he put the blame for those pathologies squarely on "the weakness of the family structure." By "weakness," Moynihan meant the prevalence of single mothers and female-headed households. This "matriarchal structure," Moynihan wrote, was dangerous "because it is so out of line with the rest of the American society."[92] For Moynihan, there was something unusual and therefore threatening about the very idea American families being structured around women's authority.

Criticism of the Moynihan Report came quickly—so quickly that, after being made public in August of 1965, it was disavowed by the Johnson administration in November of the same year.[93] But Moynihan's argument that Black mothers were somehow to blame for poverty, crime, and a more generalized crisis of family values had a lasting influence on public debate and on mainstream views of minority families. As Hortense Spillers has famously argued, the Moynihan Report effectively succeeded in turning "matriarchy" into a synonym for racial "pathology."[94] Along similar lines, the critic Habiba Ibrahim describes the 1970s as a decade when "US nationalism cast Black women as mothers beyond the pale of proper citizenship."[95]

Bambara herself was no stranger to Moynihan's work. In 1970, she edited the anthology *The Black Woman*, a landmark collection of Black feminist writing. Bambara explained in the book's preface that one of her ambitions in putting it together was to push back against stereotypes about Black femininity and Black motherhood, to "set the record straight on the matriarch and the evil Black bitch."[96] Several writers in the volume called out Moynihan directly. In the essay "Motherhood," Joanna Clark observed, "there are people like . . . Moynihan carrying on about our matriarchy and inferring that we've botched up the job."[97] And in "Is the Black Male Castrated?" Jean Carey Bond and Patricia Peery lamented that "the myth of the Black female matriarchy," while hardly new, had recently been dredged up by "the highly publicized and highly touted work *The Negro Family: The Case for National Action*, by Daniel Patrick Moynihan." Bond and Peery wondered whether Moynihan's "assumptions and conclusions" had been so "successfully popularized" that they were beginning to affect how Black families were viewed even by Black commentators.[98]

Bambara's *Those Bones Are Not My Child* can be read as a continuation of the early Black feminist response to the Moynihan Report. Indeed, this response would have felt newly urgent to Bambara in the years she was working on her novel, as Moynihan's ideas found renewed popularity and traction in the 1980s, a decade that became obsessed once again with the ostensible pathologies of Black mothers. (The magazine *Ebony* dubbed 1986 "the year of the Black Family."[99]) *Those Bones* references Moynihan explictly, mocking the report for enjoining Black men to "escape from Black matriarchs who're fucking up your male minds." At a broader level, Bambara meticulously details how her protagonist Zala navigates assumptions about her failures as a mother. Sometimes the assumptions are based on her physical appearance ("Had she come across as incompetent somehow? Had she forgotten to button her clothes or comb her hair?"). Sometimes they are linked to stereotypes about Black female sexuality (a cop asks Zala about her children, "Are they all natural siblings? . . . They all have the same father?"). And sometimes they are exposed as the raw language of class struggle ("Mrs. Spencer, you list three work numbers, and you're the only adult in the house"). Zala explains to her kids at one point that "if I lived in a different part of town, people would call me a working mother" and applaud her for "taking courses at college and working three jobs." But in their working-class Black neighborhood, she's viewed as something else entirely: a "terrible mother" whose multiple jobs are a symbol not of industriousness but of neglect, "always going off here and there, leaving her kids all alone. How awful." Again and again, Zala is forced to say to state authorities, "I am not a neglectful mother."[100] The authorities remain unconvinced.

Bambara's key insight in *Those Bones*—born from watching Moynihan's ideas retain their influence across three decades—is that the endurance of stereotypes about Black families and Black mothers inevitably informed the state's response to the missing children in Atlanta. What Bambara sees in this tragic situation is the logical endpoint of the moral panic about Black families, whereby Black mothers would no longer simply be blamed for the so-called cultural pathologies of poverty and crime; they would now be held legally responsible for them. We're a long way from Cape Cod.

In a pivotal scene in the first half of *Those Bones*, Zala agrees to take a lie detector test at a local police station. Zala thinks she is there to share information she's discovered about the patterns of the kidnappings, but she is instead asked a series of inappropriate personal questions: "Do you masturbate?" "Do you resent it if your husband has an orgasm and you do not?" "Have you ever stolen anything, Mrs. Spencer?" "Does Sonny use drugs?" Eventually, Zala realizes that these queries about sexual deviancy, criminality, and juvenile delinquency have all been leading to one climactic question: "Did you kill your son, Mrs. Spencer?" This question closes the circuit between the imagined pathologies of the Black family (sex, stealing, drugs) and the explicit criminalization of the Black mother. It is a question Zala has been expecting, since it's one all the other mothers of missing children had been asked as well: "Did you kill your child? She'd heard the parents at STOP comparing notes. Did you kill your very own child?" Could a mother really be a murderer? The difference between Clark's version of this question and Bambara's is that there is no answer the working-class Black women of Atlanta can give that will satisfy the state agents who are asking it. Eventually, Zala starts "hearing about mothers who wound up in jail after going to court about their curfew-defying children and ringing off the metal detector." She notices that media coverage of "the mothers cracking open the investigation" is always paired with a story "about parental neglect and abuse."[101] And she realizes that the more Black mothers do to expose the external sources of violence that are harming their children, the more strongly state and media institutions insist that it is really the mothers themselves who are to blame.

The mother who is both heroic investigator and perpetual suspect is the defining figure of the story Bambara wants to tell about family violence at a moment of renewed moral panic about what Moynihan reductively dubbed "the Black family." Yet it is important to note that the novel is not, in the end, actually about incidents of family violence. Rather, *Those Bones* is about how the issue of family violence provided a convenient moral framework for deflecting attention away from the larger forms of racial, state, and structural violence that played a role in the children's disappearances. (Indeed, at a certain point Zala and Spence begin to suspect that the police themselves may be the ones responsible for all the "kidnapping and murder.") For Bambara—working both with and against the conventions of an established genre—the criminalized Black family is a red herring. This helps explain one strange part of the novel, wherein Spence, in his grief over Sonny's disappearance, becomes obsessed with statistics about family crime. These statistics seep into the language of the narrator: "Family. Six out of ten nightly calls to the police were to report domestic violence. Twenty percent of all homicides were family related. One-third of all female deaths were at the hands of husbands or boyfriends.... lately had Spence perused data concerning children murdered by relatives." Later, on a phone call with Zala, Spence again rattles off "a bunch of statistics.... More children under five were murdered by their parents than died from natural causes.... Over a million children were sexually abused per annum. Over five hundred thousand children were reported missing per annum." This data is deeply upsetting, for the reader as much as for Zala. But Zala also admits that she doesn't know what to do with all these numbers: "What did that have to do with bringing the children home?... what were his statistics about? It was all so stupid. How could anyone carry on a conversation with a person who said 'per annum?' "[102] These are all good questions. Here's another one: What kind of person says "per annum" anyway? The answer is: a bureaucrat. That Spence has adopted the language of government bureaucracy makes sense. His tendency to view the family as an accumulation of crime data was, at this time, also the tendency of the government. According to the criminologist Jonathan Simon, "crime control and family governance" became tightly intertwined starting in the 1980s. The state began to view "the family as a site of crime... and criminals," and crime thus became "the framework by which oversight of the family" took place.[103] The rendering of the family as a crucible of crime and danger is the reason that mothers like Zala are always the first and often the last people suspected in cases involving children. To focus so obsessively on family crime is to refuse to see the deeper sources of class- and race-based violence that structure American life. Ultimately, Bambara's novel suggests that American culture's obsession with the hidden ills of child abuse, domestic violence, and family pathology in the 1980s made it impossible to see that what was really happening to the children of Atlanta had nothing to do with families at all.

Near the end of the novel, Spence notices a library book on the family's kitchen table: "Spence sat down in the chair and opened the paperback his eldest had checked out of the library, *The Exorcist*. 'Great,' he said, and put his head down on the table."[104] Why does Bambara choose *The Exorcist*? And why is Spence so disheartened to see it? As the critic Palmer Rampell has convincingly detailed, *The Exorcist* was one of the first attempts by a writer of genre fiction to address what was then considered the hidden epidemic of child abuse in wealthy white families.[105] Its appearance in *Those Bones* throws into sharp relief the very different kind of novel Bambara has been writing: a novel about the crisis of family violence assumed to be happening in Black working-class homes even when it isn't. The cultural narrative of the pathological Black family and the neglectful Black mother is, like *The Exorcist*, a lurid if compelling fiction. And fiction is a category with which Bambara's novel has little patience. As Zala realizes, "There was no Kojak to grab a creep out of a car.... There'd be no Virgil Tibbs arriving on the scene all scientific and articulate.... Only in stories was there a detective" who could be counted on to find the key clue in the nick of time. What was there instead? "Real life; she had to stick to real life."[106] Zala, a fictional character, commits to the idea of real life as a riposte to the outlandish stories she knows society has been telling about her as a Black mother.

Read together, Bambara's and Clark's related versions of the missing-child narrative show us the complex, racially charged ways that the figure of the "bad" or criminalized mother was forced to shoulder the blame for cultural anxieties about the decline of the nuclear family. Because family values and child safety were rooted in ideologies of maternal responsibility, women deemed unable to protect their children were frequently cast as criminals, held responsible for violence visited on them by men or by larger systems of oppression. In *Where Are the Children?*, Clark offers an important proto-feminist defense of the criminalized mother; yet in doing so, she falls back on an essentialist idea of maternal identity and a bourgeois ideal of the white nuclear family. In *Those Bones Are Not My Child*, Bambara tells a parallel story about working-class Black women's inability to escape the more deeply entrenched cultural narratives that cast doubt on their fitness as mothers. To Clark, the criminalization of motherhood is a misperception to be gently corrected. To Bambara, it is woven into the very fabric of racial and class inequality in the United States.

The sharp interplay between these two novels brings us back, finally, to Clark's famous title. *Where Are the Children?* is not a question asked by any character in the novel. It comes to us instead as the voice of collective concern, an example of the idealized way that community institutions are imagined to join forces and share resources in situations of missing children—specifically, white middle-class children, who are, in the language of Clark's title, not a particular person's children, certainly not *your* children, just *the* children, as if they were everyone's children. In the prologue to *Those Bones Are Not My Child*, Bambara poses a more acute version of the same question: "Where the hell is your child?"[107] The use of second-person address here might be taken as universalizing, asking readers to put themselves in someone like Zala's shoes, the "your" meant to feel like "our." But it could also be the kind of lonely rhetorical question you ask yourself, in panic as well as steely self-reliance, when you realize there is no one else you can count on to ask it with you. Sometimes "your child" (an echo of the individuated *My Child* in Bambara's title) really means yours alone. Sometimes you know the cops aren't going to listen to you. Sometimes you know you're on your own.[108]

CARCERAL FEMINIST FICTION

Times change, and laws do too. If in the 1970s and early 1980s it was difficult for novelists like Clark and Grafton to imagine that the police would take women's claims about being abused seriously, by the 1990s the situation had changed substantially. In 1996, the prosecutor turned crime novelist Linda Fairstein was able to celebrate the new seriousness with which domestic and sexual assault was being policed and the new success people like her were having in prosecuting it. "There have been a lot of improvements," she wrote, "a lot of changes in the law."[109] Those changes included mandatory and presumptive arrest, no-drop prosecution, stricter sentencing guidelines, and "prosecution-favoring evidentiary rules" in cases of domestic and sexual violence.[110]

As these legal changes took hold, a new kind of feminist crime novel emerged to publicize them. In place of the unaffiliated private detective or the persecuted mother, this type of novel offered the female police officer or prosecuting attorney. In the 1980s, only a handful of police procedural novels starred women; when they did, their focus was on the difficulty of professional advancement in the face of workplace sexism. Surveying the situation in 1988, the critic Maureen T. Reddy concluded that "the police procedural ultimately seems an unpromising genre for the woman creator of a woman detective."[111] If the genre subsequently became more promising for female crime novelists, and more amenable to what Reddy called "feminist questions," this was because it was a natural literary mode through which to track the collaboration between antiviolence feminists and police departments—a collaboration that succeeded in establishing new legal procedures for handling gender-based violence. The feminist police and prosecutor novels of the 1990s shored up this collaboration by expressing an untroubled faith in the just workings and deterrent effects of the legal system as a solution to violence against women. In doing so, they staked out a unique position in the landscape of women's crime fiction.

The feminist anthropologist Elizabeth Bernstein coined the influential phrase "carceral feminism" to describe the enmeshment of feminism and law enforcement that became dominant in the 1990s. For Bernstein, carceral feminism names the feminist "commitment... to a law and order agenda" as well as "a drift from the welfare state to the carceral state as the enforcement apparatus for feminist goals."[112] A similar drift began to occur in women's crime novels around the same time. We might call this the emergence of *carceral feminist fiction*: a subgenre that fused the lineage of feminist crime writing to an explicit pro-police agenda. Where hard-boiled detective novels and missing-child narratives in this period evinced a lingering ambivalence about the help law enforcement agencies were willing and able to offer, police and prosecutor novels presented the criminal legal system as the best—if not the only—hope for women's safety.

Eleanor Taylor Bland's innovative Marti MacAlister series was the first to feature a Black female police detective as a protagonist. Set in a fictional Illinois suburb called Lincoln Prairie (which bears some resemblance to Springfield), the first MacAlister novel, *Dead Time* (1992), slots easily into the literary history I've been sketching in this chapter, as it features both battered women and children in danger. The plot revolves around a murder at a hotel for the transient and mentally ill.[113] The killing turns out to be linked to a decades-old attempt by a naval officer to smuggle jewels out of Vietnam. But what makes the crime particularly urgent for MacAlister and her white male partner Vik is that they believe a group of homeless children witnessed the murder and can identify the killer. The suspense of the novel is less about solving the crime than it is about finding the children.

Dead Time imagines a world in which child endangerment and domestic violence are constants.[114] The siblings who witnessed the crime, we learn in sections focalized through their perspective, left home after their mother's abusive boyfriend was imprisoned for killing her. Earlier, MacAlister describes her involvement in a case in which a man with "a previous record of beating his wife" ended up stabbing her. Toward the end of the novel, the cops find themselves involved in another domestic abuse case: "A sixty-seven-year-old woman had stabbed her son-in-law because he was beating her daughter." This case leads Vik to fondly recollect his own father, also a police officer, who once "had to go to a neighbor and speak with him about not hitting his wife again." Yet another of the novel's subplots concerns a fourteen-year-old girl on trial for killing her baby by shaking it.[115]

In Bland's telling, there is a specific culprit for this epidemic of violence against children and women: bad parents. At the start of the novel, a character sees the homeless children—who are Black—and thinks, "No need asking where the kids' parents were. Odds were there wasn't any daddy around, the mother, prostitute maybe, or a junkie or a drunk." This description of an absent father and a mother involved in either sex work or drugs conjures the specific racial ideologies that inhered in the post-Moynihan moral panic about single-mother households. The idea that derelict parents produce a cycle of poverty, pathology, and crime in their children is articulated repeatedly throughout the novel. Reflecting on the trial of the teenager accused of shaking her baby, Vik decides that the young woman's bad parenting is *itself* the product of bad parenting: "Need to lock her parents up."[116]

At this moment, Bland was hardly alone among crime writers in diagnosing a world that seemed to present a unique set of dangers to women and children. What sets *Dead Time* apart is that it views this world as one that can only be salvaged, if not redeemed, by the police. If children are endangered and their parents have failed to protect them, then law enforcement must step in to do the parenting. "This was not a safe or caring world if you were a child," MacAlister thinks. Her job as a police officer is to correct that. As she explains to the rescued children in the novel's final pages, "We're police officers . . . You're safe now."[117]

Fusing aspects of the feminist detective novel (MacAlister is a tough female detective) with aspects of domestic suspense (who is searching for missing and endangered children), *Dead Time* altered these established genre frameworks by making MacAlister a police officer. On duty during what the novel repeatedly claims is an unprecedented moment of parental delinquency and family crisis, MacAlister and Vik are called on repeatedly to protect children and reconstitute families. They play the role of surrogate parents. Such roleplaying becomes more literal at the end of the novel, when, having successfully rescued the missing kids, MacAlister helps place them in the foster system. Three "would live together in a foster home." Two others "would become wards of the state of Illinois; a judge and DCFS would have to approve." As far as MacAlister is concerned, this is a happy ending. In the novel's final line, our hero settles into a feeling of contentment, "a serenity that she hadn't felt in a long time."[118] Though it is at best an equivocal fate for the children, and in reality something likely worse, it makes all the sense in the world that putting the runaways in the care of the Department of Child and Family Services would fill MacAlister with a newfound feeling of "serenity." That's because it confirms the novel's belief that it is the job of law enforcement institutions to step in for failing parents. Although MacAlister cannot adopt the children herself, having "the state of Illinois" do so is the next thing.

Bland thus depicts the police as the only viable replacement for the extinct family structures that once served to protect women and children. The novel emphasizes the state's role in child protection and makes multiple references to cops' interventions in violent domestic situations. Even the main villain, Bernard Greyson, isn't just a killer but an abuser—he's been stalking his ex-wife, and late in the novel he murders his current one. Through all of these plot turns, *Dead Time* offers a spirited defense of the necessity of the police for the prevention of partner and child abuse. What makes the police necessary, according to Bland, is not only their capacity to punish and apprehend bad parents. It is also their ability to reconstitute the sort of stable family unit that bad parents let dissolve.

Dead Time is convinced that this crisis of the nuclear family has reached a historically new degree of severity. Vik laments, "Things weren't like this ten years ago." Another character agrees: "Folks wasn't responsible no more, not like when she was coming up." MacAlister herself recalls growing up on Chicago's South Side, where, despite being poor, "she had been safe." Now her class mobility as a successful professional has ironically resulted in a loss of safety for her own children, a loss determined not by geography (given that she has moved from the city to the suburbs) but by history: "For all that she could buy her children that her parents had not been able to provide for her, she couldn't promise them safety."[119] The problem with all of these versions of the same declension narrative—that parents were more responsible and kids were safer thirty years before, twenty years, heck, even "ten years ago"—is that they are flatly untrue. As we saw in the previous section, moral panic about the bad parenting habits of poor people, especially poor people of color in urban areas, had been a staple of public discourse since at least the 1960s. So what is going on here?

Narratives of decline and nostalgia for bygone eras of social harmony are essential tools for justifying why we need more police. For Bland's characters, decreasing public safety can only be corrected by an increase in cops on the street. Bland ensures we don't miss this point by having MacAlister wax nostalgic about the patrolman who ably protected her own childhood neighborhood: "The beat cop wasn't always friendly but he was there, on foot, and whether they liked him or not everyone knew him. They all knew his top priority was a crime-free shift."[120] Setting aside the fact that this is not generally what the increased foot patrols in places like Chicago accomplished or were meant to accomplish in the 1960s, MacAlister's nostalgia for the age of the benevolent beat cop allows Bland to connect the dots between family responsibility, community safety, and a strong police presence. If parents of the 1980s are less responsible and kids are less safe, the reason must be that there are fewer cops keeping the former in line and the latter secure. Parenting, as Bland presents it, is at heart a police matter.

Nevertheless, *Dead Time*'s impassioned case for the importance of the police in protecting children does produce some moments of cognitive dissonance. At one point, an officer specializing in child safety admits that "there might not be any way to help" the children they're looking for. "After their families get through with them the system gets them. What one starts the other finishes. The end of the line is prison or the morgue."[121] These lines paint a very different picture of a carceral system that doesn't safeguard neglected children so much as further entrap them. Here "the system"—which comprises not just prisons but also the police who help fill them, as well as the child welfare agencies that partner with law enforcement[122]—is not a corrective to family violence but an extension of it. What starts in families, the carceral system finishes. In a passage like this, *Dead Time* seems suddenly to become aware that the police—essential cogs in a punitive and inescapable system of state supervision—may not be much of an improvement on the violence of family life after all. Yet the awareness is fleeting. At the novel's end, MacAlister and the state of Illinois—which MacAlister has entrusted, with a feeling of serenity, to take care of the children—are presented to readers as the book's two primary heroes. MacAlister has been warned about how the system really operates, but she can't hear it. She's too deep inside it. In that sense, you could say that *Dead Time* is really a story about what it takes for the police to convince themselves, and us, that they are not so much part of this country's vast system of social control as they are part of the family.

The character of the sympathetic police officer capable of protecting children and intervening in unstable family situations embodied what had become, by the end of the 1980s, the conventional wisdom that "arrest is best." Yet arrest was only one piece of the puzzle. An equally significant concern for many antiviolence activists was how difficult it was to successfully prosecute cases involving domestic and sexual violence. Given that, it makes sense that the figure of the prosecutor would begin to play a more prominent role in crime fiction about violence against women. The most consequential writer of carceral feminist prosecutor fiction was Linda Fairstein. In her day job, Fairstein was the assistant district attorney leading the Sex Crimes Prosecution Unit in New York City. The job made her something of a local celebrity.[123] It also put her smack in the middle of, among other things, the 1989 Central Park Five case, which resulted in the false convictions of five innocent young men of color accused of assault and rape. (Their convictions were vacated a decade later.) Shortly after securing those convictions, Fairstein began work on a series of crime novels celebrating female prosecutors and emphasizing how dangerous the world would be for women without them.

Fairstein's career as a fiction writer was launched in 1996 with the publication of *Final Jeopardy*, the first novel in her Alexandra Cooper series. Cooper is the assistant district attorney in New York's Sex Crimes Prosecution Unit and, as such, an unmistakable stand-in for Fairstein. *Final Jeopardy* is in many ways a standard-issue procedural murder mystery, weaving a yarn about a movie star named Isabella Lascar who is killed while staying at Cooper's vacation home in Martha's Vineyard. Cooper attempts to solve the crime with the help of a male cop assigned to protect her. Eventually, Cooper's suspicion falls—unsurprisingly, as we've been taught to expect by our earlier readings in the genre—on the man she is dating, Jed Segal, who had been having an affair with Lascar behind Cooper's back. In the end, the killer is not Jed (though Cooper breaks up with him anyway) but a female stalker who had been following him. In an especially brazen choice, Fairstein sets the climactic stand-off between Cooper and the stalker in Central Park.

But the solving of Isabella's murder was subordinate to Fairstein's more immediate aim in writing *Final Jeopardy*, which was to teach readers about the important work being done by sex-crimes prosecutors like her. In fact, Fairstein had already written a book on this topic: *Sexual Violence: Our*

War Against Rape (1993), a nonfiction account of her work as a prosecutor in the Manhattan Sex Crimes Unit. Fairstein explains that she was inspired to write *Sexual Violence* in order to advertise the "extraordinary change in the legal process" pertaining to crimes against women that had taken place in the previous decade. The book methodically narrates how her office "accomplished extraordinary results in the course of a very few years," seeing conviction rates "soar" while treating victims with care and respect. The story of these procedural changes and promising results was, Fairstein felt, something people needed to know. The purpose of *Sexual Violence* was, in her own words, "the education of the public."[124] Unfortunately, the public wasn't as interested as she hoped; the book didn't garner much attention or sell many copies. Fairstein seems to have decided that this might be a genre problem. She set about rewriting *Sexual Violence* as a mass-market mystery novel.

The result was *Final Jeopardy*. Throughout the narration of its central mystery, Fairstein weaves in a good deal of pedagogical exposition taken verbatim from *Sexual Violence*, including descriptions of how laws have changed, how witness interviews work, how prosecutors collaborate with the police, how the D.A.'s office is bureaucratically organized, and what the Manhattan Criminal Courts Building looks like. Read through these borrowed paragraphs, *Final Jeopardy* turns out to be more than a standard potboiler. Instead, it marks a pivotal moment when women's crime fiction was transformed into an explicit tool for carceral feminist advocacy.

One thing *Final Jeopardy* wants to teach its readers is how the legal system works to "better the plight of women" and to secure for them the "justice" they "had long been denied." The other, more elemental thing it wants to teach is that the system does in fact work. This is a running theme throughout *Final Jeopardy* (and *Sexual Violence*, too). Cooper believes that the biggest remaining obstacle to prosecuting gender-based violence cases is that victims are primed to believe the legal system won't work for them. As she explains, again closely echoing an explanation Fairstein had written for her nonfiction book, "Most women who survive a sexual assault come to the criminal justice system not expecting that any kind of justice will be done. They doubt that the rapist will be caught, and both fiction and made-for-TV movies have taught them that even if he is, he'll never be convicted. It's great to be part of changing that, of making the system work in these cases, of putting these bastards away." There is no doubt that, in the preceding decades, the legal system had very little interest in pursuing or punishing men who committed acts of violence against women. But for Fairstein, that's old news. Now "the system work[s]," and the "bastards" who hurt women are regularly put away. The real problem now, as Fairstein sees it, is that women are misled into thinking that the legal system isn't on their side. She places the blame for this misperception on "fiction and made-for-TV movies," which have "taught" women the wrong lessons about the policing and prosecution of gendered violence. As Cooper puts it, "there have been a lot improvements... this stuff isn't like all those awful made-for-TV movies." This belief in the power of fiction to shape women's relation to the law helps explain why Fairstein chose to write her own work of crime fiction. She wanted to teach a different kind of lesson than she saw on offer in other novels being written about women and crime. After securing another guilty verdict from a jury, Cooper congratulates herself, noting that "as usual, justice was done."[125] What's important here isn't just the justice of the verdict. It's also that it happened as usual. The premise of *Final Jeopardy* is that legal victories for victimized women are the new normal.

How does Fairstein's novel succeed in convincing readers, and itself, that the best solution to violence against women is to be found in the courts and the prisons? A key feature of *Final Jeopardy* is its depiction of gender-based violence as a constant threat. Although the novel's title is supposed to be a sly nod to Cooper's love of the television game show, it also indicates a worldview that sees all women—including Cooper herself—as being in perpetual jeopardy. Fairstein depicts New York City as a cesspool of danger, overflowing with criminals and rapists. Cooper is constantly trying to clear her thoughts of the "stalkers and rapists and murderers who loomed before me every day." She has nowhere to "turn for safe haven," especially at night—"evil spirits... crept around the city after dusk." Sitting on a train, all Cooper sees is danger; her "peripheral vision was scanning the car for the usual assortment of freaks and perverts." The perpetual threat of stranger rape looms over everything Cooper does, including where she chooses to live: "Too many years of investigating break-ins of brownstones and townhouses, with rapists climbing in from fire escapes or pushing in vestibule doors behind unsuspecting tenants, had driven me to a luxury building—low on quaintness and charm but high on doormen and rent."[126] A luxury building sounds great if you can afford it. But it is hard not to notice the paradox that creeps into the novel here, as it insists simultaneously that women are protected by the legal system and that women, no matter where they live—from "brownstones" to "townhouses"—are endlessly at risk of being victims of violence.

But maybe it's not a paradox, because maybe Fairstein doesn't think that women are protected by the law. Maybe she thinks they are merely avenged by it ("justice was done"). The idea that the vengeance of the carceral system is necessary because the prevention of gender-based violence is impossible is supported by the novel's obsession with recidivism. The problem, according to *Final Jeopardy*, is that the men who go to jail for violence against women get out too quickly—and go right back to committing the same sorts of crimes. In a key subplot, Cooper and a police detective pursue a serial rapist in Manhattan. Eventually they identify him as a man "who just got out of state prison in New Jersey." Earlier Cooper had instinctually guessed that the assailant was a repeat offender, and now she finds she was "right all along. Four counts of rape, Bergen County." Why was the man released, then? Because "he was in that treatment center in the Jersey system"—a treatment center, Cooper says sarcastically, "where they rehabilitate rapists" and "send 'em back to us all cured and well behaved."[127] The implied scare-quotes around the word *rehabilitate* practically leap off the page. Frank disbelief in the possibility of rehabilitation is a crucial pillar of the novel's carceral ideology.[128] Several other side plots in the novel also involve suspects with prior convictions. Eventually Cooper says outright what the novel has long been implying: "The therapist hasn't been born yet who can rehabilitate one of these predators."[129] If rehabilitation is not possible and the danger to women is ever-present, then carceral solutions—more prosecutions, longer prison sentences, less parole—will seem the only viable option. Perfectly encapsulating the ethos of carceral feminism, *Final Jeopardy* is an attempt to teach readers that the best hope for safety from gender-based violence is to keep putting more people in prison, and to work harder to make sure they never get out.

Cooper, no doubt speaking for Fairstein, notes at the start of the novel how much she enjoys "being on the side of the angels."[130] Yet her side in the war against sexual and domestic violence was one that activists had long warned was also the side of the carceral state—a side that, by the middle of the 1990s, had succeeded in creating the largest population of imprisoned people in the world. The runaway imprisonment rates of the 1990s confirm that, as many abolition feminists have argued, it is not so easy to distinguish interpersonal violence from state violence, modes of harm that are ideologically as well as practically linked.[131] The violence of prison is not the opposite of violence against women, and is no solution to it. Surely, it is hard to say that the false imprisonment of the five innocent teenagers in the Central Park Five case—let alone the full-blown crisis of mass incarceration—was really something "the angels" would have endorsed.

One thing's for sure: Whether Fairstein was on the side of the angels or not, she was certainly on the side that won. Although *Final Jeopardy* represents itself as swimming against the current of popular crime narratives when it makes the case for the success of the legal system in securing justice for women (unlike "all those awful made-for-TV movies"), in fact the case had already been decided. By the middle of the 1990s, carceral feminism, led by prosecutors just like Fairstein, had won the day. The framing of gendered violence as a criminal justice issue had become an unshakable form of bipartisan common sense. Who could disagree that the state needed to protect women? Nowhere was this common sense more vividly demonstrated than in the widespread public support for the Violence Against Women Act, which passed with the help of intensive lobbying by several feminist groups. Folded into the landmark 1994 Violent Crime Control and Law Enforcement Act (otherwise known as the Clinton crime bill)—which added the death penalty to more than fifty new federal offenses and poured billions of dollars into prison-building and police-hiring—the Violence Against Women Act earmarked $1.6 billion for the prevention of gender-based crimes.[132] Some of this funding went toward the creation of more shelters and a national domestic violence hotline.[133] But most of it was funneled into police departments, prisons, and prosecutors' offices. In this way, VAWA bolstered the idea that increased criminalization was the answer to gendered violence, and it backed up the idea with cash. Carceral solutions to domestic and sexual violence were now fully mainstream. *Final Jeopardy* was just the victory lap.

Abolition feminism teaches us that this victory was not inevitable. What I have tried to do in this chapter is reconstruct how women's crime writing from the 1970s to the 1990s functioned as an essential popular arena for reckoning with the rise of carceral solutions to gender-based violence, and for exploring the possibility of alternatives. For every Linda Fairstein arguing for the need to "put these bastards away," there was a

Barbara Neely insisting that putting more men in jail won't "change a thing." Make no mistake, most of the novelists I have discussed in these pages would hardly have described themselves as prison abolitionists. Yet a surprising number of them were perceptibly ambivalent about trusting law enforcement to protect women. They were right to be. Empirical evidence continues to confirm that the government-sponsored war on violence against women did not make women safer. "The criminalization of gender-based violence championed by carceral feminists has been ineffective in decreasing that violence," Leigh Goodmark has concluded.[134] Writing during the decades when this type of criminalization grew from contested grassroots strategy to reigning common sense, crime novelists did not agree on the best way to solve gender-based violence. But in the midst of an unprecedented buildup of U.S. police and prison capacity, they turned the genre into a place where concerned readers could reliably go to see what different solutions might look like.

4

TWO PATHS FOR PATHOLOGY, 1984–1998

> Disease is neutral. Homicide's not.
>
> —*C IS FOR CORPSE* (1986)

SICK DAYS

It would be fair to say that, by the start of the 1990s, serial killers had a stranglehold on popular crime fiction. In May of 1991, two of the top three spots on the *New York Times* paperback bestseller list were occupied by Thomas Harris's Hannibal Lecter novels—novels that the *Times*'s characteristically pithy plot synopses rendered practically indistinguishable. On *Red Dragon*: "An F.B.I. agent hunts a serial killer." On *The Silence of the Lambs*: "An F.B.I. man and woman track a serial killer."[1] These summaries suggest two things. First, Harris was working within the confines of a fairly rigid formula. Second, it was a formula that worked. The term *serial killer* had only been coined in the mid 1970s; less than two decades later, it was an inescapable part of popular literary culture. The modern serial killer formula—which Harris is credited with more or less inventing—was so successful that it quickly "glutted and saturated the market."[2] Writers as varied as Patricia Cornwell, James Ellroy, and Dean Koontz took Harris's formula and ran with it. Scholars have mused extensively on why so many readers have been drawn to serial killer fiction.[3] Here I want simply to emphasize the subgenre's sheer ubiquity. At the end of the twentieth century, serial killer novels were the dominant form of crime fiction. Suddenly every crime writer seemed to be writing one. Recalling this moment in publishing, the critic Leonard Cassuto writes that it was starting to feel as if bookstores were being stocked directly by "the assembly line at the serial killer fiction factory."[4]

While fictional serial killers stalked bookstore shelves and bestseller lists in the 1980s and '90s, however, a completely kind of criminal dominated the nightly news. This was the criminal type—young, Black, and living in a city—created by the War on Drugs. As Michelle Alexander has written, by the mid 1980s, "the media was saturated with images" of drug use and violence "that seemed to confirm the worst negative stereotypes about impoverished inner-city residents."[5] Such stereotypes helped drum up widespread support for the Comprehensive Crime Control Act of 1984—one of the most sweeping efforts in American history to amend the federal criminal code—which abolished the federal parole system, increased penalties for drug offenses, established civil forfeiture provisions that enriched local police departments, and introduced mandatory minimum sentencing. The legislation was passed by a Democrat-controlled House by a vote of 406–16. Elizabeth Hinton argues that the Comprehensive Crime Control Act "marked the official beginning of the War on Drugs."[6] Over the next decade, politicians from both parties eagerly supported the aggressive punishment of nonwhite drug users, dealers, and gangs, which led to the Anti-Drug Abuse Acts of 1986 and 1988, the Violent Crime Control and Law Enforcement Act of 1994, and the Federal Death Penalty Act of 1994; these acts established severe penalties for drug possession, introduced three-strikes legislation, and expanded the number of crimes punishable by death.[7] The drug war was in full swing.

Without question, the "central villain" in the eyes of policymakers in the 1980s and '90s was Black youth.[8] Yet the distinctive villain of the era's serial killer fiction was almost uniformly white. "White guys are always the serial killers," Sherman Alexie wrote in his serial killer novel *Indian Killer* (1996).[9] The discrepancy between these two very different character types vying for attention in the last decades of the twentieth century raises some important questions about the relation between popular fiction and the criminal legal system. How are we to explain a cultural moment in which the widespread circulation of stories about racialized drug use and urban violence went hand in hand with the equally widespread circulation of stories about white psychos? And what does it mean that the contest, if not the contradiction, between these two kinds of stories played out in precisely the years when the American prison population began its vertiginous upward climb? More simply: Why were so many Americans reading about white serial killers while hundreds of thousands of young Black men were being imprisoned? What tune was genre fiction fiddling while justice burned?

Confronted with the discordance between the type of criminal who prowled the pages of popular crime fiction and the types of people who were preyed on by the War on Drugs, it is tempting to assume that the former was nothing but a distraction from the brutal, biased reality of the latter. That's surely part of the story here: the guilty pleasures of serial killer fiction as a displacement of American society's presumption of Black guilt.[10] The logic of displacement at the heart of the serial killer narrative is made explicit in the early work of one of the genre's foremost practitioners, James Ellroy. In the mid 1980s, Ellroy published two serial killer novels that began in exactly the same way: with a riot scene that juxtaposed a Black or Brown mob with a lone white psychopath. Ellroy's *Blood on the Moon* (1984) begins with the Watts uprising of 1965, while his bestselling *The Black Dahlia* (1987) begins with the Zoot Suit riot of 1943.[11] Why did Ellroy use this device twice? This repeated method of differentiating the solo psychopath from the urban mob offered a tidy allegory of generic and cultural succession. It announced the arrival of a whole new kind of crime novel in the 1980s: one that had shifted its attention from urban social conditions to serial killing; from Black and Brown communities to white men; from indivisible masses of street criminals to individual psychos; and, most importantly, from sociological explanations for crime to the enshrinement of a kind of purely inexplicable violence—something like what Ellroy calls, in *Blood on the Moon*, "the vortex of divinely evil compulsions."[12] By beginning his novels with race riots that birth serial killers, Ellroy was trying to narrate where crime fiction had been in recent decades, and where he now wanted it to go. This narrative doubled as a savvy marketing ploy. It gave readers permission to enjoy the transgressive thrills of the serial killer novel (Mike Davis has described Ellroy's work, not inaccurately, as "an almost unendurable wordstorm of perversity and gore"[13]) without having to think that what they were reading had anything to do with real-world crime control measures that were destroying low-income minority neighborhoods and filling up prison cells.

The major claim of this chapter, however, is that the literary figure of the serial killer actually had a lot to do with the policies and ideologies of the War on Drugs. Consider, for instance, the uncanny resemblance between fictional serial killers and "super-predators," the venomously popular term coined by the arch-conservative thinker John DiIulio. In a 1995 article introducing the concept, DiIulio warned of a coming wave of "morally impoverished" youth who were "perfectly capable of committing the most heinous acts of physical violence for the most trivial reasons."[14] The specter of the super-predator became a bipartisan rallying point for urban crime control in the 1990s, invoked approvingly by everyone from Bob Dole to Hillary Clinton. But of course, DiIulio's description of amoral criminals "committing the most heinous acts ... for the most trivial reasons" could just as easily apply to the serial killers who were single-handedly powering book sales in the same decade. The striking similarity between the conscienceless, inhuman psychopaths invented to sell crime novels and the "remorseless," dehumanized super-predators invented to sell the drug war provides one initial clue to the entanglement of the era's literary and criminal imaginaries.

Another clue can be found in a question that crime novels frequently asked about their serial killers: Are they evil or are they sick? This question mattered a great deal during the drug war. That's because the same thing was being asked at the time about drug addicts. By the mid 1980s, *crime* was effectively a synonym for *drugs*. Yet the conception of drug addiction as a crime was a relatively recent development. Between 1945 and 1978, the dominant social tendency was to understand addiction as a public health concern and to give doctors the primary responsibility for managing it. Broadly speaking, the policy response to drug use in these decades was one of tolerance.[15] A 1971 poll in New York City, for instance, found that nine out of ten respondents believed that "drug addicts should be treated as sick people, not criminals."[16]

Over a very brief period of time, tolerant, treatment-based attitudes toward addiction were replaced by exceedingly punitive laws criminalizing drug users as well as dealers. In the California prison system, the proportion of people incarcerated for drug infractions more than tripled between 1977 and 1990.[17] In 1986, *Time* magazine named crack cocaine its "issue of the year."[18] The same year, policymakers introduced the infamous 100:1 sentencing disparity for crack versus powder cocaine possession (meaning that possessing five grams of crack cocaine would automatically trigger the same number of years in prison as five *hundred* grams of powder). The War on Drugs was now officially under way. Between 1984 and 1990, a full 90 percent of people who received federal mandatory minimum sentences did so for drug offenses.[19] Today drug offenders still constitute close to a quarter of all incarcerated people and nearly half of the federal prison population.[20]

This is how U.S. drug policy decisively shifted from a "treatment regime" to a carceral regime.[21] One of the enabling forces behind the War on Drugs was the transformation of a health problem—addiction—into a crime problem. As Ruth Wilson Gilmore puts it, "The number of prison beds has gone up, as the number of hospital beds has gone down."[22] It is no wonder that addiction and mental illness are now crushingly common among incarcerated people. Angela Davis estimates that "there may be twice as many people suffering from mental illness who are in jails or prisons than there are in all psychiatric hospitals in the United States combined."[23] In the midst of all of this, the idea of medical treatment for addicts abruptly vanished from view. The drug epidemic that decimated so many American cities in the 1980s was treated primarily as an issue of law enforcement, not an issue of public health.[24] Addiction itself was not officially classified as a disease until 1987. By then it was too late. The doctors had been swapped out for cops, the treatment centers replaced with prisons.

This chapter catalogs the surprising number of crime novels that depicted the War on the Drugs as a contest between carceral policy and medical care. These texts circled knowingly around the multiple meanings of *pathology*, a term that could refer either to physical and mental illness or to putative underclass disorder. According to the tough-on-crime perspective that fostered bipartisan support for the drug war, it was a "pathological culture" of poverty that "predisposed" young Black men "to drugs, crime, vice, and urban destruction."[25] This way of thinking about the alleged defects of poor communities of color was popularized in 1965 by the Moynihan Report, which described African American culture as a "tangle of pathology."[26] In the decades that followed, the idea of cultural and racial pathology became a standard way of redescribing the structural conditions of poverty as the behavioral failings of poor people[27]—behaviors (such as "poor parenting" and "welfare dependency") that were invariably characterized as "personal pathologies."[28] The process of racial pathologization was a perfect fit for the drug war, where the prevalence of certain drugs like crack was taken as yet another sign of the pathology or dysfunction of poor inner-city communities. As the political scientist Naomi Murakawa astutely points out, both the War on Crime and the War on Drugs were rooted in the persistent characterization of "black crime as black sickness."[29] Yet this sickness wasn't to be found in actual bodies. It was the metaphorical infection of a whole community, the pathology of an entire racialized culture.

While the drug war added a new chapter in the enduring legacy of pathologizing Black culture, more literal understandings of pathology and illness were being reestablished as core features of professional criminology. The once-marginalized fields of biocriminology and psychophysiology (which lost credibility in the wake of World War II) gained renewed acceptance among criminologists in the 1990s as biological explanations of crime began to displace sociological ones. The biological turn in criminological research shifted scholarly attention to a different kind of criminal. Street crime and its need for a broader sociological explanation were out. The psychopath was in.[30]

The concept of pathology thus splintered in the midst of the drug war, as entrenched logics of racial criminalization, recently recovered ideas of biologically determined criminality, and new forms of fear and prejudice tied to the AIDS epidemic (which, due to anxieties about needle sharing, was closely associated with drug use) created competing frameworks for understanding the relation between crime and illness.[31] At the heart of each of these frameworks was the same set of unresolved questions. Who, in the eyes of the state, was truly sick: a single unwell individual or a whole class? And which system was responsible for managing that sickness: the health care system or the criminal legal system? This chapter follows pathology's forking path through crime novels of the 1980s and '90s, which became fixated on the intersections of murder, illness, and institutional care. My aim is to persuade you that crime fiction's prevailing obsession with the pathological acts of serial killers also served, in more covert and complex ways, as a means of wrestling with the criminalization of addiction and the racialization of medicine in the heyday of the War on Drugs.

DIAGNOSING MURDER

The War on Drugs weighed heavily on the minds of writers in the early 1990s. A wide range of novels, from pulpy works of genre fiction to National Book Award nominees, testifies to its looming influence. Lawrence Block's *A Walk Among the Tombstones* (1992) tells the story of a private detective hired to investigate the murder of the wife of a drug trafficker. Walter Mosley's *White Butterfly* (1992) features a visit to Oakland where detective Easy Rawlins sees a woman sitting on a porch "oblivious to the war going on around her."[32] Barbara Neely's *Blanche on the Lam* (1992) describes a world in which people assume that a Black woman living in New York City would "automatically" be "a junkie."[33] Patricia Cornwell's *All That Remains* (1992) finds medical examiner Kay Scarpetta working for the national drug policy director, "one of the most powerful and admired women in America," who got her start prosecuting "high-profile drug cases in the federal system."[34] James Ellroy's *L.A. Confidential* (1990) revolves around a plan by a diabolical police captain to flood heroin into Black neighborhoods—a mirror of concern in Ellroy's own time about the U.S. government's alleged role in seeding the crack epidemic.[35] Even Joyce Carol Oates's *Because It Is Bitter, Because It Is My Heart* (1990), a critically acclaimed work of naturalism set in the 1950s, feels called upon to comment on the tragedy of "black men killing one another" in the context of "the drug trade."[36]

All six of these novels have something else in common. They're also about serial killers. *L.A. Confidential* includes an extended B-plot (cut completely from the better-known film adaptation) about a serial killer responsible for a string of unsolved child murders. *White Butterfly* is about a serial killer targeting Black sex workers in Watts and Oakland. *Blanche on the Lam* features a rich white woman who turns out to have been a murderous psychopath since she was a child. *Because It Is Bitter* revolves around a twelve-year-old sociopath with "heavy-lidded eyes like killers in the movies" who serially accosts "every girl he sights between the approximate ages of twelve and twenty."[37] *All That Remains* is about an unidentified serial killer murdering couples in Virginia. And in *A Walk Among the Tombstones*, a duo of serial killers turns out to be butchering the wives and daughters of suspected drug dealers. This array of double-sided novels raises a fascinating and important question, which this section strives to answer: What did it mean to think of the drug war and the serial killer as two sides of the same story?

Block's novel offers one tempting answer. In *A Walk Among the Tombstones*, the serial killers are two men who used to work for the Drug Enforcement Agency. They are "evidently obsessed with the subject" of drugs. This "low-grade obsession about dope dealers" leads them to serial killing. It probably also explains why they became DEA agents in the first place; such psychopathic obsession, the novel's hero Matt Scudder reasons, could only have been "an asset in that line of work."[38] Block's plot all but begs to be read allegorically, offering a neat parable for how the government enterprise of the War on Drugs, in its relentless persecution of communities connected to the drug trade, had itself begun to operate with the sadistic obsession of serial murder.

That reading works for me. Still, something more specific is being hashed out in these novels. It is commonplace for novelists to describe killers using the language of insanity, madness, and mental illness.[39] The "contemporary serial killer," Leonard Cassuto suggests, is invariably offered to us as a "case study of mental illness." In most serial killer fiction, these case studies tend to involve some sort of nebulous personality disorder, a condition often figured by novelists as "inscrutable," "mysterious," and "incurable."[40] The novels by Block, Cornwell, Neely, Mosley, Ellroy, and Oates seem to follow this trend. They all include conventional descriptions of serial killers as "crazy"[41] or "insane."[42] "All murderers were probably crazy," Blanche decides in *Blanche on the Lam*, a novel that ends with the killer being sent to "a cushy asylum."[43] But another term keeps cropping up in these books as well: *sick*. The murderer in *Blanche on the Lam* is "sick.... Very sick."[44] In *L.A. Confidential*, the serial killer Douglas Dieterling isn't mad, he's "quite *physiologically* ill. He gets brain inflammations periodically."[45] The physiological effects of brain inflammation are, unexpectedly, also emphasized in *White Butterfly*, where the big reveal about serial killer J. T. Saunders is that he suffers from syphilis, which has affected his brain. As Rawlins's wife, Regina, a nurse, explains to him, "VD can make you insane."[46] Cornwell makes the sickness more literal still. Her novel's serial killer is finally identified after it is discovered that he suffers from "aplastic anemia."[47]

"What kind of people act like that?" a character asks of the killers in *A Walk Among the Tombstones*. Block's detective answers, "Sick ones or evil ones, take your pick."⁴⁸ This was the same choice society was facing when trying to explain drug-related crime. Was it criminality or was it sickness? The fine line between "sick" people and "evil" people was similarly foregrounded in Cornwell's debut novel, *Postmortem* (1990). Talking about the serial killer she's pursuing, Scarpetta insists, "He isn't *sick*, okay? He's antisocial, he's evil." Her colleague disagrees: "Has to be some kind of sickness. He knows he's sick." Although Scarpetta wants to hold on to a more old-fashioned conception of "evil," she eventually discovers that her colleague is right. As in *All That Remains*, the key break in *Postmortem* comes when Scarpetta discovers that the killer has a rare "metabolic disorder" whose symptoms help identify him.⁴⁹ The killer is truly sick after all, and the medical work of diagnosing that sickness turns out to be essential to the process of catching him.

These writers saw that the literary serial killer needed to be understood as "sick," not metaphorically or even emotionally but in physiologically specific ways (metabolic disorder, brain inflammation, venereal disease). This focus on the link between criminality and physiological illness was the unique product of an era defined by the sweeping punishment of a crime that had only recently been treated as an illness. That crime was addiction. It is no accident that all of the novels whose references to serial-killer sickness I have cited here doubled as commentaries on the social and racial drama of the drug war. Once the War on Drugs brought the illness of addiction under the oversight of the criminal legal system, crime novelists were forced to reconsider the relation between illness and crime. Cornwell's *All That Remains* concludes with the drug policy director shooting the serial killer herself, as if to signal the crime writer's sense that serial killing was now a problem that fell directly under the purview of U.S. drug policy. In *Blanche on the Lam*, one of the serial killer's murder weapons is an empty syringe. As a figure of terror whose criminality was rooted in overlooked forms of sickness, the serial killer thus became an unexpected double of the addict—and an important limit case in the showdown between crime politics and medical ethics. In *A Walk Among the Tombstones*, Block makes this doubling crystal clear. Serial killing, the detective surmises, "seems to be addictive, like any strong drug."⁵⁰ In *Postmortem*, Cornwell describes her serial killer in exactly the same way: "He's a friggin addict, Doc."⁵¹

Explaining the shift toward carceral antidrug policy in the 1980s, the historian Julilly Kohler-Hausmann writes, "What program administrators and politicians had presented as efforts to cure addicts of their disease they now framed as efforts to protect 'the public' from the addict and pusher." In this way, policymakers "moved pushers from being considered *diseased* to being cast *as the disease*."[52] A key feature of the drug war, in other words, was the strategic reframing of disease as crime—and of crime as its own kind of community-wide pathology, a metaphorical "disease." At the center of this new crime control framework were drug users, who were widely seen as vectors not only of criminal acts but also of communicable diseases.[53] But mental illness was not immune from the intensified effort to punish sick people; the Insanity Defense Reform Act of 1984 made it significantly harder for defendants to be found not guilty by reason of insanity. Between the criminalization of addicts and the criminalization of the mentally ill, there was a clear political imperative to shift the management of illness from the medical realm to the legal one.[54] Crime novelists found themselves compelled to navigate this rapidly shifting terrain. In doing so, many of them discovered the hidden link between the era's two dominant criminal types, the drug user and the serial killer—literary characters who looked like mirror images but in fact stood on opposing sides of America's criminalization of illness, which transformed punishment at the end of the twentieth century.

Consider the fate of Douglas Dieterling, the killer in *L.A. Confidential*. At the end of Ellroy's novel, Dieterling is located by LAPD lieutenant Ed Exley—the same cop who, earlier in the book, murdered three innocent Black suspects during a raid. When Exley confronts Dieterling, the reader is led to believe that he will murder this suspect, too. But Exley doesn't kill Dieterling. Instead, he gives the killer his medicine: "Ed threw the pills at him ... [Douglas] grabbed them, gagged them down. Ed aimed at his mouth, couldn't pull the trigger.... [Douglas] fell asleep, his lips curled over his gums. Ed looked at his face, tried for some outrage. He still couldn't kill him." A page later, Exley drives Dieterling to the Pacific Sanitarium in Malibu Canyon. He has one request for the sanitarium's director: "That man taken care of on a locked ward for the rest of his life." In this way, Dieterling becomes a staging-ground for the definitive choice of the drug war era between incarceration and hospitalization. Punishment or pills? Eventually, Ellroy's novel decides that what Dieterling needs isn't capital punishment or even prison, just medical care. The "remedy" for Dieterling's serial killing is "the proper drugs applied for life."[55]

TWO PATHS FOR PATHOLOGY

This climactic burst of sympathy for the guilty white serial killer (about whom Exley wants to feel "some outrage" but can't) is especially jarring for the way that it reverses Exley's earlier decision to kill the three falsely accused Black men. One may quite reasonably conclude from these parallel storylines that Ellroy simply found white illness a more sympathetic cause than Black criminalization. Nevertheless, it's worth pausing to note that these two storylines in *L.A. Confidential* are not merely distorted images of one another. They are literally, if somewhat circuitously, linked. Douglas Dieterling's father is Raymond Dieterling, and "Ray Dieterling was friends with Pierce Patchett—a chemist" whose hobbies include manufacturing the antipsychotic drug that Douglas takes. Douglas Dieterling thus spends his life medicated by homemade drugs produced by Pierce Patchett. This is noteworthy, because Patchett also happens to be the drug supplier who helps mastermind the Nite Owl killings (the primary mystery in *L.A. Confidential*), which were an attempt to corner the greater Los Angeles heroin market. Patchett, then, is both a prescriber of medicine and a supplier of heroin, a chemist who cooks antipsychotics in his spare time when he's not fine-tuning his special recipe for horse ("he's been developing a special blend for years. . . . I've heard it puts regular heroin to shame").[56] He is the medical establishment and the drug trade all in one.

Patchett is thus the thread that connects the two kinds of crime prominently featured in *L.A. Confidential*, serial killing and drug dealing. He links the psychotic killer Dieterling not only to the drug trade but also to the anti-Black violence that surrounds it—Patchett is working for Captain Dudley Smith, a racist who plans to push Patchett's "special blend" of heroin specifically into Black neighborhoods in order to "contain" and "sedate" residents.[57] Not for nothing is Smith's right-hand man named Bud White.

This series of narrative crosshatchings shows how the generic figure of the psychopath was now located at the center of a web of crime, race, and illness that was woven by the War on Drugs. The serial killer Douglas Dieterling gets the medicine for his mental and physiological illness from the same drug manufacturer who is involved in a conspiracy not just to sell illegal drugs but to blame drug-related violence on young Black men. As I have been suggesting throughout this chapter, there were two divergent yet interdependent paths for the idea of pathology in the years Ellroy was writing *L.A. Confidential*. Dieterling represents one of these paths, the wrongly accused suspects the other. Pierce Patchett, meanwhile, walks both of them, aiding in the construction and pathologization of Black criminality while also revealing that medical treatment was indeed a conceivable alternative to warrior policing—provided one was lucky enough, or simply white enough, to get the proper diagnosis.

The serial killer J. T. Saunders in Mosley's *White Butterfly* bears a strong resemblance to Douglas Dieterling. Both are described as physically ill. Both require—and lose access to—medication to manage their conditions. And both become unexpected objects of sympathy for the detectives pursuing them. The difference in Mosley's novel is that Saunders is Black, and he is murdered, not given his medication, by the police. Saunders's alternative fate significantly reframes how we are invited to read *White Butterfly*'s intervention in ongoing debates about crime and illness. It is no accident that Mosley chose to have Saunders diagnosed with syphilis. In a general sense, the choice highlights how racialization has often operated through stereotypes about both illness and sexuality. "White doctors at one time thought that almost all Negroes were rife with venereal disease," one character in *White Butterfly* explains.[58] More specifically, the detail about Saunders's medical condition connects him to the infamous Tuskegee Experiment, the forty-year study run by the United States Public Health Service in which Black men with syphilis were left untreated so that doctors could "observe the course of the disease as it wreaked havoc on its victims."[59] Patients in the Tuskegee study were barred from receiving penicillin or any other treatment that might have helped them manage their disease. The critic Britt Rusert reads the Tuskegee Experiment as emblematic of a "dialectic of social control and social abandonment." She argues, "It was the intensive oversight of this particular population in the Black Belt that justified and obscured their actual abandonment by the state."[60]

The same dialectic is powerfully exemplified by the War on Drugs, where the pathologization of Black urban communities justified both the violent intrusion of police and the violent withdrawal of state services in the form of everything from drug treatment programs to school funding and affordable housing. "As the stigma associated with drug-selling reached a crescendo," writes Kohler-Hausmann, "those ensnared by law enforcement and the drug economy found they were entitled to fewer and fewer rights and services from the state."[61] With the drug war's dialectic of state violence and state abandonment playing out for Mosley as he wrote *White Butterfly* while living in New York City, it becomes much easier to understand what a character like J. T. Saunders was supposed to represent. Saunders is ultimately killed by the cops because he suffered from precisely the mind- and body-ravaging sickness that happens to be the single most famous example of the long, shameful history of African Americans' mistreatment by the public health system. Mosley mobilized the literary cliché of the serial killer character, which flourished directly alongside the real-world devastation of the War on Drugs, as an entry point for thinking about the longer history of race and health care. A kind of racial rewriting of the more famous *The Black Dahlia*—Ellroy's bestselling novel about the unsolved murder of a white woman—*White Butterfly* reimagines the stock serial killer character as an ill Black man abandoned by the state.[62] In doing so, the novel invites us to consider that the secret history of serial killer fiction is the racialized history of American public health. Published at the height of the drug war (in 1992 alone more than one million people were arrested on drug charges), *White Butterfly* sought to show how the U.S. carceral state's tendency to treat addicts and other sick people as criminals needed to be understood as the logical extension of the state's longstanding disinclination, as evidenced in the forty-plus years of the Tuskegee Experiment, to offer adequate medical treatment to Black Americans.

The literary confrontation between addicts and killers, illness and crime, was not limited to conventional crime novels. It appeared across the literature of the late twentieth century, including in some unlikely places. One of these was Don DeLillo's postmodern satire *White Noise* (1985). *White Noise*, narrated by Professor Jack Gladney, is famously concerned with the popularization of psychopharmaceuticals. Less noticed about DeLillo's novel is that this concern is framed by very specific ideas about both drug addiction and serial killing. Early in the novel, Jack's son Heinrich mentions that he is playing correspondence chess with a "fellow in prison" who killed six people. Jack and Heinrich's conversation about the killings quickly turns to the topic of "brain chemistry." As Heinrich explains, "It's all this activity in the brain and you don't know what's you as a person and what's some neuron that just happens to fire or just happens to misfire. Isn't that why Tommy Roy killed those people?"[63] Echoing Ellroy's later reference to "chemical brain imbalance," DeLillo's description of a mass murderer's misfiring neurons and dysregulated brain chemistry similarly indexes how medical and neurological frameworks had begun to remake the popular understanding of criminality.

White Noise isn't just about the brains of serial killers. It's also about what happens to brains that are on drugs. The climax of *White Noise* revolves around the brain chemistry of Jack's wife, Babette, who, her family discovers, is secretly taking an unregulated psychopharmaceutical called Dylar. This causes her daughter Denise to worry, "Is my mother a drug addict?" Jack dismisses the concern, later explaining, "Your mother is not a drug addict. Dylar is not that kind of medication." When Jack says that Dylar is *not that kind of medication*, he does not mean that Dylar doesn't produce addiction. He simply means that it doesn't produce the particular kind of people—poor, nonwhite—Denise associates with the phrase *drug addict*. The precise racial and class meanings of the character type of the drug addict are made abundantly clear when Jack decides to kill Willie Mink, the man who illegally sold Babette the Dylar and who embodies all of those meanings rolled into one. He is a drug dealer, an addict, and one of the novel's only nonwhite characters. (Mink's actual ethnic identity is left unclear; in one of the novel's most cringe-inducing passages, Jack notes that "his skin was the color of a Planter's peanut" and wonders, "Was he Melanesian, Polynesian, Indonesian, Nepalese, Surinamese, Dutch-Chinese?"[64])

After getting his revenge on the dealer-addict Willie Mink, Jack feels some remorse and decides to take him to the hospital. While driving around looking for an emergency room, Jack says, "I would take whatever they had, even an emergency ward in the worst part of town. This is where we belonged, after all, with the multiple slash wounds, the entry and exit wounds, the blunt instrument wounds, the traumas, the overdoses."[65] Having become the kind of person who goes to a motel to murder a drug dealer, Jack concludes that he now belongs in the "worst part of town," by which he clearly means the inner city: a place, as he imagines it, where emergency clinics are inundated with precisely the kinds of drug-related violence (shootings, stabbings, overdoses) that the public associated with racially segregated urban areas. Put simply, Jack's pursuit of Mink has taken him into the urban teeth of the War on Drugs.

Meanwhile, one cannot help but be struck by the contrast between the drug-dealing Mink and the serial killer whom Jack and Heinrich were discussing earlier. These two easily overlooked figures in *White Noise* represent parallel instances of the era's distinctive intersection between criminal and medical pathology, even as they indicate the divergent ways that neurobiology could be used to ground conceptions of criminal responsibility and justifiable punishment. Heinrich's pen pal is separated from his agency and responsibility by his own brain chemistry, neurons firing or misfiring beyond his control. By contrast, Jack judges Willie Mink personally responsible for distributing the very drugs that alter one's brain chemistry (including Mink's own). At once addicted and responsible for the scourge of addiction, and racially disposable to boot, Mink alone is figured in the novel as both deserving of and requiring punishment. Jack obliges, congratulating himself on his shooting of Mink. "I was pleased to see how well it was going," he thinks during the assault.[66]

Mark Seltzer has described serial killer modernity as a cultural "addiction" to "addictive violence."[67] Yet he never mentions what the politics of addiction really meant in the 1980s and '90s, the crucial decades when the figure of the addict fully shifted from a case study in medical treatment to an emblem of pathological criminality—"from being considered *diseased* to being cast *as the disease*," as Kohler-Hausmann put it. What I've tried to demonstrate in this section is how the literary figure of the serial killer gave authors an opportunity to sort through the public health issues that were deeply entangled with the racial stereotypes of the War on Drugs. With those issues now more vividly in view, we may conclude that the signature problem of the late-twentieth-century crime novel was less that readers were "addicted" to reading about violent crime, and more that they were swept up in a cultural moment when the very difference between crime and addiction was in the process of being swept away.

HOSPITAL DRAMA

The serial killer, I've suggested, served as a kind of funhouse mirror for the figure of the racialized drug addict. But this was not the only way that the politics of the drug war entered into the era's crime fiction. Many novels offered more direct depictions of the debates surrounding drug criminalization and addiction treatment. No one offered franker fictional commentary on these issues than Barbara D'Amato, whose mystery novel *Hardball* (1990) revolves around the murder of a Chicago activist who has been advocating for drug decriminalization. D'Amato served as president of the Mystery Writers of America from 1999 to 2000; *Hardball* was the first entry in her Cat Marsala series. As the novel opens, the journalist Catherine (Cat) Marsala attends a conference at the University of Chicago to interview Louise Sugarman, a sweet, elderly woman who leads an organization working to decriminalize drugs in Illinois. At the conference, a bomb explodes, killing Sugarman and wounding Marsala, who vows to get to the bottom of what happened. The rest of the novel is partly an investigation into Sugarman's murder and partly an interrogation of her politics. The process ends up changing Marsala's mind: "I went into this whole project thinking, sure, drugs are evil; they should be illegal. I mean, it was a *given*. Now I'm not so sure." She begins the book believing that "Drugs are one of the plagues of modern times" and that decriminalization "sounded dangerous." She ends it with a more skeptical question: "This war on drugs. Is it working?" But D'Amato was interested in giving voice to all sides of the issue. Thus, over the course of the novel, Marsala listens to arguments from an economist who believes criminalization has "created a pusher class" by artificially elevating drug prices; a schoolteacher who has seen firsthand how drug use wrecks families; a psychiatrist who believes young people shouldn't be punished for risk-taking; and a police captain who is "mad" at what the drug war "is doing to the black community."[68]

In the end, Marsala discovers that Sugarman was killed by two organizations working in cahoots: the Chicago Mafia, which the novel claims stood to lose a lot of money if drugs were legalized, and the leader of an antidrug group called PASA (Parents Against Drug Abuse), which the mob was secretly funding. *Hardball* thus provocatively depicts the moral crusade against drugs as a front for murderous economic interests. But what should everyday readers think about drug laws? The novel repeatedly returns to one talking point in particular: that "addiction—any addiction—is a medical problem, not a criminal problem." Addiction is an illness. Even two of the novel's staunchest pro-criminalization characters agree, each referring to drug use as a "plague" that is "worse than AIDS." A public health problem surely requires a public health solution, not "stronger laws" and "stiffer penalties." "You treat a medical problem with medical arrangements," one character says reasonably.[69]

In fact, D'Amato goes to great lengths to point out that we already do this with one addiction in particular: alcoholism. Two separate scenes in the novel involve Marsala spending time with an alcoholic man who drinks himself into a stupor. One of the men is a cop who runs the city's drug task force and drunkenly admits that the drug war is a farce; he'd rather be arresting "somebody who really hurts people." The other man is Marsala's boyfriend. When he relapses, she calls his sponsor to come help. The sponsor reminds her, "It's a disease. Treat it, don't fight it."[70] Written as a direct response to the early years of the War on Drugs, *Hardball* implores its readers to extend the same kind of grace to other kinds of addicts, to stop fighting them and start treating them.[71]

A number of late-twentieth-century crime novels channeled the unfolding saga of the drug war into stories about medical treatment, health care, and hospitals. In Block's *A Walk Among the Tombstones*, a drug trafficker whose daughter has been kidnapped confesses that the only reason he continues to deal drugs is his sick wife's "hospital bills, the doctors, my God, what it cost."[72] Meanwhile, *Hardball* makes a pitch for the importance of hospitals in its opening pages, as Marsala distances herself from the traditional detective's antipathy toward health care institutions: "In all the mystery novels I read—and I read lots; they relax you at the end of a ghastly day the way nothing else ever does—the heroine or hero, badly injured, is always raring to get out of the hospital. . . . Such was not my instinct."[73] Taking seriously her convalescence and enjoying being cared for, Marsala cannot relate to the desire to "get out of the hospital," an institution she warmly embraces. Several other of the decade's fictional detectives investigated a similar set of attachments.

Both the politics of addiction treatment and the economics of hospitals play central roles in Sue Grafton's *C Is for Corpse* (1986), the third book in her blockbuster Alphabet series. Detective Kinsey Millhone has been hired by Bobby Callahan, a young man suffering from amnesia after a car accident who thinks someone is trying to kill him. To solve the case, Millhone must navigate Bobby's wealthy white family, including his stepsister Kitty, who is a drug addict. When Millhone first visits the Callahan home, Kitty overdoses, and the family finds "a stash of pills that would have felled an elephant. They were in a Ziploc bag, maybe two hundred capsules: Nembutals, Seconals, blue-and-orange Tuinals, Placidyls, Quaaludes." Kitty, according to her stepmother, has "been stoned since she walked in my front door."[74] In this way, she is the veritable poster child for what the historian Matthew D. Lassiter calls "the suburban imperatives" of the War on Drugs, which "positioned white middle-class youth as innocent victims" who had to be protected not only from dangerous inner-city dealers but also from the harsh criminal drug laws designed to target those dealers.[75] The white suburban drug user was a key component in the complex architecture of the drug war, justifying the expansion of police power in urban areas while showcasing the medical alternative to that power in suburban neighborhoods, where public health campaigns like "Just Say No" were localized.[76] African Americans caught up in the urban drug war went to prison; white users and dealers in the suburbs went to rehab.

Antidrug public health campaigns in the suburbs and militarized policing in segregated urban neighborhoods were two sides of the same coin. In Grafton's telling, the hospital is a space that captures both sides at once. That's because it plays a crucial role in sorting the ill from the criminal, the white from the nonwhite, and the middle class from the poor. Sure enough, Kitty is sent to the hospital after her overdose, where Millhone expects to find that she has been "admitted to Detox." But she hasn't been; instead, she's been placed in a "locked psychiatric ward."[77] A site where choices about medical treatment intersect and sometimes overlap with choices about imprisonment, the hospital interests Grafton precisely insofar as it has the capacity to hold these two opposing faces of the drug war—the suburban and the urban, the medical and the carceral—in view at the same time.

Grafton's novel is thoroughly obsessed with hospitals. Bobby had tried and failed to get into medical school, so his mother helped him land a part-time job at the Santa Teresa Hospital, locally known as St. Terry's, where he worked in medical records and later as a "clerk-typist in Pathology." Bobby was thus at one point employed in the same hospital where Kitty is now imprisoned. Grafton lays out all of this with an eye toward the town's broader transformation at the hands of a growing health care industry. Sitting in a bar near St. Terry's, Millhone observes that "the area has by now been infiltrated by medical buildings, clinics, convalescent homes, pharmacies, and various other suppliers to the health-care industry, including a mortuary two blocks away to service folk when all else fails." The health care boom that has literally changed the landscape of Santa Teresa is at

TWO PATHS FOR PATHOLOGY

heart a boom in real estate development and private industry. As such, it hastened the disappearance of more accessible kinds of state-sponsored medical care. As Millhone discovers, the pathology department where Bobby worked operated partly out of "the morgue out in the old county medical facility"—a facility that had otherwise been abandoned in lieu of the privatized health care options that sprang up around St. Terry's:

> County General had once been a flourishing medical facility, designed to serve the entire Santa Teresa community. It was secondarily earmarked as the treatment center for the indigent, funded through various social-services agencies. As the years passed, it came to be associated with the underprivileged: welfare recipients, illegal aliens, and all the unfortunate victims of Saturday-night crime sprees. Gradually, County General was shunned by both the middle-class and the well-to-do. Once MediCal and Medicare came into effect, even the poor opted for St. Terry's and other local private hospitals, turning this place into a ghost town.

Grafton depicts the abandonment of state-run health facilities as an effort on the part of the upper and aspiring classes to distance themselves from the welfare recipients, street crime victims, and immigrants who ostensibly crowd the hallways of County General. "The very air" of County General "was permeated with abandonment and neglect," Millhone opines when she visits.[78] The neglect registers what Grafton renders here as a kind of *health care white flight*, as middle- and upper-class whites avoid clinics and hospitals that serve the racialized ("illegal aliens") and criminalized ("victims of Saturday-night crime sprees") poor.

All of this ties back, in a roundabout way, to Bobby's case. One night Bobby leaves Millhone a message on her answering machine with a pivotal clue about his case: "Hi, Kinsey. This is Bobby . . . One thing came to me. I know this doesn't make much sense, but I thought I'd pass it on anyway. I think the name Blackman ties into this. Somebody Blackman. I don't know if that's who I gave the little red book to or the guy who's after me." Millhone runs with it: "I reached in my top drawer for the telephone book and hauled it out. There was one Blackman listed, an S. . . . Maybe Sarah, or Susan, or Sandra Blackman knew Bobby and had his little red book." The novel keeps up this charade for more than a hundred pages, as Millhone dutifully tries to track down the owner of this mysterious surname

("Have you ever heard the name Blackman? S. Blackman? Anybody Blackman?") to no avail.⁷⁹ In the end, as you've probably been able to guess, no one has "heard the name Blackman" because it isn't a name at all. It's a racial description. Bobby had simply written down: *Black man*. The particular Black man Bobby is talking about is not even a living person. He is the corpse referenced in the novel's title.

This corpse is the thread that braids together Grafton's story of the abandonment of public health infrastructure with the story of racial criminalization. Because the abandoned and neglected County General hospital no longer serves the living of the Santa Teresa community, it now serves the dead as an overflow morgue. The morgue stores mostly "indigents," as an attendant explains to Millhone: "A couple of 'em are John Does we're holding in hopes we'll get a positive I.D. . . . Two we've had around for years. Franklin and Eleanor." Franklin—one of the unclaimed, unidentified bodies that has been abandoned to an already abandoned public hospital—is the Black man Bobby mentions on Millhone's answering machine. Once Millhone puts all this together, she goes to the morgue to find Franklin's body, which contains, quite literally, the solution to Bobby's predicament. Bobby had stumbled across a blackmail plot involving a missing gun, and Millhone now finds it in the most unexpected of places, and only after a crash course in amateur radiology enables her to operate the morgue's X-ray machine: "In the center of Franklin's belly was the solid white silhouette of a handgun."⁸⁰ Yes, you're reading that right. Bobby hid the missing gun in an abandoned hospital . . . inside the corpse of an indigent African American man . . . who is named after FDR.

"What did the corpse of a black man have to do with the murder of Dwight Costigan and the blackmailing of his former wife?" Millhone wonders earnestly.⁸¹ We might ask ourselves the same question! What sense are we supposed to make of this truly astonishing plot twist, in which what had seemed a standard mass-market mystery novel content to spin a yarn of blackmail and murder among the white coastal elite suddenly turns out to revolve around the fact that a white handgun has been physically implanted inside a Black body stored at a former public hospital?

Published the same year that Reagan signed the Anti-Drug Abuse Act, which devoted almost four billion dollars to the War on Drugs, most of it for local police departments, *C Is for Corpse* was an attempt to highlight the major social antagonisms—between rich and poor, suburban and urban, and white and Black—that were expressed through drug policy.[82] It was also an effort to explain how those divisions might have their roots in a longer history of social welfare and public health. Not for nothing are the two unidentified bodies stored at the morgue named Franklin and Eleanor, as if to say that the birth of the War on Drugs can be traced all the way back to the death of the New Deal order, and to the collapse of the array of social services that once promised to care for the poor, not punish them. (Of related interest is Roosevelt's decision, under political pressure, to remove national health insurance from the 1935 Social Security Act; he had planned to make universal health care "his next great political crusade" before he died.[83]) For Grafton, writing in the first years of the drug war's official launch, what the death and abandonment of "Franklin and Eleanor" symbolizes is the fateful shift, over the second half of the twentieth century, from welfare programs to crime control. Grafton's repeated descriptions of the demise of public health infrastructure and her allusions to addiction's contradictory management through both treatment and imprisonment (detox versus the locked ward) culminate in the discovery of an anonymous Black body into which a white person has inserted a white gun. Putting these pieces together, we could say that Franklin embodies both the procedures of racial criminalization and the defunding of public health institutions that worked hand in hand to propel the War on Drugs.

At the center of this complicated symbolic tangle is the pathologist Dr. Fraker, who is unmasked as the novel's villain. Dr. Fraker killed Bobby for discovering his blackmail scheme; he also planted the bag of pills in Kitty's drawer in order to get her locked up. Kitty—the white suburban drug addict—thus turns out to have more in common with Franklin than it might appear. Both symbolize the ways in which anxieties about drugs and guns are artificially affixed to certain kinds of bodies. One body is stored in a public hospital that has been abandoned, the other brought to a private hospital that treats her like a prisoner. Kitty represents her era's exemplary white suburban victim in one way (her family calls an ambulance, not the police) but not another (she is locked up, not sent to a treatment program). To be sure, Grafton is in no position to undo the difference between urban and suburban drug policy. But she does make Franklin and Kitty curiously parallel case studies in how bodies that enter the health care system are subject to the punitive whims of an institution that covertly traffics in criminalization and that is primed to see drug abuse as a proxy for race. By making Dr. Fraker the real criminal of her novel, Grafton makes sure we don't miss the point. In *C Is for Corpse*, it's not racial or behavioral pathology that kills people. It's the pathologist.

Throughout *C Is for Corpse*, Millhone has a mantra she repeats several times. It is meant to remind her, and us, of the fundamental difference between illness and crime. "Diseases don't require an underlying motivation in the same way homicide does," she explains at one point. At another: "Disease is neutral. Homicide's not."[84] This seemingly unobjectionable bit of common sense acquires a sharper edge when we read it in the context of the nation's drug war, which Grafton was closely observing.[85] The War on Drugs had just recently transformed addiction into a crime (one that was closely tied, in the popular imagination, to homicide). Distinguishing crime from disease was therefore a task that had only become necessary after the recent wave of antidrug legislation, which demonstrated the federal government's willingness to mistake one for the other.

One year after *C Is for Corpse* hit shelves, Sara Paretsky published *Bitter Medicine* (1987), which took Grafton's critique of for-profit hospitals a step further. *Bitter Medicine* imagines a private hospital so hell-bent on protecting itself from a malpractice suit that it hires a Latino gang to kill a doctor who has knowledge of the malpractice. Early in the novel, Paretsky's series detective V. I. Warshawski says that the violence taking place in Chicago is "like a cholera epidemic" that can't be "cured" by a single person; instead, it's the kind of situation for which "you'd call in the state public-health people and leave it to them." Her friend, a doctor, appreciates the analogy: "Maybe the epidemic of gang violence is too big for anyone, even the state, to solve." If gang violence was really an epidemic, then it makes sense to think of detective work as a kind of health care work. *Bitter Medicine* argues exactly that. At one point, Warshawski's boyfriend comments that her job sounds "a lot like medicine." Later, Warshawski infiltrates the evil hospital by literally dressing up as a doctor.[86]

Paretsky clearly understood herself to be writing at a moment when medical care and crime control were increasingly hard to tell apart. In her novel, the conflation flows in both directions. On one hand, gang violence is an epidemic that can only be solved by hospitals and other large public health institutions; on the other, hospitals, engaged in their own crimes, are now directly hiring gangs to help cover them up. Consequently, an

TWO PATHS FOR PATHOLOGY

investigator like Warshawksi has to think a bit like a doctor and a bit like a detective as she battles both corrupt hospital administrators and racialized street criminals who are repeatedly described as "sociopaths," "hoodlums," "punks," and "creeps." Again, one particular word does much of the heavy lifting to link these two different kinds of crime and two different ways of characterizing criminals. The word is *pathology*. It's a word Warshawski should know. As one of the detective's friends tells her, "You'd be a good pathologist, Vic."[87]

Yet another hospital-themed crime novel of the time was Richard Price's *Freedomland* (1998). No writer did more to popularize the category of "literary crime fiction" than Price, whose lengthy, stand-alone novels eschewed traditional mystery conventions and aspired to a pseudo-ethnographic level of realist detail. His 1992 novel *Clockers* had already been turned into a film by Spike Lee and would soon be known as one of the main inspirations behind David Simon's TV show *The Wire*, for which Price became a regular writer. *Freedomland* was less positively received, but it is the stranger and more interesting book, focused less on humanizing the figure of the Black criminal (which *Clockers* endeavored to do in a way that some found patronizing—as the author Ishmael Reed clearly did when he dismissed Price as someone "who has made a fortune writing fake ghetto books"[88]) than on cataloging the way such a figure is invented and circulated as a racial fiction in the first place. *Freedomland* is about a white woman named Brenda Martin who turns up at an emergency room one night claiming to have been carjacked by a Black man who threw her out of the car and drove off with her young son in the backseat. After roughly 450 pages, Brenda admits that the story is bullshit. She invented a supremely generic Black carjacker ("black male, five foot ten to six feet tall, shaved head"[89]) in order to cover up the fact that her son Cody had overdosed on Benadryl one night due to her own negligence; she buried him herself. *Freedomland*, in other words, is literally a story about the white invention of Black criminality. Perhaps in that sense it will be remembered as Price's one great work of metafiction.

Freedomland opens with a view of one hospital—"the Dempsey Medical Center, vast, Gothic, and half shut down, the emergency room entrance shedding the only eye-level light before the city hit the river"—and its climactic scene, in which Brenda confesses to making up the story about the carjacker, takes place on the grounds of another. This second hospital is the fictional William Howard Chase Institute for the Mentally and Physically Incapacitated, which operated from 1904 until the early 1970s. In its early years, the privately run Chase Institute was "the standard by which all other rehabilitation facilities were judged," but during the Great Depression it went bankrupt and was taken over by the state of New Jersey. At that point, it became "a surly and abusive little corner of hell" that was "overpopulated and understaffed" and ruled by cruel attendants "in the same intimate way that prisons are owned by the guards." The final analogy is not an accident; Price repeats it a page later, describing Chase's three thousand patients as "imprisoned" at the facility. What does it mean to describe a hospital as functioning in "the same way that prisons" do, as a site of overpopulation, incapacitation, and "murderous abuse?"[90] It means, as I've been arguing throughout this chapter, being attuned to a historical moment when people in need of clinical medical care—from addicts to AIDS patients—were more likely to be treated as criminals.

Framed by depictions of two different failing medical centers, one shuttered and one "half shut down," *Freedomland* is about the increasing interchangeability of prisoners and patients, the criminal and the ill. The War on Drugs persistently conflated Black crime with Black sickness, to return to Murakawa's instructive way of phrasing it. Price renders this conflation in several ways, including through the fictional history he bestows on the Chase Institute—whose collapse "in the summer of 1967," leading to "weeks of national media coverage" and eventually "hearings, investigations, audits, and commissions," seems an intentional echo of the 1967 Newark rebellion, a major event in the early years of the War on Crime that was extensively covered in the media and that led to a series of riot commissions (as discussed in chapter 2).[91] Dempsey, the fictional city where *Freedomland* and several others of Price's novels are set, happens to be based on Newark. If the inmates at Chase are meant to serve as allegorical stand-ins for the rioters in Newark, this is because *Freedomland* understands that the history of Black criminalization—a history that connects the rebellions of the 1960s to Brenda's fake carjacker story—can no longer be separated, at the height of a war on drug addiction, from the history of institutionalized medicine.

In the 1990s, crime and illness were regularly covered in the media as if they were a single issue. "Media reports on early death in black American communities now routinely yoke together AIDS, teen homicide, and infant mortality," one scholar observed at the time.[92] Just so, in *Freedomland*, Price depicts the Armstrong housing project, where Brenda's fake Black criminal is purported to live, as a space of both rampant criminality and widespread health problems. "At any given time there were always a goodly number of Armstrong tenants checked into the medical center," Price writes, including "two relatively young women . . . battling AIDS-related illnesses, and an older, heavier woman who suffered from diabetes."[93] A passage like this certainly does little to dislodge the era's malicious stereotypes about the pathologies of Black communities. But it does call our attention to the way that medical and carceral institutions collaborate in managing marginalized populations who have been labeled, in one way or another, pathological. No wonder Brenda's climactic confession—in which she admits to inventing yet another story about Black criminal pathology— takes place on the grounds of an abandoned hospital that was once indistinguishable from a prison.

As crime writers, Price and Grafton aren't often talked about in the same breath. Yet an unforgettable image connects *Freedomland* back to *C Is for Corpse*. When Brenda first enters the ER at the start of Price's novel, she sees an "overweight young black man on the gurney directly across the room" and is "unable to look away." The man is barefoot, and Brenda "stared at the pale-skinned soles of his feet as if hypnotized by this hidden whiteness."[94] Where Kinsey Millhone sees a "solid white silhouette" when X-raying a Black body housed in an abandoned morgue, Brenda glimpses a "hidden whiteness" in the feet of a Black man lying on a gurney in the Dempsey Medical Center. These remarkably similar images of *hidden whiteness* concealed in hospitalized Black bodies invite several interpretations. One thing we are surely meant to see in both novels is white society's role in cultivating the fictions of racial pathology that drove the War on Drugs—fictions that relied on the willful misreading of ill people as criminals. On a more practical level, there is the fact that hidden whiteness is the answer to each book's mystery. The secret guilt of both Brenda (in *Freedomland*) and Dr. Fraker (in *C Is for Corpse*) is initially projected onto Black men. Finally, though, we may decide that the hidden whiteness that informs these novels actually refers to Grafton and Price themselves. Here were two white liberal crime writers attempting to depict the drug war as the calamitous product of white-authored fictions about Black crime—yet sharply aware that their own books could reasonably be described in similar terms.

What did the racial drama of the hospital mean to writers working in other genres at the time? Consider a famous work by one of the most celebrated science fiction writers of the late twentieth century, Octavia Butler. Technically classed as a novelette, "The Evening and the Morning and the Night" (1987) was first published in the fiction magazine *Omni* and was nominated for several major science fiction awards, including the Nebula. It tells the story of a new illness called Duryea-Gode disease, or DGD, which has created a new kind of social stigma and fear. The disease "has inspired restrictive laws, created problems with jobs, housing, schools." Sufferers are considered dangerous and frequently locked away. Facilities for patients—"state-approved, custodial-care places"—are sites of abuse and neglect; often, they resemble "prisons." The main symptoms of the disease are "suicide or murder," and sufferers account for a larger-than-average "share of criminals."[95] The disease is passed down from parents to children. It is the result of taking a particular drug.

"The Evening and the Morning and the Night" has been read incisively by critics as a text about AIDS, disability, and race.[96] Yet it is hard to shake the sense that this particular way of recounting its plot—which highlights the intersection of illness, homicide, drugs, and the effects of drug use on unborn children—sounds suspiciously like the moral panic over crack, which was a major part of the culture of the War on Drugs as it ramped up in the years when Butler was completing her story.[97] The critic Sami Schalk points out the clear "connection between DGD institutions and prisons," while Butler herself has explained that the story emerged from her "ongoing fascinations with biology, medicine, and personal responsibility"—a set of concerns that, in pairing the medical with the juridical, aptly capture the contradictions of crime policy during the drug war.[98] I am not trying to say that it matters a great deal whether we label "The Evening and the Morning and the Night" *science fiction* or *crime fiction*. I am saying that, without understanding its relation to the ideologies of crime, race, and drug use that were flourishing at the time, we won't get the full picture of what Butler's story was about.

While Butler's invention of DGD had several real-world sources, there are key aspects of her description of the disease that tie it to the War on Drugs.[99] One character describes DGD as an illness of "self-destructiveness," while the repeated emphasis on self-mutilation—an impulse the text describes as a desperate attempt to dig your way out of your own skin—sounds a lot like the physiology of withdrawal. Most evocatively, we are told that sufferers of the disease "all drifted—went off into a world of their own and stopped responding to their surroundings," like a user of crack or heroin. (Even the constant swirl of *d*s and *g*s from the story's two most repeated words—*DGD* and *Dilg*—seem meant to conjure a society that has been fully immersed in an ambient atmosphere of drug use.) Finally, it is worth noting that the specific thing that "makes people afraid" of DGD patients is not the fear of contagion. It is the fear of violence. What it means to be sick in "The Evening and the Morning and the Night" is to be stricken with the impulse to hurt yourself and others. This is why the narrator admits that "we did produce our share of criminals," and it is why she says—in an especially telling metaphor—that a "maximum security prison wouldn't have been as potentially dangerous" as a DGD ward.[100]

In this way, Butler's story narrates the criminalization of illness that, this chapter has sought to show, was part and parcel of the drug war. "Evening" is a story in which being sick literally makes a person a criminal. One such criminal is the narrator's father, a sufferer of DGD who passed it on to her: "Dad killed Mom then skinned her completely. . . . It was an especially bad example of the kind of thing that makes people afraid of us."[101] The gruesomeness of this passage would not be out of place in a Thomas Harris novel, nor would the story's more general interest in the genetics of extreme violence. Yet Butler ultimately takes things in a different direction. Her story is not a sci-fi serial killer narrative (though at times it seems like it could be). It's a story about rehab.

Indeed, it is easy to overlook the fact that the story's single plot arc involves two prospective patients touring a private medical clinic. "Evening" follows the unnamed narrator and her boyfriend, Alan, both "double DGDs" (a more extreme manifestation of the disease inherited not from one parent but from both), as they tour the Dilg clinic, a beautiful property "where not only the patients but much of the staff has DGD." The patients at Dilg spend their time making things. "Our people work instead of tearing at themselves or staring into space," the clinic's director, Beatrice, tells them. "It's only a stopgap, I know. Genetic engineering will probably give us the final answers, but for God's sake, this is something we can do now!"[102] This feels to me like a key moment where Butler abandons the pretense of writing speculative fiction (this is a story that quite pointedly *doesn't* imagine the future answers proffered by genetic engineering) and instead turns her attention to the murky realities of addiction, criminalization, and imprisonment that were then becoming a starkly visible presence in the greater Los Angeles area where Butler lived. The private hospital at the center of "The Evening and the Morning and the Night" presents itself as "something we can do now": something to combat the twin failures of the criminal justice system and the health care system to manage an illness that looks like a crime. What exactly a place like Dilg can do now depends on the double meaning of *rehab* as both a place for treating addiction and an abandoned aim of criminal justice. In the end, "The Evening and the Morning and the Night" is an attempt to imagine what it would look like not only for people who are ill but also for people who are criminals to have access to humane institutions whose aim is to rehabilitate them.

If hospitals became a dominant setting for crime novels in the late twentieth century—I haven't even had time to mention Mary Wings's *She Came Too Late* (1987) or Linda Fairstein's *Likely to Die* (1997) or many others—this had everything to do with the conflict between medical and carceral institutions during the War on Drugs. The drug war functioned by selectively conflating illness with criminality. Hospitals held out the hope of a more accurate diagnosis concerning what was and wasn't crime—not to mention the possibility of offering a therapeutic rather than punitive response to it. But they also ran the risk of lending official cover to bankrupt ideas about criminal and racial pathology. Some crime novelists saw hospitals as bastions of healing; others worried that they might just be prisons by another name. Then there's the persistent question of privatization to which these authors keep returning. Butler and Price valorized the shifting of neglected government-run health facilities into private hands, while Grafton and Paretsky depicted for-profit hospitals as downright deadly, criminal in their own right. In both cases, though, an important truth was being aired. The federal government was the most prominent face of the War on Drugs. But the drug war was not exclusively a government affair. It had as much to do with the forces of privatization, deregulation, and deindustrialization that at that very moment were dramatically reorganizing American society. The private hospital was a bellwether.[103]

As these writers grasped, it was not only a site where criminalization had to contend with other forms of diagnosis and treatment. It was also itself a symptom of declining economic health.

DEINDUSTRIALIZING THE CRIME NOVEL

Thus far I've sought to show how a wide range of literary texts from the 1980s and '90s were prompted by the War on Drugs to reconsider the relation between crime and illness. At this time, the illness of addiction was both heavily criminalized and deeply racialized. Treatment programs and public health campaigns were reserved for wealthier suburbs, while merciless drug laws and invasive police surveillance were unleashed on poorer urban areas. And yet, for all of that, it was not simply the abandonment of drug treatment programs that led to the imprisonment of millions of people and devastated communities of color. It was not solely public health failures that fueled the furious engine of mass incarceration, and it was not the criminalization of addiction alone that drove the federal War on Drugs, which was, it is important to understand, about more than just drugs.

The drug war was also an economic fix—a response to what is often called "the long downturn," which transformed the United States after 1973, gutting the manufacturing sector, scaling back social services, increasing unemployment, and deepening income inequality. The sociologist Douglas Massey has suggested that the very "character of American poverty changed significantly during the 1970s," becoming at once "more geographically concentrated" and more racially specific.[104] The new character of poverty prompted a new type of government response, which, as the legal scholar Kaaryn Gustafson puts it, "treat[ed] the poor as a criminal class."[105] In practical terms, this meant that welfare policy was increasingly accompanied and finally supplanted by penal policy. The authors of the sober policy analysis *Disciplining the Poor* bring the receipts: "In 1980, the United States spent 58 percent more on AFDC [Aid to Families with Dependent Children] than on jails and prisons; by 1995, U.S. spending on jails and prisons exceeded investments in AFDC (132 percent greater) as well as Food Stamps (69 percent greater)."[106] The radical changes to practices of policing, norms of punishment, and the scale of imprisonment implemented through the drug war thus represented a political solution to an economic problem: the problem of "the crumbling labor market for low-skilled workers" in the 1980s and '90s.[107] The problem was most acute in working-class Black communities. Peter Ikeler and Calvin John Smiley have called the racial concentration of poverty and job loss in the postwar period "the racialization of unemployment."[108] As the crisis of racialized unemployment worsened in the final decades of the twentieth century, law enforcement supplanted welfare as the primary tool for managing it.

How do intensified policing and increased imprisonment work as anti-poverty measures? Prisons can be a place to "warehouse" a racialized labor reserve that is no longer needed.[109] They can apply a "Keynesian, stabilizing effect" to the economy by "artificially lower[ing] the official unemployment rate."[110] And they can serve—through the "work-enforcing supervision" that takes place under this country's colossal parole system—to force people back into the lowest-waged, most exploitative sorts of jobs.[111] With all this in mind, we may begin to see the War on Drugs in a somewhat different light: as a wide-ranging government response not to illegal drugs alone, but to the deeper conditions of poverty indexed by informal economies such as drug dealing—a punitive reaction not only to shifting ideologies of illness but also to the declining health of inner-city labor markets.

"The need for work is at the heart of any real war on crime," Christian Parenti shrewdly remarks.[112] Did the crime novels of the drug war era grasp this? Frequently they did. Almost all of the novels I've discussed in this chapter depict the discourses of pathology and illness as a vortex swirling around a more elemental void: the absence of jobs. Different authors were inclined to interpret the meaning of this absence in different ways. In *Clockers*, Richard Price seems genuinely conflicted on the question of whether drug dealing constitutes a legitimate career path. The novel's protagonist, Strike, "never considered himself a criminal: clocking was just what he did, what he considered his best shot at having a life, like going to the army or working for UPS." Yet Price remains unsure how far to follow this line of thinking, according to which drug dealing is the one kind of work that remains after other prospects for employment have vanished from neighborhoods like Strike's. Despite the novel's formal attention to the parallel procedures of drug work and cop work (a parallel that would go on to influence shows like *The Wire*), *Clockers* is nevertheless seduced by the neoliberal fantasy that the way to end the War on Drugs is for drug dealers to make better life choices, which would start with choosing to get better jobs. At the very end of the novel, Price sentimentally dramatizes exactly this choice, as Strike finally decides to "get a job" by suppressing his "urge to hustle." By thinking of work in these terms—as a rational choice one makes by conquering one's more criminal urges—Price appears to validate what a beat cop condescendingly tells Strike a few chapters earlier: "You'd rather sell dope than take home a paycheck like a real human being."[113]

Of course, simply being "a real human being" was not the sole prerequisite to getting a steady paycheck if you lived in a racially segregated urban core in the midst of the War on Drugs. Ideas of cultural and criminal pathology have long shaped employers' assumptions about job applicants in postindustrial inner cities.[114] Moreover, "the mark of a criminal record" constitutes its own separate and "powerful barrier to employment," as Devah Pager demonstrates in her seminal study of crime and labor markets. "Mere contact with the criminal justice system," Pager notes, "severely limits subsequent job prospects." One year after leaving prison, more than 75 percent of ex-inmates remain unemployed.[115]

Perhaps that's why Butler's "The Evening and the Morning and the Night" ultimately reads as a story not just about rehab but also about prisoner retraining and reentry: a story about how to put people who have been stigmatized by ideas of racial criminality and pathology back to work. Recall that the director of the Dilg clinic tells the narrator and her boyfriend, "Our people work instead of tearing at themselves or staring into space." A few pages later, the narrator observes of the patients, "It would have been an ordinary scene except that some people had half their faces ruined or had only one hand or leg or had other obvious scars. But they were all in control now. They were working." The ideas of control and focus are paramount for Butler. She is drawn to the idea that a genetic predisposition to violence could be rerouted to a different outlet for obsessive focus: industriousness. "We passed through more workrooms. People painted; assembled machinery; sculpted in wood, stone; even composed and played music.... I watched a woman work quickly, knowledgeably, with a power saw."[116] Ultimately, Dilg reveals itself to be not a hospital at all but a kind of vast utopian workplace. What the narrator sees as she tours the clinic is a vision of how to reincorporate the criminalized sufferers of DGD back into the labor force. Butler's image of an institution capable of rechanneling self-destructiveness into industriousness suggests that what she thinks the systematically criminalized need most is not necessarily treatment. What they need are jobs.

The need for work as well as for work-related benefits informs the narrative arc of *Blanche on the Lam*. Neely's novel begins with Blanche on the run for writing bad checks because of her precarious work situation ("If four of her employers hadn't gone out of town without paying her, she'd have had enough money in the bank to cover the checks"). It ends with her receiving a "job offer" that "made her eyes sparkle." In between, she is mistaken for a different maid sent by a domestic service, which is how she ends up working—under specifically racialized pretenses (the association of Black women with domestic work)—in the house owned by Grace, the book's "sick" serial killer. As for that job offer that arrives in the very last pages of the novel, there's one more thing Blanche needs to negotiate, something that reminds us yet again of the multiple kinds of sickness that shape Neely's novel. "I got kids," Blanche counters. "They need health insurance."[117]

Even the historical crime novels of this period—*L.A. Confidential*, *White Butterfly*, and *Because It Is Bitter, Because It Is My Heart* are all set in the 1950s—are preoccupied with the politics of race and work. In *Because It Is Bitter*, the life of Jinx Fairchild, a budding high school basketball star, is derailed not because he kills Red Garlock but because he discovers that there are no jobs for him in the factory town of Hammond, New York. Here Jinx confronts the racial division of labor in an industrial sector that was about to enter a state of prolonged and precipitous contraction. A new plant is opening in Hammond, but "word's out early on before the new processing plant at National Lead even posts its openings that management isn't hiring blacks except for janitorial work." This isn't surprising to Jinx, who remains haunted by "that humiliation last year about 'Negroes' finally being let in the UAW local, then getting laid off almost as soon as they started work."[118]

Walter Mosley's detective Easy Rawlins has a similar experience. In the first novel in the series, *Devil in a Blue Dress*—published in 1990 and set in 1948—Rawlins has just been fired from his job at a manufacturing plant. "He worked at Champion Aircraft up to two days ago.... They laid him off." This, in fact, is the reason he agrees to take on informal work as a private eye in the first place. As Rawlins's friend Joppy explains, introducing him to the nefarious DeWitt Albright, "Mr. Albright lookin' for a man to do a li'l job, Easy. I told him you outta work an' got a mortgage t'pay."[119] Thus, in Mosley's telling, the very emergence of the Black private investigator as a literary protagonist is made possible by the history of industrial contraction and its consequences for Black workers. Ultimately, the racialized history of deindustrialization represents the solution to a lingering mystery that has been hanging over both Mosley's novel and Oates's: the mystery of why the economic conditions of the 1950s would seem like a relevant topic for a crime writer in the 1990s.

As for *L.A. Confidential*, it approaches this same history from the opposite direction, spotlighting the economic processes that decisively shifted jobs and wealth away from the working class. These processes are land speculation (Raymond Dieterling, the father of serial killer Douglas, made his fortune in Southern California real estate) and financialization. Lo and behold, Pierce Patchett doesn't see himself as a drug dealer at all. In his own words, "I'm a financier."[120]

Patchett's savvy professional rebranding provides one final clue for decoding the brisk ascendence of serial killer fiction. After the ravages of deindustrialization, what is left but the murderousness of high finance? Think less Hannibal Lecter, more Patrick Bateman. In Bret Easton Ellis's infamous serial killer novel *American Psycho* (1991), Bateman's well-known translation of "mergers and acquisitions" into "murders and executions" is first signaled by his own murder of an unhoused Black man whom he tells, "Get a goddamn job."[121] Bateman, you could say, *is* the War on Drugs: not simply because he is a rich white man killing an unemployed Black man (though when you put that way . . .), but in a more precise sense, because he embodies the specific criminal justice priorities of the Reagan era, in which the intensified policing of poor communities of color was part of a broader imperative to de-emphasize white-collar crime and deregulate financial markets.[122] Massive financial deregulation was the Janus face of mass incarceration. As the criminologist John Hagan explains, the Reagan administration simultaneously "demand[ed] increased imprisonment of street criminals and a reduced scrutiny and enforcement in the financial sector," a trade-off that was justified by making white-collar crime appear an "acceptable and expected" fact "in the life of a market."[123] The "acceptable and expected" fact of financialized criminality is a pretty on-the-nose description of Patrick Bateman himself. Recall that the running joke of *American Psycho* is that the other characters in the novel find it impossible to imagine Bateman to be a criminal at all.[124]

Representing the high-water mark of deindustrialization as it wiped out jobs, hollowed out American cities, and produced a racialized swell of unemployed workers, Patrick Bateman—financialized criminal par excellence—was no less central a character in the drama of the War on Drugs than the mythical Black super-predator or the low-level drug dealer. Ellis's uniquely American psychopath—at once white and white-collar—personifies the extended economic crisis of declining productivity, stagnating wages, and disappearing jobs to which financialization was one response and the drug war another.[125] He is also a practical representative of the class that stood to profit most from the wedding of drug criminalization to deregulation, which helped solve the crisis of falling industrial profitability by opening up financial markets to investment bankers like Bateman on one hand and opening up prisons to the poor, the addicted, the out of work, and the racially marginalized on the other. Unable to be seen for the compulsive killer he is, Patrick Bateman is what it looks like for the pathologies of finance capital to be masked by the pathologization of the poor. He is what you get when the terminal sickness of a deindustrialized economy is successfully concealed behind the criminalization of the unemployed and the sick.

5

THE NOVEL IN THE AGE OF MASS INCARCERATION, 1992-2023

> I was too upset to deal with the prison system this morning.
>
> —*HARD TIME* (1999)

PROLOGUE: BENEATH THE PAVING STONES, THE PRISON

In the mid 1970s, a forensic psychiatrist named Roland Jefferson tried his hand at writing a crime novel. The result, *The School on 103rd Street* (1976), was based on recognizable elements of the era's Black radical fiction, including a heroic revolutionary who embodies the tensions of an emergent Black bourgeoisie.[1] Although Jefferson's plot was familiar in its broad strokes, it revolved around one key detail that was at once strikingly original and disturbingly prophetic. *The School on 103rd Street* tells the story of a Black doctor who begins investigating the suspicious death of a teenager in the Los Angeles neighborhood of Watts. With the help of some friends, he discovers that the teenager was killed because he had accidentally stumbled upon an explosive government secret, what the novel dubs "the most frightening discovery in the history of black America": an underground prison facility hidden beneath his neighborhood school. As one character puts it, "A motherfucking *jail*—right here in the community under the motherfucking *school!*"[2]

The novel's heroes quickly realize that there must be more secret prisons spread across the country. They decide "that every city with any sizable black population" could be harboring one. A bit of public-records digging exposes both the expansive scale and the racial specificity of the nation's hidden prison system. The group uncovers "underground prison compounds in the following cities: Detroit, underneath a health clinic on the edge of the ghetto; in Chicago on the West Side beneath a Baptist church... in Bedford-Stuy underneath a tenement house; in Harlem... underneath the new wing of the Harlem hospital." They find more underground prisons beneath a junior high school, a library, a medical clinic, and a "day care center for children of working mothers."[3] The point is hard to miss. Hidden directly beneath schools, health clinics, public housing, and day care centers, prison interpenetrates the social services and public institutions that serve the poor and minority communities of major urban centers.[4] State-funded care turns out to be the alibi for state-funded containment.

Jefferson was not the only novelist writing about prison at this time—Donald Goines and James Baldwin jump to mind—but he stood out in his attempt to portray prison as a large-scale system: a coordinated network of racial containment centers distributed across the country. On one hand, his novel offers a prescient vision of the central role that prison would come to play in managing the racial and class antagonisms of the late twentieth century. On the other hand, the particulars of the novel's plot raise an interesting question. What did it mean, in 1976, to conceive of prison as something that was hidden beneath the façade of American life? What did it mean to represent the prison system as something that needed to be excavated or exposed—as a tool of domination that, being literally concealed underground, most people couldn't see?

Another way to phrase this question is to ask what role prison *did* play in American life in the years when Jefferson wrote *The School on 103rd Street*. In 1972, the total number of people incarcerated in the United States was roughly the same as it had been in 1957, and had been steadily decreasing since the early 1960s. Not only was the prison population in decline; so was public support for prisons. This was the result of a variety of factors, including an increasingly active prisoners' rights movement as well as the writing and activism of Malcolm X, George Jackson, Angela Davis, and other imprisoned Black intellectuals. Calls for prison reform steadily gained traction with the general public. As a result, the prison system faced "a very real crisis of legitimacy" in the early 1970s, as "policymakers temporarily soured on the idea of prison" as a solution to social ills.[5]

THE NOVEL IN THE AGE OF MASS INCARCERATION

Prison's faltering legitimacy came to a head with the uprising at New York's Attica State Correctional Facility in September 1971. Over 1,200 inmates, most of them Black, rose up against the facility's "harsh conditions, capricious rules, and racial discrimination." During the rebellion, prisoners gave prison officials a list of demands that included calls for political and religious freedom, an end to censorship, changes to the parole system, better training for prison guards, and access to education, health care, and "realistic rehabilitation programs for all inmates."[6] Unwilling to negotiate, Governor Nelson D. Rockefeller ordered the retaking of the prison by force. When the standoff was over, thirty-nine people were dead.

The Attica uprising brought a new level of public scrutiny to the prison system. As the historian Heather Ann Thompson explains in *Blood in the Water*, her Pulitzer Prize–winning history of the events, the prison rebellion helped spur "vital victories for prisoners across the country" and revealed "the extraordinary power and possibility of prisoner rights activism."[7] In Attica's immediate aftermath, there was "an outpouring of public and scholarly interest in how to make prisons more humane and in how to reduce the prison population."[8] For a brief yet meaningful moment, the use of prison as a crime control strategy was "viewed with skepticism." In 1973, the National Advisory Commission on Criminal Justice Standards and Goals (a brainchild of the LEAA) suggested freezing new prison construction for ten years.[9]

There was a very real chance at this moment that America was moving toward decarceration. Sadly, the moment was fleeting. Political skepticism toward prison proved temporary. In a bitter irony, even as it demonstrated what prisoner-led activism could accomplish, the Attica rebellion also prompted significant backlash against prison reform, effectively turbocharging the rise of mass incarceration. In the wake of exaggerated stories of prisoner barbarism and intensified fear of the dangers posed by militants and people of color, Attica "directly, albeit unwittingly, helped to fuel an anti-civil-rights and anti-rehabilitative ethos in the United States," Thompson concludes.[10] The unexpected result, as the sociologist David Garland would ruefully remark, is that "in a matter of 30 years," the U.S. prison system went "from being a failed correctional facility, destined for abolition, to being a major and apparently indispensable element of modern social order."[11] Starting in 1973, the total number of people in U.S. state and federal prisons increased *every year* until 2010.

The early 1970s, then, were something like the eye of the carceral storm: a deceptive moment of calm between the federalized transformation of policing in the 1960s and the unprecedented explosion of imprisonment that occurred in the early 1980s. Jefferson's novel aptly captures this transitional moment. It is tempting to read *The School on 103rd Street* as an allegory for a moment when the racial and class dimensions of incarceration were effectively hidden underground, concealed from view for the majority of citizens and commentators who believed the country's reliance on prison was on the wane. But we also need to account for the fact that the novel was predicting a future that, in its own telling, had not yet arrived. As one character puts it upon seeing the underground prison, the U.S. government "would *love* to put that jail to use, just love it!" To state the matter this way is to view the prison system as something ready to be used—but also as something that isn't in use just yet. In the novel, the discovered prison is so brand-new that "the mattresses were still wrapped, the lighting fixtures were taped."[12] The future of racially targeted mass imprisonment, as Jefferson foresaw it, was still in the process of being furnished.

GROWTH MINDSET

This chapter is not about prison in the 1970s. It's about what happened next. To Roland Jefferson, writing in the transitional year of 1976, the idea of a massive network of prisons secretly structuring American society seemed like a future that wasn't yet here. Little did he know it was waiting right around the corner. What Jefferson depicted as the hidden truth of secret prisons would soon be the open secret of America's full-blown prison crisis. This chapter pursues three questions pertaining to that crisis. When did incarceration become a truly mass phenomenon? When did it start to be described as such? And what did it look like when the distinctive historical situation we now call *mass incarceration* finally entered the consciousness of American fiction writers?

The future of imprisonment steadily materialized in the two decades directly following the publication of *The School on 103rd Street*. Between 1976 and 1986, America's prison population doubled. Eight years later, it had doubled again. Between 1994 and 2006, it increased by another

50 percent. In 1993 alone, the United States added more than 100,000 new people to its penal institutions; it managed the same feat again in 1994, and again in 1997. Amid these dizzying increases, the racial demographics of prison changed significantly. White people had made up the main share of the U.S. prison population for the first three-quarters of the twentieth century; by 1989, however, a majority of prisoners were Black.[13] When all was said and done, the total number of people in U.S. prisons and jails had grown from roughly 326,000 in 1970 to a peak of more than 2.3 million in 2008.[14] A total social catastrophe had just unfolded in the span of a single generation, remaking the political, economic, and racial landscape of the United States in the process.

The exponential growth of the prison population was matched, if not fueled, by a frenzy of correctional spending. "Between 1980 and 1995," the sociologist Loïc Wacquant recounts, "the country increased its carceral expenditures sevenfold," initiating a substantial transfer of resources away from social welfare programs. In 1996 President Bill Clinton famously claimed that "the era of big government is over," but this would prove false in one major respect: government-funded prison projects. As Wacquant notes, it would be more accurate to call this *"the era of carceral 'Big Government.'"*[15] The Clinton administration's 1994 Violent Crime Control and Law Enforcement Act put $7.9 billion toward new prison construction.[16] (The crime bill was also meant to include the Racial Justice Act, to help detect racial disparities in capital punishment, but Clinton, afraid the provision would tank the legislation as a whole, dropped it.) Fresh prisons were the country's new "public works," Eric Schlosser suggested in a widely read article for *The Atlantic*: "a 3,100-bed jail in Harris County, Texas; a 500-bed medium-security prison in Redgranite, Wisconsin; a 130-bed minimum-security facility in Oakland County, Michigan; two 200-bed housing pods at the Fort Dodge Correctional Facility, in Iowa; a 350-bed juvenile correctional facility in Pendleton, Indiana; and dozens more."[17] At the state level, the 1980s saw California "embark on the biggest prison construction program in the history of the world," as Ruth Wilson Gilmore meticulously details in her indispensable book *Golden Gulag*. "In less than a decade," Gilmore writes, "the amount of state debt for [California's] prison construction project expanded from $763 million to $4.9 billion." During that time, the California Department of Corrections turned itself "into the state government's largest department."[18] Nationwide, the growth of the penal sector was so extraordinary that, by 1998, state and county correctional operations had become the country's third-largest employer. U.S. prisons and jails now employed more people than either General Motors or McDonald's.[19]

Schlosser's *Atlantic* article helped to popularize the idea of "the prison-industrial complex." Schlosser did not coin the phrase, however. That would be Mike Davis, who warned in 1995 of an "emergent 'prison-industrial complex'" that was gaining a disturbing amount of economic and legislative power. The prison-industrial complex was a "monster that threatens to overpower and devour its creators," Davis wrote, and "its uncontrollable growth ought to rattle a national consciousness now complacent at the thought of a permanent prison class."[20] But people did not seem to be rattled. The monster kept growing. "Prison construction in the United States" had acquired "a seemingly unstoppable momentum."[21] A raft of new crime control legislation helped to fill newly built prison cells.[22] Mass incarceration was here.

Its arrival did not go unnoticed. In the early 1990s, evidence of the distressing human scale of mass incarceration was already starting to circulate. Major newspapers ran stories on the disproportionately high number of Black people being imprisoned under the auspices of new drug laws, and nonprofit groups such as The Sentencing Project began to carefully document the country's worsening prison crisis. The year 1990 was a turning point. As the legal scholar James Forman Jr. explains, that year The Sentencing Project "published a report with an explosive and unprecedented finding: one in four young black men were trapped in the criminal justice system—either through probation, parole, prison, or jail. The next year, the group issued a report showing that the United States had surpassed South Africa and Russia to become the world's largest jailer." According to Forman, "Both reports were widely disseminated and discussed."[23]

The debate sparked by these and similar findings eventually reached the ears of the nation's top lawmakers. In 1992, George H. W. Bush's attorney general, William Barr, penned a government report called *The Case for More Incarceration*. "Build more prisons," Barr recommended. "The problem is too much crime, and the simple fact is that the best way to stop crime is to put criminals in prison."[24] Neither Barr's bloodlust for prison-building nor his casual faith in the effectiveness of incapacitation is particularly surprising; both were commonplace features of tough-on-crime politics in the 1990s.[25] What *is* noteworthy about the report is that Barr had written it as a response to a growing chorus of worries about overimprisonment. The occasion for the report was "all the concern we hear about high incarceration rates for young black men"—concern that Barr was eager to debunk but unable to ignore. "Ask many politicians, newspaper editors, or criminal justice 'experts' about our prisons," Barr wrote in the report's opening paragraph, "and you will hear that our problem is that we put too many people in prison." Barr didn't believe this.[26] But the very fact that he felt compelled to address it is a powerful indication that the view of mass incarceration as a serious social problem was starting to gain public traction.

In 1995, Mike Davis referred to the overuse and overcrowding of the American prison system as "super-incarceration."[27] Similar terms quickly followed. In 2001, David Garland used the phrase *mass imprisonment* to describe "an unprecedented event in the history of the USA and, more generally, in the history of liberal democracy." He reasoned that "an extraordinary phenomenon of this kind deserves a name of its own." He proposed "'mass imprisonment'—a new name to describe an altogether new phenomenon." Garland identified two "defining features" of this phenomenon: "One is sheer numbers. Mass imprisonment implies a rate of imprisonment and a size of prison population that is markedly above the historical and comparative norm for societies of this type. The US prison system clearly meets these criteria." The second "is the social concentration of imprisonment's effects. Imprisonment becomes mass imprisonment when it ceases to be the incarceration of individual offenders and becomes the systematic imprisonment of whole groups of the population." In the U.S. context, that group was "young black males in large urban centres. For these sections of the population, imprisonment has become normalized. It has come to be a regular, predictable part of experience."[28] Immense, systematic, racialized, and normalized: These were the distinguishing characteristics of mass incarceration that marked it off as a unique development in American history.

This chapter details how the "altogether new" scope, scale, and racial character of U.S. mass incarceration became an explicit topic for novelists starting in the 1990s.[29] I map the variety of ways that writers incorporated mass imprisonment into their narratives and worked to cultivate in their readers a particular ethical or affective stance toward prison. That stance steadily evolved over three decades. In the mid 1990s, wrongful-conviction novels by popular writers such as Stephen King and John Katzenbach ruminated on the concept of guilt—primarily the guilt readers themselves could be expected to feel about the increasingly irrefutable racial disparities of mass incarceration. Around the same time, detective novels by genre mainstays such as Michael Nava, Walter Mosley, and Sara Paretsky were preoccupied with a sense of their own complicity: how to narrate both the detective's and the detective genre's longstanding implication in a correctional system now suddenly perceived as irredeemably flawed. In the early 2000s, Sister Souljah and Vickie Stringer helped popularize the genre of street literature, turning women's upward mobility narratives into metafictional cautionary tales about the risk prison increasingly posed to their books' predominately Black female readership. Finally, after 2010, major works by Colson Whitehead, Jesmyn Ward, Margaret Atwood, George Saunders, and Nana Kwame Adjei-Brenyah demonstrate what happened once the topic of mass incarceration became fully entrenched in public discourse: Novelists started writing about the prisons of the past and the prisons of the future. These two contemporary versions of the prison novel reveal an unresolved tension between a sense of historical inevitability and a sense of shared responsibility in reckoning with mass incarceration. Stories of past and future prisons provide opposing ways of answering a pair of lingering questions about the overfilled prisons of our present. Did mass incarceration have to turn out the way it did? Or might we once have had, at some point in the past, the freedom to choose a different future for ourselves?

The archive I assemble in this chapter may strike some readers as idiosyncratic if not incomplete. To be sure, there are a number of compelling ways to take up the topic of the novel in the age of mass incarceration. Some scholars might opt to study writing done by incarcerated people. Others might focus on the recent history of novels set inside prisons. These are both essential lines of inquiry, which I hope my approach in the following pages will be seen to supplement. Here, though, my aim is to figure out how mass incarceration—as a specific historical formation, and as a specific way of talking about that formation—made its way into mainstream fiction, remaking established genres (detective fiction, speculative fiction) and fostering the creation of new ones (street lit) in the process. In his excellent book *From Slave Ship to Supermax*, Patrick Elliott Alexander argues that "mass incarceration is the most critically underexplored allusive framework for the contemporary African American novel."[30] I agree and would add only that, since the 1990s, its significance as a narrative framework has not been limited to African American fiction alone. Building on Alexander's groundbreaking work at the intersection of literary studies and prison studies, the remaining sections of this chapter show how the concept of mass incarceration became central to the evolution of a variety of contemporary genres and literary traditions. It was not until the end of the twentieth century that the enormous growth of the American prison population—which had been occurring, unchecked, for nearly two decades—was widely understood as an indisputable and "altogether new" historical phenomenon. This chapter tells the story of how American novelists slowly but steadily awakened to the fact that they were living in a new world of mass imprisonment, and what happened to the forms of popular fiction once they did.

SONGS OF INNOCENCE

The attorney general who oversaw the creation of the War on Crime was Nicholas Katzenbach. In 1965, Katzenbach chaired the National Commission on Law Enforcement and Administration of Justice, which produced the first of several reports on crime issued during the Johnson administration. Though less well known than the famous 1968 Kerner report, the Katzenbach commission's 1967 report, *The Challenge of Crime in a Free Society*, arguably did more to lay the foundation for the Wars on Crime and Drugs, as its recommendations focused on replacing social programs with increased police presence in Black urban communities.[31] When turning to the issue of how justice was dispensed in American courtrooms, the authors of *The Challenge of Crime* drew important attention to the "overwhelming evidence of institutional shortcomings" in the legal system and to the general impression of "assembly line justice."[32] But when it came to making it easier for imprisoned people to appeal their convictions, the Katzenbach report was torn between the rights of the accused and the desire for closure: "Finality, the conclusive end of a case, is desirable, but so is providing a man in prison or under sentence of death every opportunity to press his claim that he is wrongfully held."[33] There was also the danger of recidivism to consider. On its opening page, the report notes the public's tendency to blame "parole boards that release prisoners who resume their criminal activities."[34]

The problem of how to balance the rights of the "wrongfully held" with the public's persistent fear of released prisoners only intensified in the ensuing decades as the prison population swelled far beyond what Katzenbach and his collaborators could have imagined. By 1992, a different attorney general was walking a less nuanced line. "When convicted offenders have been placed on probation or released early from prison, many of them have committed new crimes," William Barr asserted without evidence. The era's obsession with recidivism was most vividly demonstrated by the George H. W. Bush campaign's infamous 1988 Willie Horton TV ad, which inflamed public fears about releasing Black people from prison. For his part, Barr was confident that the growing number of people being sent away to prison all belonged there. "If we were actually over-incarcerating," he reasoned, "surely we could find numerous prisoners who do not deserve to be in prison."[35]

In fact, in those very years, observers found many such prisoners. During the prison buildup of the 1980s and '90s, exaggerated stories of spectacular recidivism began to vie for public attention with sobering accounts of wrongful imprisonment. The year 1989 marked the first time that an American was exonerated based on DNA evidence.[36] Several more DNA-based exonerations quickly followed. In 1992, the lawyers Barry Scheck and Peter Neufeld founded the Innocence Project, with the mission of using newly available DNA evidence to reopen old cases and exonerate wrongfully convicted prisoners. By 1995, there were already twenty-eight instances of DNA exonerations in the United States. Scheck and Neufeld described these cases of scientifically-confirmed wrongful imprisonment as "just the tip of a very deep and disturbing iceberg."[37]

The Innocence Project and the Willie Horton ad were two sides of the same coin, representing inverse responses to a single question that preoccupied the public at a pivotal moment in the prison boom: Did everyone in the rapidly growing prison population truly deserve to be there? Ultimately, the metastasis of mass incarceration in the 1990s came to be defined in the popular imagination by the tension between these two directly contradictory feelings: the fear of locking innocent people up and the fear of letting guilty ones out.

From Scott Turow's *Presumed Innocent* (1987) to Barry Siegel's *Actual Innocence* (1999) (which came out one year before a different book called *Actual Innocence* written by Scheck and Neufeld), this was a moment when novelists and novel-readers were keen to figure out how effective the legal system was in distinguishing the innocent from the guilty. In this section, I delve into two of the most popular and fascinating wrongful-imprisonment novels of the period: *The Green Mile*, by the indefatigable Stephen King; and *Just Cause*, by the reporter turned novelist John Katzenbach—who, in a strange twist, happens to be Nicholas Katzenbach's son. One might suppose that writing about the potential innocence of the incarcerated was a way to make readers confront the "disturbing iceberg" of false imprisonment and perhaps even indict the prison system as a whole.[38] For Katzenbach and King, however, the false imprisonment narrative served a more complex function. Their novels were not intended to call attention to the failings of a system that imprisons the innocent. They were about absolving a predominately white readership of the guilt they might feel for continuing to support that system despite its flaws. *Just Cause* and *The Green Mile* worked simultaneously to criticize mass incarceration and to naturalize it. These two hugely popular stories about misconstrued guilt were ultimately ways of staging, and assuaging, their readers' guilty feelings about the injustices that were now widely known to be essential to the accelerated growth of the prison system.

In 1967, Nicholas Katzenbach wrote that "a man in prison" should be given "every opportunity to press his claim that he is wrongfully held." In 1992, his son wrote a novel worrying about what might happen if a prisoner pressed his claim to innocence too far. Emerging out of the same set of conversations about racism and injustice in the legal system that produced the Innocence Project, and reevaluating the elder Katzenbach's earlier ideas about the need to balance a concern for justice with a fear of recidivism, *Just Cause* presents readers with a baroque and cynical thought experiment: What if a person could be falsely imprisoned and truly guilty at the same time? The novel tells the story of white Miami journalist Matt Cowart. One day Cowart receives a letter from a Black inmate on Death Row named Bobby Earl Ferguson, who claims he is innocent of the charge of killing and raping a young white girl, Joanie Shriver, in a rural Florida town. Cowart, known for his anti–death-penalty editorials, becomes interested in Ferguson's case, which he discovers was based on shoddy evidence and a coerced confession. He also learns that another inmate on Death Row—Blair Sullivan, a Ted Bundy-esque serial killer—has taken responsibility for Joanie's murder. With this information in hand, Cowart writes a series of articles about the case, arguing for Ferguson's innocence, Sullivan's guilt, and the general racism of the legal system in rural Florida. As a result of the articles, the charges against Ferguson are dropped and he is released from prison. For his efforts, Cowart collects a Pulitzer Prize.

That story alone could be a novel, but it isn't Katzenbach's novel. It's only the first half. Midway through *Just Cause* comes a twist: Cowart realizes he's been duped.[39] The two prisoners, Ferguson and Sullivan, had made a deal. Sullivan would take responsibility for the murder of Joanie Shriver despite not having done it; in return, Ferguson, once freed, would kill Sullivan's abusive parents for him. Perceiving that he has helped "set a killer free," Cowart is distraught.[40] To make amends, he teams up with Tanny Brown, the police detective who initially tortured Ferguson into confessing. Together, the detective and the journalist pursue Ferguson from Florida to New Jersey and back, convinced that he is responsible not only for Joanie's murder but for the disappearances of several young Black girls after his release from prison. In the novel's climactic showdown, Brown kills Ferguson during a chase through the Florida swamps. He and Cowart decide to hide Ferguson's body and keep his death a secret, lest they be held legally responsible for killing a man who seemed to them extremely guilty but was, in fact, judged by the courts to be innocent.

In effect, *Just Cause* is telling two stories at once: a story of wrongful imprisonment, and a story about the danger of believing that there are such things as cases of wrongful imprisonment. These two stories are clearly incompatible. Yet Katzenbach seems to want both of them to be true at the same time. When Ferguson first writes to Cowart, his letter explains, "*I am an innocent man, facing the supreme punishment because of a racist system that was stacked against me.*" Although the novel will later cast doubt on Ferguson's innocence, it never disagrees with the second part of this statement. It repeatedly demonstrates that Ferguson really was the victim of a "racist system that was stacked against" him. His "conviction had been based on the flimsiest evidence concocted in a prejudicial atmosphere," not to mention a coerced confession. So is Ferguson innocent or guilty? Is he the perpetrator of a heinous crime or the victim of a rigged system? Was he rightfully or wrongfully convicted? Which is it? In the end, *Just Cause* suggests that it's both. "They were right to convict him," one character concludes; it was just "for all the wrong reasons."[41]

In this way, *Just Cause* becomes a revealing document of the contradictory attempt to reconcile longstanding anxieties about Black criminality with a new national conversation about prison's racial disparities. What if, Katzenbach proposes darkly, prison is both racist and right? Yet despite the novel's both/and sensibility, it does find subtle ways to cast doubt on emergent criticisms of the carceral system. Its most devilish strategy is the decision to have those criticisms voiced by the suspected murderer himself. It is no accident that the first thing Ferguson does after his release from prison is learn more about the criminal legal system. He does this by resuming his studies at Rutgers as a criminology major. His research centers on trying to "explain why fairly a quarter of the young black male population in this nation is or has been behind bars," and he has written papers exploring how white fears about urban crime help "feed the criminal justice system with its daily quota of black men."[42] Put simply, what Ferguson is studying is mass incarceration.

When *Just Cause* says things like *a quarter of the young black male population in this nation is or has been behind bars*, it distinguishes itself as a novel that has a surprisingly good grasp of the racialized crisis of mass incarceration in the United States. Katzenbach knows the statistics about mass incarceration. He knows that the legal system constitutes "a perfect formula for prejudice." Yet he also represents this knowledge as something that could itself become a tool of deception, a way for well-intentioned liberals to end up being "duped by [a] killer."[43] What if believing that the nation imprisons too many Black men is exactly what a killer like Ferguson wants you to think? This is, of course, paranoid silliness. But it reveals how anxious *Just Cause* is about critiques of mass incarceration going mainstream. Katzenbach was writing at a moment when evidence of the deep-rooted prejudice of prison was both undeniable and destabilizing. The result is a novel working at cross-purposes with itself, detailing the structural flaws of the correctional system while at the same time attempting to downplay them. The novel's split personality ultimately allows it to perform a kind of magic trick: It makes the entire problem of a racist carceral system disappear. Now you see the injustice of wrongful conviction. Now you don't.

Throughout the novel, Bobby Earl Ferguson is a man "suspected of everything, with evidence of nothing."[44] This is true. We never see Ferguson commit a crime, nor are we at any point presented with clear evidence that he ever has.[45] The fact that "there is no real evidence" against Ferguson becomes an increasingly uncomfortable problem for the novel, and ultimately leads us toward a slightly different way of interpreting it.[46] What began as a wrongful-conviction story that then became the tale of a falsely acquitted criminal who is actually guilty—call it a "wrong wrong man" narrative—is in fact the story of a man who has been legally exonerated and yet for some reason *is still assumed by everyone to be guilty*. Viewed in this way, *Just Cause* looks more like the story of a criminalized Black man being obsessively hunted by police and media institutions that, despite there being "no real evidence" of his guilt, are feverishly unwilling to believe he is innocent. As such, the novel is perhaps best read as an unwitting allegory for the lengths to which the public will go to preserve its faith in mass imprisonment: a faith rooted in the idea, no matter how unprovable, that everyone who goes to prison must be guilty of something.

In the final pages of *Just Cause*, detective Tanny Brown executes Ferguson and buries his body in the swamp. He then tells Cowart that the newspaperman's job is to write a story to convince readers of Ferguson's guilt, which they were never able to legally prove. When the courts fail, Katzenbach suggests, try the court of public opinion.

> "Write the story," Tanny Brown said.
> "I'll write the story," Cowart replied.
> "Make them believe," the policeman said.
> "They'll believe," Cowart answered.[47]

If, at the of end *Just Cause*, Ferguson's guilt remains merely rumor or legend, that's no problem. Just print the legend. The lesson of Katzenbach's novel is that believing in the guilt or innocence of incarcerated people—and by extension, in the justice or injustice of the systems that convict, confine, and execute them—isn't a matter of courtrooms or procedures, evidence or facts. It's a matter of the stories we tell about those people. On this score, Katzenbach was way ahead of us. With *Just Cause*, he wrote the story to make us believe.

At a moment when narratives of wrongful imprisonment were a major feature of popular culture across literature, television, and film, Katzenbach's novel made a splash. (You may remember the film adaptation starring Sean Connery and Laurence Fishburne that came out a few years later.) But it is likely that no work of wrongful-conviction fiction was more widely read than Stephen King's *The Green Mile*, published in six separate serial installments throughout 1996 and as a "complete serial novel" later that same year. Each individual installment of *The Green Mile* was a bestseller. It was released as a feature film at the end of 1999, and that, too, was a massive success, grossing more than $280 million and garnering several award nominations. King claims that he wrote *The Green Mile* because "the electric chair...has fascinated me since my first James Cagney movie."[48] But there's more to the novel than its nostalgia for gangster cinema or its macabre fascination with electrocution. At its core, *The Green Mile* is a vigorously cleansing confession of guilty feelings about the carceral system. As American prisons overflowed with Black men in the 1990s, King's novel stood as a sentimental monument to the undeniable racial injustice of prison, while implying the powerlessness of white observers to do anything to change it.

Set in the 1930s, *The Green Mile* is narrated by Paul Edgecombe, a white guard at the Cold Mountain Penitentiary who oversees the men on Death Row and handles their executions. In 1932, Paul gets a new prisoner, a Black man named John Coffey, whose large size and limited intelligence King mentions repeatedly. John is set to be executed for the rape and murder of two nine-year-old white girls. But John is innocent. He is no murderer; in fact, he's a magical healer. Discovering this, Paul hatches a plan with the help of his fellow prison guards to sneak John out of prison in order to cure the warden's wife of an inoperable brain tumor. The plan works; John cures her, then returns to prison. In the novel's final section, Paul performs a bit of amateur detective work to prove John's innocence, only to realize the proof won't help. The county's racist sheriff refuses to reopen the case, and the state of Georgia has no interest in commuting the death sentence of a Black prisoner. In the end, Paul is compelled to execute the falsely convicted John Coffey, having decided that it's his job to guarantee John a "good" death. For his part, John reassures Paul by telling him he wants to die anyway: "I *want* to go, boss." Hearing this, Paul decides, "Yes, it was a terrible thing we'd be doing, nothing would ever change that . . . and yet we'd be doing him a favor."[49] The essential alchemy of *The Green Mile* lies here, in its solemn attempt to transform the imprisonment and execution of a falsely convicted Black man into a gesture of sympathy—a "favor" doled out by the big-hearted representatives of the carceral state who simply want to help put hopeless poor people out of their imagined misery.

As in *Just Cause*, race is not incidental to imprisonment in *The Green Mile*. Paul points out that "most of the men who came to stay for awhile in E Block" are Black—an observation that clearly echoes the increasingly manifest racial disparities of imprisonment at the time when King was writing. And it's not just that. After one of the several electrocutions narrated in the novel, King writes that a white inmate's face "had gone blacker than John Coffey's."[50] We can gloss this line by saying that, as the novel depicts it, prison is what produces the cultural idea of Blackness itself.

Yet *The Green Mile* is not ultimately a novel about the plight of overrepresented Black prisoners. It is a novel about the plight of virtuous white prison guards. In a foreword, King explains that he is especially proud of the narrator Paul's "essentially decent voice; low-key, honest, perhaps a little wide-eyed."[51] The honesty and naïveté of Paul's narration is meant to reassure us that even if prisons are deeply regrettable places, they are nevertheless being run by "essentially decent" people. Paul Edgecombe and his crew are all dignified, humane men. Paul explains that as a guard on Death Row, "talking was our biggest, most important job"; his primary task is "to comfort" the men facing execution. There is one racist and abusive prison guard, Percy Wetmore, who is Paul's nemesis and whose role in the novel is to show us what a bad apple looks like so we can better recognize the essential decency of the other guards. It is exemplary of the book's thinking about prison that Paul's right-hand man, a former football tackle named Brutus Howell, is nicknamed "Brutal" purely as "a joke, he wouldn't hurt a fly unless he had to, in spite of his size." In King's carceral universe, prison brutality is an irony—"a joke"—that only highlights the moral fiber of prison guards. The prisoners are largely made to agree with this rosy portrait of the men guarding them. As one tells the group while sitting in the electric chair about to be executed, "You a good man, Boss Howell. . . . You too, Boss Edgecombe. . . . You all good men."[52]

The goodness of the correctional officers is brought into full relief by the story of the terrible but unavoidable act they are required to perform: execute a man, John Coffey, whom they know to be innocent. John is unfailingly gentle, his eyes are constantly filled with tears, and he has magical healing powers. One immediate conclusion to draw from this portrait is that King has set a fairly high standard for thinking about the politics of wrongful conviction. You can't just be innocent or good-hearted; you have to literally be Jesus—as John Coffey, per his initials, is clearly meant to be. "It was as if it was sorrow for the whole world he felt," Paul says revealingly of John.[53] As a proper Christ figure, it is John's job to bear that sorrow on behalf of others. This is what his healing hands do. With a touch or a kiss, Coffey takes on other people's physical suffering. "The sickness ... the pain.... the hurt," Paul explains. "He takes it in, then lets it out into the open air again." If John Coffey is Jesus Christ, this allows *The Green Mile* to put a surprisingly redemptive spin on mass incarceration. "God sacrificed John Coffey, who tried only to do good," Paul informs us.[54] In King's novel, incarcerated Black men are sacrificed for our sins.[55]

What sin, exactly, is John called on to bear? It seems that he is sacrificed for the sin of the prison system itself. In the climax of *The Green Mile*, John saves the life of the wife of the prison warden, sucking out her cancer and taking it into his own body, nearly killing himself in the process. Seeing his wife magically saved, the warden emerges from a deep depression and returns with renewed vigor to his job, which is ... running the prison that is about to execute John. Here prison is figured simultaneously as social cancer and original sin, and it is Christ-like prisoners such as John Coffey who are made to die both of it (the cancer) and for it (the sin). John dies for the prison's sins, yes, but it is also his death that eases the warden's suffering and allows him to get back to doing what he does best: efficiently running a state penitentiary. John dies so the prison can live.

He also dies so one prison guard in particular can live. In the last of the book's several twists, we learn that on the day of his execution, John touched Paul with his magic hands, giving him an electric shock and passing on some kind of protection against death: "John Coffey inoculated me with life. *Electrocuted* me with life, you might say." Paul, it is now revealed, has been narrating the book from the Georgia Pines nursing home, where he currently lives at the age of 104. Notice the reversal of the electrical metaphor: John, killed in the electric chair, has *"electrocuted"* Paul "with life." And this version of electrocution, Paul explains, is no less of a punishment than being put to death. Paul has been condemned to the life sentence of having his life last longer than he wants it to: "I will have wished for death long before death finds me. Truth to tell, I wish for it already."[56]

Might *The Green Mile* be suggesting that prison itself—as embodied by its exemplary employee Paul Edgecombe—has lived too long, become an aging aberration or withered anachronism in the context of modern America? Possibly. Yet even as King hints that the prison system may have, like Paul, lived past its appropriate expiration date, he also develops a set of parallels that enable Paul to take John's place as the focal point of our sympathy, the book's most pitiable prisoner. Now it is Paul who has been "electrocuted"; Paul who has been given his own version of a life sentence; Paul who, in the novel's very last line, describes himself as walking "the Green Mile"—which refers to the stretch of painted corridor in Cold Mountain that condemned prisoners must walk to get to the electric chair. "Sometimes, oh God, the Green Mile is so long," Paul says of his protracted wait for death. With all of these parallels, King encourages us to shift our sympathy away from the executed man and toward his executioner. To this end, it is little wonder that what Paul's wife says when she learns Paul must perform John's execution is not *Poor John Coffey*. What she says is, "Poor Paul."[57] With this elaborate transposition of victimhood, the novel discloses that its deepest sympathy is reserved not for those who are trapped in an unjust, inhumane prison system. It is reserved for those who, with nobility and decency, and despite their understandable guilt, help run it.[58]

In *The Green Mile*, the ritualistic imprisonment of Black men is made to seem at once a natural expression of original sin and a humane alternative to being forced to go on living in a world that is cruel enough to, among other things, have mass imprisonment. Indeed, Paul's distress at still being alive at 104 turns out to have a lot to do with the shame of having to live in the particular political climate of the mid 1990s. At the Georgia Pines nursing home where Paul currently resides, there is an evil orderly named Brad Dolan who reminds Paul of the racist prison guard he once worked with back at Cold Mountain, Percy Wetmore. At Georgia Pines, Brad Dolan surveils, torments, and threatens Paul, making his life miserable. But perhaps his most alarming character flaw is the bumper sticker on his car: "Brad Dolan . . . drives an old Chevrolet with a bumper

THE NOVEL IN THE AGE OF MASS INCARCERATION

sticker that says, I HAVE SEEN GOD AND HIS NAME IS NEWT." This detail is important enough to the novel that King mentions it again 150 pages later: "He got into his old Chevrolet with the bumper sticker reading I HAVE SEEN GOD AND HIS NAME IS NEWT."[59] Brad Dolan is not simply a sadist who torments the elderly. Worse, he's a Republican.

Famous as the pugnacious minority whip of the U.S. House of Representatives from 1989 to 1995 and speaker of the House from 1995 to 1999, Newt Gingrich was in many ways an obvious figure for King—a famously outspoken Democrat—to choose as the face of Republican sadism. But *The Green Mile* is a book about prison, and Gingrich has a more specific relation to the realignment of prison politics in the Clinton years. On one hand, Gingrich embodied the pro-punishment, pro-prison ethos of the Republican party to a T. "You want to lock prisoners up and . . . build as many prisons as you need," he advised in 1996.[60] On the other hand, Gingrich was actually best known at one point for successfully stalling the passage of Clinton's 1994 crime bill. Gingrich's maneuvering, which pitted him directly against Clinton in media appearances, led to an even more Republican-friendly version of the crime bill, with significant cuts to proposed social programs and more stringent crime control measures around the margins. Yet taking the slightly longer view, what Gingrich's hampering of the Clinton crime bill revealed was the broad political consensus that had formed around the issues of crime control and prison expansion. Liberals were outraged at the possibility that the crime bill might fail. A 1994 *New York Times* op-ed accused Gingrich, through his "deceitful and dishonorable" attacks on the crime bill, of "thwarting the will of the American people."[61] If Clinton's sweeping crime legislation really represented the will of the American people, then Gingrich's stalling of it could make him seem a bit like a criminal himself. "Gingrich Mugs the Crime Bill," the *Times* headline read.

Clinton had signed the Violent Crime Control and Law Enforcement Act into law a full two years before the first serial installment of *The Green Mile* was published, so it is implausible that King would have seen Gingrich as the sole face of the prison boom. More likely, he saw Gingrich as the devil to whom Democrats had just sold their souls. While Brad Dolan's bumper sticker looks at first simply like an auxiliary sign of his bad character, what it really represents to Paul is something whose implications are more disturbing. It is the fact that Paul has been alive long enough to see the ostensible difference between Republicans and Democrats erased by the consensus on prison-building. This brings *The Green Mile*'s own political views into significantly sharper focus. It is crucial to Paul's self-identity that he be seen as the complete opposite of both Percy Wetmore and Brad Dolan: caring rather than cruel, benevolent rather than sadistic. But he is like them in one indisputable way as well. He, too, is a prison guard. Despite the differences among these men, they are all equal participants in the administration of incarceration. To struggle to salvage some subtle difference from this elemental sameness is to glimpse the core truth of *The Green Mile*. In King's novel, the difference between liberals and conservatives—between Paul and Percy, Paul and Brad, Bill and Newt—is not that only one side supports a project of racially biased mass imprisonment. The difference is that only one side is enlightened enough to feel guilty about it. Poor Paul; poor Stephen. Paul makes the stays of his prisoners more comfortable, and they are grateful to him when they go. This may sound like cold comfort at Cold Mountain, but it was the best King could imagine offering in the face of a massive prison system that, like the ageless Paul Edgecombe, wasn't going anywhere any time soon—precisely because it had the full support of the country's two major political parties.

By the middle of the 1990s, prison was a widespread aspect of life in the United States. Paul was right: Sometimes the Green Mile seems long indeed. As two massively successful novels of wrongful imprisonment, *The Green Mile* and *Just Cause* are indicative of a historical moment when mass incarceration had become a problem that felt, to many people, at once too prevalent to ignore and too big to solve. Where Katzenbach warned readers that emerging critiques of mass incarceration could pose a threat to American safety, King resolved that the only thing left for decent people to do was acknowledge those critiques and bravely bear the guilt. Both writers agreed, however, that the scale, lethality, and prejudice of the prison system was an unchangeable fact. For their two protagonists, participation in the system is unavoidable; it's just a question of how they justify it to themselves. Early in *Just Cause*, a minor character spells out the truth: "Prison is a bad deal for everybody."[62] In their strikingly similar depictions of mass incarceration as an ineluctable ritual in which innocence doesn't matter but race does, *Just Cause* and *The Green Mile* both demonstrate just how had a deal prison really is. They also show how it became a deal that liberal society was willing to live with: a sacrifice it was willing to make.

THE PRIVATE EYE GOES TO PRISON

In *The Green Mile*, there is a classic literary work that King keeps mentioning: Edgar Allan Poe's "The Murders in the Rue Morgue," published in 1841 and generally considered the first detective story written in English. *The Green Mile* alludes to Poe's story at least four separate times. Early in the novel, Paul says that cleaning up after an execution "made me feel like a character in an Edgar Allan Poe story." In the same scene, Paul's friend and fellow guard Brutus casts a shadow on the wall "like the shadow of that ape in the story about the Rue Morgue." Later, "our shadows danced huge and misshapen on the walls, like shadows in that Poe story about the big ape in the Rue Morgue."[63] Why this specific Poe story? The choice seems surprising at first, given that *The Green Mile* would be expected to have more in common with Poe's gothic and horror stories than with his detective fiction. But it begins to make more sense once we recall the extent to which Poe wrote "The Murders in the Rue Morgue" as a racial allegory. Poe's fictional "conflation of black man and orangutan," the literary historian Richard Kopley suggests, was clearly connected to "race-related fears that the orangutan's attack on two white women would have suggested, including slave rebellion and miscegenation."[64] The politics of racial criminalization link Poe's story to King's novel. But with a key difference. It's not that John Coffey is supposed to be the threatening ape. It's that he is misperceived that way: transformed from an innocent man into the "misshapen" "shadow" of a dehumanized Black criminal who society falsely believes has, just like Poe's character, killed two white girls.

The shadow thing is worth pausing on. King refers to it several times: "the shadow of that ape in the story about the Rue Morgue"; "like shadows in that Poe story about the big ape." As it happens, there is not a single mention of the orangutan's shadow in Poe's story. This is odd. Did King invent the detail or simply misremember it? Either way, it is a telling image. The shadow is an obvious metaphor for racial and criminal stereotype: the projection of exaggerated or outsized fears that don't necessarily match reality. A shadow is also something that requires a physical screen to be projected onto. To this end, "the walls" of the prison on which the "shadows danced" are not incidental; they are, in fact, the required backdrop onto which the racially exaggerated ideas about John Coffey's criminality are cast. To the extent that King has somewhat inexplicably added the detail about shadows to Poe's story, he has also added the physical surface needed to make those shadows visible. In other words, he has added prison walls. We might say he has added these not just to one story where they're never mentioned but to the whole history of the genre that this particular story helped birth. What's being staged here, I would suggest, is a process of generic succession hastened by mass incarceration. If the genre of detective fiction was forged in the 1840s as a way of processing hidden anxieties about nonwhite criminals, then by the 1990s, King suggests, those same anxieties no longer need to be detected or unveiled. They can now be viewed directly, an exaggerated shadow play playing out across the interior walls of every prison in America.

Detective fiction is American culture's preeminent genre of crime and punishment. Yet for a genre that is all about catching criminals, it rarely mentions what happens to its criminals after they are caught. Detective novels almost never talk about prison. King's allusions to Poe can be read as an attempt to reckon with this generic blind spot: with prison's shadowy, unacknowledged presence in the literary tradition descended directly from "The Murders in the Rue Morgue." Rewriting (or just misremembering) the story as one about shadows and walls—about criminal stereotypes and the penal institutions onto which we project those stereotypes—*The Green Mile* compels us to realize that the concrete walls of the prison have been casting their own shadow over the genre of detective fiction for a long time.

This one-sided intertextual dialogue taking place across more than a century raises some natural follow-up questions. What exactly *was* happening to conventional detective novels in the years when mass incarceration went from being a half-glimpsed shadow to a full-bodied presence in American life? How did detective novelists, working with a generic template that was effectively invented in "The Murders in the Rue Morgue," reposition themselves to be able to acknowledge the increasingly incontrovertible evidence of America's prison crisis? In short, how did the genre of the detective novel adapt to mass incarceration? How did it read the writing on the prison wall? The rest of this section aims to get to the bottom of these particular mysteries.

THE NOVEL IN THE AGE OF MASS INCARCERATION

It took Sara Paretsky until the ninth book of her V. I. Warshawski series to address the connection between the detective genre and what was beginning to be called the prison-industrial complex. She gave the book a great title: *Hard Time* (1999). It begins with Warshawski encountering a woman dying in the middle of the road. The woman turns out to be an illegal immigrant and an escaped prisoner from the nearby Coolis detention center for women, a privately run institution that is a combination prison and jail. (This type of institution is Paretsky's invention; it doesn't exist in real life.) As the plot progresses, Warshawski discovers that a private firm called Carnifice Security, which owns and operates the Coolis prison, has teamed up with the media conglomerate Global Entertainment to use Coolis as a sweatshop to produce Global-branded merchandise. The woman in the street had been working in the sweatshop and was murdered by the guards running it. Her body was moved to the streets of Chicago and spun as a prison escape in order to cover up the secret factory within the private prison.

Hard Time had clearly metabolized the emerging discourse around mass incarceration. Paretsky's novel is peppered liberally with very specific facts about the prison system. Warshawski informs us that "women prisoners make up the fastest growing segment of the fast-growing U.S. prison population"; that it only takes a "minute amount of crack ... to send someone to prison"; that the "private prison business" was growing rapidly; and that the prison population tended to be majority "Spanish or black," with "very few white faces." But I don't want to give the impression that *Hard Time* is only a bloodless recitation of data points. It also earnestly documents the conditions in American penal institutions. Paretsky based her depiction of prison on a Human Rights Watch report detailing the abuses in U.S. women's prisons, and she makes that report vivid for her readers by having Warshawski herself become a prisoner at Coolis. Abruptly transformed from heroic detective to helpless inmate, Warshawski experiences firsthand the total "misery" that prison produces, from the denial of needed medical care to the constant threat of sexual and physical abuse by prison guards to the forms of mental dissociation needed to bear it all. "Prison was a destructive environment," Warshawski reports. "It wore on you physically as well as mentally." At the end of *Hard Time*, Paretsky insists that imprisonment must be understood as a form of torture (Warshawski's friend says to her: "You were in a helpless situation, at the mercy of the law, shot with an electric weapon, beaten, and then chained to a bed. I think you were tortured") and as a lasting trauma. In the final sentence of the novel, Warshaswki confesses that "my sleep was still disturbed . . . the images of terror still sometimes woke me."[65] Paretsky seems to have intended her novel's images of the terror and trauma of prison to keep readers up at night, too.

While the emotional plea at the heart of Paretsky's novel is straightforward, the mechanics of its plot are anything but. Taking her cue from the deep vein of anticorporate populism that runs through the tradition of hardboiled detective fiction—"To hell with the rich," Raymond Chandler famously wrote in *The Big Sleep* (1939)[66]—Paretsky depicts the Coolis prison as a top-down corporate conspiracy whose aim is to create more favorable labor conditions for American conglomerates. Like most of the new prisons built in the 1990s, the Coolis facility is sited in a town suffering the consequences of deindustrialization. Yet the new jobs created in the region are nothing, in Paretsky's telling, compared to the profits reaped by the media behemoth Global Entertainment through the operation of its prison sweatshops. In *Hard Time*'s climactic scene, Warshawski explains to a group of assembled journalists how the arrangement stood to offer cheaper labor than developing nations, given that both the facility and the equipment at Coolis were paid for by the state of Illinois. "You can't get lower production costs for this kind of operation, even if you go to Burma, because you can't beat free space and machinery," the detective explains. "And you have a labor force that can never go on strike, never balk at the working conditions, never complain to OSHA or the NLRB. It's a beauty for the bottom line in these days of the global economy."[67] *A beauty for the bottom line*: This is Paretsky's unified theory of mass incarceration in the age of late capitalism. Prison helps American corporations get ahead in "the global economy."

The rise of the prison-industrial complex and the economics of prison labor were a source of much media attention in the years leading up to the publication of *Hard Time*. Angela Davis points out that "it was during the decade of the 1980s that corporate ties to the punishment system became more extensive and entrenched than ever before."[68] *Hard Time* clearly took those ties seriously. In actual fact, however, the economic value of prison labor is hard to pin down. Many scholars of the prison system have cast doubt on the assumption that prisons operate as direct sources of profit.

THE NOVEL IN THE AGE OF MASS INCARCERATION

Christian Parenti notes that "less than 5 percent of the entire incarcerated population" works for prison industries. He argues that "in the state sector most prison industries end up costing the government money, or at best break even," while private businesses "are threatened by the idea of facing state-subsidized competitors" and are loath to enmesh "their operations in the treacherous ganglia of correctional bureaucracies." In Parenti's view, "prison labor is a sideshow."[69]

What is the appeal of the prison-labor story for a writer like Paretsky? The answer, I think, is that it is a story that involves concealment and revelation: something hidden that must be exposed. In other words, it is a story that requires detecting. Eric Schlosser cautioned readers in 1998 that the "prison-industrial complex is not a conspiracy, guiding the nation's criminal-justice policy behind closed doors."[70] Yet it is simpler for Paretsky to imagine that it is, because it is simpler to fit a conspiracy into the existing templates of the detective genre. In Paretsky's telling, Coolis looks on the surface like a regular prison but is in truth a conspiratorial attempt to secure cheap sweatshop labor behind the backs of the American public. The conspiracy also involves an elaborate cover-up; private corporations, local politicians, and shady police all conspire to guard the terrible secret of what's happening at Coolis. To understand prison in these terms is to view it as something enabled by secrecy—and therefore threatened by exposure. No wonder that, in *Hard Time*, Warshawski the detective is positioned as the double of a new ally, a human-rights journalist named Morell (a man whose name is a further indicator of the novel's interest in digging things up and bringing them to light.) Setting up an analogy between detective work and investigative reporting, Paretsky has Warshawski go undercover at Coolis in order to secretly document the poor conditions and abuse. At one point, Warshawski has the opportunity to leave the prison—her lawyer comes to bail her out—but opts to stay in order to continue her investigation. The decision, perverse as it is, pays off. She collects enough material evidence of what's going on behind closed doors at Coolis to expose it to the public.

At the end of *Hard Time*, Warshawski presents her photographic evidence to a roomful of assembled reporters. With the aid of a slideshow, the detective discloses the formerly invisible truth about prison: that it is an unregulated, privately run space of abuse, torture, and forced labor. Having brought this calamity to light, Warshawski feels hopeful that she's changed something. She explains that the aim of her presentation is to try to bring an end to "some of the misery at Coolis." She calls on Carnifice's CEO to resign "because of the degradation of prisoners that goes on hourly in a prison that his company built and runs," and she brings a "suit against the Department of Corrections for inflicting grievous bodily harm" on her during her incarceration, which has already resulted in two prison guards being fired. All of this damning public exposure is an attempt to get the prison sweatshop shut down so that Coolis can finally be "run along humane lines."[71]

The problem with pretending that prisons are secretly sweatshops, however, is that it implies that the way to solve the problem is to close the sweatshops but keep the prisons. And the problem with imagining that publicly exposing "the degradation of prisoners" will lead to more humane treatment is that it assumes that such degradation isn't what the public already expects from the prisons it sanctions. "We law-abiding citizens don't necessarily want prisoners rehabilitated," Warshawski acknowledges during her climactic speech, "but we sure do want them punished."[72] Just so. What if the most shocking truth about the American prison system is that it is not a scandal or an exception but the norm? What if the dehumanizing treatment of prisoners is built in to both the institution of prison and American culture's beliefs about the purpose of punishment? What, in that case, is exposure really worth?

Hard Time wants readers to believe that the abusive excesses of the prison are a product of its falling into the unregulated hands of private corporations; that reforms are necessary to make prison more "humane"; and that the exposure of the facts about prison will make such reforms inevitable. Yet the final pages of Paretsky's novel cast doubt on all of this. In the concluding chapter, Warshawski receives payment for her services from a movie star represented by Global Entertainment—the very star whose picture was on the shirts being sewn at the Coolis sweatshop. Accepting the check, Warshawski thinks, "Money made from T-shirts sewn by women in prisons here or abroad. It was in my hands, too. I could have turned it down but I didn't." The fact that Warshawski is paid with money made from the very sweatshop she was trying to shut down suggests a kind of unavoidable complicity in the global division of labor— her entanglement in the systematic exploitation of vulnerable workers both here and abroad, whether they work in "an Illinois prison" or in

"Myanmar's forced labor camps."[73] Warshawski could have turned down the money but she didn't. She, too, is part of the nastiness of the prison economy now.

In this way, *Hard Time* turns out to be less about reform than it is about complicity. Or perhaps those are just two sides of the same coin. It's hard to change something when you're also enmeshed in it. Morrell comforts Warshawski by pointing out that her complicity is so unavoidable as to be universal: "You have to live in the world," he says. And that world has prisons. By insisting on the continuity between sweatshops in the Global South and forced labor in U.S. prisons, *Hard Time* implies that our complicity in mass incarceration is rooted primarily in consumption: that, like Warshawski's, our lives and livelihoods are made possible by the products that prisoners are forced to make. This isn't really true, however. Goods manufactured in prisons make up only a tiny fraction of the commodities that circulate in the United States. If we are indeed complicit in mass incarceration, it is not because of the things we buy or the checks we cash. Our complicity is not sewn into the clothes we wear. It would be more apt to say it's woven into the fabric of our cultural imagination. This is most obviously the case when we try to imagine what justice ought to look like in the face of injury. On the last page of *Hard Time*, Morrell tries to lift Warshawski's spirits by reminding her that one of the prison guards who abused her is "likely to go to prison himself." "There's a measure of justice there," he points out, trying to cheer her up.[74] Even two such enlightened souls as Warshawski and Morrell—a woman still living with the trauma of her incarceration and a man whose job is to interview torture survivors—can't separate their conception of justice from the institution of the prison. This may explain why Warshawski isn't actually trying to close Coolis, just to get it "run along humane lines": because she, or the genre she represents, still uses incarceration as the standard measure of what counts as justice. Certainly, it is hard to feel good about living in a world with prisons. But the hardest time that *Hard Time* has is imagining a world—or even just a detective novel—without them.

Around this time, another well-known detective novelist was asking similar questions about what mass incarceration meant for the genre on which he'd staked his reputation. At the end of the 1990s, Walter Mosley was at a crossroads. He had written six successful detective novels featuring Easy Rawlins. Over the course of the series, Rawlins had evolved from an unemployed machinist to a homeowner, a landlord, and a gainfully self-employed private eye. From the start, Mosley's series used the figure of the Black detective to think about race and class in American society. It was never lost on Mosley that these forms of social marginalization were intimately connected to the threat of imprisonment. In *Devil in a Blue Dress* (1990), Rawlins describes himself as "poor and black and a likely candidate for the penitentiary."[75] A few years later, however, Mosley found himself wondering how much the genre of the detective novel was really able to say about the worsening reality of prison in America. He needed a new approach.

He found one in *Always Outnumbered, Always Outgunned* (1998). It was Mosley's eighth work of fiction but only the second not to feature Easy Rawlins. *Always Outnumbered* is no detective novel. It's a series of linked stories starring Socrates Fortlow, a formerly incarcerated man now living in Watts and barely scraping by. The stories are short, enigmatic, and philosophical. They document Socrates's struggles to find a job, to build a supportive social network, and to avoid going back to prison. *Always Outnumbered* thus begins where Mosley's detective novels usually end—with a guilty protagonist apprehended and sent to prison—and proceeds in the reverse direction. In doing so, the book poses a new set of narrative questions for readers most likely to have come to Mosley through his previous works of genre fiction. What happens when prison is the starting point rather than the goal of the crime story? How does this reversal affect the genre's standard plots and underlying moral system? These questions clearly mattered to Mosley; he didn't return to his detective series for another four years.[76] *Always Outnumbered* is thus a fascinating document of the way a detective novelist who was already using the genre to address American racism felt compelled to reimagine his work in the face of the prison crisis.

Like *Hard Time*, *Always Outnumbered* explicitly situates itself amid the emerging discourse about mass incarceration. Mosley's book takes place at a moment when the inhabitants of prison are "mostly young men, mostly black and Latino." His characters recognize that the demographic makeup of the incarcerated population is no accident. As one of Socrates's friends says, "the court wanna put ev'ry black man they can in the can." In Mosley's telling, conditions inside jails and prisons are inhumane or worse ("Anything's better than prison or death," Socrates says), while reentry has its own steep challenges, from the difficulty a convicted felon has in securing a job to the impression others have of him as someone who, having once been incarcerated, is likely to commit more crimes. In all, Mosley's stories set out to narrate the "long history of felony trailing in Socrates's shadow."[77] That history encompasses both the character's traumatic experience in prison and his dawning realization that he has returned to a society that seems intent on sending him back.

Always Outnumbered is a meditation on genre at a pivotal moment in its author's career. As mass incarceration burst into public view, Mosley began to wonder whether the literary figure best suited to illuminate this new world of crime and punishment might be someone other than a detective. Throughout the book, Socrates confronts a number of criminals, but he solves no crimes. Instead, his interactions with criminal characters repeatedly foreground the question of how a community might collectively decide to handle transgression. In this way, Socrates is less a detective than he is a judge, and *Always Outnumbered* becomes an interrogation of the logic of judgment that had implicitly structured Mosley's previous detective fiction. Socrates "knew, from his days in prison, that many judges got rich off of the blood of felons."[78] Yet he keeps being asked by his community to make consequential ethical judgments himself. What happens not just to criminals but also to crime narratives, *Always Outnumbered* asks, when we attempt to pry apart the naturalized relation between judgment and imprisonment?

Mosley tests out several answers to this question over the course of the book. In the story "Midnight Meeting," Socrates and his friends meet to discuss the problem of a neighborhood man named Petis who has robbed and killed several people to support his crack addiction. One person at the meeting wants to go to the police. Another wants to kill Petis. A third wants to do nothing. Socrates maintains that killing is "no answer for civilized men," but he also refuses to turn Petis in: "I don't believe in goin' t'no cops . . . A black man—no matter how bad he is—bein' brutalized by the cops is a hurt to all of us. Goin' to the cops ovah a brother is like askin' for chains." Having rejected both vigilante violence and police violence, Socrates still has to help his community solve a problem. What to do? In the end, Socrates and the rest of the group go to Petis's house, rough him up, and tell him to leave town. He complies. But with nowhere else to go and suffering from addiction, Petis "drift[s] downtown" and dies while living on the street. At the end of the chapter, one of Socrates's friends suggests that they hold "a regular group meeting" to deal with nuisances in the neighborhood. Socrates refuses; the act of being responsible for deciding Petis's punishment was too great a burden for him, and he is not keen to repeat the experience. "We did what we had to do," he says. "But you know, I don't know if I'd have the heart to ever do it again."[79]

Unfortunately, he is compelled to do it again. A later story, "Firebug," puts Socrates back in the position of having to act as judge and mete out punishment. An arsonist has been setting fires throughout Watts. The first few have no casualties, but then two unhoused people are killed by another fire while sleeping in an abandoned building. Socrates knows who the arsonist is but isn't sure he should incriminate him. "What would you do if you knew, or thought you knew, that a man had killed two people?" he asks a friend. And what "if it wasn't on purpose?" This time, Socrates decides to go to the cops. He meets an off-duty police officer and tells him that he'll reveal the arsonist's name on one condition: "I want him treated like a man, officer. . . . I don't want him beat, or cursed, or cheated. I want a fair deal for the man I give you." The fair deal doesn't happen; it may never have been possible in the first place. As events transpire, the arsonist sees the cops coming for him and kills himself. Socrates gets the reward money for helping identify the culprit yet ends up regretting his decision. "I thought maybe I could make a difference," Socrates tells a friend, in a way that suggests he knows he didn't. When his friend replies, "You cain't blame the cops for ev'rything," Socrates "wanted to hit" him.[80] Cooperating with the cops, Socrates seems to think, was exactly his mistake.

Why does he decide to work with the police at this late moment in the book? The decision suggests not only a kind of social pressure but also, we might surmise, a kind of *genre pressure* exerted on Mosley's novel—the sense of an inexorable gravitational pull in crime narratives from criminal transgression to state correction. In this way, the "long history of felony trailing in Socrates's shadow" seems also to be trailing Mosley's book. Socrates's series of judgments about how to punish others start to look less like alternatives to the correctional system and more like allegories for it. *Always Outnumbered* is ultimately about the violence embedded in official as well as unofficial acts of moral judgment—acts that linger in Mosley's stories about crime even after the character of the detective has been sidelined. Socrates rejects prison and the police yet repeatedly finds himself in the position of having to punish people. Clearly, it doesn't go well; the two men whose sentences he is made to decide—the addict and the arsonist—both end up dead. From these discouraging results, we can draw two larger conclusions about the literary experiment of *Always Outnumbered*. First, by the late 1990s, Mosley was keenly interested in what it would look like to explicitly renounce prison as the natural endpoint for narratives about criminal wrongdoing. Second, he remained concerned that certain habits of carceral thinking might nevertheless be hard to break.

Published just one year apart, *Always Outnumbered* and *Hard Time* are, beneath the surface, surprisingly similar projects. Paretsky gives us a private eye who becomes a prisoner, while Mosley employs the character of the ex-prisoner to replace his private eye. Both books indicate a clear desire on the part of established detective novelists—writers who had built their careers on stories about fighting crime and catching criminals—to investigate the problem of incarceration from the other side. This shift of perspective is at least a little ironic. In both cases, the detective finds him- or herself on the inside looking out, caught up in the very carceral machinery whose gears they had once helped oil. Facing down the crisis of mass incarceration, Paretsky and Mosley may have felt themselves caught up, or complicit, in a similar way. We can read *Hard Time* and *Always Outnumbered* as expressions of this complicity.[81] They are books in which the detective's—no less than the detective novelist's—ideological implication in mass imprisonment is conveyed through the story of a detective who literally winds up in prison.

If late-twentieth-century detective fiction was really in the midst of changing its mind about the penal system—and in the process, changing how it wrote about prison—there is no clearer evidence for this than the case of Michael Nava. Nava attended Stanford Law School and went to work for the Los Angeles City Attorney's office in the 1980s. His debut novel, *The Little Death* (1986), established him as a pioneering voice in gay and Chicana/o detective fiction. *The Little Death* introduced readers to Henry Rios, a gay Latino criminal defense lawyer who would go on to star in six subsequent detective novels by Nava. Although Nava himself had been a prosecutor, he chose to make Rios a public defender. As a literary choice, this was a clever idea; it put his protagonist in much closer proximity to the everyday reality of prison than most fictional detectives had been up to that point. (We could also read it as a subtle mea culpa for the more punitive role that Nava played as an attorney in the L.A. prosecutor's office.) The opening pages of *The Little Death* describe Rios visiting the county jail in Palo Alto to meet with clients. (Nava had worked at the same jail while in law school.) "Jails," Rios says as he enters, "were the cornerstones" of "human misery." Yet, he admits, "I minded the jail less than most." It is "not so much different from a courtroom." Plus, he's heard that time spent in the county jail is "easy time.... County was relatively uncrowded and the sheriffs relatively benign."[82]

Nava was ahead of his time in recognizing the detective genre's proximity to the prison system. Yet *The Little Death*'s account of the jail is notably inconclusive. Jail is at once a pillar of "human misery" and "relatively benign." It is a place of suffering but also of ethnographic fascination, even allure, for Rios; it is, in fact, the unlikely setting of the meet-cute that takes place between Rios and his lover in the novel. Nava deserves a lot of credit for having the foresight to use his debut detective novel to comment on the injustice of the prison system as early as the mid 1980s. Nava himself, however, seems to have felt differently about his contribution to the topic. Several decades later, in an act of literary revision with few precedents, Nava acquired the copyrights to the Henry Rios series and began to intensively rewrite the books. Exactly thirty years after *The Little Death*, Nava published a substantial revision of the novel, retitled *Lay Your Sleeping Head* (2016). The revised version is about fifty pages longer than the original, more sexually explicit, and more focused on Rios's Chicano identity. But for our purposes, what is most interesting about *Lay Your Sleeping Head* is how it documents the dramatic transformation in Nava's view of prison that took place between 1986 and 2016.

The opening scene of *Lay Your Sleeping Head* is once again set at the Palo Alto jail, but the scene has doubled in length from two pages to four. The extra pages give Nava more space to comment on problems such as prison overcrowding in "places like Folsom or San Quentin."[83] They also give him the chance to clarify Rios's potentially odd-sounding comment in the original novel that he "minded the jail less than most." In the revision, Rios explains that what he didn't mind was being reminded of the high stakes of his job as a public defender: "It was salutary to have to encounter the misery on a regular basis because otherwise it became too easy to believe that trials were a contest between lawyers to see who was the craftiest. It was good to be reminded that when I lost a case someone paid a price." These lines put a different spin on the recurring theme of the detective's complicity in incarceration. As a defense attorney, Rios does not send people to prison himself, but he understands that imprisonment is the steep price his clients pay for his professional failures. As for Rios's feelings about correctional institutions, they are no longer ambivalent. He is full of unequivocal outrage. In fact, Nava adds a new plot detail, informing us that Rios has recently been demoted from the public defender's office in San Jose specifically for expressing his outrage in court. After having an innocent client found guilty of murder, Rios jumped up and shouted, "This isn't a jury, it's a lynch mob." He remarks, "My courtroom outburst had been the culmination of years of frustration with the criminal law system."[84]

We may infer that those "years of frustration" are the very years that elapsed between the initial publication of *The Little Death* and its republication as *Lay Your Sleeping Head*. Public opinion about prisons changed substantially between the 1980s and the 2010s. Part of the purpose in rewriting *The Little Death* for the twenty-first century seems to have been to account for that change at a personal level: to register Nava's own experience of what he calls, in *Lay Your Sleeping Head*, an "awakening about the criminal law system."[85] Such an awakening was hardly Nava's alone. His ambitious project of self-revision was only an extension of the narrative adjustments that genre writers like Paretsky and Mosley had begun to make a decade earlier. But Nava's novel offers direct testimony about the imperative detective novelists felt to revise the genre for an age of mass incarceration. On this score, even the new title of Nava's revised novel is instructive. Driven by a shared sense of complicity, if not self-recrimination, Nava, Mosley, and Paretsky were all in search of more effective ways to address the crisis of human captivity that they knew detective fiction had for too long been asleep to.

WORDS OF WARNING

It's impossible to talk about American fiction's relation to mass incarceration without talking about the emergence of the genre known as street literature. Pioneered by Black women and aimed at a predominately Black female readership, street lit was one of the most significant developments in American publishing in the late twentieth century. The genre drew on elements of romance, upward mobility narratives, and the Black pulp tradition of Iceberg Slim and Donald Goines in order to tell stories of Black women navigating the worlds of crime, drugs, and love. Street lit was initially a self-made phenomenon. Rejected by mainstream publishers, authors such as Vickie Stringer and Teri Woods printed their novels themselves and sold them on street corners and out of the trunks of their cars.[86] This enterprising spirit paid off. Both Stringer's *Let That Be the Reason* and Woods's *True to the Game* were success stories of self-publishing, and each author went on to start her own influential publishing company: Stringer began Triple Crown Publications, while Woods founded Meow Meow Productions, later rebranded as Teri Woods Publishing. Corporate publishers took note, signing street lit authors to lucrative contracts and creating new imprints to distribute them.[87] By the early twenty-first century, Kinohi Nishikawa writes, the genre of street lit "had become big business."[88]

From the beginning, street lit was inseparable from the transformation of the American prison system. The critic Aneeka Ayanna Henderson persuasively argues that the genre "was a direct product of the [1994] crime bill and the Welfare Reform Act," probing the limits of the marriage plot in the face of "the prison state's decimation of Black communities."[89] The books' link to the prison state was reflected not just in their content but also in their modes of production and circulation. Justin Gifford, Kristina Graaf, and other critics have shown how the prison plays a central role in the business of street lit, as works in the genre are frequently written by, read by, and marketed to incarcerated people. "America's correctional facilities," Gifford explains, have "become cultural centers for the creation, distribution, and consumption of street literature."[90] Graaf points out that "the list of primarily African American writers who penned their popular novels while incarcerated comprises hundreds of authors," and she quotes one independent street lit publisher who estimates that "90 percent of the submissions I get ... are from prisoners."[91] With all of these aspects of the genre in mind, it is perfectly logical to conclude, as Gifford does, that "street literature's growing popularity" is "a reflection of the larger influence of prison culture in African American and American life."[92]

THE NOVEL IN THE AGE OF MASS INCARCERATION

Street lit attended to the lives of working-class Black women in a way few fictional genres had done before. It did so at a moment when this exact demographic happened to be the fastest-growing segment of the U.S. prison population. The target audience for street lit thus had significant overlap with the new targets of an expanding carceral state. This convergence was a decisive factor in the kinds of stories street lit authors chose to tell. Two of the genre's founding texts, by Sister Souljah and Vickie Stringer, expressly fashioned themselves as cautionary tales for female readers.[93] The language of self-help that critics have long noticed suffusing the genre here took on a more specific function, encouraging readers to take responsibility for educating themselves about the workings of the prison system.[94] These two pioneering works of street literature were attempts to alert their readers that conventional fantasies of empowerment and upward mobility for women of color had been upended by mass incarceration. Once there might have been hope of hustling one's way to a higher class. Now all plots led to prison.

The activist and hip-hop artist Sister Souljah published her debut novel, *The Coldest Winter Ever*, in 1999. It was an absolute smash, going on to sell more than a million copies and spawning several best-selling sequels. In Henderson's estimation, the novel's popularity "rivals that of Public Enemy's best-selling singles."[95] A magazine feature on Souljah describes *The Coldest Winter Ever* as "among the 100 'most-loved' books featured as part of PBS's *The Great American Read* series and 'a Bible for a generation of Black women.'"[96] *The Coldest Winter Ever* is an inspired reimagining of the naturalist tradition, a new spin on Richard Wright and Ann Petry for the self-empowerment '90s. The novel is narrated by Winter Santiaga, the sixteen-year-old daughter of a Brooklyn drug kingpin. As the book opens, Winter's family has just relocated from Brooklyn to a fancy house on Long Island. But things quickly unravel. Her father is arrested and his assets seized, her younger sisters are taken by the Bureau of Child Welfare, her mother descends into crack addiction, and Winter is left to hustle for herself, tirelessly pursuing her goal of marrying a wealthy man. Eventually she connects with an old flame, Bullet. Bullet is rich but possessive, abusing Winter by keeping her locked in their apartment, "held hostage" by vicious dogs. One day Bullet and Winter are driving to a major drug deal when their car crashes; Bullet flees the scene and leaves Winter to take the fall for the drugs and guns found in the car. The novel concludes with Winter halfway through "a mandatory fifteen-year prison sentence."[97]

The narrative of Vickie Stringer's *Let That Be the Reason*, self-published in 2001, follows a similar arc. Based closely on Stringer's own life and written while she was serving time in federal prison on drug trafficking charges, it tells the story of Pamela, who at the start of the novel is abandoned by her boyfriend Chino and left to raise their baby son alone. Having lost Chino's financial support, Pamela channels her inner hustler—creating an alter ego she dubs Carmen—and pursues a series of increasingly lucrative entrepreneurial ventures. She starts her own escort service, then moves into drug dealing. She makes a connection with a powerful supplier in New York City and becomes a major figure in the drug game in Columbus, Ohio, by innovating the idea of using hidden panels in vans to transport drugs. Eventually, Pamela decides that she wants to get out of the drug business, but before she can, she is arrested by federal agents. Chino informs on Pamela in order to win his own release, while Pamela refuses to provide the name of her supplier in New York. She ends the novel in county jail awaiting her sentence, which, she is told by her lawyer, is required by new mandatory minimum laws to be at least eleven years.

Together, Souljah's and Stringer's novels helped to establish the lucrative market for street lit. The two novels also share a noteworthy formal feature. They use modes of direct address and metafictional interruption to speak to their readers directly. Stringer explains her reasons for writing her novel in an afterword that was included with the initial self-published run of the book. "I've exposed myself with the prayer that my life can be used as an example to warn others of the awful dangers of the drug Game," she says. "It is for the people in the streets that I write."[98] Souljah understood the aims of her writing in similar terms, though she expressed them in a more formally elaborate way. In *Coldest Winter*, Souljah appears as a character in her own novel, functioning as a spiritual guide to self-improvement and self-empowerment. If the novel operates largely as an address to female readers, it mirrors this in fictional scenes involving Souljah the character literally dispensing advice to women on the radio and in support groups she runs in her home. "When we hate ourselves we destroy our bodies with alcohol, drugs, casual sex, and a bunch of stuff," she advises her followers in one scene. Winter won't listen, but Souljah the writer clearly hopes that her readers will. This helps explain the sharp irony of the book's closing lines, when Winter, now incarcerated, sees her sister Porsche living well and wonders about the legality of her situation: "I said nothing at all. Hell, I'm not into meddling in other people's business. I definitely don't be making no speeches. Fuck it. She'll learn for herself."[99] The refusal to meddle may be Winter's defining flaw—a sign of her narcissistic self-interest—but it is the novel's principal virtue. As a book, *The Coldest Winter Ever* is willing to do precisely what Winter won't: risk "meddling" and seeming preachy ("making speeches") in order to intervene in "other people's business." Souljah's self-positioning as a committed teacher offers a clear contrast to Winter's willingness to leave other women to learn for themselves.

What made these books' attempts to "meddle" (Souljah) and "warn others" (Stringer) necessary? Both novels give the same answer: mass incarceration. In *The Coldest Winter Ever*, Souljah the character writes a series of letters to a love interest criticizing him for his involvement in the drug trade. "*Drugs is a government game*," Souljah writes, and prison a form of "*slavery*." As a result of "*hundreds, thousands, and millions of drug-related convictions*," the U.S. prison system now holds "*the majority of black men, and increasingly women*." The sense that prison had increasingly become a threat to Black women clarifies the purpose of Souljah's novel. In another letter, her fictionalized self asks, "*how do we get men and women before they are hunted like foxes and trapped like rats and treated like ants to understand the concepts of unity, working, building, living together?*"[100] Part of her answer to this question is a novel precisely like *The Coldest Winter Ever*, which pitches itself as an attempt to teach the concepts that Souljah believes have the best chance of keeping women from being "hunted" and "trapped" by the prison system.

As for Stringer, she believes that the best defense against the carceral system is a better understanding of how it works. *Let That Be the Reason* aims to raise awareness not only about the fact that American prisons are "filling at a rapid pace with young promising men and women," but also about the specific ways this growth is happening: through racially biased drug policies and draconian sentencing laws. At one point, Pamela learns the "nauseat[ing]" facts about mandatory minimum sentencing from her lawyer: "I need to tell you what you are facing. They have new federal guidelines that start at a mandatory minimum of ten years to life. Your drug sale puts you in the minimum . . . as it stands, you are at a guideline level of 34 based upon which you are facing 151–188 months in prison. Which is give or take 11 to 15 years." Stringer did not want to leave the instructive aims of fictional passages like this implicit. She expands on many of the same issues, including mandatory minimums, in the afterword. "Attention definitely needs to be given to the federal Mandatory Minimums that are in effect as 'Justice,'" Stringer writes. "The Mandatory sentencing Guideline is inhumane. It imposes punishment that does not fit the crime.... This 100 to 1 ratio is a further outrage. It is a biased law and evident by whom it effects the most—People of Color." Here Stringer enumerates the specific aspects of crime control legislation that increased racial bias in the legal system and played a central role in making mass incarceration a crisis for nonwhite communities: mandatory minimums, the infamous 100:1 sentencing disparity for crack possession, and the government's "unfair" use of conspiracy charges, which frequently targeted women. (Winter, too, rails against the absurdity of the conspiracy charge.) The afterword continues, "I implore you to become aware of the laws governing your actions and the actions of those you love. What you find may amaze you. These guidelines have been law since 1987. I came face to face with them in 1994.... Please be cognizant. Your awareness may save someone else."[101] Stringer's repeated emphasis on *awareness*—"become aware," "be cognizant," "Your awareness may save someone"—makes clear the pedagogical thrust of her literary project. "Awareness" of mass incarceration is, as Stringer puts it, a way to save others and perhaps yourself. The salvational power of readers' cognizance is, I think, key to both Stringer's and Souljah's novels. *Let That Be the Reason* and *The Coldest Winter Ever* were attempts to help their readers "become aware" not just of what was happening in American prisons, but of the fact that it could very well happen to them.

In writing to a predominately female audience about women's increased vulnerability to prison, Souljah and Stringer highlight the experience of what the feminist scholar Beth E. Richie has influentially called "gender entrapment." As Richie documents, vulnerable and victimized women are often "compelled to crime" through situations of abuse.[102] Building on Richie's work, the legal scholar Leigh Goodmark discusses what she calls "the criminalization of survival," which occurs when survivors of gender-based violence become caught up in the prison system themselves.[103] Gender entrapment plays a key role in both *The Coldest Winter Ever* and *Let*

That Be the Reason.[104] In Souljah's novel, Winter finds herself in an abusive relationship—surveilled by her boyfriend's employees, imprisoned in her own apartment—and is eventually set up to take the fall for a drug deal she had nothing to do with. In Stringer's novel, Pamela is compelled to enter the drug game after being abandoned by her abusive boyfriend and left to raise their son alone; once she starts making a living as a trafficker, she is intimidated by various men into continuing to deal. In the end, just like Winter, Pamela is set up by other men and left to take the fall by her ex-boyfriend, who abandons her yet again in the novel's final pages. Both novels thus draw a clear set of connections between partner violence, gender entrapment, the exploitative function of conspiracy charges, and the incarceration of Black women. As Henderson puts it, these novels highlight the link between "intimate partner and state violence"[105]—the line that stretches from abuse to incarceration.

It is true that, even as they emphasize important systemic aspects of women's oppression, the novels also indulge in moralizing critiques of women's personal behavior. Henderson is disappointed to find that Souljah leans on a neoliberal "ideology of personal responsibility aimed at Winter," relying on a set of "regressive gender ideals" that "criminalize Winter's marry up goals and sexual 'excess.'"[106] *Coldest Winter* repeatedly implies that Winter's problem is her unwillingness to improve herself; as the fictional Souljah says at one of her women's group meetings in the novel, "What could we [women] change about our own actions to cause [men] to treat all of us better?"[107] *Let That Be the Reason* similarly involves a certain degree of moral disapproval, as Pamela's early dreams of moving to the suburbs give way to the shame she feels after realizing the suffering she has personally caused by dealing drugs. Seeing "the effects of drugs" on other women in prison, Pamela is forced to confront the consequences of her choices; she can't "believe I had my hand in contributing to this."[108]

Yet despite these lapses into what Henderson justifiably calls a "conservative, gendered spiel of personal responsibility," both novels are ultimately about female protagonists who are caught in the gears of a carceral system that they wish they had understood sooner.[109] Winter is incredulous that she could get a fifteen-year sentence for being unknowingly involved in someone else's trafficking scheme ("I rented a car that was being used to transport guns and cocaine. But they wasn't my drugs. They wasn't my guns"[110]). Pamela is "nauseated" to learn that the charges against her carry a minimum of eleven years. In both cases, the texts' investment in the ideology of self-help rests in part on the imperative to readers to educate themselves about the prison system and thereby avoid Winter's and Pamela's fates. In *The Coldest Winter Ever* and *Let That Be the Reason*, attempts at self-actualization and at achieving economic independence culminate in harsh prison sentences. The uplift narrative had become a cautionary tale. "Fuck it. She'll learn for herself," Winter says of her sister at the end of her narrative. As authors, Souljah and Stringer took the opposite tack. They didn't want women to have to learn for themselves; they wanted to help teach them before it was too late. In the face of an out-of-control prison system that was at best racially "biased" (Stringer) and at worst a form of "slavery" (Souljah), and that was increasingly entrapping Black women, they wrote their novels in order to "warn others" about the personal threat that mass imprisonment posed—especially to those who didn't yet understand the complicated ways that new drug laws worked. Prison was fast becoming a reality for a growing number of working-class women of color. As Pamela's mother tells her at the end of *Let That Be the Reason*, "You're not the first to be arrested, and you won't be the last."[111]

CHOOSE WISELY

In 1976, an amateur pulp novelist imagined a massive and, at that point, largely fictional prison system hidden underneath a school in Watts. By the start of the 2010s, little about mass incarceration remained hidden. Numerous books, studies, and articles about the prison crisis appeared in the first decade of the twenty-first century, culminating in Michelle Alexander's enormously influential *The New Jim Crow*, first published in 2010. Alexander explains that she wrote *The New Jim Crow* with "a specific audience in mind—people who care deeply about racial justice but who . . . do not yet appreciate the magnitude of the crisis faced by communities of color as a result of mass incarceration."[112] In her own telling, Alexander was writing at a moment when the fact of mass incarceration had not yet fully entered the consciousness of racial justice advocates, let alone that of the general public. Her book played a major role in changing this, drawing a whole new level of attention to the magnitude of the prison crisis.[113] *The New Jim Crow* "quickly became required reading for anyone concerned about mass incarceration," James Forman recalls, as likely to be a book club pick as it was to be cited in legislative and policy debates.[114]

After 2010, the national conversation about prison took a sharp and surprising turn. Liberals and conservatives alike finally acknowledged that the size of America's prison population was a problem, and support for the project of mass imprisonment waned. In 2011, the Supreme Court issued its decision in *Brown v. Plata*, which ordered California to reduce the number of people in its prisons. In 2015, President Barack Obama created an agenda for criminal justice reform, with a focus on keeping nonviolent drug offenders out of prison. "I have . . . despaired about the magnitude of the problem" of mass incarceration, he told one audience, echoing Alexander's language.[115] Framing prison as an issue of government spending, conservative firebrands such as Newt Gingrich and Grover Norquist became unlikely Democratic allies in the development of bipartisan legislation on sentencing reform. Meanwhile, city councils moved to decriminalize drug possession, something that would have seemed politically inconceivable just a decade earlier.[116] While all of this was happening, U.S. incarceration rates did begin slowly to decline. Taking stock of these shifts, Marie Gottschalk cautiously observed in 2015 that "developments over the past year suggest that criminal justice reform has finally arrived as a leading public policy and political issue—at least for now."[117] It was not just the political class that had changed its tune on mass incarceration. A 2017 poll found that 71 percent of respondents believed "it is important to reduce the prison population in America"; two-thirds acknowledged that the criminal legal system treated African Americans unfairly.[118] By 2019, the authors of a policy brief titled "Ending Mass Incarceration" could plausibly suggest that any politician who didn't focus on fixing the prison crisis "risk[ed] being out of step with the American people."[119]

As mass incarceration became widely recognized as a serious problem, it also became a more frequent topic for serious novelists.[120] In a span of just three years at the end of the 2010s, Colson Whitehead, Jesmyn Ward, Rachel Kushner, and Tayari Jones published acclaimed novels about the prison system. Ward's *Sing, Unburied, Sing* (2017) won the National Book Award. Whitehead's *The Nickel Boys* (2019) won the Pulitzer Prize. Kushner's *The Mars Room* (2018) was shortlisted for the Man Booker Prize. Jones's *An American Marriage* (2018) was an Oprah's Book Club pick. As a privileged subject for prestige fiction, prison's time had clearly come. An ever-expanding list of authors have taken up the topic of mass imprisonment since. Here in the final section of this book's final chapter, I don't have room to discuss all of them. But I do want to take the time to follow two of the more interesting directions in which twenty-first-century prison fiction has been trending. One of these tracks back toward the prison system's past. The other leads forward into its future.

Whitehead's *The Nickel Boys* and Ward's *Sing, Unburied, Sing* are the most famous examples of the historical novel of mass incarceration.[121] *The Nickel Boys* tells the heartbreaking story of a brutal reform school in Tallahassee in the 1960s called the Nickel Academy. The novel is based on the true story of the Dozier School for Boys, which operated from 1900 to 2011 and on whose grounds investigators later discovered the graves of students who had been killed by guards. In writing it, Whitehead drew not just on the history of the Dozier School but also, he has explained, on histories of solitary confinement and of the Arkansas prison system. The story of the fictional Nickel Academy thus combines the history of abuse and excess at a reform school with facts about the normal functioning of U.S. prisons. At Nickel, "the boys were called students, rather than inmates," and yet, for Whitehead, what's important is how little this distinction matters. Nickel Academy is a place where young poor people, many of whom are Black, are confined for no reason; where an ostensible mandate to rehabilitate hides a sadistic commitment to punishment; where, in the words of one character, justice exists "in theory" but not in practice. In a telling detail, we learn that beatings at the school take place in a small white shed nicknamed the White House. "The White House delivered the law and everybody obeyed," Whitehead's narrator explains.[122] With this line, we are invited to view Nickel not as a single, aberrant reform school but as a punishment system whose highest level of authority is "the White House." *The Nickel Boys* is the story of how a system of punitive confinement—one that operates along the vectors of both race and class—outlived the Civil Rights movement and became an open secret in American society with the help of the federal government. Put that way, it's clear that what the novel is really talking about is mass incarceration.

Yet Whitehead opts to tell this story from a distance, as a prehistory (what came before mass incarceration) that doubles as an allegory, with Nickel Academy standing in for the contemporary correctional system. In fact, the concept of the stand-in constitutes a crucial feature of Whitehead's plot. The narrative of *The Nickel Boys* alternates between Elwood Curtis's experiences at Nickel in the early 1960s and his life in New York City in the 2010s. But in the novel's big plot twist, we learn that Elwood actually died trying to escape Nickel, and that the person now living under Elwood's name is really his friend Turner, who got away during the same escape attempt. The secret identity plot clinches Whitehead's central point even as it calls attention to the allegorical method he's using to make it. Elwood is Turner. Reform school is prison. Sometimes one thing can be a way of talking about another. Ultimately, *The Nickel Boys* is about what it would mean to discover that the present is, like Turner himself, simply the past in disguise.

In *Sing, Unburied, Sing*, Ward tells a similar story about the prison system's connection to the past—in this case, to the longer histories of Jim Crow and plantation slavery. Ward's primary tool for telling this story is not allegory's technique of disguise but the ghost story's mechanics of haunting. *Sing, Unburied, Sing* is about a woman named Leonie, who takes her adolescent son and young daughter on a road trip to pick up her boyfriend, Michael, upon his release from the Mississippi State Penitentiary. The novel does not say much about Michael's recent experience in prison, however. Instead, it narrates the horrors of prison through a series of extended flashbacks featuring Leonie's father, Pop, who did time in the same prison as a young man during the Jim Crow era. A boy with whom Pop was imprisoned, Richie, appears in the novel as an occasional narrator and as a ghost who is now haunting Leonie's son. The logic of haunting also applies to the Mississippi State Penitentiary itself, otherwise known as Parchman Farm, which was founded in the early twentieth century and, according to one historian, "looked like a typical Delta plantation, with cattle barns, vegetable gardens, mules dotting the landscape, and cotton rows stretching for miles."[123] Parchman thus brings together in one physical place the past of slavery, the past of Jim Crow, and the present of mass incarceration. Ward's novel strives to do the same thing. In *Sing, Unburied, Sing*, the past haunts the present in the form of phantoms that resemble lost loved ones no less than in the form of prisons that resemble plantations. Ghosts like Richie are hanging around because they need closure. Prisons like Parchman, the novel suggests, need closure too. The word's double meaning indicates that, for Ward, ending mass incarceration in the present requires understanding it as the product of an unresolved past.

It would be simplistic, though not incorrect, to point out that these two novels about the contemporary prison system's links to the pre–Civil Rights past strongly echo Michelle Alexander's argument about mass incarceration as a "new" version of the prior legal regime of Jim Crow. An emphasis on historical continuity is paramount in both novels. How, they wonder, did we get here? In a crucial passage in *The Nickel Boys*, Whitehead swiftly sketches the long continuum of racial violence stretching from chattel slavery ("Their daddies taught them how to keep a slave in line") to Jim Crow laws ("vagrancy, changing employers without permission, 'bumptious contact'") to the "dark cells" of reform schools like Nickel to police killings in the present ("another boy shot dead by a cop"). He sees these moments as parts of a single, ongoing story about Black dehumanization: "They treat us like subhumans in our own country. Always have."[124] Ward evokes the same continuum with even greater economy. "Parchman was past, present, and future all at once," she writes.[125] Passages like these are meant to put the current prison crisis in historical perspective. Mass incarceration, Ward and Whitehead insist, did not emerge out of nowhere. It is not a new way of racializing, controlling, and dehumanizing large segments of the population. It is, in fact, a very old way. It may even be an unavoidable way. In both *The Nickel Boys* and *Sing, Unburied, Sing*, mass imprisonment is identified as only the most recent chapter in the much longer history of American systems of racial control. This is a history that has repeated itself so many times it can begin to feel inevitable: like something that, in Whitehead's words, has "always" been there, and if we're not careful, always will be.

In the same years that Whitehead and Ward set out to excavate mass incarceration's buried past, other novelists were trying to speculate about its undecided future.[126] Set in a near-future America where a financial crisis has left most citizens out of work, Margaret Atwood's *The Heart Goes Last* (2015) tells the story of Charmaine and Stan, a married couple brought low by "the big financial-crash business-wrecking meltdown," now living out of their car and fending off roving gangs of thieves and rapists. Desperate for safety and stability, Charmaine and Stan sign on to join Consilience, a new planned community that promises full employment. There the couple will get jobs, a house, and protection from the dangerous, ravaged outside world. The catch? Consilience is able to offer all of this by cycling its citizens in and out of the town's prison, Positron. Everyone alternates on a monthly basis: "prisoners one month, guards or town functionaries the next." By warehousing half the community in any given month, the prison makes it possible for every job and every home to serve not one person but two. "Unemployment and crime solved in one fell swoop," goes the advertising pitch. "Think about that!"[127]

Summed up like this, the premise of Atwood's science fictional novel seems to be: What if we used prisons to solve an unemployment crisis? From one perspective, the question is fairly easy to answer. That *is* what we use them for. Loïc Wacquant and other researchers have argued for decades that mass incarceration is a response to the racialized crisis of un- and underemployment that came with deindustrialization. (I pursue this line of argument in chapter 4.) Yet on a purely literal level—and not to be too terribly pedantic here—the idea of swapping out prisoners and citizens each month makes very little economic sense. As Newt Gingrich would be happy to explain, housing and feeding incarcerated people is terribly expensive. In 2021, it cost $106,000 per year to incarcerate one person in California.[128] And that's before we take into account the fact that, in *The Heart Goes Last*, the Positron prison is extremely comfortable and has excellent food. "It's like having a vacation every month," Charmaine thinks to herself at one point.[129] As the ostensible solution to an economic problem, a luxury prison where workers vacation is baldly illogical. Something else must be going on here.

Something else is. What really interests Atwood in *The Heart Goes Last* is how the prison provides a staging ground for questions of free choice and free will. To what extent is freedom—prison's supposed opposite—realized through the exercising of choice? *The Heart Goes Last* is bookended by choices that are framed as demonstrations of freedom. When Stan and Charmaine first consider signing the contract for Consilience, they're told, "If you signed up, it would be of your own free will." Then at the very end of the novel, having gotten free from Consilience and Positron, Charmaine's freedom is expressed as a new horizon of choices. In the book's final lines, Charmaine is told, "you're free to go. The world is all before you, where to choose."[130] If there is an irony to this ending, it is that what looks at first like the difference between Charmaine's past confinement in Positron and the free choices of her future—"where to choose"—is not as much of a difference as it should be. After all, Positron, too, was Charmaine's and Stan's choice, one that was made of their "own free will." Here lies the central paradox of Atwood's rather wild carceral fable. The paradox is not that prison should be economically useful but isn't. It's that prison, presumed to be the definitive other of free choice, somehow turns out to be a prime expression of it.

Atwood was not the only author puzzling out the significance of choice to the future carceral state around this time. George Saunders's "Escape from Spiderhead" (which appeared first in the *New Yorker* in 2010 and later in Saunders's 2013 collection *Tenth of December*) is about a futuristic correctional facility called Spiderhead where prisoners are used to test experimental drugs. The main plot involves a prisoner and test subject named Jeff, who as part of a drug trial is forced to choose which of two fellow inmates will be tortured. That's not the first difficult choice Jeff has had to make. Just being at Spiderhead is already a choice: an alternative to prison to which inmates have freely chosen to be transferred. Once confined there, prisoners are legally required to give their consent each time a drug is administered, a call-and-response that becomes the story's refrain ("'Drip on?' Abnesti said over the P.A.... 'Acknowledge,' I said."). Yet inmates have no choice but to consent; it's part of the agreement to come to Spiderhead in the first place. This absurdity comes to a head when, faced with Jeff's growing unwillingness to participate in the trial, the CEO of Spiderhead, Abnesti, considers administering him a drug that will chemically produce consent. He is then reminded by his technician that they need Jeff's consent to give him the consent drug. "See, that, to me, makes zero sense," Abnesti complains. "What good's an obedience drug if we need his permission to use it?"[131] Finally he remembers a workaround. They just need to fill out a waiver. The outlandish farce of this scene—a waiver that bypasses the need to get Jeff's consent to give him a drug that produces consent—reveals what we've known all along: that all of the choices Jeff has made as a prisoner at Spiderhead have not really been choices at all. That includes the final choice Jeff makes, which gives the story its title. In the end, Jeff decides that he no longer wants to consent to being part of the drug trial that requires him to make difficult choices. But what Saunders optimistically calls his "Escape" is in truth a dispiriting euphemism.

THE NOVEL IN THE AGE OF MASS INCARCERATION

Unwilling to choose which of his fellow inmates will be tortured with a suicide-inducing drug called Darkenfloxx™, Jeff makes the one other choice available to him. He chooses to ingest the drug himself. His escape from Spiderhead only happens once he has killed himself.

The genre of future-prison fiction reached the apex of its critical and commercial appeal with Nana Kwame Adjei-Brenyah's *Chain-Gang All-Stars* (2023). (Adjei-Brenyah was an MFA student of Saunders's at Syracuse.) A finalist for the National Book Award as well as a celebrity book club pick, *Chain-Gang All-Stars* is yet another story about the intersection between the future of prison and the problem of free choice. In the future world of *Chain-Gang All-Stars*, incarcerated people are given the choice to leave prison by signing up with Criminal Action Penal Entertainment (CAPE), a corporation that forces inmates to fight to the death in packed arenas and on live television. Adjei-Brenyah tempers this seemingly fantastical premise by repeatedly reminding readers about the facts of mass incarceration in the present. A series of footnotes running throughout the book offers real-world statistics about the current U.S. prison system ("It is estimated that between 2.3 percent and 5 percent of incarcerated people in America are innocent"). His characters even quote Ruth Wilson Gilmore. Details like these help readers grasp that the speculative future described by Adjei-Brenyah is only a thinly disguised stand-in for the prison abolitionist struggle in the present. Yet like *The Heart Goes Last* and "Escape from Spiderhead" before it, *Chain-Gang All-Stars* is especially fixated on the language of choice. Describing those in the CAPE program, one character says, "It is a choice. A choice we all made." This is true. What distinguishes CAPE from traditional prison is that it is (just like Positron and Spiderhead) freely chosen by those who participate in it. Indeed, the legislation passed to allow prisoners to opt in to CAPE is called the Rightful Choice Act, which "states that under their own will and power, convicted wards of the state may elect to forgo a state-administered execution or a sentence totaling at least twenty-five (25) years' imprisonment, to instead participate in the CAPE program." The "rightful choice" made by prisoners "under their own will and power" is, in truth, something significantly more coercive: a choice made under the extreme duress of technologically enhanced punishments that are indistinguishable from torture. Yet the supposition that we all have the freedom to choose our fate is an idea to which even the book's heroes cling. Wracked by guilt over the crime that sent her to prison in the first place, the novel's heroine, Loretta Thurwar, insists on owning her choices: "I did have control. I had choices."[132]

All three of these texts narrate pivotal moments of people choosing or consenting to their own imprisonment. On the face of it, this seems like an inaccurate if not outwardly cruel way of describing how real people actually end up in prison.[133] Perhaps, though, these repeated scenes aren't meant to indict the choices made by imprisoned people. Perhaps they're meant to indict the choices made by those who have consented to the whole system of mass imprisonment. Think again about that line from *Chain-Gang All-Stars*: "It is a choice. A choice we all made." What would it mean to think of mass incarceration as a choice that "we"—the American public—"all made?"

To be sure, when it comes to their incarcerated characters, these texts stress the forms of economic, legal, and bodily coercion that lurk beneath the neoliberal shibboleths of free choice and personal responsibility. At the same time, they raise the possibility that mass imprisonment as such is a phenomenon that American citizens have freely chosen. In *The Heart Goes Last*, Atwood repeatedly emphasizes her characters' collusion in their own incarceration. Stan and Charmaine sign their Positron contract of their "own free will"; later, Stan wonders, "Who had caged him and walled him off? He'd done it himself."[134] In *Chain-Gang All-Stars*, Adjei-Brenyah describes the popularity of CAPE programming in the same terms of shared responsibility, writing that "they, we, you, them—everyone agreed to the arrangement."[135] The fact that Adjei-Brenyah's particular vision of the future prison centers on its fusion with the entertainment industry suggests that the "everyone" in this sentence includes his readers. Entertainment is its own form of consent. If the violence of prison were a televised spectacle, would you choose to watch it? Or, to put a finer point on it, if the spectacle were a novel—called, say, *Chain-Gang All-Stars*, and filled with dozens of pages of meticulously described fight scenes that are, depending on your perspective, either thrilling or sickening—would you choose to read it?

The freely signed contract or consent form that figures prominently in all three of these future-prison narratives is thus not simply a parody of coerced choice. It is also an allegory for the collective responsibility borne by free citizens—including these texts' own readers—for consenting to the social compact that has defined American society since the end of the twentieth century: a compact that has promised jobs and safety to some people in exchange for the imprisonment of others. "Look," say Atwood's Positron entrepreneurs: "safe streets, no homelessness, jobs for all!"[136] It is on the basis of this particular pitch that Stan and Charmaine agree to send themselves to prison. And it is on this same basis, Atwood implies, that the tragedy of mass incarceration became something that the nation did to itself. For Atwood, Saunders, and Adjei-Brenyah, the future of an even crueler and more massive prison-industrial complex is not some unforeseen calamity that will unexpectedly befall us. It is, on the contrary, precisely the arrangement we have already chosen for ourselves.

Mass incarceration is, indeed, a system to which many Americans have long consented. Reflecting back on this state of affairs from the vantage of an imagined future, the novel of the future prison is at heart a parable of regret about the choice a free populace has made, over six decades, to wage war on crime and to create a society that imprisons more people than any other on the planet. That said, there is certainly a risk in depicting the carceral state as a matter of choice. Mass incarceration was not the result of a single choice or even a single actor; it was the product of thousands of individual, local, state, and federal decisions and processes—some racist, some sadistic, some stupid, some well-intentioned—made over the course of more than half a century. So why use the future prison as a literary site for ritually staging scenes of people choosing their own imprisonment? Perhaps it is because choice remains a powerful symbol of making as well as unmaking. It signifies individual responsibility, yes, but it also introduces contingency. Novels such as *The Nickel Boys* and *Sing, Unburied, Sing* narrate a historical continuum of racial violence on which mass incarceration appears as a kind of inevitability: prison as the unavoidable end point of a past long ago inscribed in blood. By contrast, a novel such as *Chain-Gang All-Stars* clings to choice in order to envision the possibility that things might have gone differently. "I had choices," Adjei-Brenyah's hero says. This is another way of saying: I could have made different ones.

At the heart of these two contrasting types of twenty-first-century prison fiction—the novel of prison's past and the novel of its future—is a single question, one no doubt informed by the reflective mood of a historical moment when it seemed, however fleetingly, that incarceration rates were finally in decline: Did things have to turn out the way they did?[137] While it is not true that the prison crisis was made through choice alone, it is understandable why some writers and readers might prefer to think that it was. Mass incarceration was one of postwar America's most ruinous mistakes. How nice to imagine—looking back from the protected perch of a fictional future—that, given the chance, we wouldn't choose to make the same mistake again.

Epilogue

AND THE LAW WON

why the hell was he wearing this badge?

—*ALL THE SINNERS BLEED* (2023)

This book has told the story of how the War on Crime was waged across the pages of novels. That story has spanned eighty years of literary and social history, from paperback thrillers probing new versions of racial and criminal ideology in the 1940s to speculative fiction confronting the dystopia of mass incarceration in the twenty-first century. You have pretty much reached the end of *American Literature's War on Crime*. But we have not yet reached the end of the story.

Midway through the 2010s—with pressure to end mass imprisonment coming from both the left and the right, and city governments moving to support drug decriminalization—it was possible to believe that U.S. society might finally be losing its appetite for unchecked policing and imprisonment. Now, less than ten years later, it is impossible to deny that the American public seems as hungry as ever for punitive anticrime policy. The swift recrudescence of law-and-order politics is as ironic as it is tragic. A decade that witnessed a sea change in public opinion about prisons and small but real shifts in incarceration rates culminated, after the murder of George Floyd in Minnesota, in nationwide protests against police violence. In 2020, the radical rallying cry "defund the police" went mainstream. The long-running TV show *Cops* was cancelled. A "certain collective mood" prevailed at this time, the critic Jonathan Flatley has pointed out, when at times it could feel as if nearly "everybody hates the police."[1] The prospect of real social change seemed to be in the air. But the political winds shifted direction, and that change never arrived.

Instead, from 2020 to 2025, law and order theatrically returned to the main stage of American politics. (*Cops*, too, returned to the air.) As crime rates were reported to rise, a pro-punishment consensus took hold. And as ever, the data paint a more complex picture. In 2020, the rate of violent crime saw a sharp spike, while property crime declined to a historic low. Over the next few years, property crime rose back up (a predictable result of the end of pandemic lockdown orders) while violent crime returned to its lower baseline of recent decades.[2] In other words, since 2020, crime rates have been stabilizing. All the breathless talk of crime waves over the past few years has been mainly that—talk driven less by increased crime than by increased use in the media of phrases such as *crime wave*.[3] By the first half of 2024, the incidence of eleven different types of crime had dropped either to or below pre-pandemic levels.[4] But it was too late. A single political and media narrative had already taken hold: that rising crime rates and decreased public safety were the direct result of a few short years of modest criminal justice reforms and justified anger toward the police.[5]

The statistical falsity of the narrative has not made it feel less true.[6] Crime has once again become a major anxiety among voters, and public support for harsh punishment has increased. Recent polls have shown that "overall confidence in American police agencies has grown substantially since 2021," with favorable views of the police rising by eight percentage points.[7] Gallup adds that Americans' increased confidence in the police between 2023 and 2024 "was the largest year-over-year change in public perceptions of 17 major U.S. institutions."[8] According to the Pew Research Center, "violent crime" was as important an issue in the 2024 election as "immigration" and "foreign policy."[9] Crime was perhaps an even more decisive issue in state and local elections, which saw the sweeping success of punitive anticrime ballot measures and the high-profile defeats or recalls of progressive prosecutors.[10] Even something as reasonable as bail reform has not survived the backlash. By the time all the 2024 election results were in, it felt like the end of a very short-lived era. In the words of the Congressional Black Caucus Foundation, "After progressive reforms were passed in the wake of George Floyd's death, the election results suggest the

EPILOGUE

pendulum is swinging the other way: voters in states across the country have chosen to increase prison sentences and levy fines to deter future crime."[11]

The reminder that all of this is a choice ("voters... have chosen") has a special sting. At the end of the previous chapter, I suggested that some recent novelists had sought to imagine that, with the benefit of hindsight, we wouldn't make the mistake of choosing mass incarceration again. So much for that. Now here we are, making the same mistake again. More police, more prison time, more punishment: These are once again the order of the day. The idea of an even slightly more progressive, slightly more humane approach to criminal justice that seemed to be on the horizon in the 2010s already feels like a distant memory. Today it's as if the War on Crime never ended. Perhaps that's because it never did.

This abrupt about-face on the crime war betrays, among other things, a profound ambivalence on the part of the American people. Do we want progressive prosecutors or punitive ones? Do we want shorter prison sentences or longer ones? Defunding or more funding for the police? And how could we have changed our minds so quickly on all of these issues? The difficulty of deciphering the country's contradictory stance toward law enforcement is similarly apparent in some of today's best crime fiction. Police novels now regularly criticize the practice of American policing. This isn't necessarily a paradox. We can think of it, instead, as an earnest investigation into the remarkable equivocation around criminal justice that characterizes our current moment. The rise of the antipolice police procedural suggests a desire to figure out how it is possible to know the extensive failings of the past six decades of U.S. crime policy and still not know how to live without it.

One of the most complex fictional commentaries on race and policing of recent years is *All the Sinners Bleed* (2023), a bestselling novel by "one of America's hottest writers," S. A. Cosby.[12] *All the Sinners Bleed* is the story of Titus Crown, an ex–FBI agent who has recently become the sheriff of a rural Virginia county. While dealing with the fallout from a shooting committed by his deputies, Crown uncovers a grisly plot involving the unreported disappearances and ritual murders of Black boys and girls. He sets about tracking down the racially motivated serial killer his county didn't know it had, while also attempting to keep the peace at an upcoming white supremacist rally (a scene that bears a strong resemblance to the tragic events in Charlottesville, Virginia, in 2017). Ultimately, it turns out that the sadistic killer is a mixed-race man passing for white who took part in the rally and who also happens to work at the local flag factory—a key detail. It's like Cosby is trying to tell us that all of these threads of racial violence are woven, flag-like, into the very fabric of American society.

But what makes *All the Sinners Bleed* most interesting as a crime novel is its repeated acknowledgment that one of the main historical sources of racial violence is the police—this despite the fact that the novel's hero is himself an officer of the law. As a Black sheriff, Crown is cognizant of the compromise built in to his chosen profession. He is well "aware of the long history of bias and bigotry that persisted, not only in the Charon County Sheriff's Office but in many police departments across the country." He recognizes "the fury that some people felt toward his department," and in many ways he shares it. "The history of policing in America, especially south of the Mason-Dixon" has made it necessary even for someone like Crown to remain skeptical of how police power is used and abused. "Too many Black men and women had been executed by folks with badges" for him to feel any different.[13]

Indeed, Crown decided to seek office in the first place because he wanted to "change things from the inside." He explains, "I ran for sheriff because I didn't want anyone here to get away with the things they did to us when we were growing up because they were the law."[14] In this sense, Cosby's novel seems intended to test out the value of police reform. What difference would it make to replace a racist white sheriff with a compassionate Black sheriff? Cosby's answer is not entirely optimistic. By the end of the novel, Crown comes to realize that changing things from the inside is "a lot easier said than done." He has "sworn that he'd change things," but quickly discovers that he may not be able to. Instead, in an event that sets the novel's plot in motion, he finds himself in charge of a department whose white deputies shot a mentally ill Black man who had been about to surrender. Crown is devastated that "his deputies had killed a man ... who had needed his help." He is also dismayed to realize that this may be how the whole system is designed to work. "What if you couldn't change the system because it was working as intended?" he reflects. "And if that was true, then why the hell was he wearing this badge?" Crown doesn't ultimately know how to answer this question. So at the very end of *All the Sinners Bleed*, he resigns as sheriff. Then he uses his car to pull down the town's Confederate monument on his way out of town. "Fuck that noise," he says to himself.[15] Is it really possible to "change the system" by working inside it—especially when that system is itself a monument to an American past steeped in racial bloodshed? Crown seems to have decided that it isn't.

Similar questions about the role of Black police officers, the possibility of police reform, and the persistent allure of law enforcement drive the three novels of Attica Locke's widely acclaimed (and justly so) Highway 59 series. Locke's series stars Darren Matthews, a Black Texas Ranger. Matthews was raised by two uncles who had opposing views of whether American law enforcement could be made "fundamentally hospitable to black life." One uncle was a Texas Ranger who believed "the law would save us by *protecting* us." The other is a defense attorney turned law professor who maintains that "the law is a lie black folks need protection from—a set of rules that were written against us from the time ink was first set to parchment." Matthews follows in the footsteps of the first uncle but remains influenced by the views of the second. He has "spent his life straddling the family's ideological divide."[16] His love for his warring uncles—each believing the other was "on the wrong side of the law"—has "cleaved his soul in two."[17]

We might say the same thing about Locke's novels: that they are cleaved in two—attempts to straddle the ideological divide between policing and its skeptics. Matthews's decision to join the Rangers is based on his belief that the legal system can protect Black communities "by prosecuting crimes against us as zealously as it prosecutes crimes against whites."[18] Matthews embodies this reformist promise. He pursues cases involving Black victims that might otherwise have been ignored, investigates white supremacist groups, even "propose[s] establishing a hate crimes unit." Yet he is also keenly aware of reform's limits. For one thing, the hate crimes unit idea is "roundly dismissed" by his superiors.[19] For another, Matthews knows that police violence against Black communities is continuing unabated. In one scene, he opines that he cannot bear to hear people "question the point of rioting in Ferguson or Baltimore," when the point surely is obvious—both were cities whose uprisings in the mid-2010s took place in direct response to the police murders of Black men.[20] Finally, there's Matthews's lingering sense that the system isn't really designed to administer justice in certain situations: situations like that of his neighbor Mack, an elderly Black man whom Matthews thinks may have shot a white supremacist, and whose crime he helps cover up. The stressful situation with Mack, along with Matthews's persistent sense of the professional "resentment" felt by "more than a few" of his white colleagues, leads him to start "questioning his allegiance to the Rangers."[21] At the end of the series' second novel, *Heaven, My Home* (2019), a despondent Matthews buys a bottle of Jim Beam, drives to his house, and puts on a record. The first song he hears is Little Milton's "I Can't Quit You, Baby"—a germane choice for conveying Matthews's intensely equivocal attraction to his job.[22]

Eventually, like Titus Crown, Darren Matthews does quit. At the start of *Guide Me Home* (2024), the third and most recent Highway 59 novel, Matthews resigns after learning he is about to be indicted for obstruction of justice. He quickly regrets his resignation, discovering how much more difficult it is to investigate a case (here, involving a Black college student who has gone missing from a white sorority) without "the power of the badge" behind him. Trying to get answers from various people, he realizes that he "had no real authority" to question them. This is disconcerting, if not outright concerning; at several points, Matthews is confronted by threatening cops and made to feel his own vulnerability to them. He misses "the authority of the Texas Rangers." He wishes "he still had his badge." At the end of the novel, having located the missing student and avoided the obstruction charge, it seems that Matthews may get his wish. His former lieutenant calls to offer him his old job back. His fiancée, Randie, asks the question that readers have likely been wondering about themselves: "So, you going back to work?" But Locke coyly and quite intentionally leaves the question up in the air. She ends her book without giving a straight answer. Matthews remains torn; he isn't sure whether he should return to the Rangers or go to law school. It's okay, Randie reminds him. The question "wasn't anything that he had to decide tonight."[23]

Crown isn't quite as undecided, though he, too, has a harder time walking away from it all than we might have expected. After resigning as sheriff, he decides to accept a university position in Baton Rouge. As he explains to his brother in the book's final pages, "I'm teaching criminology, so it's not like I'm completely giving up on law enforcement." Crown has left the sheriff's department yet can't bring himself to abandon law enforcement as such. He acknowledges and has often leaned into the "darker aspects of his position" as a police officer, its violent tendencies and systemic flaws. Yet he's still not "completely giving up on" it. Crown's ambivalent feelings about the job are powerfully summed up in one striking passage late in the novel: "Sometimes the star felt like a shield over your heart, sometimes it felt like an anchor dragging you down, and other times, well, other times it felt like a cheap-ass piece of tin."[24] Call this three ways of looking at a badge. From one angle, we see the false ("cheap-ass") promises of policing; from another, the burden ("an anchor") of the institution's violent history; and from a third, its continued allure as a beacon of security ("a shield"). The tormented brilliance of Cosby's novel lies in its attempt to make us see all three angles at once.

Is a badge precious silver or cheap tin? Is it an ideal or a delusion? A shield or a weapon? Is it there to protect others or only the person wearing it? Neither *All the Sinners Bleed* nor the Highway 59 novels offer definitive answers to these questions. That may be what makes these works such apt emblems of our time. Sometimes the police novel and the defund-the-police novel are one and the same book. We are currently living through a moment when more Americans are more well-versed in the extensive failings of the carceral state—more thoroughly schooled in its racism, its classism, its depravity, and its unaccountability—than ever before, and when they nevertheless decide to keep casting their lot (and their vote) with it. Ten years of ghastly episodes of police violence circulating on social media have now mixed with five years of law-and-order backlash and media-stoked crime panics to create a cloudy brew of deep criminal justice indecision. Ambivalent citizens are "cleaved" right down to their "souls," sympathetic to the anger and distrust that many people feel toward the police but not yet ready to "completely giv[e] up on" the most punitive tendencies of U.S. law enforcement institutions. Cresting the wave of such mixed feelings, the War on Crime has just celebrated its sixtieth anniversary as a pillar of American social policy. In that time, we have amassed all the evidence we could ever need of the abiding cruelty and basic ineffectiveness of this war. We know that it is flawed in a way that is not local or provisional but structural and unavoidable. We know that vulnerable people who need support will continue to be killed by the police and that mass incarceration will remain a humanitarian crisis of colossal and heartbreaking proportions. In short, we know we should be done with the War on Crime. But it's like Locke's Little Milton record says. We just can't seem to quit it.

ACKNOWLEDGMENTS

Writing this book has been, more than anything, a profound learning experience. I owe an immeasurable debt to all the scholars, writers, and activists who have labored to understand the past and to alter the present of policing and imprisonment in the United States. Without their scrupulous, tireless, inspiring work, this book would not exist.

Writing is hard; at least it is for me. Luckily, I've received a great deal of support from many marvelous people. I feel quite fortunate to have the opportunity to thank the following friends, neighbors, colleagues, readers, teachers, and conversation partners: Jonathan Alexander, Elizabeth Allen, Tamara Beauchamp, Adrienne Brown, Amy Chen, Youngmin Choe, Miles Corwin, Ricky Crano, Joe Darda, Becky Davis, Chris Fan, Kennan Ferguson, Laura Finch, Josh Gang, Ben Garceau, Richard Godden, Amanda Goldstein, Kyle Grady, Andrea Henderson, Thomas Heise, Gordon Hutner, Joe Jeon, Travis Linnemann, Colleen Lye, J. B. Manchak, Meka Manchak, Xander Manshel, Kate Marshall, Tom McEnaney, Tobias Menely, Valentina Montero Roman, Liron Mor, Kinohi Nishikawa, Andrew Pepper, Kent Puckett, Palmer Rampell, Caroline Reitz, James Robertson, Tara Rodman, Margaret Ronda, Chelsea Schields, Natalie Shapero, Rebekah Sheldon, Dan Sinykin, Michael Szalay, Claire Vaye Watkins, and Jesse Wolfson. Thank you, too, Ben and Solon. Thank you again, Margaret and Tobias. A special note of gratitude is owed to the brilliant and bracingly honest writing group (Michael, Richard, Chris, Joe, Annie) that was generous enough to have me, and whose skeptical questions and piercing insights made this book a whole lot better.

Thank you to Philip Leventhal and his incomparable team at Columbia University Press. Philip believed in this project from the beginning and provided his wisdom, expertise, and support until the very end. It is a privilege to be able to say this is our second book together. Thank you to the esteemed editors of Literature Now—Rebecca Walkowitz, David James, and especially Matt Hart—for welcoming me back to the series. Thank you to Emily Simon for answering my constant questions about everything; to Kathryn Jorge for expertly shepherding this book through production; and to Katherine Harper for her wise and generous copyedits. Thank you to Kimberly Glyder for another incredible book cover. Thank you to my two anonymous press readers, who offered valuable guidance on needed repairs, as well as some generous words of encouragement. Portions of chapter 1 originally appeared as "Crime Fiction and Black Criminality" in *American Literary History* 30, no. 4 (Winter 2018): 703–29, published by Oxford University Press and reprinted with permission. Portions of chapter 2 originally appeared as "War-on-Crime Fiction," *PMLA* 136, no. 2 (2021): 213–28, published by Cambridge University Press on behalf of the Modern Language Association of America and reprinted with permission. Thank you to the editorial boards and peer reviewers of both journals for giving these ideas a chance. Publication support for this book was generously provided by the UCI Humanities Center.

Thank you, wonderful family: Jon, Han, Erin, Jonathan, Rick, Josh, Jen, Cia, Anne, and Billy. We still miss you, dad. Thank you for everything forever, Ma.

This book is dedicated to Annie and Lulu McC, who have shaped my life so elementally and so profoundly that it would take a whole separate book to explain.

Appendix

CAST OF CRIME NOVELS

1. INVISIBLE MEN, 1940-1966

Native Son by Richard Wright (1940)
The Man Who Lived Underground by Richard Wright (written 1942; published 2021)
If He Hollers Let Him Go by Chester Himes (1945)
The Street by Ann Petry (1946)
Country Place by Ann Petry (1947)
In a Lonely Place by Dorothy B. Hughes (1947)
Strangers on a Train by Patricia Highsmith (1950)
Invisible Man by Ralph Ellison (1952)
The Killer Inside Me by Jim Thompson (1952)
The Outsider by Richard Wright (1953)
Yesterday Will Make You Cry by Chester Himes (1953)
Runaway Black by Evan Hunter (1954)
Savage Holiday by Richard Wright (1954)
Pick-Up by Charles Willeford (1955)
The Talented Mr. Ripley by Patricia Highsmith (1955)
Cop Hater by Ed McBain (1956)
Psycho by Robert Bloch (1959)
The Expendable Man by Dorothy B. Hughes (1963)
Run Man Run by Chester Himes (1966)

APPENDIX

2. RIOT ACTS, 1967-1974

Cop Hater by Ed McBain (1956)
The Man Who Cried I Am by John A. Williams (1967)
The Algiers Motel Incident by John Hersey (1968)
Death for a Playmate by John Ball (1969)
Sons of Darkness, Sons of Light by John A. Williams (1969)
The Spook Who Sat by the Door by Sam Greenlee (1969)
The New Centurions by Joseph Wambaugh (1970)
Shaft by Ernest Tidyman (1970)
The Vulture by Gil Scott-Heron (1970)
Death Wish by Brian Garfield (1972)
The Friends of Eddie Coyle by George V. Higgins (1972)
The Lynchers by John Edgar Wideman (1973)
Crime Partners by Donald Goines (1974)

3. DETECTING DOMESTIC VIOLENCE, 1975-2000

Where Are the Children? by Mary Higgins Clark (1975)
A Is for Alibi by Sue Grafton (1982)
Bitter Medicine by Sara Paretsky (1987)
Marriage Is Murder by Nancy Pickard (1987)
Postmortem by Patricia Cornwell (1990)
Dead Time by Eleanor Taylor Bland (1992)
Blanche Among the Talented Tenth by Barbara Neely (1994)
Final Jeopardy by Linda Fairstein (1996)
Those Bones Are Not My Child by Toni Cade Bambara (1999)
Blanche Passes Go by Barbara Neely (2000)

4. TWO PATHS FOR PATHOLOGY, 1984-1998

Blood on the Moon by James Ellroy (1984)
White Noise by Don DeLillo (1985)
C Is for Corpse by Sue Grafton (1986)
Bitter Medicine by Sara Paretsky (1987)

APPENDIX

The Black Dahlia by James Ellroy (1987)
"The Evening and the Morning and the Night" by Octavia Butler (1987)
Because It Is Bitter, Because It Is My Heart by Joyce Carol Oates (1990)
Devil in a Blue Dress by Walter Mosley (1990)
Hardball by Barbara D'Amato (1990)
L.A. Confidential by James Ellroy (1990)
Postmortem by Patricia Cornwell (1990)
American Psycho by Bret Easton Ellis (1991)
All That Remains by Patricia Cornwell (1992)
Blanche on the Lam by Barbara Neely (1992)
Clockers by Richard Price (1992)
A Walk Among the Tombstones by Lawrence Block (1992)
White Butterfly by Walter Mosley (1992)
Freedomland by Richard Price (1998)

5. THE NOVEL IN THE AGE OF MASS INCARCERATION, 1992-2023

The School on 103rd Street by Roland Jefferson (1976)
The Little Death by Michael Nava (1986)
Just Cause by John Katzenbach (1992)
The Green Mile by Stephen King (1996)
Always Outnumbered, Always Outgunned by Walter Mosley (1998)
The Coldest Winter Ever by Sister Souljah (1999)
Hard Time by Sara Paretsky (1999)
Let That Be the Reason by Vickie Stringer (2002)
"Escape from Spiderhead" by George Saunders (2010)
The Heart Goes Last by Margaret Atwood (2015)
Lay Your Sleeping Head by Michael Nava (2016)
Sing, Unburied, Sing by Jesmyn Ward (2017)
The Nickel Boys by Colson Whitehead (2019)
Chain-Gang All-Stars by Nana Kwame Adjei-Brenyah (2023)

APPENDIX

EPILOGUE: AND THE LAW WON

Bluebird, Bluebird by Attica Locke (2017)
Heaven, My Home by Attica Locke (2019)
All the Sinners Bleed by S. A. Cosby (2023)
Guide Me Home by Attica Locke (2024)

NOTES

INTRODUCTION: CRIME AND FICTION

1. Lyndon B. Johnson, "Special Message to the Congress on Law Enforcement and the Administration of Justice," March 8, 1965, The American Presidency Project, https://www.presidency.ucsb.edu/documents/special-message-the-congress-law-enforcement-and-the-administration-justice.
2. In telling the story of mass incarceration as something that unfolded over more than three-quarters of a century, I am following the lead of groundbreaking scholarship by Heather Ann Thompson, Elizabeth Hinton, Naomi Murakawa, Ruth Wilson Gilmore, Stuart Schrader, and Jordan T. Camp, among others. As Camp explains it, "the making of the postwar carceral state was as much a product of civil rights struggles over policing and law and order in the 1940s and 1950s as it was a response to" the social upheavals and economic crises of later decades. Jordan T. Camp, *Incarcerating the Crisis: Freedom Struggles and the Rise of the Neoliberal State* (University of California Press, 2016), 7.
3. These numbers are from the Prison Policy Initiative (prisonpolicy.org).
4. Jonathan Simon, Ian Haney López, and Mary Louise Frampton, Introduction, *After the War on Crime: Race, Democracy, and a New Reconstruction*, ed. Mary Louise Frampton, Ian Haney López, and Jonathan Simon (New York University Press, 2008), 3.
5. Heather Ann Thompson, "Why Mass Incarceration Matters: Rethinking Crisis, Decline, and Transformation in Postwar American History," *Journal of American History* 97, no. 3 (2010): 734.
6. Stuart Schrader, *Badges Without Borders: How Global Counterinsurgency Transformed American Policing* (University of California Press, 2019), 1.

INTRODUCTION

7. Elizabeth Hinton, *From the War on Poverty to the War on Crime: The Making of Mass Incarceration in America* (Harvard University Press, 2016), 2.
8. Dominique Kalifa, *Vice, Crime, and Poverty: How the Western Imagination Invented the Underworld*, trans. Susan Emanuel (Columbia University Press, 2019), 5.
9. Alex Vitale, *The End of Policing* (Verso, 2017), 33.
10. David Correia and Tyler Wall, *Police: A Field Guide* (Verso, 2018), 100.
11. Criminal law is a way of "punishing the poor," Loïc Wacquant has argued. It also "function[s] to produce race," Micol Siegel suggests. Wacquant, *Punishing the Poor: The Neoliberal Government of Social Insecurity* (Duke University Press, 2009); Siegel, *Violence Work: State Power and the Limits of Police* (Duke University Press, 2018), 21.
12. Sal Nicolazzo, *Vagrant Figures: Law, Literature, and the Origins of the Police* (Yale University Press, 2020), 3.
13. Saidiya Hartman, *Wayward Lives, Beautiful Experiments: Intimate Histories of Riotous Black Girls, Troublesome Women, and Queer Radicals* (W. W. Norton, 2019), 242.
14. Hartman, *Wayward Lives, Beautiful Experiments*, 224.
15. Christian Parenti, *Lockdown America: Police and Prisons in the Age of Crisis* (Verso, 1999; repr. 2008), 242.
16. Hinton, *From the War on Poverty*, 12.
17. This is a process whose outcome Douglas S. Massey and Nancy A. Denton once famously described as "American Apartheid." According to their analysis, "No group in the history of the United States has ever experienced the sustained high level of residential segregation that has been imposed on blacks in large American cities for the past fifty years." Massey and Denton, *American Apartheid: Segregation and the Making of the Underclass* (Harvard University Press, 1993), 2. This high level of residential segregation is also what scholars call ghettoization. On "the ghetto as paramount mechanism of ethnoracial domination" in American life from the 1920s to the 1960s, see Loïc Wacquant, "From Slavery to Mass Incarceration: Rethinking the 'Race Question' in the U.S.," *New Left Review* 13 (2002): 48. For an intellectual history of the concept of the ghetto in the twentieth-century social sciences, see Mitchell Duneier, *Ghetto: The Invention of a Place, the History of an Idea* (Farrar, Strauss, and Giroux, 2016).
18. Thomas J. Sugrue, *The Origins of the Urban Crisis: Race and Inequality in Postwar Detroit* (Princeton University Press, 1996; repr., 2014), 4, 3.
19. Hinton, *From the War on Poverty*, 19.
20. Writing about the period of economic recession in post-1960 Britain, Stuart Hall, Chas Critcher, Tony Jefferson, John Clarke, and Brian Roberts famously argued that "*race* has come to provide the objective correlative of crisis—the arena in which complex fears, tensions, and anxieties, generated by the impact of the totality of the crisis on the whole society, can be most conveniently and explicitly projected and ...'worked through.'" Thus, in a way that parallels what was happening in the United States, "black crime becomes the *signifier* of the crisis in the urban colonies." Hall et al., *Policing the Crisis: Mugging, the State, and Law and Order*, 2nd ed. (Palgrave Macmillan, 2013), 327, 333.

INTRODUCTION

21. Ruth Wilson Gilmore, *Abolition Geography: Essays Towards Liberation* (Verso, 2022), 495.
22. Ruth Wilson Gilmore, *Golden Gulag: Prisons, Surplus, Crisis, and Opposition in Globalizing California* (University of California Press, 2007), 7.
23. In Joshua Clover's words, "racialization [is] both feature and engine of class recomposition" in the postwar era. Clover, *Riot. Strike. Riot: The New Era of Uprisings* (Verso, 2016), 169.
24. Gilmore, *Abolition Geography*, 479. Gilmore is referring to Hall's famous formulation that "race is the modality through which class is lived." As Hall and his coauthors elaborate in *Policing the Crisis*, "It is through the modality of race that blacks comprehend, handle and then begin to resist the exploitation which is an objective feature of their class situation.... It is in the modality of race that those whom the structures systematically exploit, exclude and subordinate discover themselves as an exploited, excluded and subordinated class" (340–41).
25. Marie Gottschalk, *Caught: The Prison State and the Lockdown of American Politics* (Princeton University Press, 2015), 4. This was already happening well before Donald Trump was elected president.
26. See Judah Schept, *Coal, Cages, Crisis: The Rise of the Prison Economy in Central Appalachia* (New York University Press, 2022); Jack Norton, "Why Are There So Many People in Jail in Scranton, PA?," Vera Institute of Justice, January 4, 2017, https://www.vera.org/in-our-backyards-stories/why-are-there-so-many-people-in-jail-in-scranton-pa; and Gottschalk, *Caught*, 6.
27. As of 2024, according to The Sentencing Project (sentencingproject.org).
28. The historian Kahlil Gibran Muhammad has scrupulously reconstructed how, as early as the 1890s, white social scientists helped to make "the notion of black people as a race of criminals ... pervasive and ubiquitous." Muhammad, *The Condemnation of Blackness: Race, Crime, and the Making of Modern Urban America* (Harvard University Press, 2010), 86.
29. There are two particularly important chapters in the recent history of racial criminalization that this book isn't able to address: One is about the politics of border control, the other the War on Terror. American anxieties tied to both immigration and terrorism have been central to how policing, imprisonment, and racial formation have evolved together in the contemporary United States. My decision not to cover them in this book should be taken, first and foremost, as an indication of the limits of my own expertise. But it is equally a product of my conviction that these histories of race and policing, though unquestionably intertwined, are also distinct in meaningful and irreducible ways. To that end, I've elected to keep this book focused specifically on the emergence of mass incarceration in the U.S. context, with the understanding that readers interested in these other, closely related histories—and in the parallel cultures of racial criminalization they helped foment—already have much excellent scholarship to consult. For groundbreaking studies of how the criminalization of Latin America has shaped U.S. popular media, see Kristy L. Ulibarri, *Visible Borders, Invisible Economies: Living Death in Latinx Narratives* (University of Texas Press, 2022), and Jason Ruiz, *Narcomedia: Latinidad, Popular Culture, and America's War on Drugs* (University of Texas Press, 2023). On the role of criminalization in contemporary Asian North American fiction in the wake of 9/11, see Monica Chiu,

INTRODUCTION

Scrutinized! Surveillance in Asian North American Literature (University of Hawai'i Press, 2014). For an ambitious cultural and literary history of Euro-American imperialism and the global War on Terror, see Anjuli Fatima Raza Kolb, *Epidemic Empire: Colonialism, Contagion, and Terror, 1817–2020* (University of Chicago Press, 2021). Finally, some formidable scholars have, indeed, produced major accounts synthesizing the processes of policing, race-making, and war-making in the United States: Nikhil Pal Singh, *Race and America's Long War* (University of California Press, 2017); Joseph Darda, *Empire of Defense: Race and the Cultural Politics of Permanent War* (University of Chicago Press, 2019); and Erica R. Edwards, *The Other Side of Terror: Black Women and the Culture of US Empire* (New York University Press, 2021).

One other topic that I regret not having more space to discuss in these pages is the policing of homosexuality and the role that such policing played in bolstering the punitive ideology and expanding the carceral machinery of the postwar United States. Important books on the policing of gay life in the twentieth century include David K. Johnson, *The Lavender Scare: The Cold War Persecution of Gays and Lesbians in the Federal Government* (University of Chicago Press, 2004); Margot Canaday, *The Straight State: Sexuality and Citizenship in Twentieth-Century America* (Princeton University Press, 2009); Chandan Reddy, *Freedom with Violence: Race, Sexuality, and the US State* (Duke University Press, 2011); and Ann Lvovsky, *Vice Patrol: Cops, Courts, and the Struggle over Urban Gay Life Before Stonewall* (University of Chicago Press, 2021). For a more conceptual account of the relation between queerness and carceral power, see Stephen Dillon, *Fugitive Life: The Queer Politics of the Prison State* (Duke University Press, 2018). Finally, to learn more about the rich tradition of LGBTQ crime fiction that emerged after the 1960s, see Judith A. Markowitz, *The Gay Detective Novel: Lesbian and Gay Main Characters and Themes in Mystery Fiction* (McFarland Press, 2004), and Phyllis M. Betz, *Lesbian Detective Fiction: Woman as Author, Subject and Reader* (McFarland Press, 2006).

30. Like many beliefs, the narratives we tell ourselves about crime are notoriously impervious to correction. Since the 1960s, polling has repeatedly shown that Americans firmly believe that crime rates are going up at times when—or in places where—they are not.
31. Mark Seltzer, "The Crime System," *Critical Inquiry* 30, no. 3 (2004): 559. Seltzer expands this argument in *True Crime: Observations on Violence and Modernity* (Routledge, 2007).
32. Lee Horsley, *Twentieth-Century Crime Fiction* (Oxford University Press, 2005), 139.
33. Nicolazzo, *Vagrant Figures*, 6, 26.
34. Hall et al., *Policing the Crisis*, 2, 175.
35. Kalifa, *Vice, Crime, and Poverty*, 6, 7.
36. On how acts of "imagining" crimes and punishments often "feed recursively into public policy," see Michelle Brown, *The Culture of Punishment: Prison, Society, and Spectacle* (New York University Press, 2009), 18.
37. Horsley, *Twentieth-Century Crime Fiction*, 138–39.
38. In a memorable formulation, the sociologist Travis Linnemann writes that "a vibrant symbolic economy—a flow of texts and images, of social media

news feeds, of true crime documentaries and reality television programs—draws us into the drama of crime and violence and the political theater of police." Linnemann, *The Horror of Police* (University of Minnesota Press, 2022), 25.

39. Christopher P. Wilson efficiently sums up the research on the media coverage of crime: "Studies have repeatedly shown that the media's representation of the crime rate, and thus public fears, accelerate far beyond crime's actual occurrence; that the media is enamored with violence and street disorder . . .; and that it commonly sides with innocent victims, colors its criminals with little regard to statistical accuracy, and demonizes young criminals into predatory, irrational psychopaths." Wilson, *Learning to Live with Crime: American Crime Narrative in the Neoconservative Turn* (Ohio State University Press, 2010), 6. For a major study of how the process of Black criminalization has been abetted by more than a century of American crime reporting, see Carol A. Stabile, *White Victims, Black Villains: Race, Gender, and Crime News in US Culture* (Routledge, 2006).

40. In *Cracked Coverage: Television News, The Anti-Cocaine Crusade, and the Reagan Legacy* (Duke University Press, 1994), media scholars Jimmie L. Reeves and Richard Campbell reconstruct how between 1981 and 1988, "network news . . . facilitated the *staging* and *legitimating* of Reagan's war on drugs as a major political spectacle" (15). In *The Suburban Crisis*, historian Matthew Lassiter offers a good example of that televised spectacle. At one point in 1986, attempting to help build support for the passage of the Anti-Drug Abuse Act, "Ronald and Nancy Reagan addressed the nation in a prime-time televised address while holding hands and sitting on a couch in the residential wing of the White House. 'Drugs are menacing our society,' the President began. 'They're killing our children.'" Lassiter, *The Suburban Crisis: White America and the War on Drugs* (Princeton University Press, 2023), 518.

41. Nicole Rafter, *Shots in the Mirror: Crime Films and Society* (Oxford University Press, 2000), 7. Rafter explains that she was moved to write a book on crime films after years of talking with students whose "ideas about legality and illegality, the volume of various types of crime, and the motives of lawbreakers" seemed to be drawn primarily from movies (vii). Rafter extended this line of inquiry in her coauthored book with Michelle Brown, *Criminology Goes to the Movies: Crime Theory and Popular Culture* (New York University Press, 2011).

42. Jonathan A. Grubb and Chad Posick, Introduction, *Crime TV: Streaming Criminology in Popular Culture*, ed. Jonathan A Grubb and Chad Posick (New York University Press, 2021), 2.

43. See, for instance, Diana Rickard, *The New True Crime: How the Rise of Serialized Storytelling Is Transforming Innocence* (New York University Press, 2023).

44. Seltzer, "Crime System," 574. As he puts it elsewhere in the same essay, "Make believe makes belief" (558).

45. As Paula Rabinowitz explains in her magisterial history of the pulps, the proliferation of pulp magazines dedicated to true and fictional crime stories throughout the 1920s and '30s meant that "the working-class reading public was immersed in the language of crime reporting." She explains, "Magazines, as a collective form, were everywhere, and everywhere they were, they invited readers into their

crypt of sex and death." Rabinowitz, *American Pulp: How Paperbacks Brought Modernism to Main Street* (Princeton University Press, 2014), 44, 90.

46. With the invention of the mass-market paperback, genre categories—predominately romance, science fiction, and mystery fiction—became essential to the enterprise of American publishing. The conglomeration of publishing houses after 1970 only increased the reliance on familiar formulas, which could reliably attract readers in the absence of a brand-name author. For the premier account of the importance of genre categories to both the mass-market era and the "conglomerate era" of literary publishing, see Dan Sinykin, *Big Fiction: How Conglomeration Changed the Publishing Industry and American Literature* (Columbia University Press, 2023).

47. Patrick Anderson, *The Triumph of the Thriller: How Cops, Crooks, and Cannibals Captured Popular Fiction* (Random House, 2007), 4. Analyzing ninety years' worth of *New York Times* hardcover fiction bestseller lists, the critic and data scientist Jordan Pruett finds that "over nearly a century, the lists' two biggest genres are 'historical' and 'detective and mystery,' by a fairly large margin." But these two genres were trending in opposite directions. Whereas the popularity of historical fiction peaked in the 1940s, both the "thriller and suspense" and the "detective and mystery" categories saw an enormous spike after 1980. Pruett, "What Counts as a Bestseller?," Public Books, October 11, 2022, www.publicbooks.org/what-counts-as-a-bestseller/.

48. Patricia Highsmith, *Strangers on a Train* (Harper & Brothers, 1950; repr., Norton, 2001), 30.

49. Brian Garfield, *Death Wish* (David McKay, 1972; repr., Overlook Duckworth, 2013), 46–47.

50. Lawrence Block, *A Walk Among the Tombstones* (William Morrow, 1992), 199.

51. Donna Tartt, *The Secret History* (Vintage, 1992), 488.

52. Toni Cade Bambara, *Those Bones Are Not My Child* (Vintage, 1999), 174, 156.

53. John Ball, *Death for a Playmate*, originally published as *Johnny Get Your Gun* (Little, Brown, 1969; repr., Bantam, 1972), 59.

54. "From at least the seventeenth century on, narrative literature insistently reflects on the effects of literature, just as novels insistently reappear in novels, cautioning about the effects of reading novels and about the risks to behavior as a consequence of print" (Seltzer, "Crime System," 558).

55. Ed McBain, *Hail to the Chief* (Random House, 1973). I picked a McBain novel off my shelf at random to cite here, but as far as I can tell, these sentences appear at the start of every one of the 87th Precinct novels.

56. Richard Wright, *Savage Holiday* (Avon, 1954; repr., University Press of Mississippi, 1994), 31.

57. Thomas Heise, *The Gentrification Plot: New York and the Postindustrial Crime Novel* (Columbia University Press, 2022), 12.

58. Recent contributions to the study of crime fiction have already begun to depart from narrower ways of defining the genre. Heise's *The Gentrification Plot* is the most thoughtful example of this tendency, but there are others. The edited volume *Crime Fiction as World Literature* announces its intention to treat crime fiction as a "globalized and hybridized genre" transformed by the transnational literary marketplace. Another collection, *The Centrality of Crime Fiction in American Literary Culture*, makes the case for cataloging "the myriad ways in which acts of crime and detection shape the entire range of American fiction."

INTRODUCTION

Louise Nilsson, David Damrosch, and Theo D'haen, "Crime Fiction as World Literature," in *Crime Fiction as World Literature*, ed. Lousie Nilsson, David Damrosch, and Theo D'haen (Bloomsbury, 2017), 4; Alfred Bendixen, "Re-Searching the Premises: The Centrality of Crime Fiction in American Literary Culture," in *The Centrality of Crime Fiction in American Literary Culture*, ed. Alfred Bendixen and Olivia Carr Edenfield (London: Routledge, 2017), 6.

59. See Sean McCann, *Gumshoe America: Hard-Boiled Crime Fiction and the Rise and Fall of New Deal Liberalism* (Duke University Press, 2000); Paula Rabinowitz, *Black & White & Noir: America's Pulp Modernism* (Columbia University Press, 2002); Leonard Cassuto, *Hard-Boiled Sentimentality: The Secret History of American Crime Stories* (Columbia University Press, 2009); and Andrew Pepper, *Unwilling Executioner: Crime Fiction and the State* (Oxford University Press, 2016).

60. See Stephen F. Soitos, *The Blues Detective: A Study of African American Detective Fiction* (University of Massachusetts Press, 1996); Andrew Pepper, *The Contemporary American Crime Novel: Race, Ethnicity, Gender, Class* (Edinburgh University Press, 2000); Maureen T. Reddy, *Traces, Codes, and Clues: Reading Race in Crime Fiction* (Rutgers University Press, 2003); Ralph E. Rodriguez, *Brown Gumshoes: Detective Fiction and the Search for Chicana/o Identity* (University of Texas Press, 2005); Jinny Huh, *The Arresting Eye: Race and the Anxiety of Detection* (University of Virginia Press, 2015); and M. Michelle Robinson, *Dreams for Dead Bodies: Blackness, Labor, and the Corpus of American Detective Fiction* (University of Michigan Press, 2016).

61. See Megan Sweeney, *Reading Is My Window: Books and the Art of Reading in Women's Prisons* (University of North Carolina Press, 2010); Caleb Smith, *Prison and the American Imagination* (Yale University Press, 2011); and Patrick Elliott Alexander, *From Slave Ship to Supermax: Mass Incarceration, Prisoner Abuse, and the New Neo-Slave Novel* (Temple University Press, 2018).

62. See Jonathan Munby, *Under a Bad Sign: Criminal Self-Representation in African American Popular Culture* (University of Chicago Press, 2011); Jeannine Marie DeLombard, *In the Shadow of the Gallows: Race, Crime, and American Civic Identity* (University of Pennsylvania Press, 2012); and Jared Sexton, *Black Masculinity and the Cinema of Policing* (Palgrave Macmillan, 2017).

63. See Justin Gifford, *Pimping Fictions: African American Crime Literature and the Untold Story of Black Pulp Publishing* (Temple University Press, 2013); Kinohi Nishikawa, *Street Players: Black Pulp Fiction and the Making of a Literary Underground* (University of Chicago Press, 2018); and Brooks E. Hefner, *Black Pulp: Genre Fiction in the Shadow of Jim Crow* (University of Minnesota Press, 2021).

64. See William J. Maxwell's incredible book *F. B. Eyes: How J. Edgar Hoover's Ghostreaders Framed African American Literature* (Princeton University Press, 2015). If you haven't read it, go read it right now!

65. See Wilson, *Learning to Live with Crime*, and Heise, *Gentrification Plot*.

66. While the War on Crime has not been given much attention by literary critics, there is one important exception. That would be Wilson's *Learning to Live with Crime*, a knowledgeable and nuanced work of scholarship that sought to challenge overly generalized political narratives about the War on Crime by looking more closely at "the 'micropolitics' of law enforcement that often worked beneath

INTRODUCTION

the radar of the superheated and often polarized public debate" (2). Wilson's close attention to these micropolitical processes is essential reading in its own right. But it also makes for a very different book from the one you're reading now, which does more or less the exact opposite: reconstructs how the macro-narratives and fervid debates of the War on Crime were woven into the fabric of the era's crime fiction.

67. Quoted in Erin A. Smith, *Hard-Boiled: Working-Class Readers and Pulp Magazines* (Temple University Press, 2000), 21.
68. Jonathan Kramnick has a wonderful way of putting this: "Literature may only be one part of the world," he writes, "but it interacts with the rest." Lee Konstantinou and Dan Sinykin offer another nice formulation: "Aesthetic production is thoroughly intertwined with social history, and social history is never free of aesthetic mediation and categories." Kramnick, *Criticism and Truth: On Method in Literary Studies* (University of Chicago Press, 2023), 97; Konstantinou and Sinykin, "Literature and Publishing, 1945–2000," *American Literary History* 33, no. 2 (2021): 235.

1. INVISIBLE MEN, 1940–1966

1. By midcentury, "the private eye had pretty much run his course," according to the pulp historian and eventual editor of the Library of America Geoffrey O'Brien. The market share of detective-driven mysteries was in steady decline; whereas mysteries had accounted for half of all paperbacks published in 1945, in 1955, they accounted for only 13 percent. Part of that market share had been taken over by a new kind of paperback original, which, as the literary historian Sean McCann explains, "remade the hard-boiled [detective] story into a drama of psychopathology," a drama whose "typical protagonist became a freak, a loser, or a sociopath." O'Brien, *Hardboiled America: Lurid Paperbacks and the Masters of Noir*, expanded edition (Da Capo, 1997), 139; McCann, *Gumshoe America: Hard-Boiled Crime Fiction and the Rise and Fall of New Deal Liberalism* (Duke University Press, 2000), 199.
2. For other accounts of the relation between visual perception and racialization, see Irene Tucker, *The Moment of Racial Sight: A History* (University of Chicago Press, 2012), and Jinny Huh, *The Arresting Eye: Race and the Anxiety of Detection* (University of Virginia Press, 2015).
3. Thomas J. Sugrue, *The Origins of the Urban Crisis: Race and Inequality in Postwar Detroit* (Princeton University Press, 1996; repr., 2014), 6–7.
4. Ira Katznelson, *When Affirmative Action Was White: An Untold History of Racial Inequality in Twentieth-Century America* (Norton, 2005), 14
5. Carol A. Horton, *Race and the Making of American Liberalism* (Oxford University Press, 2005), 129.
6. Sugrue, *Origins of the Urban Crisis*, 217. Sugrue is talking specifically about postwar Detroit, which he suggests offers a paradigmatic case study of how deindustrialization transformed social and economic life in the United States.
7. David Roediger, *Working Toward Whiteness: How America's Immigrants Became White —The Strange Journey from Ellis Island to the Suburbs* (Basic Books, 2005), 234.

1. INVISIBLE MEN

8. *We Charge Genocide: The Historic Petition to the United Nations for Relief from a Crime of the United States Government Against the Negro People*, ed. William L. Patterson (Civil Rights Congress, 1951), 8.
9. Sugrue cites a neighborhood association poster from 1950s Detroit that demonstrates how white homeowners fought integration by leveraging racialized fears about crime: "Home Owners Can You Afford to . . . Have your children exposed to gangster operated skid row saloons? . . . Gamblers and prostitution? You Face These Issues Now!" (*Origins of the Urban Crisis*, 217).
10. Quoted in Jordan T. Camp, *Incarcerating the Crisis: Freedom Struggles and the Rise of the Neoliberal State* (University of California Press, 2016), 27.
11. Naomi Murakawa, *The First Civil Right: How Liberals Built Prison America* (Oxford University Press, 2014), 66, 52, 53.
12. Khalil Gibran Muhammad, "Where Did All the White Criminals Go? Reconfiguring Race and Crime on the Road to Mass Incarceration," *Souls* 13, no. 1 (2011): 74, 83.
13. On the forms of racial exclusion built into the New Deal, see Katznelson, *When Affirmative Action Was White*.
14. Muhammad, "Where Did All the White Criminals Go?" 79, 81, 88.
15. For more on the history of white racialization in the United States, see Matthew Frye Jacobson, "Becoming Caucasian: Vicissitudes of Whiteness in American Politics and Culture," in *Race and Immigration in the United States: New Histories*, ed. Paul Spickard (Routledge, 2012), 131–47; Thomas A. Guglielmo, *White on Arrival: Italians, Race, Color, and Power in Chicago, 1890–1945* (Oxford University Press, 2003); and Roediger, *Working Toward Whiteness*.
16. Daniel Bell, "Crime as an American Way of Life," *Antioch Review* 13, no. 2 (Summer 1953): 151.
17. Khalil Gibran Muhammad, *The Condemnation of Blackness: Race, Crime, and the Making of Modern Urban America* (Harvard University Press, 2010), 271.
18. Patricia Highsmith, *Strangers on a Train* (Harper & Brothers, 1950; repr., W. W. Norton, 2001), 45, 68, 90, 274.
19. Patricia Highsmith, *The Talented Mr. Ripley* (Coward-McCann, 1955; repr., W. W. Norton, 2008), 233.
20. Robert Polito, *Savage Art: A Biography of Jim Thompson* (Vintage, 1995), 338.
21. Jim Thompson, *The Killer Inside Me* (Lion, 1952; repr., Mulholland, 2014), 4, 26.
22. Dorothy B. Hughes, *In a Lonely Place* (Duell, Sloane & Pearce, 1947; repr., New York Review of Books, 2017), 93, 32, 40.
23. Robert Bloch, *Psycho* (Simon & Schuster, 1959; repr., Overlook, 2010), 132, 126, 29, 147.
24. Highsmith, *Strangers on a Train*, 30, 22, 278.
25. Andrew Wilson, *Beautiful Shadow: A Life of Patricia Highsmith* (Bloomsbury, 2004), 320.
26. Wilson, *Beautiful Shadow*, 321.
27. W.E.B. Du Bois, "Courts and Jails," in *The Selected Writings of W. E. B. DuBois*, ed. Walter Wilson (New American Library, 1970), 126.
28. Highsmith, *Strangers on a Train*, 98.
29. It is not the only genre to do so. For an invaluable account of how other popular genres generate worlds defined by race, see Mark C. Jerng, *Racial Worldmaking: The Power of Popular Fiction* (Fordham University Press, 2018).

1. INVISIBLE MEN

30. Richard Kopley, *Edgar Allan Poe and the Dupin Mysteries* (Palgrave Macmillan, 2008), 38, 35. For a captivating analysis of why it is both difficult and necessary to see the racial meaning of "The Murders in the Rue Morgue," see Ed White, "The Ourang-Outang Situation," *College Literature* 30, no. 3 (2003): 88–108.
31. See Maureen T. Reddy, *Traces, Codes, and Clues: Reading Race in Crime Fiction* (Rutgers University Press), 2003, and Megan E. Abbott, *The Street Was Mine: White Masculinity in Hardboiled Fiction and Film Noir* (Palgrave Macmillan, 2002). For an important account of the role of white nativism in the development of early hardboiled crime fiction, see McCann, *Gumshoe America*, 37–86.
32. Dashiell Hammett, *Red Harvest* (Alfred A. Knopf, 1929; repr., Vintage Crime, 1992), 163.
33. Raymond Chandler, "Pickup on Noon Street," in *The Simple Art of Murder* (Vintage, 1998), 187–230; first published as "Noon Street Nemesis," *Detective Fiction Weekly*, May 30, 1936. For a compelling analysis of how this story established the racial assumptions of Chandler's later work, see Justin Gifford, *Pimping Fictions: African American Crime Literature and the Untold Story of Black Pulp Publishing* (Temple University Press, 2013), 18–25.
34. Carroll John Daly, "Knights of the Open Palm," in *The Black Lizard Big Book of "Black Mask" Stories* (Vintage Crime, 2010), 429–41; first published in *Black Mask*, June 1, 1923.
35. Norman Mailer, "The White Negro: Superficial Reflections on the Hipster," *Dissent*, Fall 1957, 277, 284–85.
36. For an essential account of the role that racial masquerade played in the era of midcentury liberalism, see Michael Szalay, *Hip Figures: A Literary History of the Democratic Party* (Stanford University Press, 2012).
37. Mailer, "White Negro," 290. For a different—though, I think, revealing—use of Mailer's essay as a framework for reading Thompson's fiction, see Polito, *Savage Art*, 338.
38. Bloch, *Psycho*, 81, 40, 41.
39. Hughes, *In a Lonely Place*, 41, 160.
40. Hughes, *In a Lonely Place*, 161, 181, 182, 30, 34.
41. Himes is of course best known for his cycle of Harlem police novels starring detectives Grave Digger Jones and Coffin Ed Johnson, which began with *For Love of Imabelle* (later retitled *A Rage in Harlem*) in 1957. The Harlem novels are amazing works of surrealist detective fiction, and much scholarship has been written on them. For this chapter, I reluctantly decided to set those novels aside in order to focus on some of the lesser-known texts in which Himes directly addressed white investment in the myth of Black criminality.
42. Chester Himes, *Run Man Run* (G. P. Putnam's Sons, 1966), 135, 133, 137, 132, 44.
43. Himes, *Run Man Run*, 8, 22, 99, 117.
44. Lawrence P. Jackson, *Chester B. Himes: A Biography* (W. W. Norton, 2017), 348.
45. Hughes, *In a Lonely Place*, 144.
46. Ralph Ellison, *Invisible Man* (Vintage, 1952), 300, 500, 566, 4–5.
47. Michel Fabre, *The World of Richard Wright* (University Press of Mississippi, 1985), 93.
48. Richard Wright, *Native Son: The Restored Text Established by the Library of America* (original Harper & Brothers, 1940; repr., Harper Perennial, 1993), 44, 219, 113.

1. INVISIBLE MEN

49. Wright, *Native Son*, 407, 408, 428–29.
50. Wright, *Native Son*, 429.
51. Abdul JanMohamed, *The Death-Bound Subject: Richard Wright's Archaeology of Death* (Duke University Press, 2005), 134.
52. Paula Rabinowitz, *American Pulp: How Paperbacks Brought Modernism to Main Street* (Princeton University Press, 2014), 149.
53. Rabinowitz, *American Pulp*, 148.
54. Ann Petry, *The Street* (Houghton Mifflin, 1946; repr., Mariner, 1974), 198, 425, 434.
55. Petry, *The Street*, 432, 432–33.
56. Lawrence P. Jackson, *The Indignant Generation: A Narrative History of African American Writers and Critics, 1934–1960* (Princeton University Press, 2011), 232.
57. Quoted in Jackson, *Indignant Generation*, 233.
58. James Ivey, "Mrs. Petry's Harlem," *The Crisis*, May 1946, 154–55.
59. Gunnar Myrdal, *An American Dilemma: The Negro Problem and Modern Democracy* (Harper and Bros, 1944), xlvii, li, 968, 967, 958, 764, 978, 976, 969, 970, 763 (emphasis in original).
60. Leonard Cassuto, *Hard-Boiled Sentimentality: The Secret History of American Crime Stories* (Columbia University Press, 2009), 213.
61. Joseph Darda, "The Race Novel: An Education," *MELUS* 45, no. 3 (2020): 11.
62. For more on how the Chicago School influenced Wright's focus on social disorganization and sexual dysfunction, see Roderick A. Ferguson, *Aberrations in Black: Toward a Queer of Color Critique* (University of Minnesota Press, 2004), 31–53.
63. Richard Wright, introduction to *Black Metropolis: A Study of Negro Life in a Northern City* by St. Clair Drake and Horace R. Cayton, lix–lxxiv (Harcourt, Brace, 1945; repr., University of Chicago Press, 2015), lx.
64. Jackson, *Indignant Generation*, 189.
65. Richard Wright, "How 'Bigger' Was Born," in *Native Son: The Restored Text*, 448.
66. Darda, "Race Novel," 12.
67. Jodi Melamed, "The Killing Joke of Sympathy: Chester Himes's *End of a Primitive* and the Limits of Midcentury Racial Liberalism," *American Literature* 80, no. 4 (2008): 775.
68. Darda, "Race Novel," 2. For a longer history of how the ideology of "racial realism" has shaped the canon of African American literature, see Gene Jarrett, *Deans and Truants: Race and Realism in African American Literature* (University of Pennsylvania Press, 2007), 1–17.
69. Myrdal, *American Dilemma*, 763.
70. Myrdal, *American Dilemma*, 763.
71. Wright, "How Bigger Was Born," 459.
72. Richard Wright, *The Man Who Lived Underground* (Library of America, 2021), 24.
73. Richard Wright, "Memories of My Grandmother," in *Man Who Lived Underground*, 163.
74. "Note on the Texts," in *Man Who Lived Underground*, 223.
75. Jackson, *Indignant Generation*, 221–22.
76. Quoted in Jackson, *Chester B. Himes*, 208.

1. INVISIBLE MEN

77. Chester Himes, *If He Hollers Let Him Go* (Doubleday, Doran, 1945; repr., Chatham Bookseller, 1973), 87–88. On *If He Hollers* as a major work of Los Angeles noir, see Mike Davis, *City of Quartz: Excavating the Future in Los Angeles* (Verso, 1990), 43.
78. Jackson, *Indignant Generation*, 224.
79. Petry, *The Street*, 436, 298–99, 349–50.
80. Charles Willeford, *Pick-Up*, in *Crime Novels: American Noir of the 1950s*, ed. Robert Polito (Library of America, 1997), 509, 571.
81. McCann, *Gumshoe America*, 239.
82. Willeford, *Pick-Up*, 435, 512, 503.
83. Willeford, *Pick-Up*, 538, 539.
84. McCann, *Gumshoe America*, 241.
85. Willeford, *Pick-Up*, 563.
86. Willeford, *Pick-Up*, 563, 522.
87. Cassuto, *Hard-Boiled Sentimentality*, 216.
88. Ed McBain, introduction to *Cop Hater* (Signet, 1956; repr., Thomas and Mercer, 1989), x.
89. Palmer Rampell discovered that when editor and publisher Marcel Duhamel was trying to convince Chester Himes to write what would become his famous series of novels about Black cops in Harlem, the book he gave to Himes as a model was *Runaway Black*. Himes read it and responded that it was "pretty shoddy stuff." Rampell interprets Himes's entire Coffin Ed and Grave Digger series as a reaction to *Runaway Black*, though he admits that Himes's "most overt response" to Hunter's exploitative novel was clearly *Run Man Run*. Rampell, *Genres of Privacy in Postwar America* (Stanford University Press, 2022), 48, 55.
90. Evan Hunter, *Runaway Black* (Fawcett, 1954), 11, 43–44, 85, 134.
91. Hunter, *Runaway Black*, 68.
92. Hunter, *Runaway Black*, 24, 86, 87.
93. Hunter, *Runaway Black*, 82, 31, 83, 102.
94. McBain, introduction, *Cop Hater*, xi.
95. McBain, *Cop Hater*, 21.
96. Dorothy B. Hughes, *The Expendable Man* (Random House, 1963; repr., New York Review of Books, 2012), 146, 147–48, 213, 243.
97. Hughes, *Expendable Man*, 152, 139.
98. Hughes, *Expendable Man*, 6, 7, 183, 171.
99. Hughes, *Expendable Man*, 56, 224, 189.
100. Hughes, *Expendable Man*, 223, 221.
101. Hughes, *Expendable Man*, 224.
102. Rachel Watson, "Parent to *Mockingbird*: Harper Lee and a Novel Deferred," Post45: Peer Reviewed, June 14, 2018, post45.org/2018/06/parent-to-mockingbird-harper-lee-and-a-novel-deferred/.
103. Hughes, *Expendable Man*, 244.
104. Hughes, *Expendable Man*, 241, 226, 242.
105. Not every Black-authored novel about white criminals was a commercial failure. But the history of such "crossover" novels is complicated, and the successes are as telling as the flops. Willard Motley's 1947 debut novel *Knock on Any Door*, for instance, was a critical and commercial hit and was swiftly made into a film

1. INVISIBLE MEN

starring Humphrey Bogart. Yet the success of *Knock on Any Door* may have had something to do with the fact that early readers didn't know Motley was Black. Motley asked his publisher to conceal his racial identity, and in the novel's first printings, no author photo appeared on the dust jacket. Lawrence Jackson believes that Motley's "choice to hide his race from the public" was a determining factor in his debut novel's positive reception and financial success. He writes, "there was as good a chance that if Motley's racial identity had been known, he might have alienated his audience and signaled to his reviewers that he supported a clandestine racial agenda" (*Indignant Generation*, 242, 246). For a different account of the role of race in the reception of *Knock on Any Door*, see Joseph Darda, *The Strange Career of Racial Liberalism* (Stanford University Press, 2022), 112–17.
106. On the phrase "white-life novel," see John C. Charles, *Abandoning the Black Hero: Sympathy and Privacy in the Postwar African American White-Life Novel* (Rutgers University Press, 2012).
107. Emily Bernard, "'Raceless' Writing and Difference: Ann Petry's *Country Place* and the African-American Literary Canon," *Studies in American Fiction* 33, no. 1 (2005): 89.
108. Rabinowitz, *American Pulp*, 144.
109. Darda, *Strange Career of Racial Liberalism*, 106–7.
110. Jackson, *Indignant Generation*, 272.
111. Rabinowitz, *American Pulp*, 143.
112. Bernard, "'Raceless' Writing and Difference," 107.
113. Ann Petry, *Country Place* (Houghton Mifflin, 1947; repr., Northwestern University Press, 2019), 16, 135, 4.
114. Rabinowitz, *American Pulp*, 137; Bernard, "'Raceless' Writing and Difference," 98.
115. Petry, *Country Place*, 266.
116. Richard Wright, *The Outsider: The Restored Text Established by the Library of America* (original Harper & Row, 1953; repr., Harper Perennial, 1991), 385, 195, 501.
117. In *The Outsider*, radical criminality appears to be inscribed directly into Black art. Listening to the radio one night, Cross reflects that "Blue-jazz was the scornful gesture of men turned ecstatic in their state of rejection; it was the musical language of the satisfiedly amoral, the boasting of the contentedly lawless, the recreations of the innocently criminal" (178). It is possible that the lawlessness Cross hears in Black music was also a feature that Wright saw in his own artistic commitment to the crime novel.
118. Keneth Kinnamon and Michel Fabre, eds, *Conversations with Richard Wright* (University Press of Mississippi, 1993), 239.
119. Richard Wright, *Savage Holiday* (Avon, 1954; repr., University Press of Mississippi, 1994), 217, 221, 109.
120. Wright, *Savage Holiday*, 31.
121. Wright initially planned *Savage Holiday* to be the first in a trilogy that represented, in Gerald Early's words, "a thoroughgoing critique of the religious foundations of the western mind." The second volume, "to be called 'Strange Daughter,' was to have as its subject a white American girl working through her sexual repression in a perverted relationship with a Nigerian and her subsequent murder. The

third, 'When the World Was Red,' was to be an exploration of the psyche of the Aztec ruler Montezuma, as well as a psychohistory of western religion at the time of the Cortez expedition." Early, afterword to *Savage Holiday* by Richard Wright (University Press of Mississippi, 1994), 233.
122. Hazel Rowley, *Richard Wright: The Life and Times* (University of Chicago Press, 2001), 473.
123. In another letter to Wright, Aswell made the racial significance of this distinction even more explicit: "It seems to me—and of course I am only guessing now—that as you have found greater peace as a human being, living in France and not made incessantly aware that the pigmentation of your skin sets you apart from other men, you have at the same time lost something as a writer" (quoted in Rowley, *Richard Wright*, 472).
124. Rowley, *Richard Wright*, 440.
125. Jackson, *Chester B. Himes*, 99.
126. Quoted in John A. Williams, afterword to *Dear Chester, Dear John: Letters Between Chester Himes and John A. Williams*, ed. John A. Williams and Lori Williams (Wayne State University Press, 2008), 175.
127. Melvin Van Peebles, "... His Wonders to Perform," introduction to *Yesterday Will Make You Cry* by Chester Himes (Old School Books, 1999), 20.
128. Jackson, *Chester B. Himes*, 253.
129. "Baleful of Laughs," *Times Literary Supplement*, January 20, 1966, 37.
130. Based on a reading of a letter that Himes sent to Highsmith in the mid-1960s, Jackson contends that Himes harbored the belief that Highsmith had stolen some of the ideas in *Strangers on a Train* from him (*Chester B. Himes*, 254).
131. Himes, *Run Man Run*, 132.
132. Highsmith, *Strangers on a Train*, 274.

2. RIOT ACTS, 1967–1974

1. Joshua Clover argues that riots were a key technology of racial ascription in the twentieth century. "It is not that race makes riots," he writes memorably, "but that riots make race." Clover, *Riot. Strike. Riot: The New Era of Uprisings* (Verso, 2016), 168.
2. George V. Higgins, *The Friends of Eddie Coyle* (Alfred A. Knopf, 1972; repr., Holt, 2000), 8.
3. Higgins, *Friends of Eddie Coyle*, 15, 27.
4. Higgins, *Friends of Eddie Coyle*, 26.
5. Lyndon B. Johnson, "Special Message to the Congress on Crime in America," February 6, 1967, The American Presidency Project, https://www.presidency.ucsb.edu/documents/special-message-the-congress-crime-america.
6. Lyndon B. Johnson, "Special Message to the Congress on Law Enforcement and the Administration of Justice," March 8, 1965, The American Presidency Project, https://www.presidency.ucsb.edu/documents/special-message-the-congress-law-enforcement-and-the-administration-justice.
7. Michael W. Flamm, *Law and Order: Street Crime, Civil Unrest, and the Crisis of Liberalism in the 1960s* (Columbia University Press, 2005), 52.
8. Barry Goldwater, "Text of Goldwater's Speech Formally Opening Presidential Campaign," *New York Times*, September 4, 1964.

2. RIOT ACTS

9. Flamm, *Law and Order*, 101, 143.
10. Lyndon B. Johnson, "The President's Address to the Nation on Civil Disorders," July 27, 1967, The American Presidency Project, https://www.presidency.ucsb.edu/documents/the-presidents-address-the-nation-civil-disorders. It is worth noting that allegations of sniper fire during riots were a frequent justification for police violence in the period but were rarely corroborated.
11. Elizabeth Hinton, *From the War on Poverty to the War on Crime: The Making of Mass Incarceration in America* (Harvard University Press, 2016), 110.
12. Quoted in Flamm, *Law and Order*, 54.
13. *The Kerner Report: The National Advisory Commission on Civil Disorders* (U.S. Government Printing Office, 1968; repr., Princeton University Press, 2016), 1.
14. Hinton, *From the War on Poverty*, 130.
15. Heather Schoenfield, *Building the Prison State: Race and the Politics of Mass Incarceration* (University of Chicago Press, 2018), 33.
16. Micol Siegel, *Violence Work: State Power and the Limits of Police* (Duke University Press, 2018), 46.
17. Julilly Kohler-Hausmann, *Getting Tough: Welfare and Imprisonment in 1970s America* (Princeton University Press, 2017), 23.
18. Hinton, *From the War on Poverty*, 89.
19. Hinton, *From the War on Poverty*, 132–33.
20. Hinton, *From the War on Poverty*, 112.
21. The particular version of the War on Crime I trace in this chapter came to an end in the late 1970s, when President Jimmy Carter sought to halt the crime war by dismantling the LEAA.
22. LeRoy Lad Panek, *The American Police Novel: A History* (McFarland, 2003), 34.
23. Christopher P. Wilson, *Cop Knowledge: Police Power and Cultural Narrative in Twentieth-Century America* (University of Chicago Press, 2000), 59.
24. Ed McBain, *Cop Hater* (Signet, 1956; repr., Thomas and Mercer, 1989), 185, 184, 67, 112.
25. John Ball, *Death for a Playmate*, originally published as *Johnny Get Your Gun* (Little, Brown, 1969; repr., Bantam, 1972), 70, 86, 94.
26. Ball, *Death for a Playmate*, 149.
27. McBain, *Cop Hater*, 205, 204.
28. Wilson, *Cop Knowledge*, 97.
29. Mike Davis and Jon Wiener, *Set the Night on Fire: L.A. in the Sixties* (Verso, 2020), 42.
30. Joseph Wambaugh, *The New Centurions* (Little, Brown, 1970; repr., Grand Central, 2008), 25–26, 216, 67, 476, 82.
31. Davis and Wiener, *Set the Night on Fire*, 40.
32. Wambaugh, *New Centurions*, 196, 384.
33. Wambaugh, *New Centurions*, 82, 113.
34. Wilson, the scholar who has studied Wambaugh most extensively, cautions that while it is tempting to pursue a purely "ideological reading" of his work, this "is a little too pat." He argues that Wambaugh's fiction did not dutifully parrot the LAPD party line but broke from department orthodoxy by depicting everyday street-level interactions (as opposed to official police academy training) as the real place where police knowledge and expertise were forged. Be that as it may, the ideological horizon of Wambaugh's fiction is not so easy to ignore—not when

it is so clearly linked to the rapidly evolving racial ideology that underpinned paramilitary policing in cities like Los Angeles in the 1960s. That racial ideology was not merely, Wilson is right to note, a top-down theory (though it was that, too); as we shall see, it also grew organically out of the "brotherhood of fraternal wisdom" that positioned the beat cop as the most reliable expert on the racial character of crime (*Cop Knowledge*, 113, 98, 115).

35. Kohler-Hausmann, *Getting Tough*, 4.
36. In the aftermath of Watts, the sham McCone Commission famously blamed the rebellion on a small portion of criminal "riffraff" who had migrated to L.A. because of its excessively generous welfare handouts (Davis and Wiener, *Set the Night on Fire*, 231–33).
37. Wambaugh, *New Centurions*, 113.
38. Wilson informs us that the Kilvinsky character—who is constantly dispensing wisdom about the realities of policing, and who is the one person to use the phrase "new centurions" within the novel—was based on Police Chief William Parker (*Cop Knowledge*, 110).
39. Wambaugh, *New Centurions*, 421, 422.
40. For a longer history of the role that crime statistics have played in constructing Black criminality and propping up white supremacy since the late nineteenth century, see Khalil Gibran Muhammad, *The Condemnation of Blackness: Race, Crime, and the Making of Modern Urban America* (Harvard University Press, 2010).
41. Hinton, *From the War on Poverty*, 24.
42. The high crime rates of the period remain a notorious area of social scientific dispute. Hinton suggests that, in New York City in 1966, the dramatic increase in recorded crimes "resulted not from an actual upsurge in crime, but from the crime reporting reforms Mayor John Lindsay implemented" (*From the War on Poverty*, 6). Along similar lines, Kohler-Hausmann notes that crime statistics "were inflated to some degree in this period by demographic factors. Since the large cohort of babies born after World War II began reaching early adulthood—the age bracket most prone to commit crime—in the late 1950s, some increases in crime were predictable." Yet, she adds, "crime rates were not wholly statistical artifacts" (*Getting Tough*, 37). For an especially influential critique of crime rates, see Stuart Hall et al., *Policing the Crisis: Mugging, the State, and Law and Order*, 2nd ed. (Palgrave Macmillan, 2013), 13–21.
43. Flamm, *Law and Order*, 125; Kohler-Hausmann, *Getting Tough*, 37.
44. Hinton, *From the War on Poverty*, 156, 23.
45. Loïc Wacquant, *Punishing the Poor: The Neoliberal Government of Social Insecurity* (Duke University Press, 2009), 138, 135.
46. In contemporary crime-mapping applications like CLEARmap, "all data are organized at the scales of beats and police districts." Brian Jordan Jefferson, "Digitize and Punish: Computerized Crime Mapping and Racialized Carceral Power in Chicago," *Environment and Planning D: Society and Space* 35, no. 5 (2017): 783–84.
47. Wambaugh, *New Centurions*, 471, 474.
48. Wambaugh, *New Centurions*, 434, 114.
49. Flamm, *Law and Order*, 102.
50. Wambaugh, *New Centurions*, 453.

2. RIOT ACTS

51. John Hersey, *The Algiers Motel Incident* (Alfred A. Knopf, 1968; repr., Johns Hopkins University Press, 1998), 74, 75, 67.
52. Hersey, *Algiers Motel Incident*, 30, 37.
53. Hersey, *Algiers Motel Incident*, 33.
54. Hersey, *Algiers Motel Incident*, 35, 36, 386, 229, 221, 195.
55. Hersey, *Algiers Motel Incident*, 394.
56. Hersey, *Algiers Motel Incident*, 31.
57. Wambaugh, *New Centurions*, 114.
58. Hersey, *Algiers Motel Incident*, 36.
59. Naomi Murakawa, *The First Civil Right: How Liberals Built Prison America* (Oxford University Press, 2014), 85.
60. Davis and Wiener, *Set the Night on Fire*, 237.
61. Wambaugh, *New Centurions*, 475.
62. Clover argues that riots tend to be seen as "thoughtless . . . lacking reason, organization, and political mediation," racially coded language that has been key to their delegitimation in the second half of the twentieth century (*Riot. Strike. Riot*, 112). Along similar lines, Elizabeth Hinton observes that "Americans have become accustomed to think of" riots "as misguided at best, and meaningless or irrational at worst . . . rooted in spontaneous, uncontrollable emotion." Hinton, *America on Fire: The Untold History of Police Violence and Black Rebellion Since the 1960s* (Liveright, 2021), 4.
63. Davis and Wiener, *Set the Night on Fire*, 232.
64. Flamm, *Law and Order*, 93.
65. Hersey, *Algiers Motel Incident*, 338–39.
66. Hinton, *From the War on Poverty*, 112.
67. Ball, *Death for a Playmate*, 56, 56–57, 78, 86, 78–79, 151, 89.
68. For a more extensive reading of Ball and Tidyman, see the excellent essay by crime novelist Aya de León, "The Black Detective in the White Mind: John Ball's Virgil Tibbs and Ernest Tidyman's John Shaft," *The Armchair Detective*, Fall 1993, 34–39.
69. Ernest Tidyman, *Shaft* (Bantam, 1970), 56, 102, 96, 74.
70. Tidyman, *Shaft*, 191, 205, 214, 17, 51, 74.
71. John A. Williams and Lori Williams, eds., *Dear Chester, Dear John: Letters Between Chester Himes and John A. Williams* (Wayne State University Press, 2008), 72.
72. Hersey, *Algiers Motel Incident*, 349.
73. Valerie Babb, *A History of the African American Novel* (Cambridge University Press, 2017), 124.
74. Ashley D. Farmer, *Remaking Black Power: How Black Women Transformed an Era* (University of North Carolina Press, 2017), 50. The figure of the Black revolutionary was significantly influenced by Black women activists, as Farmer details, and eventually evolved to become more gender-inclusive than is commonly acknowledged. However, the novels of Black revolution that emerged in the 1960s and '70s were dominated by what Farmer calls "the model of black revolutionary manhood" on which the Black Panther Party was initially founded and that it helped popularize (50).
75. Loren Glass, *Counterculture Colophon: Grove Press, the "Evergreen Review," and the Incorporation of the Avant-Garde* (Stanford University Press, 2013), 151.

76. See Kali Tal, "That Just Kills Me: Black Militant Near-Future Fiction," *Social Text* 20, no. 2 (2002): 65–91; Mark Bould, "Come Alive by Saying No: An Introduction to Black Power SF," *Science Fiction Studies* 34, no. 2 (2007): 220–40; and Julie A. Fiorelli, "Imagination Run Riot: Apocalyptic Race-War Novels of the Late 1960s," *Mediations* 28, no. 1 (2014). For a different account of Black and Chicano revolutionary novels as fictions of professionalization and "class suicide," see Elda María Román, *Race and Upward Mobility: Seeking, Gatekeeping, and Other Class Strategies in Postwar America* (Stanford University Press, 2018), 67–71.
77. Babb, *History of the African American Novel*, 149.
78. Quoted in Elizabeth Reich, *Militant Visions: Black Soldiers, Internationalism, and the Transformation of American Cinema* (Rutgers University Press, 2016), 188.
79. Sam Greenlee, *The Spook Who Sat by the Door* (Allison and Busby, 1969; repr., Brawtley, 2012), 61, 97.
80. Greenlee, *Spook Who Sat by the Door*, 130, 137, 176,146.
81. See Stuart Schrader, *Badges Without Borders: How Global Counterinsurgency Transformed American Policing* (University of California Press, 2019); Siegel, *Violence Work*; and Joseph Darda, *Empire of Defense: Race and the Cultural Politics of Permanent War* (University of Chicago Press, 2019).
82. Quoted in Hinton, *From the War on Poverty*, 69.
83. Quoted in Hersey, *Algiers Motel Incident*, 21.
84. Quoted in Jordan T. Camp, *Incarcerating the Crisis: Freedom Struggles and the Rise of the Neoliberal State* (University of California Press, 2016), 53.
85. Greenlee, *Spook Who Sat by the Door*, 224, 229, 230.
86. John A. Williams, *The Man Who Cried I Am* (Little, Brown, 1967; repr., Tusk Ivories, 2004), 371, 372.
87. Williams, *Man Who Cried I Am*, 387–88, 387, 372.
88. Asked in an interview about the inspiration for the Boatwright character, Williams responded, "Boatwright is somebody I made up." Nevertheless, in the context of a novel that is largely about the life and career of Richard Wright—indeed, it is the Wright character, Harry Ames, who gives Max the pages of the King Alfred Plan—it is hard not to read Boatwright as a sly reframing of Wright's Bigger Thomas. Contra Wright's ideas about social and environmental determination, Boatwright represents a Black figure for whom a more privileged environment—including Harvard—has not in fact offered greater access to freedom from white supremacy. "John Williams at 49: An Interview," *Minnesota Review* 7 (1976): 55.
89. Williams, *Man Who Cried I Am*, 53, 58, 377, 58.
90. John A. Williams, *Sons of Darkness, Sons of Light: A Novel of Some Probability* (Little, Brown, 1969; repr., Northeastern University Press, 1999), 58.
91. Williams, *Dear Chester, Dear John*, 83.
92. Williams, *Sons of Darkness*, 59.
93. Williams, *Sons of Darkness*, 82, 58, 101, 84.
94. Williams, *Sons of Darkness*, 269, 72, 271.
95. This is another way that Williams connected the political exigencies of his own moment back to the literary lineage of his friend Richard Wright, who had articulated a version of the same problem more than a decade earlier in *The Outsider*:

2. RIOT ACTS

"In a way, he was a criminal, not so much because of what he was doing, but because of what he was feeling." Wright, *The Outsider: The Restored Text Established by the Library of America* (original Harper & Row, 1953; repr., Harper Perennial, 1991), 109.
96. John Edgar Wideman, *The Lynchers* (Harcourt Brace Jovanovich, 1973; repr., Lulu, 2010), 46, 148.
97. Wideman, *Lynchers*, 41, 134,
98. Gil Scott-Heron, *The Vulture* (World, 1970; repr., Canongate, 2010), 129, 157, 158–59, 160.
99. Gil Scott-Heron, *Small Talk at 125th and Lenox* (World, 1970), 12. *Small Talk* and *The Vulture* are something like companion pieces. A poem called "The Vulture" from *Small Talk* serves as the epigraph for the novel, and several other poems appear in the pages of *The Vulture* as the writing of one of the novel's narrators, Ivan Quinn. Quinn is a student at Columbia and a kind of poet-philosopher, and thus seems to be a character Scott-Heron modeled on himself.
100. Scott-Heron, *Vulture*, 167–68, 157; Scott-Heron, *Small Talk*, 12.
101. Farmer, *Remaking Black Power*, 79, 84.
102. William J. Maxwell, *F. B. Eyes: How J. Edgar Hoover's Ghostreaders Framed African American Literature* (Princeton University Press, 2015), 3.
103. Wideman, *Lynchers*, 221.
104. For a slightly different account of genre's place in the Black radical tradition, see Maxwell, who argues that in the 1950s and '60s, Black novelists began experimenting with forms of detective and espionage fiction as a way to imaginatively respond to the open secret that they were being surveilled by the FBI. As Maxwell views them, such experiments with genre represented a form of "novelized counterinvestigation that recoded known forms of FBI rhetoric" (*F. B. Eyes*, 23).
105. "A mystery story is a hell of a departure from *Soul on Ice*," the publisher told him, referencing Eldridge Cleaver's popular book of essays from 1968. "I think our readers are going to be into the ghetto experience more than the mystery." Clearly, even by the late 1960s, the publishing industry continued to cling to the assumption that Black literature was primarily a vehicle for racial authenticity and urban ethnography. Gil Scott-Heron, *The Last Holiday: A Memoir* (Grove, 2012), 122–23.
106. Williams, *Dear Chester, Dear John*, 93, 136. It almost kept him eating for a while longer; Williams reported that at one point ABC was interested in turning *Sons of Darkness* into a television series with the help of Bill Cosby.
107. "Books: Eye for an Eye," *Time*, July 11, 1969.
108. For more on how modernist interiority developed in part out of an interest in criminal psychology, see Matthew Levay, *Violent Minds: Modernism and the Criminal* (Cambridge University Press, 2019).
109. Donald Goines, *Crime Partners* (Holloway House, 1974; repr., Holloway House Classics, 2008), 42.
110. Kinohi Nishikawa, *Street Players: Black Pulp Fiction and the Making of a Literary Underground* (University of Chicago Press, 2018), 137. Nishikawa establishes that earlier Holloway books, including Iceberg Slim's, were marketed primarily to white readers.

2. RIOT ACTS

111. L. H. Stallings, "'Im Goin Pimp Whores!': The Goines Factor and the Theory of a Hip-Hop Neo-Slave Narrative," *CR: The New Centennial Review* 3, no. 3 (2003): 200; Justin Gifford, *Pimping Fictions: African American Crime Literature and the Untold Story of Black Pulp Publishing* (Temple University Press, 2013), 87.
112. Jonathan Munby, *Under a Bad Sign: Criminal Self-Representation in African American Popular Culture* (University of Chicago Press, 2011), 153.
113. Nishikawa, *Street Players*, 148, 188. Elsewhere, Nishikawa has maintained that "Kenyatta is, in fact, an underworld gang leader and a liberator in name only." Kinohi Nishikawa, Review of *Pimping Fictions: African American Crime Literature and the Untold Story of Black Pulp Publishing* by Justin Gifford, *African American Review* 47, no. 1 (2014): 210.
114. Goines, *Crime Partners*, 48, 99, 49.
115. Kohler-Hausmann, *Getting Tough*, 35, 64.
116. Kohler-Hausmann, *Getting Tough*, 54–55.
117. Michael Javen Fortner, *Black Silent Majority: The Rockefeller Drug Laws and the Politics of Punishment* (Harvard University Press, 2015), 184.
118. Fortner, *Black Silent Majority*, 187, 186.
119. Scott-Heron, *Vulture*, 158, 173.
120. Brian Garfield, *Death Wish* (David McKay, 1972; repr., Overlook Duckworth, 2013), 131, 62, 80.
121. Kohler-Hausmann, *Getting Tough*, 64.
122. Garfield, *Death Wish*, 80.
123. Garfield, *Death Wish*, 63.
124. Like *Death Wish*, *The New Centurions* is obsessed with toughness as the solution to liberal permissiveness. Wambaugh goes so far as to put these talking points into the mouths of everyday citizens, such as a hamburger-stand cook who explains to a cop that the reason for the Watts riots is that African Americans "don't fear the Anglo" (435). The cook continues, "If a man tried to burn your house or hold a knife at your belly you kill him no matter his color. If he broke your laws you would prove to him that it's a painful thing to do such a thing" (436–37).
125. Garfield, *Death Wish*, 124.
126. Garfield, *Death Wish*, 46–47.
127. Quoted in Merve Emre, *Paraliterary: The Making of Bad Readers in Postwar America* (University of Chicago Press, 2017), 236.
128. Emre, *Paraliterary*, 242.
129. Emre, *Paraliterary*, 244.
130. Thomas J. Sugrue, "John Hersey and the Tragedy of Race," introduction to *The Algiers Motel Incident* by John Hersey (Johns Hopkins University Press, 1998), xvii.
131. Johnson, "Special Message on Crime."
132. Christopher P. Wilson, *Learning to Live with Crime: American Crime Narrative in the Neoconservative Turn* (Ohio State University Press, 2010), 3.
133. Quoted in Emre, *Paraliterary*, 241.
134. Garfield, *Death Wish*, 119, 94.
135. Flamm, *Law and Order*, 128–29.

3. DETECTING DOMESTIC VIOLENCE, 1975-2000

1. Mary Higgins Clark, introduction to *Where Are the Children?* (New York: Pocket Books, 2005), xiv.
2. Clark, *Where Are the Children?*, 208, 47, 75, 211.
3. Clark, *Where Are the Children?*, 28, 166.
4. In focusing on how female crime novelists transformed a traditionally male-centered genre, this chapter is indebted to many formative works in the field of feminist crime fiction studies, including Kathleen Gregory Klein, *The Woman Detective: Gender and Genre* (University of Illinois Press, 1988); Maureen T. Reddy, *Sisters in Crime: Feminism and the Crime Novel* (Continuum, 1988); Sally R. Munt, *Murder by the Book? Feminism and the Crime Novel* (Routledge, 1994); and Priscilla L. Walton and Manina Jones, *Detective Agency: Women Rewriting the Hard-Boiled Tradition* (University of California Press, 1999). More recently, Caroline Reitz has written a superb study of women's crime fiction as a genre that explores the uses of female anger in response to injustice—injustice that frequently involves victimized women whose claims are ignored. See Reitz, *Female Anger in Crime Fiction* (Cambridge University Press, 2024).
5. Bill Goldstein, "Some Best-Seller Old Reliables Have String of Unreliable Sales," *New York Times*, January 20, 2003.
6. Marie Gottschalk, *The Prison and the Gallows: The Politics of Mass Incarceration in America* (Cambridge University Press, 2006), 149.
7. Mimi E. Kim, "The Carceral Creep: Gender-Based Violence, Race, and the Expansion of the Punitive State, 1973-1983," *Social Problems* 67, no. 2 (2020): 258.
8. Kim, "Carceral Creep," 256.
9. Gottschalk, *Prison and the Gallows*, 140.
10. Aya Gruber, *The Feminist War on Crime: The Unexpected Role of Women's Liberation in Mass Incarceration* (University of California Press, 2020), 51.
11. Kim, "Carceral Creep," 256.
12. Kim, "Carceral Creep," 256.
13. Gruber, *Feminist War on Crime*, 45.
14. Gottschalk, *Prison and the Gallows*, 145, 149.
15. Gottschalk, *Prison and the Gallows*, 145, 147.
16. Gruber, *Feminist War on Crime*, 67; Gottschalk, *Prison and the Gallows*, 150.
17. Beth E. Richie, *Arrested Justice: Black Women, Violence, and America's Prison Nation* (New York University Press, 2012), 83, 71.
18. Kim, "Carceral Creep," 256-57.
19. Quoted in Amia Srinivasan, *The Right to Sex: Feminism in the Twenty-First Century* (Picador, 2021), 164.
20. Robin McDuff, Deanne Pernell, and Karen Saunders, "Letter to the Anti-Rape Movement," *Off Our Backs* 7, no. 5 (June 1977), 9. 10.
21. Assata Shakur and Joanne Chesimard, "Women in Prison: How We Are," *Black Scholar* 9, no. 7 (1978): 9.
22. Angela Y. Davis, Gina Dent, Erica R. Meiners, and Beth E. Richie, *Abolition. Feminism. Now.* (Haymarket, 2022), 111.

3. DETECTING DOMESTIC VIOLENCE

23. Kimberlé Crenshaw, "Mapping the Margins: Intersectionality, Identity Politics, and Violence Against Women of Color," *Stanford Law Review* 43, no. 6 (1991): 1259.
24. Crenshaw, "Mapping the Margins," 1260, 1257.
25. The group is now called INCITE! Women, Gender Non-Conforming, and Trans People of Color Against Violence.
26. "INCITE!—Critical Resistance Statement on Gender Violence and the Prison Industrial Complex (2001)," in *Abolition. Feminism. Now* by Davis, Dent, Meiners, and Richie, 175–81, 176.
27. Kristin Bumiller, *In an Abusive State: How Neoliberalism Appropriated the Feminist Movement Against Sexual Violence* (Duke University Press, 2008), 11.
28. Richie, *Arrested Justice*, 83; Gottschalk, *Prison and the Gallows*, 160.
29. Gruber, *Feminist War on Crime*, 88.
30. Leigh Goodmark, *Imperfect Victims: Criminalized Survivors and the Promise of Abolition Feminism* (University of California Press, 2023), 12.
31. Goodmark, *Imperfect Victims*, 12, 171.
32. Angela Y. Davis, *Women, Race & Class* (Vintage, 1981), 201.
33. Because this chapter focuses on some specific subgenres of women's crime fiction, it does not discuss such towering literary figures as Toni Morrison and Alice Walker, both of whom offered important portrayals of Black women's vulnerability to abuse. For more on the historical significance of Morrison's and Walker's novels in the context of Black feminist antiviolence organizing in the 1970s and '80s, see Richie, *Arrested Justice*, 147–48. On the controversy prompted by Walker's depiction of Black male violence in *The Color Purple* and the lessons of that controversy for an intersectional feminist approach to gendered violence, see Crenshaw, "Mapping the Margins," 1256.
34. In *Female Anger in Crime Fiction*, Reitz points out some examples of the role that battered women seeking justice have played in feminist detective novels. For a pioneering study of the literary depiction of domestic abuse in an earlier period—including, notably, in the detective stories of Arthur Conan Doyle—see Lisa Surridge, *Bleak Houses: Marital Violence in Victorian Fiction* (Ohio University Press, 2005). And for a compelling analysis of how the issues of domestic and sexual violence have been central to the development of contemporary gothic fiction by women, see Sarah E. Whitney, *Splattered Ink: Postfeminist Gothic Fiction and Gendered Violence* (University of Illinois Press, 2016).
35. Lee Horsley, *Twentieth-Century Crime Fiction* (Oxford University Press, 2005), 243.
36. Quoted in Walton and Jones, *Detective Agency*, 10.
37. "Mission/Vision/Values of SinC," Sisters in Crime, sistersincrime.org.
38. "A History of Sisters in Crime," Sisters in Crime, sistersincrime.org.
39. Walton and Jones, *Detective Agency*, 11.
40. Walton and Jones, *Detective Agency*, 12.
41. Horsley, *Twentieth-Century Crime Fiction*, 248.
42. Bruce Taylor, "G Is for (Sue) Grafton," *Armchair Detective*, Winter 1989; republished in *Murder & Mayhem*, August 8, 2017.
43. Komo's novel is sometimes described as the first full-length detective novel by a Black woman. However, Komo is a mysterious figure who never published

3. DETECTING DOMESTIC VIOLENCE

another book under that name, and there is some controversy surrounding her identity.

44. Carroll John Daly, "Knights of the Open Palm," in *The Black Lizard Big Book of "Black Mask" Stories*, 429–41 (New York: Vintage Crime, 2010), 429; first published in *Black Mask*, June 1, 1923.
45. In *Detective Agency*, Walton and Jones note that hardboiled fiction has long represented the need to "act outside and often against the authorized centers of power" (190). For more on detective fiction's ambivalence toward the state, see Sean McCann, *Gumshoe America: Hard-Boiled Crime Fiction and the Rise and Fall of New Deal Liberalism* (Duke University Press, 2000), and Andrew Pepper, *Unwilling Executioner: Crime Fiction and the State* (Oxford University Press, 2016).
46. Nancy Pickard, *Marriage Is Murder* (Pocket, 1987), 57.
47. Pickard, *Marriage Is Murder*, 53, 62, 76, 77, 156, 219.
48. It is widely known that the rate of domestic violence incidents is higher among police officers than among the general public.
49. Ellen Hawkes, "G Is for Grafton: Instead of Killing Her Ex-Husband, Sue Grafton Created a Smart-Mouthed, Hard-Boiled (and Incidentally Female) Detective Named Kinsey Millhone," *Los Angeles Times*, February 18, 1990.
50. Sue Grafton, *A Is for Alibi* (St. Martin's Griffin, 1982), 42–43, 43, 45, 44, 267–68.
51. Grafton, *A Is for Alibi*, 159.
52. Gruber, *Feminist War on Crime*, 94.
53. Grafton, *A Is for Alibi*, 206, 32, 306–7.
54. Grafton, *A Is for Alibi*, 267.
55. Sara Paretsky, *Bitter Medicine* (William Morrow, 1987), 76.
56. Violent encounters with the criminal classes are standard fare in hardboiled detective fiction, whose male heroes are constantly being beaten up or sapped in the back of the head. Horsley draws an important contrast, noting that "male hardboiled protagonists . . . tend to be physically damaged on a regular basis. But the female PI, as a woman, is more vulnerable and more likely to be represented as linked to those who are victims" (*Twentieth-Century Crime Fiction*, 268). Yet the violence that detectives like Warshawski and Millhone experience is not simply a matter of female vulnerability writ large. It is represented, more specifically, as a vulnerability to intimate partner violence.
57. Richie, *Arrested Justice*, 92.
58. Grafton, *A Is for Alibi*, 295.
59. Patricia Cornwell, *Postmortem* (Scribner, 1990); republished in *Three Complete Novels: Postmortem, Body of Evidence, All That Remains* (Smithmark, 1997), 87.
60. Barbara Neely, *Blanche Among the Talented Tenth* (St. Martin's Press, 1994), 215, 214.
61. Barbara Neely, *Blanche Passes Go* (Viking, 2000), 217–18.
62. Richie, *Arrested Justice*, 90, 91, 92.
63. In her reading of the Blanche series, Reitz detects Neely's lingering resistance to a version of feminism founded on a flattened universalism. "Neely's message," Reitz suggests, is that "race trumps gender in the ways bodies are understood, and an unquestioning gender solidarity can be dangerous" (*Female Anger*, 36).
64. Paretsky, *Bitter Medicine*, 268.

3. DETECTING DOMESTIC VIOLENCE

65. Writing on *Bitter Medicine*, Sally Munt concludes that the "the text falls prey to the classism raddling the bourgeois history of liberalism, which extends the hand of democracy only to those endowed with certain means" (*Murder by the Book?*, 46). Along similar lines, Andrew Pepper observes how Paretsky's work "fuses anti-establishment and liberal feminist concerns without drawing too much attention to possible ruptures within this alliance." For him, there is something "too good to be true" about the racial politics of Paretsky's novels, which tend to feature a "rainbow coalition" that is shaped by contradictions her books don't acknowledge. Pepper, *The Contemporary American Crime Novel: Race, Ethnicity, Gender, Class* (Edinburgh University Press, 2000), 54, 56.
66. Julilly Kohler-Hausmann, *Getting Tough: Welfare and Imprisonment in 1970s America* (Princeton University Press, 2017), 183.
67. Grafton, *A Is for Alibi*, 64, 90, 274, 256, 274.
68. The philosopher Amia Srinivasan argues for the centrality of class to the feminist project. "A feminism that addresses only sexual oppression will be of little use to women whose sex is just one cause of their political predicament," she writes. "Globally, most women are poor, and most poor people are women. This is why feminism understood as the fight against 'common oppression' comes apart from a feminism that fights for the equality and dignity of all women. A feminism focused on women's common oppression leaves untouched the forces that most immiserate most women" (*Right to Sex*, 162–63).
69. Leigh Goodmark suggests that social expectations about what the "perfect victim" of gender-based violence is supposed to look like leave little room for actually existing victims. She contends that "survivors of violence had to perform their victimization in very specific ways," as they were socially pressured to match "unrealistic stereotypes of people subjected to abuse" (*Imperfect Victims*, 9).
70. Richie, *Arrested Justice*, 72.
71. Neely, *Blanche Among the Talented Tenth*, 228–29.
72. Neely, *Blanche Passes Go*, 191.
73. What should battered women do instead? Neely waits until the final pages of the last book in her series to offer an answer. No longer able to ignore the abusive domestic situation of her unnamed neighbor, Blanche "wrote down the name and the number of the new women's shelter, then slipped the piece of paper with the number on it under the woman's screen door." One woman who has experienced male violence helps another woman escape an abusive situation she can't escape on her own. This is a vision of feminist mutual aid. "Maybe the only way to end this mess," Blanche concludes, "was for every woman to stand up for every other woman, even if she couldn't stand up for herself" (*Blanche Passes Go*, 274, 273).
74. Grafton, *A Is for Alibi*, 16.
75. Melinda Cooper, *Family Values: Between Neoliberalism and the New Social Conservatism* (Zone, 2017), 8.
76. Gottschalk, *Prison and the Gallows*, 147
77. On the shifting relation between privacy and the family and the growing sense that middle- and upper-class family privacy nurtured hidden violence, see Palmer Rampell's excellent book *Genres of Privacy in Postwar America* (Stanford University Press, 2022), 101–28.

3. DETECTING DOMESTIC VIOLENCE

78. Jonathan Simon, *Governing Through Crime: How the War on Crime Transformed American Democracy and Created a Culture of Fear* (Oxford University Press, 2007), 204.
79. Gottschalk, *Prison and the Gallows*, 163.
80. Grafton, *A Is for Alibi*, 158.
81. Paretsky, *Bitter Medicine*, 114.
82. Neely, *Blanche Among the Talented Tenth*, 93.
83. Clark, *Where Are the Children?*, 93, 218.
84. Clark, *Where Are the Children?*, 79, 132, 155, 222.
85. In light of this claim, it is interesting that Clark based *Where Are the Children?* on the real case of Alice Crimmins—a woman accused of killing her children in 1965 and eventually found guilty after multiple trials and appeals.
86. Clark, *Where Are the Children?*, 287.
87. Clark, *Where Are the Children?*, 79.
88. Clark, *Where Are the Children?*, 281.
89. Toni Cade Bambara, *Those Bones Are Not My Child* (Vintage, 1999), 67.
90. Bambara, *Those Bones*, 103, 157, 5, 314, 93, 8, 6.
91. Kohler-Hausmann, *Getting Tough*, 154–55.
92. Daniel Patrick Moynihan, *The Negro Family: The Case for National Action* (Office of Planning and Research, United States Department of Labor, 1965), 30, 29.
93. Daniel Geary, *Beyond Civil Rights: The Moynihan Report and Its Legacy* (University of Pennsylvania Press, 2015), 3.
94. Hortense Spillers, "Mama's Baby, Papa's Maybe: An American Grammar Book," *Diacritics* 17, no. 2 (1987): 66.
95. Habiba Ibrahim, "'Why Talk About the Children?': James Baldwin, Octavia Butler, and the Future of Care," *American Literary History* 35, no. 1 (2023): 184.
96. Toni Cade Bambara, preface to *The Black Woman: An Anthology*, ed. Toni Cade Bambara (New American Library, 1970; repr., Washington Square, 2005), 6.
97. Joanna Clark, "Motherhood," in *The Black Woman: An Anthology*, 85.
98. Jean Carey Bond and Patricia Peery, "Is the Black Male Castrated?" in *The Black Woman: An Anthology*, 143.
99. Geary, *Beyond Civil Rights*, 212.
100. Bambara, *Those Bones*, 117, 69, 68, 69, 201, 69.
101. Bambara, *Those Bones*, 186, 187, 188, 365, 371.
102. Bambara, *Those Bones*, 178, 254, 317, 318.
103. Simon, *Governing Through Crime*, 178, 204, 179.
104. Bambara, *Those Bones*, 660.
105. Rampell, *Genres of Privacy*, 107–18.
106. Bambara, *Those Bones*, 156.
107. Bambara, *Those Bones*, 107.
108. This sense of extreme isolation from the state can paradoxically, if understandably, create the desire to be drawn closer to it. This may explain why, at the end of *Those Bones*, Zala gives an impassioned speech calling for "crimes against children" to be "dealt with more seriously." A few pages later, in the novel's epilogue, the narrator notes with some satisfaction that national coverage of the Atlanta murders had succeeded in getting "other parts of the country" to call "for stricter

3. DETECTING DOMESTIC VIOLENCE

child-protection laws." This is all a bit puzzling; surely, the preceding six-hundred-plus pages of *Those Bones Are Not My Child* have rather thoroughly demonstrated that the problem is a series of state and federal institutions unwilling to admit that the crimes are even happening—not a lack of effective laws. But fear for the safety of children (a group referred to earlier in the novel as "our most treasured resource, our most precious people, our future") is as visceral as it is relatable, and in the end the novel may not know quite where else to turn but back to the state to ask for stricter laws (*Those Bones*, 660, 666, 171). The feminist education scholar Erica R. Meiners offers valuable insight into this paradox, explaining how "the theme of saving our children refracts across the criminal justice landscape," as likely to be marshaled in an argument for less policing as in an argument for more. Meiners, *For the Children? Protecting Innocence in a Carceral State* (University of Minnesota Press, 2016), 2.

109. Linda Fairstein, *Final Jeopardy* (Pocket, 1996), 29.
110. Gruber, *Feminist War on Crime*, 44.
111. Reddy, *Sisters in Crime*, 84.
112. Elizabeth Bernstein, "The Sexual Politics of the 'New Abolitionism,'" *Differences* 18, no. 5 (2007): 143.
113. The focus on mental illness also puts *Dead Time* in conversation with the novels discussed in chapter 4.
114. At one point a character refers to the runaways as "throwaway children" (*Dead Time*, 46). The phrase comes from a 1969 book by Lisa Richette, *The Throwaway Children*, about child abuse and the juvenile justice system. It so happens that Richette, a famous Philadelphia judge, was a key figure in the national debate about domestic violence, giving impassioned testimony at the 1978 congressional hearings about battering. According to Gruber, Richette's commentary at the hearings was focused specifically on rejecting the "contention that DV was a racial and socioeconomic phenomenon" (*Feminist War on Crime*, 55–56).
115. Eleanor Taylor Bland, *Dead Time* (St. Martin's Press, 1992), 59, 161, 164, 39.
116. Bland, *Dead Time*, 6, 40.
117. Bland, *Dead Time*, 103, 204.
118. Bland, *Dead Time*, 211.
119. Bland, *Dead Time*, 40, 6, 103.
120. Bland, *Dead Time*, 103.
121. Bland, *Dead Time*, 168.
122. On the relation between the child welfare system and the carceral state, see Dorothy Roberts, *Torn Apart: How the Child Welfare System Destroys Black Families—and How Abolition Can Build a Safer World* (Basic Books, 2022).
123. Fairstein's influence would eventually cross over into television. She has said in interviews that *Law and Order: Special Victims Unit*, created by Dick Wolf in 1999, "was based on our unit." Kathryn Shattuck, "Linda Fairstein Looks Crime in the Face and Smiles," *New York Times*, September 12, 2017.
124. Linda Fairstein, *Sexual Violence: Our War Against Rape* (William Morrow, 1993), 10, 17, 272.
125. Fairstein, *Final Jeopardy*, 10, 53, 29–30, 176.
126. Fairstein, *Final Jeopardy*, 114, 98, 197, 2.
127. Fairstein, *Final Jeopardy*, 250.

4. TWO PATHS FOR PATHOLOGY

128. In the 1970s, radical abolition feminists made a similar argument that prison was unlikely to rehabilitate rapists, given the extensive amount of violence and rape that took place there. But that was an argument about the inhumane conditions of prison. Here Fairstein is saying something quite different. By emphasizing the futility of treatment centers and therapists—that is, the futility of actual rehabilitative alternatives to prison—she is making what amounts to an ontological claim about the unchangeable essence of rapists and criminals.
129. Fairstein, *Final Jeopardy*, 271.
130. Fairstein, *Final Jeopardy*, 7.
131. As Davis, Dent, Meiners, and Richie argue in their indispensable collaborative book *Abolition. Feminism. Now.*, there are crucial "connections between state violence, street violence, and interpersonal violence" and many ways of mapping those connections. Taken together, the intersections among these different scales of gender-based violence represent the "conjunction at the heart of all of the work of abolition feminism" (19).
132. Richie argues that the very fact that VAWA was packaged with the larger Clinton crime bill meant that it inherently "came with a cost—a set of harsh laws that disadvantaged some of the same communities that the population of women who are most vulnerable to male violence come from" (*Arrested Justice*, 86). For more on how the Clinton crime bill contributed to mass incarceration, see chapter 5.
133. Gottschalk, *Prison and the Gallows*, 151.
134. Goodmark, *Imperfect Victims*, 8.

4. TWO PATHS FOR PATHOLOGY, 1984-1998

1. "Paperback Best Sellers," *New York Times*, May 26, 1991.
2. Leonard Cassuto, *Hard-Boiled Sentimentality: The Secret History of American Crime Stories* (Columbia University Press, 2009), 242.
3. Highlighting the genre's link to "sexual gratification," Gill Plain proposes that "the serial-killer narrative confronts ... both our desire for violence and our most violent desires." Stephen Knight suggests that the genre's focus on "sadomasochistic detail" and "sensational violence" raises issues of "identity and subjectivity." Lee Horsley argues that the "excessive" and "gothic" elements of serial killer fiction serve to undermine "facile moral assumptions." Leonard Cassuto observes that serial killer fiction plays on the affinity between "sympathy and disgust." And Mark Seltzer maintains that serial killer narratives are most important for their emphasis on "a failure of explanation as to cause or motive ('motiveless crimes')." Plain, *Twentieth-Century Crime Fiction: Gender, Sexuality, and the Body* (Edinburgh University Press, 2001), 227; Knight, *Crime Fiction Since 1800: Detection, Death, Diversity*, 2nd ed. (Palgrave Macmillan, 2010), 212–13; Horsley, *Twentieth-Century Crime Fiction* (Oxford University Press, 2005), 141; Cassuto, *Hard-Boiled Sentimentality*, 257; Seltzer, *Serial Killers: Death and Life in America's Wound Culture* (Routledge, 1998), 162.
4. Cassuto, *Hard-Boiled Sentimentality*, 242.
5. Michelle Alexander, *The New Jim Crow: Mass Incarceration in the Age of Colorblindness*, rev. ed. (New York: New Press, 2012), 5.

4. TWO PATHS FOR PATHOLOGY

6. Elizabeth Hinton, *From the War on Poverty to the War on Crime: The Making of Mass Incarceration in America* (Harvard University Press, 2016), 310.
7. Naomi Murakawa, *The First Civil Right: How Liberals Built Prison America* (Oxford University Press, 2014), 113–14.
8. David Wilson, *Inventing Black-on-Black Violence: Discourse, Space, and Representation* (Syracuse University Press, 2005), 51.
9. Sherman Alexie, *Indian Killer* (Grove, 1996), 339.
10. One of the most striking examples of the form this disavowal took in the 1990s is the literary output of Linda Fairstein, the prosecutor turned crime novelist, whom I discuss in chapter 3.
11. James Ellroy, *Blood on the Moon* (Mysterious Press, 1984; repr., Vintage, 2005); James Ellroy, *The Black Dahlia*, 1987, in *The L.A. Quartet* (Everyman's Library, 2019).
12. Ellroy, *Blood on the Moon*, 111. Although *Blood on the Moon* signals its intention to distance itself from Black criminalization, it manages to do so only by conjoining criminality with homosexuality. The novel thus offers a distressing reminder of the extent to which early literary depictions of serial killers were rooted in homophobia and gay panic. For a provocative account of how homophobia works in serial killer narratives, see Jack Halberstam's "Skinflick: Posthuman Gender in Jonathan Demme's *Silence of the Lambs*," *Camera Obscura* 9, no. 3 (1991): 36–53.
13. Mike Davis, *City of Quartz: Excavating the Future in Los Angeles* (Verso, 1990), 45.
14. John DiIulio, "The Coming of the Super-Predators," *Washington Examiner*, November 27, 1995.
15. David Musto, *The American Disease: Origins of Narcotics Control*, 3rd ed. (Oxford University Press, 1999), 230, 273.
16. Julilly Kohler-Hausmann, *Getting Tough: Welfare and Imprisonment in 1970s America* (Princeton University Press, 2017), 79–80.
17. Ruth Wilson Gilmore, *Golden Gulag: Prisons, Surplus, Crisis, and Opposition in Globalizing California* (University of California Press, 2007), 108.
18. Hinton, *From the War on Poverty*, 317.
19. Murakawa, *First Civil Right*, 119.
20. Marie Gottschalk, *Caught: The Prison State and the Lockdown of American Politics* (Princeton University Press, 2015), 6.
21. Kohler-Hausmann, *Getting Tough*, 33.
22. Ruth Wilson Gilmore, "Covid-19, Decarceration, and Abolition," lecture at Princeton University, April 17, 2020, https://www.haymarketbooks.org/blogs/128-ruth-wilson-gilmore-on-covid-19-decarceration-and-abolition.
23. Angela Y. Davis, *Are Prisons Obsolete?* (Seven Stories, 2003), 10.
24. James Forman Jr., *Locking Up Our Own: Crime and Punishment in Black America* (Farrar, Straus and Giroux, 2017), 147.
25. Wilson, *Inventing Black-on-Black Violence*, 34. Wilson doesn't believe this himself; he's parroting the conventional discourse.
26. Daniel Patrick Moynihan, *The Negro Family: The Case for National Action* (Office of Policy Planning and Research, U.S. Department of Labor, 1965), 47. For more on the Moynihan Report and its legacy, see chapter 3.
27. For a valuable account of how "culture of poverty" discourses informed postwar American literature, see Stephen Schryer, *Maximum Feasible Participation: American Literature and the War on Poverty* (Stanford University Press, 2018).

4. TWO PATHS FOR PATHOLOGY

28. Gottschalk, *Caught*, 147.
29. Murakawa, *First Civil Right*, 147.
30. Nicole Rafter, *The Criminal Brain: Understanding Biological Theories of Crime* (New York University Press, 2008), 199–238. According to Rafter, "biocriminology's enduring poster boy" was "the psychopath" (232).
31. Musto, *American Disease*, 269.
32. Walter Mosley, *White Butterfly* (Washington Square, 1992), 213.
33. Barbara Neely, *Blanche on the Lam* (Penguin, 1992), 19.
34. Patricia Cornwell, *All That Remains* (Scribner, 1992); republished in *Three Complete Novels: Postmortem, Body of Evidence, All That Remains* (Smithmark, 1997), 555, 560.
35. Michelle Alexander writes, "From the outset, stories circulated on the street that crack and other drugs were being brought into black neighborhoods by the CIA" (*New Jim Crow*, 5).
36. Joyce Carol Oates, *Because It Is Bitter, Because It Is My Heart* (Plume, 1991), 305–6.
37. Oates, *Because It Is Bitter*, 94.
38. Lawrence Block, *A Walk Among the Tombstones* (William Morrow, 1992), 209, 273.
39. This way of describing criminal minds has a much longer history. In her study of Golden Age detective fiction, Samantha Walton explains how depictions of "emotional instability and mental pathology complicated the [genre's] pattern of reason and reassurance," presenting criminals "as victims of their own troubled minds." More sweepingly, Seltzer has argued that "the killer's madness" mirrors back to us the "normal madness" of the modern world. Walton, *Guilty but Insane: Mind and Law in Golden Age Detective Fiction* (Oxford University Press, 2015), 48; Seltzer, *Serial Killers*, 162.
40. Cassuto, *Hard-Boiled Sentimentality*, 259, 261, 262. According to Cassuto, serial killer fiction emerged partly in response to the surge in homelessness among the mentally ill that occurred in the wake of the massive defunding of state-run mental health institutions between the 1960s and the 1980s. In these decades, more than two-thirds of available inpatient beds disappeared. Once that happened, Cassuto persuasively argues, serial killer narratives emerged as a way of expressing "collective anxiety about the presence of the mentally ill in middle-class space" (262).
41. Mosley, *White Butterfly*, 146.
42. Ellroy, *L.A. Confidential*, 1043.
43. Neely, *Blanche on the Lam*, 135, 212.
44. Neely, *Blanche on the Lam*, 209.
45. Ellroy, *L.A. Confidential*, 1042 (emphasis in original).
46. Mosley, *White Butterfly*, 201.
47. Cornwell, *All That Remains*, 818.
48. Block, *A Walk Among the Tombstones*, 200.
49. Patricia Cornwell, *Postmortem* (Scribner, 1990); republished in *Three Complete Novels: Postmortem, Body of Evidence, All That Remains* (Smithmark, 1997), 162, 222.
50. Block, *A Walk Among the Tombstones*, 90.

51. Cornwell, *Postmortem*, 133.
52. Kohler-Hausmann, *Getting Tough*, 120 (emphasis in original).
53. Musto, *American Disease*, 274.
54. Stephen Kern points out the longstanding tension between medical and legal institutions in the history of insanity defenses. He explains, "The history of ideas about the causal role of insanity in murder is extremely complex because the two professions most concerned with it, jurisprudence and psychiatry, had clashing concepts, values, and goals.... As physicians, psychiatrists vowed to cure the sick, while as servants of the state, jurists vowed to judge the accused." Kern, *A Cultural History of Causality: Science, Murder Novels, and Systems of Thought* (Princeton University Press, 2004), 255.
55. Ellroy, *L.A. Confidential*, 1051, 1052, 1058.
56. Ellroy, *L.A. Confidential*, 1058, 1006.
57. Ellroy, *L.A. Confidential*, 1026.
58. Mosley, *White Butterfly*, 209–10.
59. Britt Rusert, "Naturalizing Coercion: The Tuskegee Experiments and the Laboratory Life of the Plantation," in *Captivating Technology: Race, Carceral Technoscience, and the Liberatory Imagination in Everyday Life*, ed. Ruha Benjamin (Duke University Press, 2019): 35.
60. Rusert, "Naturalizing Coercion," 38.
61. Kohler-Hausmann, *Getting Tough*, 120.
62. If *The Black Dahlia* is about the media and law enforcement frenzy stoked by the killing of a white woman (the real-life unsolved murder of Elizabeth Short), *White Butterfly* is about the way a Black serial killer preying on Black women is systematically ignored by local politicians and the police.
63. Don DeLillo, *White Noise* (Penguin, 1985), 43, 44, 46.
64. DeLillo, *White Noise*, 210, 250, 307.
65. DeLillo, *White Noise*, 315.
66. DeLillo, *White Noise*, 312.
67. Seltzer, *Serial Killers*, 2.
68. Barbara D'Amato, *Hardball* (Scribner, 1990), 140, 10, 173, 46, 177.
69. D'Amato, *Hardball*, 127, 73, 104, 73, 128.
70. D'Amato, *Hardball*, 151, 70.
71. The link between alcoholism and drug addiction is also highlighted in *A Walk Among the Tombstones*. Block's novel is filled with both addicts and alcoholics, and the novel goes out of its way to describe all of these characters as struggling with an illness. When a character refers to his brother's heroin use as a "habit," the book's protagonist, himself a recovering alcoholic, corrects him: "We generally call it a disease" (200, 204).
72. Block, *Walk Among the Tombstones*, 241.
73. D'Amato, *Hardball*, 7.
74. Sue Grafton, *C Is for Corpse* (St. Martin's Press, 1986), 40–41, 56.
75. Matthew D. Lassiter, "Impossible Criminals: The Suburban Imperatives of America's War on Drugs," *Journal of American History* 126 (2015): 127.
76. Lassiter, "Impossible Criminals," 128.
77. Grafton, *C Is for Corpse*, 63, 61.
78. Grafton, *C Is for Corpse*, 9, 64–65, 98, 99, 100.

4. TWO PATHS FOR PATHOLOGY

79. Grafton, *C Is for Corpse*, 150–51, 201.
80. Grafton, *C Is for Corpse*, 105–6, 294.
81. Grafton, *C Is for Corpse*, 278.
82. Musto, *American Disease*, 268–69.
83. James A. Morone, "Presidents and Health Reform: From Franklin D. Roosevelt to Barack Obama," *Health Affairs* 29, no. 6 (2010): 1096.
84. Grafton, *C Is for Corpse*, 96, 274.
85. In the same year that she published *C Is for Corpse*, Grafton also wrote a short story called "The Parker Shotgun," which makes clear how focused she was on the War on Drugs. "The Parker Shotgun" finds Kinsey Millhone investigating the death of a former drug dealer. Despite having cleaned up his act, the dead man is dismissed by the police as a "small-time punk" who was probably killed in a drug deal. Initially, Millhone is inclined to believe this version of events as well, noting the inherent dangers of drug dealing and the proximity of Santa Teresa to "the big time in L.A."—where, of course, the intensive policing of Black and Brown neighborhoods associated with drug use was just getting into full swing. Grafton, "The Parker Shotgun," in *The Longman Anthology of Detective Fiction*, ed. Deane Mansfield-Kelly and Lois A. Marchino, 295–308 (Pearson Longman, 2005), 296.
86. Sara Paretsky, *Bitter Medicine* (William Morrow, 1987), 239, 45, 46, 107, 227.
87. Paretsky, *Bitter Medicine*, 98, 23, 55, 44, 33.
88. Wajahat Ali, "Faking the Hood," interview with Ishmael Reed, *Counterpunch*, March 15, 2008.
89. Richard Price, *Freedomland* (Delta, 1998), 27, 4.
90. Price, *Freedomland*, 418–19, 420, 419.
91. Price, *Freedomland*, 419–20.
92. Kathryn Bond Stockton, "Prophylactics and Brains: *Beloved* in the Cybernetic Age of AIDS," *Studies in the Novel* 28, no. 3 (1996): 435.
93. Price, *Freedomland*, 414.
94. Price, *Freedomland*, 4.
95. Octavia E. Butler, "The Evening and the Morning and the Night," *Callaloo*, Spring 1991, 478, 487, 490, 482, 478.
96. See, for instance, Sami Schalk, "Interpreting Disability Metaphor and Race in Octavia Butler's 'The Evening and the Morning and the Night,'" *African American Review* 50, no. 2 (2017): 139–51; and Isiah Lavender III, "Digging Deep: Ailments of Difference in Octavia Butler's 'The Evening and the Morning and the Night,'" in *Black and Brown Planets: The Politics of Race in Science Fiction*, ed. Isiah Lavender III, 65–82 (University of Mississippi Press, 2014).
97. In her excellent treatment of Butler's story, Schalk explains that Butler "worked on 'Evening' off and on between 1966 and 1985," clipping and filing many mainstream news stories about illness and disability along the way ("Interpreting Disability Metaphor and Race," 143). Working on the story up through the mid-1980s would have given Butler plenty of time to see how the issues of illness and mental health had become inextricable from media representations of drug abuse and the government's punitive response to it.
98. Schalk, "Interpreting Disability Metaphor and Race," 144. Octavia Butler quoted in Eric Carl Link, "Introduction: Naturalism and Science Fiction," *Studies in American Naturalism* 8, no. 1 (2013): 2.

4. TWO PATHS FOR PATHOLOGY

99. According to Schalk, "Butler developed this nonrealist disease by combining aspects of three real-world diseases: Huntington's disease, phenylketonuria, and Lesch-Nyhan disease.... DGD is also explicitly compared to other eventually or potentially disabling diseases in the story, including 'leprosy'... and diabetes" ("Interpreting Disability Metaphor and Race," 142).
100. Butler, "The Evening and the Morning and the Night," 481, 482, 477, 478, 482.
101. Butler, "The Evening and the Morning and the Night," 477.
102. Butler, "The Evening and the Morning and the Night," 482, 483, 484, 491.
103. For an incisive history of the relation between deindustrialization and the health care sector, see Gabriel Winant, *The Next Shift: The Fall of Industry and the Rise of Health Care in Rust Belt America* (Harvard University Press, 2021).
104. Douglas S. Massey, "American Apartheid: Segregation and the Making of the Underclass," *American Journal of Sociology* 96, no. 2 (1990): 329.
105. Kaaryn Gustafson, "The Criminalization of Poverty," *Journal of Criminal Law and Criminology*, 99, no. 3 (2009): 643.
106. Joe Soss, Richard C. Fording, and Sanford F. Schram, *Disciplining the Poor: Neoliberal Paternalism and the Persistent Power of Race* (University of Chicago Press, 2011), 103.
107. Soss, Fording, and Schram, *Disciplining the Poor*, 107.
108. Peter Ikeler and Calvin John Smiley, "The Racial Economics of Mass Incarceration: A Critique of Clegg and Usmani," *Spectre* 1, no. 2 (2020): 97.
109. Loïc Wacquant, "From Slavery to Mass Incarceration: Rethinking the 'Race Question' in the US," *New Left Review* 13 (2002): 52.
110. Gottschalk, *Caught*, 32.
111. Soss, Fording, and Schram, *Disciplining the Poor*, 103. For a more detailed analysis of the various "connections between incarceration and labor markets," see 105–8.
112. Christian Parenti, *Lockdown America: Police and Prisons in the Age of Crisis* (Verso, 1999; repr. 2008), 243.
113. Richard Price, *Clockers* (Houghton Mifflin, 1992), 69, 586, 492.
114. In an interview conducted by the sociologist William Julius Wilson, a Chicago employer sidesteps a question about "racial discrimination" in inner-city employment by suggesting there is a lot of "fear and concern" about African Americans' putative tendency toward violence: "I think a related question is the fear on the part of the majority community of the violence and the criminal activities that generally are black people acting upon black people." Wilson, *When Work Disappears: The World of the New Urban Poor* (Knopf, 1996), 128.
115. Devah Pager, *Marked: Race, Crime, and Finding Work in an Era of Mass Incarceration* (University of Chicago Press, 2007), 145, 5.
116. Butler, "The Evening and the Morning and the Night," 483, 485, 487.
117. Neely, *Blanche on the Lam*, 5, 211.
118. Oates, *Because It Is Bitter*, 356, 351. Jinx's experiences with low-wage, deskilled work and with racial exclusion from union membership puts a slightly different spin on the way Oates renders the fate of Jinx's brother Sugar Baby, who is killed after he begins working for a drug dealer in Buffalo. Before he dies, Sugar Baby explains his decision as a response to Black people's confinement to the lowest rung of a labor market that was already beginning to shift from manufacturing

5. THE NOVEL IN THE AGE OF MASS INCARCERATION

work to service work—in hotels and, wouldn't you know it, hospitals. As he tells his family, his choice of work was a "whole lot better than janitor work or shoveling gravel or cleaning up white folks' shit at the hospital or some hotel uptown or hauling away their garbage, which is what his friends from high school do, mostly" (192).

119. Walter Mosley, *Devil in a Blue Dress* (Washington Square, 1990), 47, 48.
120. Ellroy, *L.A. Confidential*, 855.
121. Bret Easton Ellis, *American Psycho* (Vintage, 1991), 206, 130. A recurring theme in *American Psycho* is the difficulty of unseeing the devastating effects of unemployment on New York City. As Bateman's colleague Price says on the second page of the novel, "That's the twenty-fourth [beggar] I've seen today. I've kept count." It is no accident that the first person Bateman kills is a homeless man.
122. For a fuller account of how Bateman allegorizes finance capital's violent revenge on "the underpaid, the underemployed, and the unemployable" (420), see Richard Godden's excellent essay "Labor, Language, and Finance Capital," *PMLA* 126, no. 2 (2011): 412–21. For another important analysis of financial violence in Ellis's novel, see Leigh Claire La Berge, "The Men Who Make the Killings: *American Psycho*, Financial Masculinity, and 1980s Financial Print Culture," *Studies in American Fiction* 37, no. 2 (2010): 273–96. And for a detailed reading of *American Psycho* as a commentary on the era's "academic neoconservative discourse on urban poverty and crime" (136), see Thomas Heise, "*American Psycho*: Neoliberal Fantasies and the Death of Downtown," *Arizona Quarterly* 67, no. 1 (2011): 135–60.
123. John Hagan, *Who Are the Criminals?: The Politics of Crime Policy from the Age of Roosevelt to the Age of Reagan* (Princeton University Press, 2010), 2.
124. For more on the literary and racial histories of criminal invisibility, see chapter 1. For an illuminating interpretation of the meanings of vision in *American Psycho* (including the fact that part of what Bateman does in the scene with the homeless man is blind him), see Godden, "Labor, Language, and Finance Capital," 420.
125. My understanding of the shift from industrial production to financial investment after 1970 was greatly aided by Annie McClanahan's *Dead Pledges: Debt, Crisis, and Twenty-First-Century Culture* (Stanford University Press, 2017).

5. THE NOVEL IN THE AGE OF MASS INCARCERATION, 1992-2023

1. For more on the literary history of the Black revolutionary novel, see chapter 2. As far as I know, Justin Gifford is the first scholar to bring attention to Jefferson's fascinating novel. See his *Pimping Fictions: African American Crime Literature and the Untold Story of Black Pulp Publishing* (Temple University Press, 2013).
2. Roland S. Jefferson, *The School on 103rd Street* (Vantage, 1976; repr., Norton, 1997), 114, 124.
3. Jefferson, *School on 103rd Street*, 150, 163.
4. Along similar lines, Gifford argues that "Jefferson's novel makes the statement that black American neighborhoods have become spaces of incarceration for many of their black citizens" (*Pimping Fictions*, 98).
5. Christian Parenti, *Lockdown America: Police and Prisons in the Age of Crisis* (Verso, 1999; repr. 2008), 166.

5. THE NOVEL IN THE AGE OF MASS INCARCERATION

6. Heather Ann Thompson, *Blood in the Water: The Attica Prison Uprising of 1971 and Its Legacy* (Vintage, 2016), 27, 79–80.
7. Thompson, *Blood in the Water*, 560, 561.
8. Marie Gottschalk, *The Prison and the Gallows: The Politics of Mass Incarceration in America* (Cambridge University Press, 2006), 181.
9. Parenti, *Lockdown America*, 164, 165.
10. Thompson, *Blood in the Water*, 562.
11. David Garland, "Introduction: The Meaning of Mass Imprisonment," in *Mass Imprisonment: Social Causes and Consequences*, ed. David Garland, 1–3 (Sage, 2001), 3.
12. Jefferson, *School on 103rd Street*, 125, 130.
13. Gottschalk, *Prison and the Gallows*, 170.
14. The numbers in this paragraph come from the invaluable data made available by The Sentencing Project (sentencingproject.org) and the Prison Policy Initiative (prisonpolicy.org).
15. Loïc Wacquant, *Punishing the Poor: The Neoliberal Government of Social Insecurity* (Duke University Press, 2009), 159, 156.
16. Parenti, *Lockdown America*, 65.
17. Eric Schlosser, "The Prison Industrial Complex," *The Atlantic*, December 1998.
18. Ruth Wilson Gilmore, *Golden Gulag: Prisons, Surplus, Crisis, and Opposition in Globalizing California* (University of California Press, 2007), 126, 101, 122.
19. Wacquant, *Punishing the Poor*, 157.
20. Mike Davis, "Hell Factories in the Field: A Prison-Industrial Complex," *The Nation*, February 20, 1995, 229.
21. Schlosser, "Prison Industrial Complex."
22. According to Davis, "more than 1,000 bills toughening sentencing under felony and misdemeanor statutes had been enacted by the legislature between 1984 and 1992" ("Hell Factories," 232). Gilmore argues that the "scramble to sponsor new laws" and create "new crimes" in California throughout the 1980s represented a concerted effort to "produce new prisoners" to fill "all the new beds" in all the new prisons the state was building at the time (*Golden Gulag*, 107, 97).
23. James Forman Jr., *Locking Up Our Own: Crime and Punishment in Black America* (Farrar, Straus and Giroux, 2017), 205.
24. William P. Barr, *The Case for More Incarceration* (U.S. Department of Justice, 1992), 11, 14.
25. Christopher P. Wilson suggests that there were "two related planks in the neoconservative platform" relating to prison at this time: "the idea that prison should punish offenders and control crime in advance; and that its costs had to be accepted on behalf of at-risk neighborhoods." Wilson, *Learning to Live with Crime: American Crime Narrative in the Neoconservative Turn* (Ohio State University Press, 2010), 124.
26. Barr, *Case for More Incarceration*, iv–v.
27. Davis, "Hell Factories," 232.
28. Garland, "Meaning of Mass Imprisonment," 1–2.
29. I hope I have succeeded in making clear that none of this is meant to suggest that serious works of fiction didn't talk about prison before the 1990s. They absolutely did. The difference between novels about prison written before 1990 and novels

5. THE NOVEL IN THE AGE OF MASS INCARCERATION

about prison written after—the core difference that motivates this chapter—is that the earlier novels appeared before the advent of a shared idea of mass incarceration as a historically distinct phenomenon. This chapter is an attempt to understand what happened when that particular idea of mass incarceration became available to novelists—and became, moreover, their primary inducement to writing about prison in the first place.

30. Patrick Elliott Alexander, *From Slave Ship to Supermax: Mass Incarceration, Prisoner Abuse, and the New Neo-Slave Novel* (Temple University Press, 2018), 4.
31. Elizabeth Hinton, "From 'War on Crime' to War on the Black Community," *Boston Review*, June 21, 2016.
32. *The Challenge of Crime in a Free Society: A Report by the President's Commission on Law Enforcement and Administration of Justice* (United States Government Printing Office, 1967), viii.
33. *Challenge of Crime in a Free Society*, 139.
34. *Challenge of Crime in a Free Society*, 1.
35. Barr, *Need for More Incarceration*, 1, 14.
36. Robert J. Norris, *Exonerated: A History of the Innocence Movement* (New York University Press, 2017), 50.
37. Norris, *Exonerated*, 65, 69.
38. Even this angle of analysis has its limitations, as Ruth Wilson Gilmore has elaborated in her critique of "the problem of innocence" in anti-prison discourse. Gilmore contends that the fixation on finding wrongfully convicted people "establishes as a hard fact that some people should be in cages, and only against this desirability or inevitability might some change occur. And it does so by distinguishing degrees of innocence such that there are people, inevitably, who will become permanently not innocent, no matter what they do or say." Gilmore, *Abolition Geography: Essays Toward Liberation* (Verso, 2022), 484.
39. Katzenbach was likely thinking about the famous ordeal of conservative pundit William F. Buckley, who in the 1960s took up the cause of Edgar Smith, a man who claimed he was wrongly imprisoned for the murder of a teenage girl. Buckley championed the cause of Smith's innocence in magazines and on television and put up his own money for lawyers, which ultimately led to Smith's release from prison. Several years later, Smith was convicted of attempting to murder another woman, and in the course of the trial, he confessed to the first murder. For a deep dive into the Smith and Buckley saga, see Sarah Weinman, *Scoundrel: The True Story of the Murderer Who Charmed His Way to Fame and Freedom* (HarperCollins, 2022).
40. John Katzenbach, *Just Cause* (G. P. Putnam's Sons, 1992; repr., Mysterious Press, 2014), 245.
41. Katzenbach, *Just Cause*, 13, 285, 239.
42. Katzenbach, *Just Cause*, 442, 467.
43. Katzenbach, *Just Cause*, 268, 284.
44. Katzenbach, *Just Cause*, 516.
45. Late in the novel, we learn that Ferguson could not have killed Blair Sullivan's parents in Florida, as Sullivan claimed, because Ferguson was in his criminology classes in New Jersey when those murders happened. It is then discovered that Sullivan had actually bribed one of the prison guards on Death Row to arrange

5. THE NOVEL IN THE AGE OF MASS INCARCERATION

the murders. It was the guard, not Ferguson, who killed Sullivan's parents. This is a thunderous revelation, yet Katzenbach does not seem entirely to clock its consequences. The whole plot of the novel—as well as the whole shift in Cowart's belief about Ferguson's guilt—rests on the idea that Ferguson and Sullivan traded murders. The killing of Sullivan's parents was the primary evidence that this trade had taken place. If Ferguson had nothing to do with the parents' murders, that would suggest there was never a deal between him and Sullivan in the first place. And if there was no deal, then there is no longer any reason to doubt that Ferguson is exactly what he says he is: a wrongly incarcerated victim of a prejudiced legal system.

46. Katzenbach, *Just Cause*, 500.
47. Katzenbach, *Just Cause*, 572, 573.
48. Stephen King, "Foreword: A Letter," in *The Green Mile: The Complete Serial Novel* by Stephen King, v–ix (Gallery, 1996), viii.
49. King, *Green Mile*, 386, 388.
50. King, *Green Mile*, 9, 236.
51. King, "Foreword: A Letter," viii.
52. King, *Green Mile*, 97, 8, 225.
53. Paul's name has biblical connotations, too, of course: Paul the Apostle helped to persecute worshippers of Christ—just as Paul Edgecombe oversees the persecution of John Coffey in prison—before converting to Christianity himself.
54. King, *Green Mile*, 97, 259, 421.
55. The film scholar Linda Williams has an excellent account of the *Green Mile* movie, which she reads as "racial melodrama"—a story form built on the "paradoxical administration of pain and death to the black body so that white people may weep." As Williams understands it, the film "rescues white Americans from the guilt of putting the innocent black man to death." Williams, "Melodrama in Black and White: Uncle Tom and *The Green Mile*," *Film Quarterly* 55, no. 2 (Winter 2001): 20.
56. King, *Green Mile*, 421.
57. King, *Green Mile*, 422, 380.
58. Williams makes a similar point in her reading of the film, writing: "We are meant to see that what looks like evil—white guards in a Louisiana prison operating an electric chair to execute an innocent black man—is, no less than Coffey's apparently violent embrace of the two raped and murdered white girls, a melodramatic misrecognition of virtue" ("Melodrama in Black and White," 19).
59. King, *Green Mile*, 268, 408.
60. Quoted in Wacquant, *Punishing the Poor*, 151.
61. Bob Herbert, "In America; Gingrich Mugs the Crime Bill," *New York Times*, August 17, 1994.
62. Katzenbach, *Just Cause*, 34.
63. King, *Green Mile*, 94, 95, 242.
64. Richard Kopley, *Edgar Allan Poe and the Dupin Mysteries* (Palgrave Macmillan, 2008), 38, 35.
65. Sara Paretsky, *Hard Time* (Delacorte, 1999), 238, 237, 87, 275–76, 283, 280–81, 324, 385.
66. Raymond Chandler, *The Big Sleep* (Alfred A. Knopf, 1939; repr., Vintage Crime, 1992), 64.

5. THE NOVEL IN THE AGE OF MASS INCARCERATION

67. Paretsky, *Hard Time*, 373.
68. Angela Y. Davis, *Are Prisons Obsolete?* (Seven Stories, 2003), 88.
69. Parenti, *Lockdown America*, 231, 232, 236, 232. For Parenti, prison labor is a "sideshow" because it is a distraction from the real class politics of the prison system, which, he argues, functions by warehousing the immense surplus populations produced by capitalism. Parenti calls this warehousing "class struggle from above" (214), and he thinks that the truth of prison as class war is concealed behind the mistaken idea that prison labor itself is directly profitable.
70. Schlosser, "Prison Industrial Complex."
71. Paretsky, *Hard Time*, 376, 374, 382, 327.
72. Paretsky, *Hard Time*, 373.
73. Paretsky, *Hard Time*, 384, 382.
74. Paretsky, *Hard Time*, 385.
75. Walter Mosley, *Devil in a Blue Dress* (Washington Square, 1990), 168.
76. Between the sixth Easy Rawlins book (*Gone Fishin'*, 1997) and the seventh Easy Rawlins book (*Bad Boy Brawly Brown*, 2002), Mosley published, among other things, a science fiction novel, a second Socrates Fortlow novel, and a nonfiction book tellingly titled *Workin' on the Chain Gang: Shaking Off the Dead Hand of History* (2000). He also experimented with a more allegorical approach to the topic of imprisonment several years later in *The Man in My Basement* (2004).
77. Walter Mosley, *Always Outnumbered, Always Outgunned* (Washington Square, 1998), 184, 196, 188, 174.
78. Mosley, *Always Outnumbered*, 183.
79. Mosley, *Always Outnumbered*, 30, 32, 36.
80. Mosley, *Always Outnumbered*, 173, 179, 180.
81. The critic Will Norman offers a superb account of the role complicity has played in the development of hardboiled detective fiction. See his *Complicity in American Literature After 1945: Liberalism, Race, and Colonialism* (Oxford University Press, 2025), 155–79.
82. Michael Nava, *The Little Death* (Alyson, 1986), 10.
83. Michael Nava, *Lay Your Sleeping Head* (Kórima, 2016), 2.
84. Nava, *Lay Your Sleeping Head*, 2, 4.
85. Nava, *Lay Your Sleeping Head*, 3.
86. Kinohi Nishikawa, *Street Players: Black Pulp Fiction and the Making of a Literary Underground* (University of Chicago Press, 2018), 242–43.
87. Kinohi Nishikawa, "Driven by the Market: African American Literature After Urban Fiction," *American Literary History* 33, no. 2 (2021): 338.
88. Nishikawa, "Driven by the Market," 339.
89. Aneeka Ayanna Henderson, *Veil and Vow: Marriage Matters in Contemporary African American Culture* (University of North Carolina Press, 2020), 13.
90. Gifford, *Pimping Fictions*, 155.
91. Kristina Graaf, *Street Literature: Black Popular Fiction in the Era of U.S. Mass Incarceration* (Universitätsverlag Winter, 2015), 167.
92. Gifford, *Pimping Fictions*, 155.
93. By reading these novels primarily as cautionary tales, I do not mean to discount the various kinds of pleasure they offer their readers. Both *The Coldest Winter Ever* and *Let That Be the Reason* are, indeed, immensely enjoyable and entertaining

5. THE NOVEL IN THE AGE OF MASS INCARCERATION

novels to read. Their moralizing function should hardly be seen as cancelling out their entertainment value. Nevertheless, both novels *do* have a clear moral imperative—and both communicate that imperative using similar formal techniques of readerly address.

94. My argument in this section builds on and is indebted to previous scholarly accounts of Souljah and Stringer. Gifford points out that a certain kind of didacticism "represents the primarily rhetorical strategy of this brand of female street fiction," while Henderson disagrees with Gifford's reading, maintaining that this didacticism often regresses into a "feminized ethos of personal (ir)responsibility and victim blaming." Gifford, *Pimping Fictions*, 168; Henderson, *Veil and Vow*, 67.
95. Henderson, *Veil and Vow*, 74.
96. Dani McClain, "How Sister Souljah Went from Radical Activist to Scapegoat to Blockbuster Novelist," *The Nation*, December 13, 2022.
97. Sister Souljah, *The Coldest Winter Ever* (Simon & Schuster, 1999), 391, 403.
98. Vickie M. Stringer, *Let That Be the Reason* (Upstream, 2002), 243.
99. Souljah, *Coldest Winter Ever*, 261, 413.
100. Souljah, *Coldest Winter Ever*, 338, 332. All the italics here are Souljah's.
101. Stringer, *Let That Be the Reason*, 244, 228, 243, 244.
102. See Beth E. Richie, *Compelled to Crime: The Gender Entrapment of Battered Black Women* (Routledge, 1996).
103. Leigh Goodmark, *Imperfect Victims: Criminalized Survivors and the Promise of Abolition Feminism* (University of California Press, 2023), 18.
104. Souljah's and Stringer's novels were thus also part of the larger conversation that women's crime fiction was having about partner violence and carceral feminism, as I detail in chapter 3.
105. Henderson, *Veil and Vow*, 13.
106. Henderson, *Veil and Vow*, 79, 81.
107. Souljah, *Coldest Winter Ever*, 304.
108. Stringer, *Let That Be the Reason*, 238.
109. Henderson, *Veil and Vow*, 83.
110. Souljah, *Coldest Winter Ever*, 408.
111. Stringer, *Let That Be the Reason*, 232.
112. Michelle Alexander, *The New Jim Crow: Mass Incarceration in the Age of Colorblindness*, rev. ed. (New Press, 2012), xiii.
113. Despite (or perhaps because of) playing an enormous role in shaping the public conversation about mass incarceration in the early 2010s, *The New Jim Crow* has come in for its share of criticism, including from scholars who are otherwise sympathetic to Alexander's political project. One common critique is that Alexander overstated the quantitative impact of the War on Drugs on incarceration rates (an oft-repeated factoid states that if we were to release every person imprisoned for a drug-related offense, the United States would still have the largest prison population in the world). Another is that her focus on Jim Crow occluded the significant class component of mass imprisonment in the late twentieth century. See, for example, James Forman Jr., "Racial Critiques of Mass Incarceration: Beyond the New Jim Crow," *New York University Law Review* 87, no. 1 (2012): 22–69; John Clegg and Adaner Usmani, "The Economic Origins of Mass Incarceration," *Catalyst* 3, no. 3 (2019); Gilmore, *Abolition Geography*, 485; and Marie Gottschalk,

5. THE NOVEL IN THE AGE OF MASS INCARCERATION

Caught: The Prison State and the Lockdown of American Politics (Princeton University Press, 2015), 119–38. For a well reasoned and data-supported defense of Alexander's argument, see Peter Ikeler and Calvin John Smiley, "The Racial Economics of Mass Incarceration: A Critique of Clegg and Usmani," *Spectre* 1, no. 2 (2020): 78–99. For my own brief account of how we might reconcile a focus on the racial disparities of drug laws with the broader history of deindustrialization, see the section "Deindustrializing the Crime Novel" in chapter 4.
114. Forman, *Locking Up Our Own*, 220.
115. Barack Obama, "Remarks by the President on Criminal Justice Reform," November 2, 2015, https://www.presidency.ucsb.edu/documents/special-message-the-congress-law-enforcement-and-the-administration-justice.
116. Forman, *Locking Up Our Own*, 217.
117. Gottschalk, *Caught*, xix. Gottschalk was rightly skeptical of the efficacy of proposed reforms, observing that "so far it looks like the United States remains caught on track to reconfigure the carceral state—not raze it." Forman, too, warned that small legislative victories around drug decriminalization must also be taken as "a cautionary tale about the limits of recent criminal justice reform efforts" (*Locking Up Our Own*, 220). Both authors' skepticism has been vindicated in the past few years.
118. "Smart Justice Campaign Polling on Americans' Attitudes on Criminal Justice: Topline Memo," American Civil Liberties Union, November 16, 2017.
119. Ames Grawert, Bryan Furst, and Cameron Kimble, "Ending Mass Incarceration: A Presidential Agenda," Brennan Center for Justice, February 21, 2019.
120. Literary fiction had certainly reckoned with prison before; late-twentieth-century novels by James Baldwin, John Edgar Wideman, and Ernest Gaines offer ample evidence of that. Patrick Elliott Alexander's book *From Slaveship to Supermax* is an excellent guide to the development of an earlier anticarceral tradition in twentieth-century African American fiction.
121. For a pathbreaking study of how and why the publishing industry, prize judges, and other literary institutions have funneled contemporary writers of color toward the genre of historical fiction, see Alexander Manshel, *Writing Backwards: Historical Fiction and the Reshaping of the American Canon* (Columbia University Press, 2023).
122. Colson Whitehead, *The Nickel Boys* (Anchor, 2019), 212, 76, 118, 66.
123. Quoted in Rebecca Evans, "Geomemory and Genre Friction: Infrastructural Violence and Plantation Afterlives in Contemporary African American Fiction," *American Literature* 93, no. 3 (2021): 457.
124. Whitehead, *Nickel Boys*, 191, 206.
125. Jesmyn Ward, *Sing, Unburied, Sing* (Scribner, 2017), 186.
126. Rachel Kushner has suggested that the mere act of writing about the prisons of "future-facing California" in *The Mars Room* was itself a way of writing about the future. The sheer size and brutality of the California penal system, she says, "is like a menagerie in which you can see the ugly future for all the states." Rachel Kushner and Caleb Smith, "Discipline and Abolish: A Dialogue About Writing, Power, and Mass Incarceration," *Yale Review* 109, no. 2 (2021): 93, 95.
127. Margaret Atwood, *The Heart Goes Last* (Doubleday, 2015), 5, 42, 37.
128. According to analysis performed by the California Legislative Analyst's Office.
129. Atwood, *Heart Goes Last*, 50.

130. Atwood, *Heart Goes Last*, 33, 306.
131. George Saunders, "Escape from Spiderhead," *New Yorker*, December 12, 2010.
132. Nana Kwame Adjei-Brenyah, *Chain-Gang All-Stars* (Vintage, 2023), 262, 31, 346.
133. Only the most hard-hearted neoliberal ideologue would sincerely maintain that going to prison is a choice that people make freely. That said, some people do maintain this. Kushner rather brilliantly captures the chilling absurdity of this position in *The Mars Room*, when a prison guard admonishes the inmates that "if you want to be a parent, you don't end up in prison. Plain and simple. Plain *and* simple." Kushner, *The Mars Room* (Scribner, 2018), 127.
134. Atwood, *Heart Goes Last*, 151.
135. Adjei-Brenyah, *Chain-Gang All-Stars*, 398.
136. Atwood, *Heart Goes Last*, 51.
137. The decline of the U.S. prison population throughout the 2010s was real. It was also relatively small. In 2022, the number of people in prison or jail in the United States was almost identical to what it had been in 1998—which is not necessarily a banner year for comparison. According to Gottschalk, "The Sentencing Project has calculated that if declines in the prison population were to continue at a rate of 1.8 percent a year (the biggest year-to-year drop registered since the boom began), it would take until 2101—or nearly nine decades—for the prison population to return to its 1980 level" (*Caught*, xvii).

EPILOGUE: AND THE LAW WON

1. Jonathan Flatley, "'Everybody Hates the Police': On Hatred for the Police as a Political Feeling," in *The Long 2020*, ed. Richard Grusin and Maureen Ryan, 217–28 (University of Minnesota Press, 2023), 218.
2. Ames Grawert and Noah Kim, "Myths and Realities: Understanding Recent Trends in Violent Crime," Brennan Center for Justice, July 12, 2022.
3. "A 'crime wave' wave has overtaken the media," Annie Lowrey wrote in 2022. "Mentions of the phrase more than doubled from 2019 to 2021 in major U.S. print publications, according to Nexis data; the number of minutes the big cable-news networks spent on it increased exponentially." Lowrey, "The People vs. Chesa Boudin," *The Atlantic*, May 19, 2022.
4. "Homicide, Most Other Violent Crimes Drop to Pre-Pandemic Levels in U.S. Cities," Council on Criminal Justice, July 25, 2024.
5. The Brennan Center's Grawert and Kim flatly rebut this narrative: "Despite politicized claims that this rise was the result of criminal justice reform in liberal-leaning jurisdictions, murders rose roughly equally in cities run by Republicans and cities run by Democrats. So-called red states actually saw some of the highest murder rates of all. This data makes it difficult to pin recent trends on local policy shifts and reveals the central flaw in arguments that seek to politicize a problem as complex as crime. Instead, the evidence points to broad national causes driving rising crime" ("Myths and Realities").
6. The progressive San Francisco district attorney Chesa Boudin, for instance, was recalled in 2022 in response to a general impression of rising crime that wasn't supported by data. As a local reporter explained at the time, "By any statistical

EPILOGUE

measure, San Francisco is not going through a crime wave. Violent crime is at historic lows. Property crime is off the hook, of course. But it's been off the hook for more than a decade.... So, clearly, there's a disconnect between what the statistics say and how people feel." Joe Eskanazi, "The Case for Recalling DA Chesa Boudin: There Isn't One. But That Hardly Matters," *Mission Local*, May 23, 2022.

7. "Recent Polls on Policing Show Positive Trends for U.S. Law Enforcement," Lexipol, June 26, 2024.
8. Megan Brenan, "U.S. Confidence in Institutions Mostly Flat, but Police Up," Gallup, July 15, 2024.
9. "In Tied Presidential Race, Harris and Trump Have Contrasting Strengths, Weaknesses," Pew Research Center, September 9, 2024.
10. The legal scholar Lara Bazelon has declared that "progressive prosecutors are on the verge of extinction." She explains, "The progressive-prosecutor movement that began less than ten years ago with the election of bold reformers pledging to reduce incarceration by rolling back many of the tough-on-crime policies of the 1980s and '90s is on the wane." Bazelon, "The Menendez Brothers and the End of the Progressive Prosecutor," *New York Magazine*, November 24, 2024.
11. Jennie Patterson, "Post-Election 2024: The Continued Unraveling of Criminal Justice Reform," Congressional Black Caucus Foundation, December 11, 2024.
12. "Crime Fiction Author S.A. Cosby Discusses His Latest Book, 'All the Sinners Bleed,'" *CBS Saturday Morning*, February 3, 2024.
13. S. A. Cosby, *All the Sinners Bleed* (Flatiron, 2023), 45–46, 42, 175.
14. Cosby, *All the Sinners Bleed*, 284.
15. Cosby, *All the Sinners Bleed*, 284, 29, 175, 338.
16. Attica Locke, *Bluebird, Bluebird* (Mulholland, 2017), 17.
17. Attica Locke, *Heaven, My Home* (Mulholland, 2019), 290.
18. Locke, *Bluebird, Bluebird*, 17.
19. Locke, *Bluebird, Bluebird*, 46.
20. Locke, *Heaven, My Home*, 26.
21. Locke, *Bluebird, Bluebird*, 46.
22. Locke, *Heaven, My Home*, 290.
23. Attica Locke, *Guide Me Home* (Mulholland, 2024), 259, 77, 69, 96, 305, 306.
24. Cosby, *All the Sinners Bleed*, 336, 269, 306.

INDEX

A Is for Alibi (Grafton), 117–19, 121, 124–26, 128, 140
abolition feminism, 112, 149–50. *See also* carceral feminism; feminism
addiction, 154–56, 159–65, 166–67, 171–72, 178, 179
Adjei-Brenyah, Nana Kwame, 231–33
Alexander, Michelle, 152, 224–25, 228, 277n35
Alexander, Patrick Elliott, 193
Alexie, Sherman, 152
Algiers Motel Incident, The (Hersey), 79–83, 102
All That Remains (Cornwell), 157, 158, 159
All the Sinners Bleed (Cosby), 237–39, 240–41
Always Outnumbered, Always Outgunned (Mosley), 211–215, 217
American Dilemma, An (Myrdal), 40–41, 42–43
American Psycho (Ellis), 183–84
anti-domestic violence movement, 106, 108–13, 123, 126, 129, 140. *See also* domestic violence
Anti-Drug Abuse Act (1986), 152, 170
Anti-Drug Abuse Act (1988), 152

antirape movement, 109, 110–11
Atlanta Missing and Murdered Children, 132–34
Attica uprising (1972), 187
Atwood, Margaret, 228–30, 232–33

Baldwin, James, 58, 186, 287n120
Ball, John: *Death for a Playmate*, 11, 72–73, 84–85; and integrationist crime writing, 49
Bambara, Toni Cade: *The Black Woman*, 135; *Those Bones Are Not My Child*, 11, 132–140
Barr, William (attorney general), 190–91, 194
beat policing, 74, 77–78, 102, 144
Because It Is Bitter, Because It Is My Heart (Oates), 157, 182–83
Bell, Daniel, 26
Bernstein, Elizabeth, 141
Bitter Medicine (Paretsky), 119–20, 124, 128, 172–73, 178
Black Dahlia, The (Ellroy), 153, 163
Black Panther Party, 68, 87, 94, 95
Black radical fiction, 84–98, 102–3, 185
Black radicalism, 68, 71, 84, 87, 104

INDEX

Black Woman, The (Bambara), 135
Blackboard Jungle, The (Hunter), 49–50
Blanche Among the Talented Tenth (Neely), 121–22, 126–27
Blanche on the Lam (Neely), 157, 158, 159, 182
Blanche Passes Go (Neely), 122–23, 127
Bland, Eleanor Taylor, 141–144
Bloch, Robert, 28, 32
Block, Lawrence, 10–11, 157, 158, 159, 167
Blood on the Moon (Ellroy), 153
Bluebird, Bluebird (Locke), 239
Bronson, Charles, 99
Brown v. Board of Education (1954), 40, 56
Brown v. Plata (2011), 225
Brown, Michelle, 252n36
Buckley, William F., 283n39
Bumiller, Kristin, 112
Bush, George H. W., 190, 194
Butler, Octavia, 176–78, 181

C Is for Corpse (Grafton), 167–72, 175, 178
Cain, James M., 44
Camp, Jordan T., 249n2
carceral feminism, 141, 146, 148–49. *See also* abolition feminism; feminism
Carter, Jimmy, 263n21
Case for More Incarceration, The (Barr), 190–91, 194
Cassuto, Leonard, 49, 152, 158, 275n3
Central Park Five, 145, 149
Chain-Gang All-Stars (Adjei-Brenyah), 231–33
Challenge of Crime in a Free Society, The (Katzenbach), 193–94
Chandler, Raymond, 12, 31, 122, 208
child welfare system, 143, 144, 219, 274n122
Civil Rights Congress, 24–25
civil rights movement, 3, 23, 25, 53, 66
Clark, Mary Higgins: commercial success of, 108; *Where Are the Children?*, 105–7, 130–32, 133–34, 139, 140
Clinton, Bill, 149, 189, 203
Clinton, Hillary, 154

Clockers (Price), 173, 180–81
Clover, Joshua, 251n23, 262n1, 265n62
Coldest Winter Ever, The (Souljah), 219–24
Comprehensive Crime Control Act (1984), 152
Cop Hater (McBain), 52, 72, 73
Cops (television show), 235, 236
Cornwell, Patricia: *All That Remains*, 157, 158, 159; and the popularity of serial killer fiction, 151; *Postmortem*, 120–21, 123–24, 127–28, 159
correctional spending, 179, 189–90, 225, 229
Cosby, S. A., 237–39, 240–41
Country Place (Petry), 58–60
Crenshaw, Kimberlé, 111
Crichton, Michael, 108
crime: changing meanings over time, 5–6; as code word, 5, 25; and the Covid-19 pandemic, 236; and storytelling, 8–12, 22, 101–4, 236; as voting issue, 1, 236–37
crime fiction: this book's definition of, 13–15; as bottomless pit, 16–17; in the history of publishing, 9–10
Crime Partners (Goines), 97–99, 100, 102
crime statistics: flaws of, 41, 76, 236, 264n42; in novels, 76–78, 137–38; perceived as colorblind, 78; and predictive policing, 77; and racial categories, 26, 264n40. *See also Uniform Crime Reports*
criminalization: defined, 5; of addiction, 154–55, 159–60, 165, 166 172; of African Americans, 5, 7–8, 23–26, 36–38, 40–41, 53–57, 65–66, 67–71, 77–78, 134–37, 152–56, 205; of domestic violence, 108–10, 140, 149; of European immigrants, 25–26; of homosexuality, 251n29; of poverty, 5, 7, 24–25, 54–57, 75, 89, 134–5, 155–56, 179, 184; of protest, 69–70, 72–72, 84, 95–96; of riots, 68–70, 79, 83; of the U.S.-Mexico border, 7, 251n29
criminal justice reform: backlash against, 187, 236–37, 241–42; in

INDEX

handling violence against women, 113; in the 1920s, 26; in response to police killings, 235–36, 238–39; and the prison system, 186–87, 210–11, 225
criminology, 9, 156
Crisis, The, 30, 39
Critical Resistance: "Statement on Gender Violence and the Prison Industrial Complex," 112

Daly, Carroll John, 31, 115
D'Amato, Barbara, 165–67
Darda, Joseph, 41–42, 58
Davis, Angela Y., 111, 113, 155, 186, 208, 275n131
Davis, Mike, 153, 190, 191, 282n22
Dead Time (Bland), 141–144
Death for a Playmate (Ball), 11, 72–73, 84–85
Death Wish (Garfield), 10, 99 101, 102, 103–4
deindustrialization, 4, 6–7, 178–80, 183–84, 208, 229
DeLillo, Don, 163–65
Democrats, 25, 152, 203–4, 225, 288n5
Denton, Nancy A., 250n17
deregulation. *See* financial deregulation
Detroit uprising (1967), 69, 70, 79, 84, 85
Devil in a Blue Dress (Mosley), 182–83, 212
DiIulio, John, 154
Dole, Bob, 154
domestic suspense fiction, 105, 112, 130, 132, 142
domestic violence: changing legal response to, 109–10, 112, 129, 140, 146–47; congressional hearings on, 109, 274n114; and differences of race and class, 111, 123–126, 133–4, 137–38; and "everywoman narrative," 119, 123, 126; and feminist activism, 108–13, 123, 126, 129, 140, 145, 148–49; ignored by police, 108, 127, 145; and imprisonment, 111, 112, 127, 148–50; as issue in the War in the Crime, 107, 109–10; in novels, 115–128, 141, 143, 270n33, 270n34; public awareness of, 109, 113, 115, 128, 129; in relation to state violence, 110–13, 149,

223, 275n131. *See also* anti-domestic violence movement; family violence
Dragnet (radio show), 72
Dragnet (television show), 74
drug addiction. *See* addiction
drug decriminalization, 165–66, 225, 235, 287n117
Du Bois, W. E. B., 30,

Ebony, 135
Ellis, Bret Easton, 183–84
Ellison, Ralph, 36, 53, 61
Ellroy, James: *The Black Dahlia*, 153, 163; *Blood on the Moon*, 153; *L.A. Confidential*, 157, 158, 160–62; and the popularity of serial killer fiction, 151
"Escape from Spiderhead" (Saunders), 230–31
"Evening and the Morning and the Night, The" (Butler), 176–78, 181
Exorcist, The (Blatty), 138
Expendable Man, The (Hughes), 53–57

Fairstein, Linda: *Final Jeopardy*, 145–49; *Likely to Die*, 178; as prosecutor, 140, 145–46, 149; *Sexual Violence: Our War Against Rape*, 145–46
family values, 129, 131, 135, 139
family violence, 109–10, 129–30, 137–39. *See also* domestic violence
Family Violence and Prevention Act (1984), 110
Farmer, Ashley D., 87
Federal Bureau of Investigation (FBI), 9, 95, 267n104. *See also* Uniform Crime Reports
Federal Death Penalty Act (1994), 152
feminism: divisions within, 110–13, 123, 149–50; and domestic violence, 108–13, 123, 126, 129, 140, 145, 148–49; and policing, 110, 113, 115, 126–28, 140–41, 149–50; and race, 111, 123–24, 126, 135–36. *See also* abolition feminism; carceral feminism
feminist detective fiction, 114–28, 142
Final Jeopardy (Fairstein), 145–49
financial deregulation, 183–84

Flamm, Michael, 104
Floyd, George, 235, 236
Forman, James, Jr., 190, 225, 287n117
Fortner, Michael Javen, 98
Freedomland (Price), 173–75, 178
Friends of Eddie Coyle, The (Higgins), 67–68

Gardner, Erle Stanley, 16–17
Garfield, Brian, 10, 99–101, 102, 103–4
Garland, David, 187, 191
Gifford, Justin, 97, 218, 281n1, 281n3, 286n94
Gilmore, Ruth Wilson, 7, 155, 189, 231, 249n2, 282n22, 283n38
Gingrich, Newt, 203, 225, 229
Goines, Donald: *Crime Partners*, 97–99, 100, 102; influence on street literature, 218; writing about prison, 186
Goldwater, Barry, 69, 107, 134
Goodmark, Leigh, 113, 150, 222, 272n69
Gottschalk, Marie, 108, 109, 129, 225, 288n137
Graaf, Kristina, 218
Grafton, Sue: *A Is for Alibi*, 117–19, 121, 124–26, 128, 140; *C Is for Corpse*, 167–72, 175, 178; commercial success of, 108; "The Parker Shotgun," 279n85; and second-wave feminism, 114
Greenlee, Sam: as part of the Black radical literary tradition, 86–87; *The Spook Who Sat by the Door*, 87–89, 95, 96, 102–3
Green Mile, The (King), 16, 195, 199–206
Gruber, Aya, 109
Guide Me Home (Locke), 240

Hagan, John, 183
Hall, Stuart, 7, 8, 250n20, 251n24
Hammett, Dashiell, 30–31
Hardball (D'Amato), 165–67
hardboiled detective fiction, 30–31, 115, 120, 122, 208
Hard Time (Paretsky), 207–11, 215, 217
Harris, Thomas, 151, 177
Hartman, Saidiya, 5
health care system, 155, 156, 163, 167, 168, 169, 171, 178

Heart Goes Last, The (Atwood), 228–30, 232–33
Heaven, My Home (Locke), 240
Heise, Thomas, 13
Henderson, Aneeka Ayanna, 218, 219, 223, 286n94
Hersey, John, 79–83, 102
Higgins, George V., 67–68
Highsmith, Patricia: and Chester Himes, 64–65; and psychological crime fiction, 91; racist attitudes, 29–30, 49; *Strangers on a Train*, 10, 27–28, 29, 30, 64; *The Talented Mr. Ripley*, 28
Himes, Chester: correspondence with John A. Williams, 91; *Cotton Comes to Harlem*, 65; and Patricia Highsmith, 64–65; *If He Hollers Let Him Go*, 44; leaving the U.S., 35, 64; *Plan B*, 86; *A Rage in Harlem*, 258n41; *The Real Cool Killers*, 30; reading *Runaway Black* (Hunter), 260n89; *Run Man Run*, 34–35; wariness of racial stereotypes about crime, 46, 58; *Yesterday Will Make You Cry*, 63–64
Hinton, Elizabeth, 4, 6, 69, 70, 71, 76, 152, 249n2, 265n62
HIV/AIDS, 156, 166, 174, 175, 176
Horsley, Lee, 114, 271n56, 275n3
Horton, Willie, 194
Hughes, Dorothy B.: *The Expendable Man*, 53–57; *In a Lonely Place*, 28, 32–34, 35
Hunter, Evan: *The Blackboard Jungle*, 49–50; and Chester Himes, 260n89; *Runaway Black*, 50–53, 57. *See* McBain, Ed

Ibrahim, Habiba, 135
Iceberg Slim, 97, 218
If He Hollers Let Him Go (Himes), 44
immigration, 7, 251n29
In a Lonely Place (Hughes), 28, 32–34, 35
incarceration. *See* mass incarceration
INCITE! Women of Color Against Violence, 112
Innocence Project, 194, 195
Insanity Defense Reform Act (1984), 160
Invisible Man (Ellison), 36, 53, 61

INDEX

Jackson, George, 186
Jackson, Lawrence P., 39, 41, 44, 58, 260n105, 262n130
JanMohamed, Abdul, 37
Jefferson, Brian Jordan, 264n40
Jefferson, Roland: as part of the Black radical literary tradition, 86–87; *The School on 103rd Street*, 185–86, 188, 224
Jim Crow, 4, 24, 25, 47, 55, 65, 227–28
Johnson, Lyndon: and fear of crime, 102; and the Moynihan Report, 134–35; on the problem of fear, 102; response to riots, 69–70, 84; and the War on Crime, 3, 68–70, 88, 107, 109, 193
Jones, Tayari, 225
Just Cause (Katzenbach), 195–99, 204

Kalifa, Dominique, 8
Katzenbach, John, 195–99, 204
Katzenbach, Nicholas (attorney general), 70, 195; *The Challenge of Crime in a Free Society*, 193–94
Kern, Stephen, 278n54
Kerner Report, 70, 80, 193
Killer Inside Me, The (Thompson), 28, 31–32
Kim, Mimi E., 108, 109
King, Stephen: *The Green Mile*, 16, 195, 199–206; commercial success of, 108
Kohler-Hausmann, Julilly, 75, 100, 125, 159–60, 162, 165,
Komo, Dolores, 114
Koontz, Dean, 151
Kushner, Rachel, 225, 287n126, 288n133

L.A. Confidential (Ellroy), 157, 158, 160–62
Lassiter, Matthew D., 168, 253n40
Law Enforcement Assistance Act (1965), 70
Law Enforcement Assistance Administration (LEAA): creation of, 70; dismantling of, 263n21; and Family Violence Program, 109; funding anti-domestic violence initiatives, 109–10; funding computer systems for crime control, 77; funding riot control, 70; and National Advisory Commission on

Criminal Justice Standards and Goals, 187
Lay Your Sleeping Head (Nava), 216–17
Lee, Harper, 55
Let That Be the Reason (Stringer), 219–24
LGBTQ crime fiction, 215, 251n29
Linnemann, Travis, 252n38
literature: relation to history, 2–3, 16, 21–22; shaping beliefs about crime, 3, 8–12, 15–16, 101–4
Little Death, The (Nava), 215–16
Locke, Attica: *Bluebird, Bluebird*, 239; *Guide Me Home*, 240; *Heaven, My Home*, 240
Lorde, Audre, 114
Lynchers, The (Wideman), 92–93, 95, 96, 103
lynching, 24, 29, 92, 217

Mailer, Norman: "The White Negro," 31–32
Man Who Cried I Am, The (Williams), 89–91, 102, 103
Man Who Lived Underground, The (Wright), 43–44
mandatory minimum sentencing, 152, 155, 220, 221–22
Marriage Is Murder (Pickard), 115–17, 120, 127–28
mass incarceration: bipartisan politics of, 203–4; and carceral feminism, 148–49; as class war, 7; coining the phrase, 191; and correctional spending, 179, 189–90; declining public support for, 225, 235–36; and financial deregulation, 183–84; and immigration, 7; and novels, 1–2, 192–234; as part of longer social history, 3–5, 249n2; public awareness, 190–91, 224–25; and race, 7, 189, 191, 194–204, 207, 212, 218, 221–23, 225, 226–28; and rural America, 7; statistics on, 4, 7, 187, 188–89, 190; and unemployment, 7, 179–80, 181, 229; and the War on Drugs, 155, 179; and women, 112, 207, 219–224
Massey, Douglas, 179, 250n17
Maxwell, William J., 95, 267n104

McBain, Ed: *Cop Hater*, 52, 72, 73; and procedural authenticity, 11–12. *See also* Hunter, Evan
McCann, Sean, 46, 48, 256n1, 271n45
McCone Commission, 84, 264n36
Meiners, Erica R., 111, 273n108, 275n131
Melamed, Jodi, 42
militancy, 68, 71, 84, 86, 91, 95, 97, 98, 100. *See also* Black radicalism
Morrison, Toni, 133, 270n33
Mosley, Walter: *Always Outnumbered, Always Outgunned*, 211–215, 217; *Devil in a Blue Dress*, 182–83, 212; *The Man in My Basement*, 285n76; *White Butterfly*, 157, 158, 162–63
Motley, Willard, 260n105
Moynihan, Daniel Patrick: *The Negro Family: A Case for National Action*, 134–35, 137, 142, 155
Muhammad, Kahlil Gibran, 25–26, 251n28
Murakawa, Naomi, 25, 156, 174, 249n2
"Murders in the Rue Morgue, The" (Poe), 30, 205–6
Myrdal, Gunnar: *An American Dilemma*, 40–41, 42–43; friendship with Richard Wright, 43
"Mystery of Marie Rogêt, The" (Poe), 9

National Advisory Committee on Civil Disorders, 70
National Coalition against Domestic Violence, 109
National Commission on Law Enforcement and Administration of Justice, 69–70, 194
National Organization for Women, 109
Native Son (Wright), 36–38, 41–42, 44, 266n88
Nava, Michael: *Lay Your Sleeping Head*, 216–17; *The Little Death*, 215–16
Neely, Barbara: *Blanche Among the Talented Tenth*, 121–22, 126–27; *Blanche on the Lam*, 157, 158, 159, 182; *Blanche Passes Go*, 122–23, 127; mistrust of the police, 127–28, 150

Negro Family: A Case for National Action, The (Moynihan), 134–35, 137, 142, 155
Neufeld, Peter, 194–95
New Centurions, The (Wambaugh), 16, 74–78, 79, 83, 84
New Deal, 26, 171, 257n13
New Jim Crow, The (Alexander), 224–25, 228; criticisms of, 286n113
Newark uprising (1967), 70, 85, 174
Nickel Boys, The (Whitehead), 225, 226–28, 233
Nishikawa, Kinohi, 97, 218
Nixon, Richard, 4, 98

Oates, Joyce Carol, 157, 182–83
Obama, Barack, 225
Office of Domestic Violence, 109, 129
Omnibus Crime Control and Safe Streets Act (1968), 70, 88, 109
Outsider, The (Wright), 60–61, 63, 266n95

Pager, Devah, 181
Parenti, Christian, 6, 180, 209
Paretsky, Sara: *Bitter Medicine*, 119–20, 124, 128, 172–73, 178; *Hard Time*, 207–11, 215, 217; founding Sisters in Crime, 114
"Parker Shotgun, The" (Grafton), 279n85
Parker, William (LAPD chief), 74, 75, 83, 88, 264n38
parole system, 152, 180, 187, 190, 194
Patterson, William L., 25
Petry, Ann: *Country Place*, 58–60; and literary naturalism, 219; "Marie of the Cabin Club," 38; *The Street*, 38–39, 44–45, 64; wariness of racial stereotypes about crime, 46, 58
Pickard, Nancy, 115–17, 120, 127–28
Pick-Up (Willeford), 46–49, 53, 57
Plan B (Himes), 86
Poe, Edgar Allan: "The Murders in the Rue Morgue," 30, 205–6; "The Mystery of Marie Rogêt," 9; "The Tell-Tale Heart," 33
police militarization, 70–71, 168

INDEX

police procedural genre, 52, 71–74, 77, 140
Postmortem (Cornwell), 120–21, 123–24, 127–28, 159
Price, Richard: *Clockers*, 173, 180–81; *Freedomland*, 173–75, 178
prison construction, 7, 189–90. *See also* correctional spending
prison fiction: as cautionary tale, 217–24; by detective novelists, 206–17; set in the future, 228–34; set in the past, 226–28, 233; written by incarcerated people, 192, 218; about wrongful conviction, 195–205
prison labor, 208–9
prison system: crisis of legitimacy in the 1970s, 186–87; growth after 1973, 4, 187–91; public concern about after 2010, 225. *See also* mass incarceration
prisoner activism, 186–87
prison-industrial complex, 190, 207, 209
progressive prosecutor movement, 237
prosecutor fiction, 145–49
Psycho (Bloch), 28, 32
publishing industry: difficulties for Black crime novelists in, 58, 62–64, 96; importance of crime fiction to, 9–10; promoting crime fiction by women, 105, 108, 114, 217–18; promoting serial killer fiction, 151–52; role of genre categories in, 254n46

Rabinowitz, Paula, 58, 59, 253n45
race war, 71, 92
radicalism. *See* Black radicalism
Rafter, Nicole, 9, 277n30
Rage in Harlem, A (Himes), 258n41
Rampell, Palmer, 138, 260n89
Reagan, Ronald, 4, 9, 110, 115, 129, 170, 183
Red Scare, 28
Reddy, Maureen T., 140
Reed, Ishmael, 173
rehab, 98, 168, 177–78. *See also* addiction
rehabilitation, 26, 148, 168, 178, 187, 210, 226, 274n128

Report of the National Advisory Commission on Civil Disorders. See Kerner Report
Republicans, 25, 203–4, 288n5
revolutionary fiction. *See* Black radical fiction
Richie, Beth E., 110, 111, 112, 123, 126, 222, 275n131, 275n132
riots: blamed on militants, 71, 84; criminalization of, 68–70, 79, 83; as impetus for the War on Crime, 67, 69–71, 84; mainstream views of, 83–84, 265n62; and myths about snipers, 263n10; in novels, 16, 72–74, 75–76, 85, 86, 88, 89–90, 93, 153, 174, 239; policing of, 79, 88–89, 91, 95, 100, 103; as political acts, 69, 83–84, 95; and racialization, 262n1. *See also* Detroit uprising; Newark uprising; Watts uprising
Rockefeller, Nelson D. (governor), 100, 187
Run Man Run (Himes), 34–35
Runaway Black (Hunter), 50–53, 57

Saunders, George, 230–31
Savage Holiday (Wright), 61–63
Schalk, Sami, 176, 279n97, 280n99
Scheck, Barry, 194–95
Schlosser, Eric, 189, 190, 209
School on 103rd Street, The (Jefferson), 185–86, 188, 224
Schrader, Stuart, 4, 249n2
science fiction, 87, 176, 229, 285n76
Scott-Heron, Gil: as part of the Black radical literary tradition, 86–87; *Small Talk at 125th and Lenox*, 93, 94, 95; *The Vulture*, 93–95, 96, 98–99, 100, 103
Second Great Migration, 3, 6, 23, 65
Seltzer, Mark, 9, 165, 254n54, 275n3, 277n39
serial killer fiction, 120–21, 151–54, 157–65, 177, 183
Shaft (Tidyman), 85–86
Shakur, Assata, 111
Siegel, Micol, 250n11

INDEX

Simon, Jonathan, 4, 138
Sing, Unburied, Sing (Ward), 225, 227–28, 233
Sisters in Crime (organization), 114, 115
Small Talk at 125th and Lenox (Scott-Heron), 93, 94, 95
Sons of Darkness, Sons of Light (Williams), 91–92, 95, 96
Souljah, Sister, 219–24
speculative fiction, 87, 88, 178, 228–234
Spillers, Hortense, 135
Spook Who Sat by the Door, The (Greenlee), 87–89, 95, 96, 102–3
Srinivasan, Amia, 272n68
"Statement on Gender Violence and the Prison Industrial Complex" (Critical Resistance and INCITE!), 112
Strangers on a Train (Highsmith), 10, 27–28, 29, 30, 64
Street, The (Petry), 38–39, 44–45, 64
street literature, 217–19, 220
Stringer, Vickie, 219–24
Sugrue, Thomas, 6, 24, 257n9
super-predator, 154

Talented Mr. Ripley, The (Highsmith), 28
Tartt, Donna, 11
Task Force on Victims of Crime (1984), 129
temporary insanity defense, 118
Thompson, Heather Ann, 4, 187, 249n2
Thompson, Jim, 28, 31–32
Those Bones Are Not My Child (Bambara), 11, 132–140
Tidyman, Ernest, 85–86
Turow, Scott, 195
Tuskegee Experiment, 162–63

unemployment, 4, 6, 24, 68, 69, 179–81, 184, 229. See also mass incarceration
Uniform Crime Reports, 26, 77. See also crime statistics; FBI

vagrancy, 5, 228
Van Peebles, Melvin, 64
Vietnam War, 69, 71, 88

vigilante fiction, 98–101, 102, 213
vigilantism, 98
Violence Against Women Act (1994), 149
Violent Crime and Law Enforcement Act (1994), 149, 152, 189, 203, 218
Vulture, The (Scott-Heron), 93–95, 96, 98–99, 100, 103

Wacquant, Loïc, 189, 229, 250n11, 250n17
Walk Among the Tombstones, A (Block), 10–11, 157, 158, 159, 167
Walker, Alice, 270n33
Wambaugh, Joseph, 74–78, 79, 83, 84
Ward, Jesmyn, 225, 227–28, 233
War on Crime: as actual war, 70–71, 88–89, 101; and crime statistics, 76–77; as expression of fear, 102, 104; as historical period, 3–5; in novels, 67–68, 71, 74–101; origins of, 3, 68–71; prehistory of, 23–25, 65–66; and race, 5–8, 67–71; renewed support for, 236–37, 242; and riots, 68–71, 84, 96; and violence against women, 107, 109–110, 149
War on Drugs: and the criminalization of addiction, 154–55, 159–60, 165, 166 172; and deindustrialization, 178–80, 183–84; and incarceration rates, 154–55 286n113; key pieces of legislation in, 152, 160; and the media, 152, 253n40; in novels, 157, 158, 161, 166–67, 170–71, 175, 176, 279n85; and race, 152–56, 162–63, 175, 179; in the suburbs, 168, 179
War on Poverty, 3, 70
War on Terror, 251n29
Watson, Rachel, 55
Watts uprising (1965), 69, 71, 84, 88; in fiction, 72–73, 76, 79, 85, 102, 153
We Charge Genocide (Civil Rights Congress), 24–25
welfare fraud, 125–26
welfare queen, 6, 125
welfare state: contraction of, 4, 69–70, 171, 179–80, 189; perceived permissiveness of, 99–100; replaced by carceral state, 141, 179–80, 189

INDEX

Where Are the Children? (Clark), 105–7, 130–32, 133–34, 139, 140
White Butterfly (Mosley), 157, 158, 162–63
white flight, 3, 6, 25, 169
Whitehead, Colson, 225, 226–28, 233
"White Negro, The" (Mailer), 31–32
White Noise (DeLillo), 163–65
Wideman, John Edgar: *The Lynchers*, 92–93, 95, 96, 103; as part of the Black radical literary tradition, 86–87
Willeford, Charles, 46–49, 53, 57
Williams, John A.: correspondence with Chester Himes, 91; *The Man Who Cried I Am*, 89–91, 102, 103; as part of the Black radical literary tradition, 86–87; *Sons of Darkness, Sons of Light*, 91–92, 95, 96
Williams, Linda, 284n55, 284n58
Wilson, Christopher P., 74, 102, 253n39, 255n66, 263n34, 282n25
Wilson, William Julius, 280n114

Wings, Mary, 114, 178
Wire, The (television show), 173, 180
women's shelters, 109, 110, 116, 149
Woods, Teri, 218
Wright, Richard: introduction to *Black Metropolis*, 41; and literary naturalism, 219; *The Man Who Lived Underground*, 43–44; and Gunnar Myrdal, 42–43; *Native Son*, 36–38, 41–42, 44, 266n88; *The Outsider*, 60–61, 63, 266n95; *Savage Holiday*, 61–63; and sociology, 41–42; wariness of racial stereotypes about crime, 46, 58
wrongful conviction, 193–95; in novels, 195–205

X, Malcolm, 90, 94, 186

Yaddo writer's colony, 64–65
Yesterday Will Make You Cry (Himes), 63–64

GPSR Authorized Representative: Easy Access System Europe, Mustamäe tee
50, 10621 Tallinn, Estonia, gpsr.requests@easproject.com

www.ingramcontent.com/pod-product-compliance
Lightning Source LLC
Chambersburg PA
CBHW022036290426
44109CB00014B/881